# Post-war Reconstruction in Europe: International Perspectives, 194

*Ed*

*Re*

OXI

UNIVER

# OXFORD
## UNIVERSITY PRESS

1 Great Clarendon Street, Oxford OX2 6DP

Oxford University Press is a department of the University of Oxford.
It furthers the University's objective of excellence in research, scholarship,
and education by publishing worldwide in

Oxford New York

Athens Auckland Bangkok Bogotá Buenos Aires Cape Town
Chennai Dar es Salaam Delhi Florence Hong Kong Istanbul Karachi
Kolkata Kuala Lumpur Madrid Melbourne Mexico City Mumbai Nairobi
Paris São Paulo Shanghai Singapore Taipei Tokyo Toronto Warsaw

with associated companies in Berlin Ibadan

Oxford is a registered trade mark of Oxford University Press
in the UK and in certain other countries

Published in the United Kingdom
by Oxford University Press Inc., New York

A catalogue for this book is available from the British Library

Library of Congress Cataloging in Publication
Data (data available)

ISBN 0-19-969274-3
ISBN 978-0-19-969274-3

Subscription information for Past & Present is available
from:jnls.cust.serv@oup.com

Typeset by Glyph International, Bangalore, India
Printed by Bell and Bain Ltd, Glasgow, UK

**Past and Present Supplements**

Supplement 6, 2011

Post-war Reconstruction in Europe: International
Perspectives, 1945–1949
*Edited by Mark Mazower, Jessica Reinisch, and David Feldman*

# Post-war Reconstruction in Europe: International Perspectives, 1945–1949

## CONTENTS

**Index 353**

## List of Illustrations

Contributions and Communications (two copies), editorial correspondence, etc., should be addressed to The Editors, *Past and Present*, 175 Banbury Road, Oxford OX2 7AW, UK. Tel: +44 (0)1865 512318; Fax: +44 (0)1865 310080; E-mail: editors@pastandpresent. org.uk. Intending contributors should write for a copy of 'Notes for Contributors'.

© *World Copyright: The Past and Present Society, 2011.*

Photocopying and reprint permissions: single and multiple photocopies of extracts from this Journal may be made without charge in all public and educational institutions or as part of any non-profit educational activity, providing that full acknowledgement is made of the source. Requests to reprint in any publication for public sale should be addressed to Oxford University Press. This policy may be reviewed by the Past and Present Society from time to time. More information can be obtained from Rights and New Business Development, Journals Division, Oxford University Press, Great Clarendon Street, Oxford OX2 6DP, UK. Tel: +44 (0)1865 354490 or 353695; Fax: +44 (0)1865 353485; E-mail: journals.permission@ oup.com, www.oxfordjournals.org/access_ purchase/rights_permissions.html

The Past and Present Society is a company limited by a guarantee registered in England under company number 2414260 and a registered charity under number 802281. Its registered office is at 9400 Garsington Road, Oxford.

Typeset by Glyph International, Bangalore, India, and printed by Bell and Bain Ltd, Glasgow, UK

# Preface

**David Feldman**

The essays presented here (with one exception) have their origins in a conference on *Reconstruction in Post-war Europe* held at Birkbeck, University of London in June 2008. Five years earlier Eric Hobsbawm had been awarded a Balzan Prize 'for his brilliant analysis of the troubled history of twentieth century Europe and for his ability to combine in-depth historical research with great literary talent'.[1] The prize was not only a significant honour and recognition of Hobsbawm's endeavour as a scholar and public intellectual, it also endowed him with the resources to fund a research project of his own choosing. The theme for the project, he decided, would be *Reconstruction in the Immediate Aftermath of War: A Comparative Study of Europe, 1945–50*. There was a pressing need, he argued, for a history of how Europe was rebuilt, not least in a literal, material sense, following the Allies' victory. Hobsbawm placed the project at Birkbeck (his institutional home since 1947) and asked Mark Mazower and David Feldman to co-direct it.[2] Birkbeck's contribution in providing administrative support as well as office and meeting space was indispensable. The June 2008 conference was the final event organized and funded by 'the Balzan project', as it became known, and this volume marks the project's conclusion.[3]

If Hobsbawm and the Balzan Foundation inspired and underwrote the project, it also drew on the expertise and goodwill of a large number of scholars based in Britain, Europe, and the United States. Most significant were Jessica Reinisch and Elizabeth White, the two postdoctoral fellows, whose interests, insight, and energy helped to shape the project. More broadly, scores of historians participated in workshops and the final conference and

[1] http://www.balzan.org/en/prizewinners/eric-hobsbawm_0000000020.html

[2] In 2005 Mazower took up the post of Ira D. Wallach Professor of World Order Studies and Professor of History at Columbia University, New York, but from there he continued to take a full part in planning the project's programme.

[3] For a full account of the project's activities, publications, and personnel see http://www.balzan.org/it/premiati/eric-hobsbawm/progetto-di-ricerca_20_94.html

*Past and Present (2011)*, Supplement 6

delivered papers and commentary. Several became loyal supporters of the project, attending on a number of occasions. In this way the project became a collaborative effort as one workshop exerted an influence on the agenda for the next.

The comparative perspective enjoined in the project title was ambiguous and at the same time provided one recurrent theme. Which comparison were we dealing with? Were we comparing reconstructions in Eastern and Western Europe or those following the First and Second World Wars? The latter comparison had long been established in scholarship and was not to be abandoned. However, the former comparison appeared innovative when we set out on the project. It is one mark of the changes in historiography over the last decade that at the project's conclusion it seems a less radical departure than it did at its inception. At the project's conclusion the importance of the Versailles settlement to reconstruction after 1945, as well as the diplomatic and economic history of the interwar years, appears ever more conspicuous. As Harold James and Jessica Reinisch demonstrate, perceptions of this history contributed to the ways in which historical actors understood their task after 1945. One of the aims of the project was to encompass East and West Europe within the same study. The idea that this inclusive strategy should take a comparative form derives from the impact of the Cold War on both history and historiography. At the project's end, the salience of the Cold War was confirmed in some respects. David Edgerton and Adam Tooze, for example, draw attention to the continued weight of military spending in shaping economic reconstruction in Britain and Germany. Mark Harrison argues that Stalin's repression and political authority made a functional contribution to Soviet economic recovery after 1945. However, as Mark Mazower points out, the end of the Cold War has encouraged historians to question the degree to which East and West Europe were meaningful categories outside of that context. The essays here by Holly Case, Tara Zahra, and Pamela Ballinger reveal both commonalities between East and West Europe and significantly diverse trajectories within what became the Soviet bloc. More broadly, the thematic range of this volume, which encompasses imperial policy and de-colonization and the rhetoric and practice of internationalism, as well as contests to exercise a monopoly of force and legitimate power, illustrates the ways in which the historiography of the immediate post-war years now strikes out in new directions which no longer can be contained by the dichotomies of the Cold War.

A second recurrent issue has been periodization. It soon became clear that the problem of post-war reconstruction could not be treated in isolation. In part, this was because plans for peace were laid in the midst of war but also because the experience and impact of war meant that reconstruction meant different things in different places. In this respect, the British case was the outlier. Undefeated, the British state (away from the Channel Islands) enjoyed a continuity denied to other European combatants and the nation's economic and social infrastructure, though damaged by bombing and subordinated to the demands of war, was saved from the radical destruction that afflicted the battlefield states. Moreover, as the project moved further away from the emphases of Cold War historiography so too did some of the apparent certitudes concerning the way that 1945 marked a new beginning came into question. Pierre Lagrou's challenging conclusion to his study of the use of force by state agents 'in and around Belgium' is that in common with many other social norms 'the norms and praxis of policing would not fundamentally be challenged in 1945'. Of course, the powerful significance of 1945 as a historical marker is not in question. But individually and taken together these essays offer ways to think anew about the intentions and forms of reconstruction after 1945 and which lines of temporal and spatial connection best help us to make sense of that process and how it connects to longer processes of continuity and change in Europe in the twentieth century.

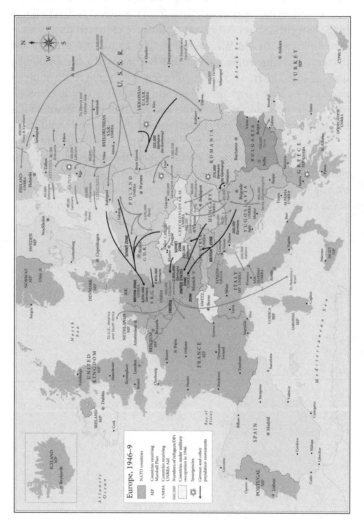

**Fig. 1.** Europe 1946–9. Map by John Gilkes.

**Fig. 2.** Ruined skyscraper, Warsaw. Photograph by John Vachon.

**Fig. 3.** Boy with bread, Boduen. Photograph by John Vachon.

**Fig. 4.** Remains of building, Wroclaw. Photograph by John Vachon.

**Fig. 5.** Coal miners. Photograph by John Vachon.

# Reconstruction: The Historiographical Issues

**Mark Mazower**

The development of interest in the problem of post-war reconstruction has a history of its own, intimately bound up with the Cold War and its impact on the historiography of modern Europe. This becomes clear once we recognize that before the fall of the Berlin Wall in 1989, the central problematic of this volume—the reconstruction effort that reshaped Europe in the years 1945–48—did not much figure in Cold War historiography. Insofar as it did, it was under two distinct rubrics.

One, the dominant one, centred upon what were already by the early 1960s the key questions: when did the Cold War start, and who started it? Charting the breakdown of Big Three understanding meant taking a position on whether the rift began in 1943, or 1945, or as late as 1947 or 1948—an issue of much more than mere academic importance for those concerned with countries such as Poland and Greece in particular. Historians who pitched it later rather than earlier tended to turn the years from 1945–48 into a moment of lost promise, the key in the international arena to the continent's division and a time when different decisions might have generated very different outcomes. Two obvious features of this historiography were firstly that it was couched almost entirely in the idiom of high politics and diplomacy, and secondly that it effectively sucked agency out of Europe itself. It was more or less accepted that 1945 represented, in Felix Gilbert's words, 'the end of the European era'.[1]

The problem in fact that these historians were grappling with was not *reconstruction* in any recognizable sense but the *construction* of two hostile opposing blocs, a kind of prehistory of the Iron Curtain. By the 1980s, the importance of European elites in shaping Superpower options—the tail wagging the dog—was already acknowledged in works on Yugoslavia, Hungary,

---

[1] F. Gilbert, *The End of the European Era: 1890 to the Present* (New York, 1970). The literature on the Cold War is vast. Early anti-Soviet accounts pushed the start date back to the takeover of Poland, if not earlier. Revisionist accounts were inclined to see the Truman Doctrine and the Marshall Plan as the turning-point.

and France among others. This development was extremely important for the future. But the fact remains that reconstruction itself was not really discussed, not even as a way of determining the means by which new post-war elites had ascended to power.[2]

The other pre-1990 rubric for thinking about the late 1940s came rather later, out of the economic crises of the 1970s and the revival of international political economy that accompanied these. It was the apparent collapse of the Bretton Woods system that led historians back into arguments about the success or failure of capitalist reconstruction after the *First* World War. Pride of place here must go to Charles Maier who posed the problem of reconstruction explicitly in his 1975 *Recasting Bourgeois Europe*, and then linked this increasingly to the issue of corporatist stabilization. He asked why things worked out in Western Europe after 1945 when they had not after 1918, and he asked this because he came to the question—as most Cold War historians did not—from the background of a historian interested in interwar fascism, well aware that people in the late 1940s had not precluded the possibility of a fascist or Nazi revival. (Elisabeth Wiskemann, a very knowledgeable commentator on Central European affairs had worried about this in the early 1950s, for example).[3] Putting the German question centre stage gave one a very different perspective on the post-1945 period. The problem was not why and how the European tail wagged the American or Soviet dog, but rather why the authoritarian German dog failed to bark. How did (West) German business elites in particular manage to come to terms with parliamentary democracy? More generally, why miracle and not slump? One way into an answer was to compare the lack of an effective hegemonic power in the 1920s in Europe with the American commitment after 1945. Not surprisingly perhaps, it was American Europeanists—such as Schuker in his 1976 *The End of French Predominance in Europe*, or the veteran economist and economic historian Charles Kindleberger in his 1986 study of economic policy failure, *The World in Depression*, who took the lead mapping out this territory.[4]

[2] E.g. I. Banac, *With Stalin against Tito* (1988); C. Gati, *Hungary and the Soviet Bloc* (1986); I. Wall, *Cold War France*; or textbooks such as D. Ellwood, T. Simons.

[3] C. Maier, *Reconstructing Bourgeois Europe: Stabilization in France, Germany and Italy in the Decade after World War 1* (Princeton, 1975); E. Wiskemann, *Germany's Eastern Neighbours: Problems relating to the Oder-Neisse Line and the Czech Frontier Regions* (Oxford, 1956).

[4] S. Schuker, *The End of French Predominance in Europe: The Financial Crisis of 1924 and the Adoption of the Dawes Plan* (Chapel Hill, NC, 1976); C. Kindleberger, *The World in*

By the late 1980s, these two approaches to the problem had fused together in the works of economic historians like Michael Hogan, John Gillingham, and Alan Milward. They debated the importance of the Marshall Plan, and of US policy and initiative generally in the recovery in Western Europe after the war.[5] Cold War historians of US foreign policy, such as Hogan, tended to take the importance of US policy-making for granted and aimed rather to engage with international relations theorists debating how and where bureaucratically policy was actually formulated. The Europeanists, on the other hand, were primarily interested in charting the proto-history of the movement towards European integration and thus directed their concern chiefly to the political and economic landscape of Europe itself, downplaying the decisiveness of the American engagement in 1947. (It is striking that it was the pioneer of this trend, Alan Milward, who brought back the term 'reconstruction', in 1984, nearly four decades after the once commonplace term had slipped almost entirely from fashion.) After 1992 their reorientation towards Europe became increasingly pronounced, even as US Cold War historians turned their attention elsewhere.

This then was the historiographical situation as the Cold War ended and new vistas opened up for historical enquiry. It was not just the Cold War that had come to an end but the whole phase of history that had begun with the division of Europe in 1945. Tracing the origins of this post-war order now became conceivable as a historical problem and the question of reconstruction assumed a new significance.[6]

Using the rubric of reconstruction meant a widening of both the spatial and temporal frames compared with earlier historical approaches. So far as the first was concerned, reunification of the continent in 1990 encouraged a greater willingness to question when and how far the East/West divide really had split Europe. Common experiences—above all in the preceding occupation—reactions and policies were traced across the continent, especially in matters of welfare and social policy, but also in the effort to

---

*Depression, 1929–1939* (Berkeley, 1973); on West German business, see V. Berghahn, *The Americanization of West German Industry, 1945–1973* (1986).

[5] M. Hogan, *The Marshall Plan: America, Britain and the Reconstruction of Western Europe,1947–52* (Cambridge, 1987); J. Gillingham, *Industry and Politics in the Third Reich: Ruhr Coal, Hitler and Europe* (New York, 1985); A. Milward, *The Reconstruction of Western Europe, 1945–51* (Berkeley, 1984).

[6] Mention should be made here of a series of conferences organized by Tony Judt on the theme of 'Rethinking Postwar Europe': some of the papers were published in I. Deak, J. Gross and T. Judt (eds), *The Politics of Retribution in Europe: World War II and Its Aftermath* (Princeton, 2000).

recuperate multi-party democracy. But so too were the radical divergences, reflecting not only wartime but also pre-war differences of experience.

As the Balzan workshops probed more deeply into the comparative histories of Western and Eastern Europe, the question arose of the usefulness of this Cold War binary, and how far it actually obscured the variety of national experiences in Europe immediately after the war. Behind this lay a conceptual question as well: how far had either 'West' or 'East' Europe really existed until the Cold War helped reify them and fill them with meaning? It is striking that the number of books with either phrase in the title increased more than tenfold between the 1920s and the 1960s. With the formation of NATO and the Cominform, the Iron Curtain became a reality, though blurred in relatively neglected zones such as Austria and Finland well into the 1950s. But in those critical years from the end of the war until 1948, it was not at all clear that Bulgaria or Romania shared more with Czechoslovakia and the German Democratic Republic than they did with, say, Greece, or that anything useful was to be gained from placing Prague and Dresden in some putative 'Eastern Europe'. The focus on reconstruction—at least at the outset a common set of responses to a common set of problems (homelessness, urban destruction, infrastructural collapse)—has helped remind us of the contingency of these Cold War categories and the lability of the idea of Europe. The war itself had been won by an alliance that claimed to speak for Europe as a whole, and the earliest planning organizations often had a pan-European remit. By 1948, this had been lost and Europe had come to be identified with something very different, exemplified by the Organisation for European Economic Cooperation and other American-backed efforts to rally the West against Communism. The older outlook lasted only in largely forgotten international bodies such as the UN's Economic Commission for Europe, whose reports were among the few after 1947 to try to see the continent as a whole.

Which brings us to another facet of the forgotten history of these years that the focus on reconstruction has helped to illuminate: the reconfiguration of internationalism out of the war effort against Nazism. Again, this involved moving away from older Cold War binaries and returning to consider the joint inheritance of both sides in the struggle against Germany. The late 1940s had been discussed in deeply normative language from the start. It was either freedom-loving liberals pitted against the evils of totalitarianism, or repressive anti-communists crushing the chances for a progressive Left. The ending of the Cold War did not dispel this moralizing but it changed its terms. There was now a new emphasis on the period's importance in the emergence of invigorated norms of international law and human rights (as in Paul Lauren's 1998 *The Evolution of Human Rights*), which presented the years 1945–48 as a series of lessons learned in the struggle with Nazi barbarism, lessons that retained their value in the late twentieth century.[7] At the same time, the hopes evident in the 1990s of a new more central role for the United Nations and other international bodies redirected attention to the post-1945 years in the emergence of a new world order, and a redefinition of internationalism itself after the gloom of the 1930s and the Nazis' own commitment to racial difference rather than universal values. And in the realm of law more broadly, the settling of scores with communism and regimes of transitional justice established in Eastern Europe after 1989 led scholars back to the war crimes trials and other kinds of reckoning that followed Liberation. In the commonly accepted late twentieth-century therapeutic model, public accounting of the past was good, cover-ups, and botched or failed purges were a sign of political ill-health or of problems stored up for the future.[8]

This return to the neglected history of law, internationalism, and judicial norm-making gained meaning too from the grim series of events that also marked the early 1990s—the eruption of ethnic cleansing in Yugoslavia, genocide in Rwanda, and the emergence of refugees as an issue for policy-makers and historians alike. Once again, the late 1940s looked pregnant with meaning. Its history of forced population movements—seguing almost seamlessly from the period of Nazi domination to the German expulsions that followed the Nazi defeat—attracted attention. So did the history of refugee movements and regimes and more broadly the impact of the demographic changes wrought by the war on conceptions of family, society, and the nation-state. Suddenly, the intensely political focus of much of the Cold War historiography looked partial and question-begging as the huge social dislocation of the 1940s swam into view.[9]

---

[7] P. Lauren, *The Evolution of Human Rights: Visions Seen* (Philadelphia, 1998).

[8] E. Borgwardt, *A New Deal for the World: America's Vision for Human Rights* (Harvard, 2005); Deak, Gross, and Judt (eds), *Politics of Retribution.*

[9] On ethnic cleansing N. Naimark, *Fires of Hatred: Ethnic Cleansing in Twentieth Century Europe* (Harvard, 1998); B. Lieberman, *Terrible Fate: Ethnic Cleansing in the Making of Modern Europe* (Chicago, 2006). Early specific studies of previously neglected cases included A. De Zayas, *A Terrible Revenge: The Ethnic Cleansing of East European Germans, 1944–50* (New York, 1994) and J. McCarthy, *Death and Exile: The Ethnic Cleansing of Ottoman Muslims, 1821–1922* (Princeton, 1995); on the former, see now B. Frommer, *National Cleansing: Retribution against Nazi Collaborators in Postwar Czechoslovakia* (Cambridge, 2005) and on the latter, A. Toumarkine, *Entre empire ottomane et etat-nation turc: les immigres mulumans du caucase at des balkans du milieu du XIXe siècle a nos jours* (Istanbul, 2000). On guilt and memory, from a vast literature, see E. Barkan, *Taking Wrongs Seriously: Apologies and Reconciliation* (Stanford, 2006). On the history of refugees, key recent works include: M. Marrus, *The Unwanted: European Refugees in the Twentieth Century* (Oxford, 1985); C. Skran, *Refugees in Interwar*

This new European narrative, which saw the period after 1945 as shaped as much by the need to cope with past experiences as with the effort to build new alliances from scratch, made it hard to sustain the old idea that 1945 had been a kind of Year Zero. If European history did not end in 1945, one had to trace instead a longer-run story of continuities across the divide of war.

A seminal article by Jan Gross in 1989 had posed the problem of how Nazi occupation, and the differential forms of Nazi occupation, might through the impact of social disintegration have paved the way for the communist take-over in Eastern Europe.[10] Perhaps therefore—and this obviously should not have needed spelling out to the extent that it did—the origins of the post war were to be found in the war years themselves. Ethnic cleansing was one phenomenon whose history ran across the 1945 watershed; but the development of corporatist partnerships in the iron and steel industries of the Ruhr was another. Gross himself had argued that total war, the destruction of the very fabric of society undertaken by the Nazis in Poland, for example, itself shaped the possibilities for post-war reconstruction. The extermination of East European Jewry, followed by the expulsion of the region's ethnic German population, meant the disappearance of much of the old bourgeois class and culture and rendered the reshaping of society by communist elites much easier. So did the legacy of German economic planning and state control of heavy industry in particular across the region, smoothing the post-war eta-tization of the commanding heights of national economies. Blurring the Left-Right divide, post-war planning often built on both wartime controls and the pre-war state plans developed by right-wing regimes in places like Poland and Bulgaria.

---

*Europe: The Emergence of a Regime* (Oxford, 1995) and a series of influential books by P. Gatrell, including: *A Whole Empire Walking: Refugees in Russia during World War 1* (Bloomington, 1999); P. Gatrell and N. Baron (eds), *Homelands: War, Population and Statehood in Eastern Europe and Russia, 1918–1924* (London, 2004), and now P. Gatrell and N Baron (eds), *Warlands: Population Resettlement and State Reconstruction in the Soviet–East European Borderlands, 1945–50* (Basingstoke, 2009). Mention should also be made of the special issue of the *Journal of Contemporary History* (July 2008) on 'Relief in the Aftermath of War', edited by Jessica Reinisch, that grew out of an earlier Balzan conference.

[10] J. Gross, 'The Social of War: Preliminaries to the Imposition of Communist Regimes in East Central Europe', *East European Politics and Societies*, 3:2 (Spring 1989), a theme explored at greater length in two masterly books: *Polish Society under German Occupation: the Generalgouvernement, 1933–1944* (Princeton, 1979) and *Revolution from Abroad: the Soviet Conquest of Poland's Western Ukraine and Western Belorussia* (Princeton, 1988).

Having accepted the obvious importance of Nazi occupation and the war, it remains to determine precisely what that legacy was. The occupation itself had, after all, affected different areas quite differently. This is obviously a vast subject and a differentiated assessment of the war's impact has hardly yet begun to be made (though the raw materials are there in the numerous analyses produced by various League of Nations bodies and by UN planning agencies such as UNRRA). To take but one example, the impact on European health remains poorly understood. Certain obvious population categories excepted, the overall impact was less catastrophic than it had been in the First World War, and outside the occupied Eastern territories, major famines and epidemics were actually rather rare. There was, for instance, no repeat of the 1918 influenza pandemic that had devastated much of the world.[11] No one has recently subjected to scrutiny the statistics for wartime mortality that were produced during and immediately after the war, despite the fact that the figures they generated were often used to justify requests for post-war aid or other kinds of assistance. Pieter Lagrou has suggested that there was considerable exaggeration in the French figures; the same may well be true for Poland and elsewhere. And this matters, since how we assess the success or failure of reconstruction is dependent on getting a proper sense of what had actually happened—as well as what people believed had happened—in the preceding few years.

A few further caveats about the post-Cold War optic may also be in order. The tendency to project back into the late 1940s the human rights norms and aspirations of the 1990s and early twenty-first century has led to a certain amount of anachronism. Accounts praising American internationalism, while explicable as reactions to trends in American foreign policy under George W. Bush, have turned out to be limited as accounts of the post-war conjuncture. One notable absence, for instance, from much of this literature has been any assessment of the Soviet role in international law and rights talk. Bringing this back in would allow the human rights/international law theme to be linked more persuasively to ideology and politics instead of presenting it as a self-evident good. And in any case, as Marti Koskenniemi has argued, one can make just as compelling a case for seeing the 1940s in terms of the crisis of law rather than the victory of law and for focusing instead on the rise of an alternative universalizing ideology of expertise, science, and technical knowledge that assumed a Leftish coloration in Julian Huxley's scientific

---

[11] I touch on this subject briefly in my *Hitler's Empire: Nazi Rule in Occupied Europe* (London, 2008), 287–90. For a contemporary assessment, see N. Goodman, 'Health in Europe', *International Affairs*, 20:4 (1944), 473–80.

humanism, and an increasingly Rightward one in the work of American modernization theorists.[12]

By the same token, one might ask in what ways precisely *were* the 1940s the crucible of internationalism? The one truth about the United Nations that could not be uttered at the time was that in many respects it was a direct continuation of the League, its predecessor. Indeed by giving more power to a directorate of Great Powers and less to the assembled membership, the new organization represented more of a return to nineteenth-century practice than an advance to a new kind of global collective diplomacy.[13]

At the same time, the state's role was much bigger, everywhere. After all, the war's generation saw that the state worked. It was national states that mobilized for war, and international agencies emerged as specialist services to assist them, working through them. Some of these turned into permanent bodies; others, like UNRRA were wound up. The International Refugee Organisation was intended to deal with a temporary problem, not to become permanent, and the International Settlement Agency that Roosevelt hoped might oversee a rational program of global colonial settlement never materialized. Those bodies that worked through the reconstruction were invariably highly contested and politicized, especially as the shadows of the Cold War lengthened. They worked with and through weakened national governments often acutely conscious of their own lack of reach or legitimacy and they operated, as Tara Zahra shows in her work on UNRRA and displaced children, by ascribing national and collective identities to their charges and acknowledging nations' rights over them. In the case of those international agencies charged with overseeing *economic* reconstruction, such as the US-driven CEEC, the renewed power of the nation-state is just as clear. Internationalism thus reached its limits quickly when it turned into an ideology indifferent to the prestige and authority of the nation-states whose political revival lay at the heart of the reconstruction effort. As the most successful strand of internationalism had insisted for the past half-century, unless international

---

[12] For a critique of works stressing human rights such as those by Borgwardt and Lauren, see S. Moyn, *The Last Utopia: Human Rights in History* (Harvard, 2010); on Soviet investment in international law after 1945, see now F. Hirsch, 'The Soviets at Nuremberg: International Law, Propaganda and the Making of the Postwar Order', *American Historical Review*, 113 (June 2008), 701–730; on the crisis of international law, M. Koskenniemi, *The Gentle Civiliser of Nations: The Rise and Fall of International Law* (Cambridge, 2001).

[13] This is argued at greater length in my *No Enchanted Palace: The End of Empire and the Ideological Origins of the United Nations* (Princeton, 2009).

institutions recognized and worked through nation-states, their success would be short-lived.

This belief in the efficacy of state power is connected with something equally germane to our subject—the self-consciousness of the reconstruction effort. Planning for post-war reconstruction began astonishingly early in the war itself. But the point is that reconstruction itself was the operative category for those involved. Karl Mannheim talked in 1940 about the 'age of reconstruction': a book characteristically anxious about the capabilities of modern mass democracy had seen reconstruction as simultaneously a political, social, ethical, and psychological challenge. But the historians were as concerned as the sociologists. Ferrero's study of the Congress of Vienna (entitled *The Reconstruction of Europe*), appearing in the same year as Mannheim's work, used the term very differently, to convey the eternal, Sisyphean task that confronted the wise statesman and diplomat in taming the disorder provoked by 'the great fear'. The subject lost none of its interest to policy-makers as the war neared an end. On the contrary. Harold Nicolson's 1946 study of the same subject testified to the search for historical insights into the post-war reconstruction problem (in Nicolson's case, the desire to avoid the break-up of the winning coalition that had ensued in 1918–20). Charles Webster, the Foreign Office historian who played such an important role in wartime peace planning, had written on the subject for the Foreign Office in the run-up to the Paris Peace Conference: his book was reprinted in 1934 and again in 1945. At least twenty-four books on the post-Napoleonic peace were published in the 1940s; the following decade saw a mere four.[14]

Reconstruction thus brought with it the desire to learn from past efforts. Only a few British diplomats sought lessons as far back as 1815. But 1914–1918 was another matter. We learn from Elisabeth White's work how the Soviet welfare authorities in Leningrad tackled the problem of child returnees on the basis of their own bitter and vivid memories of the mass childlessness and neglect that had followed the Russian civil war. But more generally, whether it was to avoid the malnutrition of the previous war, or the depression of the 1930s, most participants in planning for the post-war world were prompted by the desire to avoid whatever it was that they had thought had gone wrong last time. Historical interpretation was thus inseparable from

---

[14] K. Mannheim, *Man and Society in an Age of Reconstruction: Studies in Modern Social Structure* (London, 1940); G. Ferrero, *Reconstruction: Talleyrand a Vienne, 1814–1815* (Paris, 1940); H. Nicolson, *The Congress of Vienna: A Study in Allied Unity, 1812–1822* (London, 1946); C. Webster, *The Congress of Vienna, 1814–1815* (London, 1919).

future strategizing and institutional reform. 1815 was a challenge to the men (and a few women) of 1945 to demonstrate that a democratic order could renew itself and generate a peace as lasting as the monarchical restoration of 1815. This was the concern that animated the establishment of the United Nations, the resolution of the German question, and the problem more generally of how to make peace in a world of nation-states. The Holy Alliance lurked in the background—inspiration for some, warning for others who suspected that what they were being asked to sign up to, whether in the guise of Roosevelt's Four Policemen, or the Dumbarton Oaks proposals for a peacetime United Nations Organization, was indeed a revived Alliance operating under the cloak of the New Diplomacy.

Thus talk about reconstruction begged the question of which past people wanted, or thought they wanted, to reconstruct. To take a brief example, there were really only two alternatives for the territorial settlement in Eastern Europe after Hitler's defeat: either to return, as it were, to 1815 by creating large federal or confederal units that would look and act rather like the old empires (only without emperors) and be a match for Germany; or back to 1919, and to make good Paris' promise of a continent of nation-states, if necessary by taking up where the Nazis had left off, shunting minorities around, stripping them of any collective rights, and promoting ethnic homogeneity. The British and Americans clung to the former idea for much of the war; the East European politicians in exile and Stalin clung to the latter. From the territorial viewpoint, 1945 was a victory for *them*,—and reconstruction proceded with only slight modifications (outside Poland) to the Paris peace settlement.

If reconstruction had a powerful history, it had a future too. Assumptions about the post-war reconstruction experience in Europe helped shape post-war social science and government policy throughout the world in the 1950s and 1960s. In particular, the rise of development studies in US universities, and their transformation in the 1960s into modernization theory, were premised on all kinds of assumptions about how reconstruction had fared in Europe after 1945. Many Kennedy-era policy-makers, their advisers and mentors, had after all taken a direct role in that reconstruction effort. When Walt Rostow became Lyndon Johnson's National Security Advisor, his prescription for South East Asia was basically an extrapolation of his own experience in Europe in the 1940s: his Vietnam policy was to bomb strategic targets (as the Allies had done in Germany, on targets Rostow had helped to select) and massive development aid to restructure Vietnamese society (much as Rostow had worked, first on the Economic Commission for Europe and then in the Marshall Plan bureaucracy). And alongside Rostow were numerous others with similar life stories bringing the lessons of Europe's successful reconstruction to Asia, Africa, and South America.[15]

In short, the reconstruction of Europe became a lesson learned that shaped the globalization of the Cold War, as likely moulding Soviet as it did American development policy in the Third World. The links between Europe and its former colonial territories went both ways. As American theorists started to argue that democracy might have triumphed in Europe after 1945 for very specific reasons that did not apply to backward peoples in Africa and Asia, so historical sociologists like Harvard's Barrington Moore suggested that the emergence of authoritarian regimes in peasant societies might be able to shed light on why so many European countries had themselves succumbed to dictatorship between the wars. Thus reconstruction offers a prism through which to view Europe's rapidly changing relationship with the wider world. Europe's life after Europe, as it were, as a socio-economic model of successful political and social restructuring ensured its importance even after the 1940s had ended and the focus of the Cold War had shifted elsewhere.[16]

Finally, we might return to the political dimension of reconstruction, which has been comparatively overlooked of late. Unlike the historians of the Cold War era, recent scholarship has focused on relief agencies and the national, social, and technical aspects of the reconstruction effort. Yet there was one very important geopolitical difference between the two twentieth-century post-war eras and that was the lack of a formal or conclusive peace settlement after 1945. The Great Powers' inability to reach agreement over the future of Germany in particular meant that there was no formal break with the war so that reconstruction took place—especially in places like Italy and Greece—in an atmosphere of ambiguous political transition. Contemporary scholars are tackling the problem of legitimacy that arose in such situations, where abrupt changes in political rhetoric and values masked significant continuities in the personnel and practices of the state. They explore whether these continuities help explain the conservative restoration that some see emerging in Western Europe and ask whether they also help us understand the persistence of a quasi-war footing lasting years after the war in countries whose populations generally longed for nothing more than a return to peace.

---

[15] The link between Rostow's policy prescriptions and his understanding of the lessons of World War Two is well brought out in D. Milne, *America's Rasputin: Walt Rostow and the Vietnam War* (New York, 2008).

[16] B. Moore, *Social Origins of Dictatorship and Democracy: Lord and Peasant in the Modern World* (Boston, 1966). See also D. Smith, *Barrington Moore: A Critical Appraisal* (New York, 1983).

Yet perhaps we still need a rudimentary typology of the politics of reconstruction. After all, there were considerable differences between countries like Denmark, the Low Countries, Norway and the USSR, where reconstruction essentially involved pre-war regimes reconstructing themselves; countries like France and Greece where the democratic transformation took place amid the memories of earlier democratic collapse; and countries under occupation—Italy, Germany, Austria, and Hungary—whose transition to democracy was being managed for them. There were others too with somewhat different political trajectories of their own; but this simply means that the task of reconstruction, from the political standpoint, varied from place to place.

Finally, it may be worth asking to what extent reconstruction took place in a continent still on a kind of war footing. This is not just an allusion to the armed insurrections which continued in parts of Central and Eastern Europe into the late 1940s, and in isolated cases even longer, where the victor's peace was challenged (unlike in Germany, for example, where it was almost immediately accepted). The historian of reconstruction ought to be able to accommodate the phenomenon of armed resistance as much as the study of the preceding occupation has done. There were certainly acute fears of political instability, on both sides of the Iron Curtain, for months and even years after the war ended. Demobilization placed huge pressure on the transition to a peacetime economy in a continent whose memory of mass unemployment and agrarian underemployment had scarcely been effaced by the war years' brief span. But there was also the lingering impact of wartime restrictions of all kinds. Was it only in and after the Korean War with the ending of the Greek civil war, the collapse of anti-Soviet insurgencies in eastern Europe, and the shutting down of camps on both sides of the Iron Curtain, after their sudden growth in the late 1940s, all accompanied of course by the anti-colonial struggle beyond Europe's borders—that Europe finally found a kind of peace? When was that moment when it could at last be seen that reconstruction too was just a phase, a phase that had now ended? The British Ministry of Reconstruction was wound up in July 1945 but in comparative terms this was astonishingly early. On the continent of Europe its equivalents in places like the Netherlands, Belgium, France, Hungary, Poland, and Greece tended to last into the mid-1950s before being wound up or folded into housing, development, or public works ministries. Perhaps reconstruction was a much longer and more pervasive process than we have tended to imagine.

# War, Reconstruction, and the Nationalization of Britain, 1939–1951

## David Edgerton

The pairing 'war and reconstruction' is a central idea in the social democratic historiography of Britain between 1939 and 1951.[1] The linking reflects the implicit view that plans for reconstruction were important during the war itself, and indeed that society was being reconstructed before 1945. Reconstruction is taken to be about the building of a society very different from that of 1939, indeed one more like that of 1945. In this story the events of 1939, and especially of 1940, inaugurated a *People's War*, which put Britain on the *Road to 1945* and thus to the *People's Peace*, to give the titles of relevant and famous books.[2] It is hardly surprising then that we have 'the triumph of social democracy', or the rise of the 'benign state' used as chapter headings for periods covering both the war and post-war years.[3] Tellingly, an account of the British state which took seriously the fiscal-military state of the eighteenth century gives Britain a 'Social-Service State' between 1880 and 1939, while the period 1939 to 1979 is covered in a chapter on 'Total War and Cradle-to-Grave Welfare'.[4] Such ideas are of course linked to the suggestion that the 1940 coalition embodied a new consensus which persisted despite party government after the war; it has a political as well as a policy dimension, one in which the Left becomes more important as the welfare state was being forged in a new Britain where the People were central.

---

[1] I am grateful to Waqar Zaidi, the editors, and referees for their perceptive comments on earlier versions. Many thanks also to Adam Tooze.

[2] Angus Calder, *The People's War: Britain, 1939–1945* (London, 1969); Paul Addison, *The Road to 1945: British Politics in the Second World War* (London, 1975) and Kenneth Morgan, *The People's Peace: Britain since 1945* (London, 1989).

[3] James E. Cronin, *Labour and Society in Britain, 1918–1979* (London, 1984), chapter 7 is entitled 'The Triumph of Social Democracy, 1940–1948'. Martin Pugh, *State and Society: A Social and Political History of Britain*, 2nd edn, (London, 1999) covers the war and post-war state under the rubric of the 'benign' state, and has the usual references to the welfare state and the Keynesian era.

[4] Philip Harling, *The Modern British State: An Historical Introduction* (Cambridge, 2001).

Although older assessments of the achievements of the welfare state (and of consensus) in this period have been much criticized, the welfare state itself remains central to historical understanding. [5] Even self-conscious products of the cultural and imperial turns run on the familiar tracks of this welfarism.[6] Yet there are good reasons to reject welfarism as the central feature of the history of the state and of Britain more generally in this period. Indeed we need to reassess the whole history and historiography of the period. Alan Milward made a powerful and under-appreciated point when he noted a generation ago that his fellow historians of wartime Britain exaggerated domestic social change and downplayed economic change, especially its international aspects.[7] The same might be said of the post-war period. Among many missing dimensions to the story are two big issues. The first is the transformation of military and military industrial capacities of the British state and nation, not only in war but in peace, in short the rise of the warfare and industrial state. The second is the new importance of economic nationalism, especially from 1945.[8] By focusing on each, and particularly the latter, I show that there are important but neglected continuities and discontinuities in 1945, as well as 1939/40 and in the early 1950s.[9] This leads also to the need to distinguish quite radically between the wartime and post-war periods, and thus to rethink not only war but reconstruction.

[5] See for example, Harold Smith, (ed.) *War and Social Change: Britain in the Second World War* (Manchester, 1986); Penny Summerfield, *Women Workers in the Second World War: Production and Patriarchy in Conflict* (London, 1984) and *Reconstructing Women's Wartime Lives: Discourse and Subjectivity in Oral Histories of the Second World War* (Manchester, 1998); José Harris, 'Society and the State in Twentieth-century Britain' in F. M. L. Thompson, *Cambridge Social History of Britain*, vol. 3 *Social Agencies and Institutions* (Cambridge, 1990), 63–118; Tom Ling, *The British State since 1945: An Introduction* (Cambridge, 1998); Lawrence Black et al., *Consensus or Coercion: The State, the People and Social Cohesion in Post-war Britain* (Cheltenham, 2001).

[6] A recent example is James Vernon, *Hunger: A Modern History* (Cambridge, Mass., 2007)

[7] Alan S. Milward, *The Economic Effects of Two World Wars on Britain*, 2nd edn (London, 1984), 27. This is a new book despite being labelled a second edition.

[8] Alan Milward and George Brennan, *Britain's Place in the World: A Hstorical Enquiry into Import Controls, 1945–60* (London, 1996) is a key contribution.

[9] This paper draws on my *Warfare State: Britain, 1920–1970* (Cambridge, 2006), and *Britain's War Machine: Weapons, Resources and Experts in the Second World War* (London, 2011) and complements my 'The Primacy of Foreign Policy? Britain in the Second World War' in William Mulligan and Brendan Simms (eds), *The Primacy of Foreign Policy in British History, 1660–2000: How Strategic Concerns Shaped Modern Britain* (London, 2010), 291–304.

## Welfare

There is much to be said for the notion that the British state was a 'welfare state', and from well before the Second World War. In the interwar years welfare expenditures were greater than warfare expenditures. There is, however, a poor correlation between historians' claims for the subsequent rise of the welfare state and changes in welfare spending. Sidney Pollard cautioned long ago that: 'In spite of a widespread belief to the contrary, Britain did not spend significantly more on the social services after 1948 than she did before 1939 apart from the retirement pension.'[10] The growth in welfare spending was hardly enormous, though the figures are unclear. Tomlinson necessarily guesstimates social services expenditure by central government (excluding food subsidies) at £900 million in 1945/46 increasing to £1,265 million in 1950/51 including transfer payments.[11] In the totemic case of health expenditure, there are no real-terms cross-war estimates of expenditure, which is in itself interesting. The estimated total public and private health spending is £150 million in the mid-1930s (about 3 per cent of GNP).[12] That would have been worth around £300 million in the late 1940s, which suggests, since in the early years the NHS was spending around £400 million, a hardly revolutionary increase of about 25 per cent over a decade. Remarkably, plans for the NHS during the war involved expenditure estimates which were less (even without correction for inflation) than total 1930s health expenditure, and the early post-war plans appeared to envisage real terms expenditure that was just as niggardly.[13] As is well known, no hospital was built in the late 1940s, and what expansion in capacity there was during and after the war might not have been enough to raise bed provision per capita.[14]

Indeed in many areas concerned with public services and infrastructure, the war saw a collapse in investment, with slow recuperation in the late 1940s, typically not reaching the levels of the 1930s. It was a case of reconstruction from huge wartime cutbacks, rather than raising the level above the

[10] Sidney Pollard, *The Development of the British Economy*, 3rd edn *1914–1980* (London, 1983), 272.

[11] Jim Tomlinson, *Democratic Socialism and Economic Policy: The Attlee Years, 1945–1951* (Cambridge, 1997), 253.

[12] Charles Webster, *Health Services since the War* (London, 1988), vol. I, 12–13. Public expenditure on health was around 1.2% of GNP. T. Cutler, 'Dangerous Yardstick? Early Cost Estimates and the Politics of Financial Management in the first decade of the National Health Service', *Medical History* 47 (2003), 217–38 does not make the trans-war comparison either.

[13] See Webster, *Health Services*, 133–4, though Webster does not appear to make the crucial correction for wartime inflation.

[14] Tomlinson, *Democratic Socialism and Economic Policy*, 249.

supposedly disastrous 1930s. A key case was housing. Local authority house building at 83,000 in 1947 was less than in 1938/39 though higher than the 1935–38 average; it should be noted that private house building was a small fraction of what it had been in the 1930s (well over 200,000 houses per annum).[15] By 1950 total house building was still one half of the late 1930s average, though state-funded building was now greater.[16] Investment in school buildings did not return to 1938 levels until 1950. As Tomlinson points out, it took a very long time for the provisions of the 1944 Education Act to be felt on the ground. [17] In many important areas, especially those concerned with welfare and infrastructure, the 1940s taken as a whole were an era of disinvestment. In other words, while there is an image of building over and above what was being done in 1939, in some areas it took till the 1950s to get back to what was happening in 1939.

## Warfare

The most significant change in public expenditure between the interwar years and the war and post-war years was in defence expenditure. It increased twentyfold from 1938/39 to its wartime peak, while conventional civil expenditure (that undertaken under the usual parliamentary procedure) hardly changed through the war. While there were additional civil expenditures out of wartime votes of credit, they appear to have been limited to measures specific to the war, for example the Emergency Medical Service, the Ministry of Food, and evacuation. There was certainly no general improvement in welfare services.[18] Although defence expenditure fell radically after the war, its level remained very much higher than before the war. In relation to GDP, it was about twice as great in the late 1940s as in 1935, with rearmament in the early 1950s it became three times as great. In 1953 defence took over 30 per cent of public expenditure (net of debt interest), while health and social security took 26 per cent. In the late 1940s, and even more so the early 1950s, the warfareness of state spending had increased compared to the 1930s. The welfare state rose around the war, but the warfare state rose even more. To put it another way, we are apt to forget the deep structural impact of the Cold War on post-war Britain.

One can tell a similar story about state employment. It seemed to be widely believed that it was the welfare state which was behind its rapid growth. Thus a 1950s study of the British civil service claimed that 'The principal reason for

---

[15] *Annual Abstract of Statistics, No 70, 1937–1947* (London, 1948) Table 76.

[16] *Annual Abstract of Statistics, No 92, 1955* (London, 1955) Table 61.

[17] Tomlinson, *Democratic Socialism and Economic Policy*, 243.

[18] *Votes of Credit, 1942–43* Cmd. 6363.

the inability to slash the British Civil Service as drastically as the critics demand is the flood of new responsibilities which have fallen on public offices since the war. The welfare state requires huge staffs of officials.'[19] Yet the same book provides a table showing that between 1938 and 1954 the *non*-industrial civil service grew by 292,000, of which 100,000 were due to the defence departments (the service and supply ministries concerned with supplying them with equipment). Only 42,000 went to the social services of all sorts. Of the remainder, 56,000 went to the Post Office, and 40,000 to trade, industry, and transport, leaving 54,000 for all other departments.[20] The number of non-industrial civil servants in defence departments had been about 10,000 in 1914; it was 23,040 in 1935 and 135,270 in 1956.[21] These figures underestimate the growth of the warfare state because they exclude (and most figures on state employment do) the vast army of *industrial* civil servants. In 1929 there were 122,000 'industrial' workers in the civil service, a category which excluded the great majority of ('manipulative') postal workers.[22] During the war half of all civil servants were industrial workers. In 1943 their number peaked at 738,000, with about 650,000 in defence departments.[23] In 1957 there were a total of 418,300 industrial civil servants, of which 289,600 were in defence departments, a number which fell steadily to 154,200 by 1971.[24] By 1957 40 per cent of all civil servants were in defence departments compared with 20 per cent of non-industrial civil servants; in this year there were about the same number of civil servants in the defence departments (423,000) as in the whole British state in 1929 (434,000).[25] Here, again, the warfare state turns out to be by far the most significant area of growth of the *civilian* state. Yet we should not ignore the military servants of the state. By 1945 there were 4.5 million men in the armed services, and 0.4 million women.[26] After the war force levels fell to 689,000 in 1950, and were

[19] G. A. Campbell, *The Civil Service in Britain* (Harmondsworth, 1955), 95.

[20] Campbell, *Civil Service*, 100.

[21] D. N. Chester and F. M. G. Willson, *The Organisation of British Central Government*, 2nd edn (London, 1968), 328, Table XVIII.

[22] Royal Commission on the Civil Service, *Introductory factual memorandum relating to the Civil Service submitted by the Treasury, 1930.*

[23] Central Statistical Office, *Statistical Digest of the War,* (London, 1951), Table 32.

[24] F. M. G. Willson, 'Coping with Administrative Growth: Super-departments and the Ministerial Cadre 1957–77' in David Butler and A. H. Halsey (eds), *Policy and Politics: Essays in Honour of Norman Chester* (London, 1978), 38.

[25] Calculated from Willson, 'Administrative Growth', 38 and Royal Commission on the Civil Service, *Introductory factual memorandum relating to the civil service submitted by the Treasury, 1930.*

[26] *Statistical Digest of the War*, Table, 9.

then pushed up to a peacetime peak of 872,000, before falling below 500,000 only in 1960. In the early 1930s the figure was around 320,000. Peacetime conscription had been introduced in 1939; after the war peacetime service remained, *increasing* from one year in 1947, to eighteen months from 1948 and to two years from 1950. No men were conscripted from the end of 1960, and the last conscripts left in 1963.[27] It was not for nothing that for the twenty years between 1939 and 1959 the Ministry of Labour became the Ministry of Labour *and National Service*. By peacetime precedents, post-1945 Britain was extraordinarily militarized.

To the extent that high levels of post-war defence expenditures were noted in the standard history they were put down to an imperial hangover and/or the result of subservience to the USA in its new role as global policeman for capitalism. Such an interpretation went along with a picture of British forces being equipped with left-over material from the war. In fact British forces were re-equipped after the war and wartime levels of development and research expenditures kept up, with many new laboratories being built. One could get post-war investment in centres for the development of weapons of mass destruction, but not for new hospitals. The reason for the re-equipment was that the new modernized and large forces were kept in being to deal mainly with the Soviet Union in Europe, not for imperial policing purposes, or minor British operations overseas. The great rearmament programme of the early 1950s often misleadingly called 'Korean War rearmament', should be recognized as what it was: a building up the capacities of British forces in Britain and Europe, not those of the small numbers who fought in Korea.

### Economic nationalism

Older approaches, as well as the recent imperial view, are apt to overstress the significance of empire to British history in both foreign relations and domestic history. Yet for the war and reconstruction eras empire is in some significant respects understated. The role of empire (formal and informal) in providing troops, military equipment, and general supplies, often for deferred payment (the sterling balances) is underplayed compared with relations with the USA. For the post-war years the proportion of British trade with empire was higher than in the age of high imperialism. The colonial empire became particularly important—Malaya for dollar exports and Africa as a potential source of many materials. There was a second very technically

---

[27] On the internal politics of getting rid of conscription see, Martin S. Navias, 'Terminating Conscription? The British National Service Controversy, 1955–1956', *Journal of Contemporary History*, 24 (1989), 195–208. In the initial 1947 bill conscription was set at 18 months, but was reduced to one year.

oriented imperial occupation of Africa after the war, which went much further than the Ministry of Food's well-known ground-nut scheme.[28] But a focus on empire can too easily disconnect Britain from the rest of the world, and lead to a neglect of a supremely important change, the rise of economic and political nationalism.

The import of any sort of manufactured goods was exceedingly difficult. Very powerful import quotas, brought to light by Brennan and Milward, were used with other tools to discriminate in favour of 'strategic' and modern industries.[29] Through these and other measures industries Britain hardly had before appeared, such as oil-refining. Before and during the war Britain was the world's largest importer of petroleum but it typically came in refined. After the war big refineries were built by 1956 in Isle of Grain (BP), Shell Haven (Shell), Stanlow (Shell), Fawley (Esso), Llandarcy (BP), Heysham (Shell) and Grangemouth (BP).[30] Other examples abound: three new plants making sulphuric acid (a hugely important chemical intermediate) from domestic anhydrite were built, to add to the one existing one;[31] watch-making and alarm-clock-making were established on a large scale, as were the manufacture of photographic film base, and new kinds of colour photographic film.[32] A heavy tractor industry was established, with first the conversion of Sherman tanks into tractors called 'Sherviks' for the African groundnut scheme, then the design and manufacture of Vickers Vigor tractors, a case of tanks into tractors rather than swords into ploughshares.[33]

---

[28] Imperialism was, furthermore, forward looking. For a recent study following up on the idea of a second imperial occupation after the war, one of technicians and researchers see Sabine Clarke, 'A Technocratic Imperial State? The Colonial Office and Scientific Research, 1940–1960', *Twentieth Century British History*, 18 (2007), 453–80 and John Hodge, *Triumph of the Expert — Agrarian Doctrines of Development and the Legacies of British Colonialism* (Ohio, 2007).

[29] Milward and Brennan, *Britain's Place in the World*, 190–4.

[30] Duncan Burn, 'The Oil Industry', in Duncan Burn (ed.), *The Structure of British Industry*, 2 vols (Cambridge, 1958), vol. I, 185.

[31] In 1950 in Britain there was one anhydrite sulphuric acid plant (ICI Billingham). Of the three new ones, one was built by ICI, and another was connected with ICI. W. B. Reddaway 'The Chemical Industry' in Duncan Burn (ed.), *The Structure of British Industry*, vol. I, 239.

[32] C. Glatt, 'Reparations and the Transfer of Scientific and Industrial Technology from Germany', dissertation (European University Institute, 1994), vol. 3, 904–15. See also P. Winston, 'The British Government and Defence Production 1943–1950', PhD thesis (University of Cambridge, 1982),173–82.

[33] J. D. Scott, *Vickers: A History* (London, 1962), 324–6. Christopher Foss and Peter McKenzie, *The Vickers Tanks* (Wellingborough, 1988), 148–9.

And of course, huge efforts were made in civil aviation, deemed by many to be the key industry of the future. State purchases of manufactures were highly nationalistic: the purchase of non-British equipment was not only rare but controversial. More than this, state agencies were keen to support national technical development with public money to supply new British machines to British nationalized and national industries. Great techno-national initiatives led to new aero-engines and aircraft, both civil and military. In terms of manufactures continued high levels of defence spending were obviously important, but the nationalization of utilities in particular created large single state buyers. Thus the Ministry of Transport through its ownership of the railways, and the Ministry of Health through its ownership of hospitals, and the Ministry of Fuel and Power, through its ownership of electrical systems, the gas works, and the coal mines had a crucial say in what was bought. Government ministries were major buyers in the domestic market, indeed sometimes monopoly buyers.[34]

The move away from internationalism and indeed imperialism towards nationalism was particularly evident in the case of food. Indeed one of the best known features uniting the war and reconstruction periods is the continuation of wartime food rationing into the 1950s, with a tightening after the war in some respects, notably in the rationing of bread for a period. The questions of rationing and domestic supply need to be kept separate: most domestically produced food was not rationed whereas most imported food was. Rationing (apart from bread after the war), was confined to relatively expensive goods of which much or all the supply was imported, in war as in peace, such as meat, butter, cheese, bacon, tea, sugar. In some cases, for example meat, wartime imports were higher than pre-war, while in other cases, such as sugar, they were considerably lower.

Diets in the war and reconstruction period were distinctive. The mid-1950s saw a temporary return, in some respects, to pre-war diets. The British diet changed at the beginning of the war as some supplies became short and others more plentiful. The diet stayed essentially the same through the end of the war into the late 1940s. There is no 1945 break in the statistics—levels of vegetables, bread and cereals, meat and fat consumption remained much the same per person, while there were steady increases through the period in the availability of milk and fruit. After 1950 there was a marked change as consumption of vegetables per capita fell, along with that of bread and cereals, while

---

[34] Carlo J. Morelli, 'The Illusions, Reality and Implications of British Government Expenditure 1948–1968', Working paper 103, Department of Economics, University of Dundee, October 1999.

meat consumption increased.[35] The case of meat illustrates the depth of the control. Before the war most imported beef was chilled, but from 1939 until the early 1950s only lower quality frozen beef was acquired.[36] Chilled beef exports from New Zealand resumed only in 1952; it was agreed that Argentina would export chilled beef again in 1951, but it was not till 1953 that experimental exports began.[37]

But the pre-war pattern of food supply would not return; national self-sufficiency and radical increases in productivity would be the aim, for all kinds of food, from wheat to meat. It is one of the few cases that corresponds to a progressive 'war and reconstruction story' of wartime development exceeding that of the 1930s, and exceeded again in the 1940s. Food was one of Britain's most important imports. The permanent and serious move significantly to increase domestic production was a radical break with one hundred years of free trade and fewer of imperial preference in food supply. The break happened in 1939/40 with the beginning of a huge increase in domestic production, with no return to pre-war levels of imports. The essential story is of the ploughing up of grassland to plant much larger quantities of cereals and vegetables. This was bulky but cheap food that saved on shipping, which could be efficiently produced in relation to land and labour. The nationalization of food supply and its scientization went hand in glove.[38]

We may summarize the story by looking at the tractorization of British agriculture. This was very radically speeded up from the beginning of the war, overwhelmingly with Fordson N tractors made by Ford in Dagenham, one of the largest factories in Britain, indeed Europe. Tractor production was roughly the same as before the war; the great difference was that the majority of tractors had previously been exported. By 1947 tractor production was many times larger than it had been pre-war, while motor car production was only getting back to pre-war levels.[39] From 1945 Ford at Dagenham was producing

---

[35] See David Buss, 'The Changing Household Diet', in J. M. Slater (ed.), *Fifty Years of the National Food Survey* (London, 1991), 49, Figure 5.2. See also the data in Ina Zweiniger-Bargielowska, *Austerity in Britain: Rationing, Controls and Consumption, 1939–1955* (Oxford, 2002), 34–7 at 36.

[36] *The Times*, 6 Jan. 1951, report from Buenos Aires correspondent.

[37] *The Times*, 9 Feb. 1953, report from Buenos Aires correspondent. On the 1951 agreement see *The Times*, 24 April 1951.

[38] The years after the war saw an extraordinary leap in productivity levels, of land and labour, in agriculture, which was greater than that in industry. The number of agricultural workers fell, but output increased enormously.

[39] *Annual Abstract of Statistics 1937–1947* Tables 164–165.

a new model, the Fordson Major, while a second major producer started up in 1946. Standard Motors built the Ferguson TE20 from 1946 at Banner Lane, Coventry.[40] The Banner Lane factory was an aero-engine 'shadow' factory, which Standard had managed and now took over.

It may seem surprising that wartime Britain could afford to extend and mechanize domestic agriculture, and that after the war it could devote so much more effort to it. It does not fit with the image of a weak pre-war industrial base, and industry left clapped out by the war effort. That image was powerful after the war: it was held that British industry sacrificed itself by giving up its overseas markets and as the future Prime Minister Harold Wilson was to put it, the 'failure to make good the wear and tear of machinery overworked in war production'.[41] The idea has been influential since.[42] Yet sectors engaged in war production received huge amounts of investment; those not deemed essential suffered from lack of investment and maintenance backlogs. A huge proportion, perhaps half, of all armaments were (in my estimate) produced not in existing facilities, but in newly built, government-owned arms plants, or on specialist machines supplied by government. The Banner Lane aero-engine factory was just one instance. The overall investment was enormous: between 1936 and 1945 the state invested around £1bn in armament capacity.[43] Its comparative scale may be gauged from looking at the compensation paid for industries which were nationalized in the 1940s: £927m for the railways, £392m for the coal mines, and £246m for the iron and steel industry.[44] A. J. P. Taylor was partly right when in the penultimate paragraph of his *English History* he stated that

> the second war, unlike the first, stimulated or created new industries which could hold their own in peacetime. During the second world war, and not before, Great Britain took the decisive step into the twentieth century. Before the war Great Britain was still trying to revive the old staples. After it, she relied on new developing industries. Electricity, motor cars, iron and steel, machine tools, nylons,

---

[40] An earlier Ferguson model, built by Ford in the USA, the famous Ford Ferguson, had not been built in Britain

[41] Harold Wilson, *Post-war Economic Policies in Britain,* (London, 1957), 2. Indeed for Wilson there appeared to be no benefit whatever from war production, ibid., 3–5.

[42] E.g., A. Cairncross, *Years of Recovery: British Economic Policy, 1945–1951* (London, 1985; 1987), 13.

[43] Edgerton, *Warfare State,* chapter 3.

[44] See Sir Norman Chester, *The Nationalisation of British Industry 1945–51* (London, 1975), 238, 257, 274, 315.

and chemicals were all set for expansion, and in all of them output per head was steadily increasing. The very spirit of the nation had changed.[45]

What Taylor inevitably missed was the key role of (hidden) public investment in certain sectors.

## Turning to the nation

Within the 'war and reconstruction' frame an implicit national and nationalist rebirth is central, for it is this which brings together the wartime nation in a way which leads to reconstruction. It is indeed easy to find a nationalist moment in 1940, with talk of the being 'alone', the 'island fortress' the 'impregnable citadel of free people', and various forms of native genius, notably from the previously non-patriotic Left.[46] Yet there were other stories in play—those of imperial unity, the unity of English-speaking peoples, and also British solidarity with those under Nazi oppression. From January 1942 British propaganda makes great play of the 'United Nations', and especially but not only the 'Big Four', fighting to extirpate barbarian, nationalist, militarism. Indeed internationalism was important and an underrated and revitalized feature of wartime political/intellectual activity.[47] Internationalism was central to the British conduct of the war from 1942, both in military terms (think of the combined chiefs of staff, the supreme commanders of mixed nationality forces in various theatres) but also in supply terms. For example, through Lend-Lease Britain got nearly all its oil from refineries in the USA, whereas at the beginning of the war Britain had sought to avoid the neutral US as a source at all. Another example would be the fact that the great majority of tanks in British armoured formations were US-built Shermans. Indeed wartime saw an unprecedented level of imports of manufactures into Britain, a point not generally noted because munitions were often excluded from import statistics. This was not a straightforward matter of subservience

---

[45] At a conference of the Institute for Contemporary British History in the early 1990s Eric Hobsbawm quoted this passage as an example of complacency about the state of British industry after the war.

[46] Quotations from the film, *Britain at Bay*, by J. B. Priestley, Ministry of Information/GPO film unit, 1940.

[47] See Waqar Zaidi, 'Technology and the Reconstruction of International Relations: Liberal Internationalist Proposals for the Internationalisation of Aviation and the International Control of Atomic Energy in Britain, USA and France, 1920–1950', PhD thesis (University of London, 2008).

to a greater power, but an attempt through a division of labour to maximize the exploitation of common resources.[48]

From 1945, rather than 1939 or 1940, 'national' and 'nation' enter the language to an extraordinary extent, and to a considerable degree the British nation is separated from Empire and Commonwealth. In the Labour manifesto, *Let Us Face the Future: A Declaration of Labour Policy for the Consideration of the Nation,* the attention given to foreign affairs and trade was negligible; the word 'empire' does not figure.[49] There is a partial contrast to be made with the language of other parties at least in the 1945 manifestos. 'Mr Churchill's declaration of policy to the electors', the Conservative manifesto of 1945, gave much attention to imperial trade, but used a national rather than imperial 'we': it spoke of the 'Mother Country' and its relation to Commonwealth and Empire noting that '*We* shall never forget *their* love and steadfastness when *we* stood alone against the German Terror' [emphasis added], noting also that 'During a whole year of this great war Britain bore the burden of the struggle alone'. The free-trading Liberal manifesto, which spoke out *against* imperial preference, was much more generous in alluding to empire as a unit in 1940: it noted that the 'sacrifice and steadfastness of the people of these Islands, the British Commonwealth and Empire—standing alone for a whole year against the insolent might of Germany and her allies—have saved the world'.[50]

The Liberal manifesto's invocation of the whole empire as the unit that stood alone, or indeed fought, was not as common as might be thought. Indeed it is remarkable how empire and allies were removed from what became by 1945 a profoundly national story of the war. A 1945 government document called *What Britain has Done, 1939–1945: A Selection of Outstanding Facts and Figures* is a powerful case in point. The imperial contribution to the war was radically downplayed, as was, less surprisingly, that of the USA and other allies—the stress is on British help to these allies.[51] A profoundly national bias is also very evident in the official *Statistical Digest of the War* published in 1951.[52] For example, only in sub-categorizations of

---

[48] See R. G. D. Allen, 'Mutual Aid between the US and the British Empire, 1941–5' *Journal of the Royal Statistical Society,* 109 (1946) 243–77.

[49] See Wendy Webster, *Englishness and Empire 1939–1965* (Oxford, 2005).

[50] Ian Dale (ed.), *Conservative Party Manifestos, 1900–1997* (London, 2000), 61, 62 and corresponding Liberal volume, 61.

[51] *What Britain has Done, 1939–1945: A Selection of Outstanding Facts and Figures* issued by the Ministry of Information, 1945. Reprinted with an introduction by Richard Overy (London, 2007).

[52] Central Statistical Office, *Statistical Digest of the War* (London, 1951).

*trade* did the Empire appear (as in trade with 'British countries' as opposed to 'foreign countries'). Otherwise the figures presented are for Great Britain and Northern Ireland. Thus the armed forces are the British ones (though a footnote recognizes there were some foreigners in them) while the very closely allied Commonwealth forces, not to mention colonial ones, or allied ones, do not figure. There is no Indian Army, no Royal Canadian Air Force, no Polish Armoured Division, or Free French, and so on, even it seemed when stationed in the United Kingdom. The figures for arms production are those for production within the borders of the United Kingdom, not those for either British or Imperial forces. The result is, for example, a serious misrepresentation of rifle production for British and Imperial forces. The only movements of goods recorded (apart from Lend-Lease, and these inadequately) are those in and out of the United Kingdom, with the crucial exception of munitions, which lived in a different statistical world. Thus the very statistical picture that was produced is shot through with a particular nationalist way of understanding, and it should be noted this would become standard in nearly all the histories of war production, and subsequent accounts of the economics of the war.[53]

Post-war nationalist feeling is evident in propaganda documentaries concerned with agriculture and industry. *United Harvest* (Greenpark Productions, 1947) focused on the wartime extension and modernization of British agriculture, stressing its new found vitality. But the film struck a decidedly nationalist tone, with a strong line against importing from foreign producers (Argentina, Holland, and Spain are mentioned). Crucially there was no mention of imperial food suppliers, so the national is contrasted with the foreign only, without the slightest hint that imperial producers—Canada, Australia, and New Zealand being the main ones—were a vital part of the issue. Interestingly enough other propaganda documentaries which do mention the Empire/Commonwealth as food suppliers treat them on a par with foreign countries. An example is *The Balance*, which shows just how much of Britain's food was imported, but makes no distinction between Empire/Commonwealth and the rest of the world. Britain needed to export to all parts of the world, in order to import from them.[54] Humphrey Jennings' *Portrait of a Family* of 1951 where the family is the British nation, notes as one

---

[53] For example, Stephen Broadberry and Peter Howlett, 'The United Kingdom: "Victory at all costs"' in Mark Harrison (ed.), *The Economics of World War II: Six Powers in International Comparison* (Cambridge, 1998).

[54] *The Balance*, Paul Rotha (COI 1947). In relation to exports and imports it dealt with New Zealand, South America, Canada, West Africa, and Sweden. Canada was as foreign as Sweden.

of its features that half the family lived on food from abroad, but again does not discriminate between imperial and foreign supplies.[55] The need for the nation to export so that the nation could import in order to eat and to get raw materials was a powerful theme of post-war economic propaganda.[56]

The nation and the national interest became key terms of political discourse. For example in the Labour Party election manifesto of 1945, 'Socialism' appears once, whereas 'nation', and 'people' appear repeatedly, more so than Britain or British; by contrast the 1935 manifesto hardly invoked Britain/British or nation. The 1945 manifesto called coal 'Britain's most precious national raw material'. It is not surprising then that a National Coal Board would appear. Alongside it came a National Health Service (though a British Transport Commission and a British Electricity Authority).[57] It is interesting too that while the 1945 Labour Party manifesto called for 'public ownership' or 'socialization' of industries, 'nationalization' would become the standard term. But 'nation', and 'national' are terms that recur well outside the domain of what we now think of as nationalization, that is state ownership. Harold Wilson claimed in an important internal document 'the Government had asserted its right to ensure that there is a duty on private industry, no less than on socialised industries, to conform to the national interest. . . private ownership of industry does not of itself give any guarantee that national considerations will prevail in industrial policy', which is precisely what he wanted to ensure.[58]

We should note too the importance of the national for technocrats in the 1940s, even those of the Left. The leftist Association of Scientific Workers published a well-known manifesto called *Science and the Nation* though it was not quite as nationalistic as the title implies.[59] Figures from the Right also

---

[55] *Family Portrait*, written and directed by Humphrey Jennings 1951. The film was made for the Festival of Britain 1951. The themes were the unity of old and new, poetry and prose, science and literature.

[56] As Jim Tomlinson has noted the export drive propaganda of the time, and historical commentary since, has underplayed two crucial ways, other than exporting more, which would have reduced the balance of payments deficit: the cutting of military expenditure overseas and the control of the deliberately unrestricted investment in the overseas sterling area. See Tomlinson, *Democratic Socialism and Economic Policy*, chapter 3.

[57] To be sure, there had long been national trade unions, and national associations of one sort or another, not to mention many British and Imperial bodies, but after the war the term 'national' and formulas such as 'the national interest' became commonplace as never before.

[58] 'The State and Private Industry: Memorandum by the President of the Board of Trade' PREM 8/1183, PRO.

[59] Penguin, 1947.

embraced and noted the rise of the national. Take for example the reflections of Sir John Lennard-Jones, a senior wartime government scientist from Cambridge University. In 1947 he noted that the scientist was becoming more nationally minded as his relation to the State became closer and while there still were some of the traditionally absent minded types there were scientists who were politically and nationally conscious. At first sight he thought, the outlook for the scientist in a planned society seemed bleak— not the view of the scientific Left of course—but he thought there was a positive side, drawing positive analogies with the army as a planned organization in which spirit and enterprise had also been developed. There had to be planning for the development of new ideas and their application to national needs.[60] Indeed as is becoming clearer, the politics of British technocrats were far from exclusively of the Left.[61]

## Reflections

One can find prognostications in the 1930s of a nationalist British future, but hardly any recognition in the historical literature that something like this did come to pass. 'One begins by "buying British": one ends by shouting for a colossal air-fleet' lamented H. N. Brailsford in the early 1930s.[62] Elie Halevy, the great French student of British liberalism was brutally frank in his defence of the true liberal political-economic faith, speculating, in 1934, about where the ideological transformation he saw underway would end:

> It is queer in England to observe how the free-trade spirit, with its pacifist implications, has survived the introduction of protection. But you have to recognise that you have become a protectionist nation, and, having become protectionist, you have become nationalistic at the same time. I know several socialist intellectuals who profess to be at the same time radical protectionists and radical pacifists. I do not understand how you can be both at the same time . . . As soon as you have begun to accept protectionism, you are bound to accept something like nationalism, and can you have nationalism without something like militarism? I was struck last

[60] Sir John Lennard-Jones, 'The Scientist and the State': Address to the Dundee Rotary Club 28 August 1947, Lennard-Jones Papers 52 Churchill Archive Centre, Churchill College, Cambridge.

[61] On this see David Edgerton, *England and the Aeroplane: An Essay on a Militant and Technological Nation* (London, 1991) and for the post-war years in particular, Waqar H. Zaidi, 'The Janus-face of Techno-nationalism: Barnes Willis and the "Strength of England" ', *Technology and Culture*, 49 (2008), 62–88.

[62] H. N. Brailsford, *Property or Peace?* (London, 1934), 229.

winter in reading a speech made at a public meeting by Sir Stafford Cripps in which he declared that he was not 'an out and out pacifist'. I know that just now he is delivering highly pacifist speeches in Canada, but I cannot forget how struck I was by this former declaration of his. I am making a bold, perhaps an absurd forecast. But who knows? Sir Stafford Cripps' father, after being a Conservative, went over to Labour because he was a pacifist. Who knows whether Sir Stafford Cripps himself will not find himself going over to patriotism and perhaps something like militarism because he is a socialist? . . . [Herbert Spencer argued that] the world was evolving towards what he called new toryism—protective, socialistic and militaristic. . . who knows whether the prophecy is not going to be true?[63]

Was Halevy right? Only a decade or so later, and for years afterward, Britain had, as we have seen, a highly protected economy, it was socialistic, and had very high defence spending and conscription. This is not to say that this was by conscious choice, much less that it was the product of overt campaigns to bring it about. Yet it was in line with important ideological changes that made such developments seem normal, necessary and indeed in many respects beneficial, so much so they elicited little adverse comment. Halevy's position was a distinctly marginal one after the war. Post-war intellectual culture was itself profoundly nationalistic and militaristic, but only implicitly so.[64]

One particular reason for the neglect was that there was no overt political or intellectual embrace of militarism and nationalism. There was no British Friedrich List of the mid-twentieth century. Economic nationalism was a matter of lower-level politics, policy, national security, business lobbies, rather than the economics seminar.[65] Furthermore, the language of post-war economics was not suited to highlighting these changes. It is significant that terms like protection, autarky, or state trading, hardly figure in discussion of the post-war British economy. In the language of economics and party political economic discourse the key issue was the role of the state, through

[63] E. Halevy, 'Socialism and the Problem of Democratic Parliamentarism', address at Chatham House 24 April 1934, reproduced in *The Era of Tyrannies: Essays on Socialism and War* (London, 1967), 201.

[64] In *Warfare State* I discuss this also in relation to historiography in the 1960s, noting the importance of critiques of liberalism from the Left and Right, and the common insistence, which persists to this day, that post-war Britain was never national or nationalistic enough. See Edgerton, *Warfare State*, chapter 7.

[65] Similarly wartime and post-war planning had really no connection to the in any case very limited British economic or political thinking about planning.

Keynesian demand management, inflation, deflation, and nationalization, with a dash of planning and industrial policy. Also centre stage were moves to liberalize international trade and British governments did essentially reject alternatives to Atlanticist multilateralism.[66] And, in discussion of the state in general, a social democratic tradition emphasized the rise of the welfare state, as did critics. Yet all these concepts were inadequate for describing some of the key new developments, like the much larger warfare state, but also the exceptionally intense economic nationalism of the post-war years. There were also great difficulties in grasping, in the light of British intellectual traditions, the precise nature of British post-war militarism.[67] Within post-war thought Halevy's prophecy that a New Toryism 'protective, socialistic and militaristic' would arrive, made no sense.

Historians of the period have been strongly affected not only by contemporary reflections on these years, but also later forms of analysis. The dominant social-democratic view of mid-century history told a very particular national, nationalist, and welfarist story in which neither militarism nor nationalism were central. Conservative historians, focused on international and military history, complained that Britain had not been, and remained, insufficiently committed to armed forces, the army in particular. Post-war Britain invested, by peacetime standards, unprecedented amounts in warlike capacity, and as an economy it was, by modern standards, unprecedentedly nationalistic, yet its intellectuals, at least many of them, chided Britain for not being nationalistic or militaristic enough.

The 'war and reconstruction' pairing is a useful one for some aspects of British history. In the case of agriculture and food supply 1939/40 saw a major change not reversed after the war and the whole period to the early 1950s was one of very significant stability of patterns of food consumption, which were different from what had happened and was to happen. Generally though, both the beginning and the end of the war were major break points. The specificities of the war period, not least the obvious importance of the scale of the armed services and the arms industry, need much greater recognition, as does the internationalism of the war years. From 1945, we need to recognise, much effort was made to get back to the situation of 1939—to increase exports, house-building, and much else besides to pre-war levels. In that sense a

---

[66] See Richard Toye's papers for the view that acceptance of the US loan in 1945 did not entail Labour acceptance of Atlanticist multilateralism in trade. 'Churchill and Britain's "Financial Dunkirk"', *Twentieth Century British History*, 15 (2004) 329–60.'The Labour Party's External Economic Policy in the 1940s', *The Historical Journal*, 43 (2000), 189–215.

[67] On this see Edgerton, *Warfare State*, chapters 7 and 8.

straightforward literal meaning of reconstruction—repairing and replacing the damage and loss of war, is appropriate. But that has not been the main sense in which the term has been used. If we were to ask the question what world did British elites want to build from 1945, and how did the experience of the war affect it, we would want to say something about the building of a new kind of universalistic welfare state, but we would also need to point to what to a majority of the elite was the pressing need to deploy military power on a greater scale than in 1939. It was not just a question of building a new Jerusalem, but also a new Sparta.

# Reassessing the Moral Economy of Post-war Reconstruction: The Terms of the West German Settlement in 1952

**Adam Tooze**

The dilemma of how to come to terms with the violent conflicts of the past, how to meet the imperative for economic growth and simultaneously to satisfy the urgent demands of the Cold War was common to the battered continent of Europe after 1945.[1] But nowhere were these difficulties more acute than in the provisional, Cold War creation that was the Federal Republic of Germany. And in Germany the process of resolution was drawn out well beyond the immediate post-war years. The passage of the new West German constitution in May 1949 did not complete the founding of the state, any more than the arrival of Marshall Plan funds in the spring of 1948 or the introduction of the Deutschmark in June 1948 completed the process of economic reconstruction. Well into the early 1950s the basic parameters of the economic and political order in West Germany remained to be defined. The success of the Deutschmark and the new central bank, the Bank deutscher Länder, was not preordained and West Germany's insertion into the international economic system had barely begun in 1949. As a means of trade integration, tariff reduction through GATT was a slow-moving process.[2] European payments remained constrained by exchange and capital controls. The single most important step towards redressing the persistent shortage of dollars was the downward adjustment of all the European currencies, including the Deutschmark, led by Britain in September 1949. But the crucial next step came in 1950 with the abandonment of the impractical Bretton Woods vision and the adoption instead of the European Payments Union (EPU) as a means of facilitating multilateral trade within Western Europe. Likewise, the international political integration of West Germany did not begin in earnest until the French initiative for the Coal and Steel Community in May 1950. Only weeks later the crisis provoked by the Korean

---

[1] These are the three central themes of Tony Judt, *Postwar: A History of Europe since 1945* (London, 2005).

[2] Christoph Buchheim, *Die Wiedereingliederung Westdeutschlands in die Weltwirtschaft 1945–1958* (Munich, 1990).

war might have derailed recovery altogether, were it not for the success of the EPU in providing a framework for concerted European-wide adjustment in 1951. The truly decisive moment in the consolidation of the Federal Republic of Germany did not finally arrive until 1952.[3]

On 10 January 1952, in the face of opposition protests, Adenauer's Bundestag majority ratified German acceptance of the Schuman Plan. This was followed within weeks by a fundamental debate in the Bundestag on rearmament echoed by a parallel debate in the French chamber and an agreement on 14 February at the meeting of foreign ministers in London on the hugely sensitive issue of war criminals. A week later, also in London, the talks opened that would decide the settlement of Germany's interwar debts. And on 21 March after delicate preliminary talks, German and Israeli negotiators met face to face to hammer out a compensation agreement. Conscious of what was beginning to gel in the West, on 10 March Stalin launched his famous offer of reunification in exchange for neutralization. Rejecting this tempting proposition Adenauer pressed ahead with *Westbindung*. On 26 May he put his signature to the *Deutschlandvertrag* which restored a modicum of sovereignty to West Germany, whilst promising to end forever the era of national armies, by making Germany a member of a prospective (West) European Defence Community.[4] Ten days beforehand the German parliament discussed and decided the basic outline of one of the most dramatic welfare measures in modern history, a measure, the *Lastenausgleich* or burden sharing, which at least on paper promised to transfer half of the nation's wealth to those who had lost their assets during the war. And if that was not enough, in July 1952 the Bundestag passed the hotly contested co-determination law, which gave German workers a limited voice on the boards of its corporations.

Any one of these issues had the capacity to derail West Germany's fledgling political system and to impart to the narrative of European reconstruction a disruptive final twist. The FRG was only three years old. What was at stake was nothing less than the question of national unity, to which was coupled the question of Germany's international alignment, its domestic social and economic order and the prospect of restoring something like normality for the millions of people who had fled or been violently expelled from the East. Adenauer was clearly and irrevocably committed to the Western alliance,

---

[3] Hans-Peter Schwarz, *Die Ära Adenauer. Gruenderjahre der Republik 1949–1957*, volume 2, *Geschichte der Bundesrepublik* (Stuttgart, 1981).

[4] Hanns Jürgen Küsters, *Der Integrationsfrieden. Viermächte-Verhandlungen über die Friedensreglung mit Deutschland 1945–1990* (Munich, 2000), 554–646.

but he was far from being the dominant political figure he was later to become. His coalition government had a tiny majority in the Bundestag and in the third quarter of 1951 his personal approval rating dipped below 23 per cent.[5] On the issue of a German military commitment to NATO he faced a groundswell of resistance. On 11 May 1952 in the steel-town of Essen, an anti-rearmament protestor was killed in scuffles with the police, reawakening fears of Weimar era political violence.[6] Meanwhile, the permanence of the post-war order was questioned in a different sense by the nearly eight million bitter, traumatized German refugees, the *Vertriebene*, who presented perhaps the most fundamental domestic political problem for the Adenauer government.[7] They too gave vent to their frustrations in mass rallies, culminating in an intimidating demonstration in Bonn on 4 May. Meanwhile, the problem of balancing domestic political resentments with the demands of the international arena was hugely delicate. The first encounters with the representatives of the World Jewish Congress and Israel were, not surprisingly, extremely difficult and by May 1952 Adenauer faced the PR disaster of the Israelis walking away from the negotiations. Meanwhile, his cabinet was riven over the prospect of paying compensation to Israel and resuming service on Germany's odious interwar debts.[8] The Federal Finance Ministry, led by the combative Fritz Schäffer of the Bavarian CSU, was boycotting government meetings.[9] Outraged by Schäffer's insensitivity, the German negotiators in the Israel talks resigned amongst a blaze of international publicity. In the Bundestag the agreement with Israel faced resistance to the bitter end and achieved the necessary majority only with the votes of the SPD opposition.[10] A third of Adenauer's own party abstained or voted against the government. Those abstaining included Finance Minister Schäffer and the vocal young

[5] Schwarz, *Ära Adenauer*, 187.

[6] Hans-Erich Volkmann, 'Die innenpolitische Dimension der Adenauerscher Sicherheitspolitik in der EVG-Phase' in MGFA edn *Anfänge westdeutscher Sicherheitspolitik 1945–1956,* volume 2, *Die EVG-Phase* (Munich, 1990), 462–604.

[7] Ian Connor, 'The Radicalization that Never Was? Refugees in the German Federal Republic' in Frank Biess, Mark Roseman, and Hanna Schissler (eds), *Conflict, Catastrophe and Continuity: Essays in Modern German History,* (Oxford, 2007), 221–36.

[8] Michael Wolffsohn, 'Globalentschädigung fuer Israel und die Juden? Adenauer und die Opposition in der Bundesregierung', in Ludolf Herbst and Constantin Goschler (eds), *Wiedergutmachung in der Bundesrepublik Deutschland* (Munich, 1989), 161–90.

[9] Wolffsohn, 'Globalentschädigung', 164.

[10] Schlomo Shafir, 'Die SPD und die Wiedergutmachung gegenüber Israel', in Ludolf Herbst and Constantin Goschler (eds), *Wiedergutmachung in der Bundesrepublik Deutschland* (Munich, 1989), 191–203.

CSU deputy and former Wehrmacht lieutenant Franz Josef Strauss.[11] The proposed settlement of Germany's international debts came close to falling at the last hurdle when recalcitrant Bundestag members refused to agree to the repayment of occupation costs claimed by France. In an embarrassing scene Foreign Secretary Hallstein was forced to intervene with the Speaker of the Bundestag to have the vote declared invalid on a technicality and to allow the CDU's whips to bring the Party into line.[12] As deeply as the Germans detested the French occupation, the restoration of their national credit had priority.

It was in accomplishing this political high wire act and demonstrating the compatibility of West Germany's constrained democratic sovereignty with the emerging international and European order that Konrad Adenauer asserted himself as a figure of historic significance. Not for nothing does 1952 form the hinge of Schwarz's monumental biography.[13] This was the moment of the making of the presidential, *Kanzlerdemokratie*. In early 1953, Adenauer's approval ratings soared. The 77-year-old made a triumphant state visit to Washington and his coalition achieved a solid majority in the September general election. But this was also the moment at which the conservative nature of reconstruction was set in stone.

By piecing together key elements of the political agenda in 1952, recent historical contributions have allowed us to understand Adenauer's founding of the FRG in new ways. The new histories of the early Federal Republic stress Bonn's persistent and active efforts to ward off accusations of guilt and to achieve internal integration at the expense of openness about the crimes of the past. The kind of honest admission of guilt and responsibility advocated by the SPD under Kurt Schumacher's leadership was marginalized. Crucially, Adenauer was able to leverage West Germany's new centrality in the Cold War to secure rehabilitation for Germany. David Clay Large and Norbert Frei have shown how the agreement by the Federal Republic to rearmament in 1952 was made directly conditional on an amnesty for the Wehrmacht soldiers convicted of war crimes.[14] Robert Moeller's *War Stories* has presented a

---

[11] Michael Wolffsohn, 'Das Wiedergutmachungsabkommen mit Israel' in Ludolf Herbst (ed.) *Westdeutschland 1945–1955* (Munich, 1986), 203–18.

[12] Ursula Rombeck-Jaschinski, *Das Londoner Schuldenabkommen. Die Regelung der deutschen Auslandsschulden nach dem Zweiten Weltkrieg* (Munich, 2005), 436–8.

[13] Hans-Peter Schwarz, *Adenauer. A German Politician and Statesman in a Period of War, Revolution and Reconstruction*, volume 1, *From the German Empire to the Federal Republic, 1876–1952* (Oxford, 1995); volume 2, *The Statesman 1952–1967* (Oxford, 1997).

[14] David Clay Large, *Germans to the Front: West German Rearmament in the Adenauer Era* (Chapel Hill, 1996). N. Frei, *Adenauer's Germany and the Nazi Past: The Politics of*

discreditable panorama of the ways in which foreign claims to compensation for the crimes committed by National Socialism were balanced against Germans' well-cultivated sense of their own victimhood.[15]

What gives each of these interpretations its force is the linkage it un-covers—rearmament traded against amnesty, admissions of responsibility towards Israel traded against compensation for the German victims of the war. These connections were of course forged by the historical actors them-selves. But the choice to highlight one set of connections rather than another is the historian's. Here, for instance, is how Norbert Frei chooses to charac-terize the crucial early weeks of 1952 in his highly influential account of Adenauer's history politics (*Vergangenheitspolitik*):

> As a solution to the war criminal question entered the vortex of negotiations on security and foreign policy, the psychological hur-dles grew higher and higher... The most difficult point of conflict between West Germany and the Allies lay precisely in the questions of recognizing the judgements' validity and the pardon commis-sion's makeup... All in all, the foreign policy situation remained fragile. The European Defence Community was by no means over its hurdles, the Saar question was unresolved, since 10 March Stalin's note about German reunification was on the table. Adenauer had absolutely no need for shrill voices from the govern-ment camp...[16]

As Frei delineates it, the relevant context for resolving the question of war criminals were the realms of security and foreign policy. The hurdles were 'psychological' and concerned the legitimacy of court rulings. But what is omitted is any mention of the economic or financial questions that were at stake. One would not guess from Frei's account that at this moment in 1952 hugely delicate negotiations were underway in the Hague with Israel and in London with the pre-war creditors in which the liabilities of Germany's past were cashed out in terms of future monetary values. Nor are these omissions peculiar to Frei. Clay Large also treats West German rearmament almost entirely at the level of politics without reference to the formidable financial

---

*Amnesty and Integration* (New York, 2002). See also Bert-Oliver Manig, *Die Politik der Ehre. Die Rehabilitierung der Berufssoldaten in der fruehen Bundesrepublik* (Goettingen, 2004).

[15] Robert G. Moeller, *War Stories, The Search for a Useable Past in the Federal Republic* (Berkeley, 2001). See also Frank Biess, *Homecomings: Returning POWs and the Legacies of Defeat in Postwar Germany* (Princeton, 2006).

[16] N. Frei, *Adenauer's Germany*, 188.

commitments involved. Moeller's work, by contrast, stands out as a piece of cultural and political history that is entirely clear about the material consequences of the politics under discussion. When linking the theme of German victimhood to the defence against the claims of Germany's Jewish victims, Moeller never leaves us in any doubt that billions of DM were at stake. But his vision is overwhelmingly domestic in its focus. He passes over the international questions of rearmament and the debt negotiations in London. There are of course a mass of studies that deal with the social and economic foundation of the Federal Republic both in its domestic and international ramifications.[17] But they tend either to focus on one particular aspect of the problem, such as the notions of social justice involved in the Lastenausgleich or the politics of the London debt negotiations. Others have presented overviews of economic policy, but largely without regard to the problem of the moral and social foundation of the Republic.

The argument of this essay is simple. If we want to do justice to the complex logic of West Germany's foundation we must find ways of grasping the simultaneous and sudden resolution of a tangled mass of political and strategic problems, problems which were at once political, legal, and cultural as well as economic and social. As demonstrated by Hans-Peter Schwarz, the biographical approach through the figure of Konrad Adenauer is one way of coping with this enormous complexity. In 1952 Adenauer had his finger in every pie. And he displayed the hallmark of his political genius precisely by forcing the pace of consolidation simultaneously on every front thereby entangling his counterparts both at home and abroad in an interlocking set of obligations. As foreign observers noted with some concern, despite the weakness of his political position at home, the person of Konrad Adenauer had become central to the construction of the entire Western order.[18]

But, to gain some sense of the forces that Adenauer was juggling, we need to go beyond the realm of personal leadership. As a counterpoint, this article aims to assess the foundation of the Federal Republic through an overview of the financial accounts. As Joseph Schumpeter argued in 1918, in the wake of the first great calamity of the twentieth century, the state budget is a privileged vantage point from which to view the totality of society's priorities. 'The spirit

---

[17] Michael L. Hughes, *Shouldering the Burdens of Defeat: West Germany and the Reconstruction of Social Justice* (Chapel Hill and London, 1999). Rombeck-Jaschinski, *Das Londoner Schuldenabkommen* complemented by Constantin Goschler, *Schuld und Schulden. Die Politik der Wiedergutmachung fuer NS-Verfolgte seit 1945* (Goettingen, 2005).

[18] Ronald J. Granieri, *The Ambivalent Alliance: Konrad Adenauer, the CDU/CSU and the West, 1949–1966* (Oxford, 2003).

of the people, its cultural level, its social structure, the deeds its policy may prepare—all this and more is written in its fiscal history, stripped of all phrases. He who knows how to listen to its message here discerns the thunder of world history more clearly than anywhere else.'[19] The aim of the present essay is to piece together an image of German stabilization as it took place in 1952 in terms of the 'hard, naked facts'[20] of the state budget and the wider framework of the national accounts that lay beyond. As Schumpeter suggested, the financial accounts, by throwing a sharp light on the relative scale of the basic elements of the new dispensation, enable us to calibrate, solidify and sharpen our judgments of Adenauer's creation.

The aim is not crudely to assert a priority for the 'economic' as against an Adenauer-centric vision, or to dismiss the kind of cultural-political history pursued by Moeller, Frei and others. The macroeconomic constraints themselves were not simply given. The financial data had to be constructed and was subject to contested interpretation.[21] The 1950s saw a booming market for economic expertise in West Germany.[22] And the use to which expert opinion was put was itself dependent on political judgement. This article will have succeeded if it manages to cast some light on the subtle interplay of agency and constraint through which the key political actors in the foundation of the Federal Republic both resisted and in the end persuaded each other to accept the post-war order.

## II

Well into 1950 the Federal Republic of Germany was still struggling to establish the routines of regular public accounts. The largest single element of the budget—occupation costs—was determined in an apparently arbitrary fashion by the occupation authorities without prior notice to Bonn. By 1952, however, Fritz Schäffer and the Federal Finance Ministry were firmly in control.[23] All of the decisions taken during that fateful year—with regard to Germany's contribution to Western European defence, domestic consolidation, repayment of old debts and compensation offered to Israel—could be cashed out in financial terms, weighed against each other and measured

---

[19] J. A. Schumpeter, 'The Crisis of the Tax State', originally 1918, published in English in *International Economic Papers* no. 4 (London, 1954), 7.

[20] Schumpeter, 'The Crisis', 6.

[21] Mark E. Spicka, *Selling the Economic Miracle. Economic Reconstruction and Politics in West Germany 1949–1957* (Oxford, 2007).

[22] Alexander Nützenadel, *Die Stunde der Ökonomen Wissenschaft, Politik und Expertenkultur in der Bundesrepublik, 1949–1974* (Goettingen, 2005).

[23] Christoph Henzler, *Fritz Schäffer 1945–1967* (Munich, 1994), 327–33.

Table 1. Claims on German National Income 1952–1959

| m DM | German national income | Military expenditure including occupation costs | Refugee compensation (Lasten-ausgleich) | London debt agreement | Individual compensation (Claims Conference) | Israel |
|------|------|------|------|------|------|------|
| 1952 | 103,800 | 14,774 | 2,500 | | | |
| 1953 | 112,100 | 15,843 | 3,500 | 734 | | 268 |
| 1954 | 121,100 | 16,786 | 5,500 | 734 | 154 | 354 |
| 1955 | 139,500 | 13,217 | 4,100 | 734 | 350 | 267 |
| 1956 | 154,400 | 12,397 | 3,600 | 1,058 | 679 | 245 |
| 1957 | 168,300 | 14,334 | 3,500 | 1,058 | 1,171 | 225 |
| 1958 | 180,100 | 14,362 | 3,450 | 1,058 | 1,244 | 261 |
| 1959 | 194,000 | 17,369 | 3,500 | 1,735 | 1,472 | 266 |

*Source:* Werner Abelshauser, 'Wirtschaft und Rüstung in den *fünfziger* Jahren', in MGFA, *Anfänge westdeutscher Sicherheitspolitik 1945–1956*, volume 4, *Wirtschaft und Rüstung Souveränität und Sicherheit* (Munich, 1997), 89.

against Germany's ability to pay. Using data from a variety of sources, Table 1 summarizes the financial implications of the most salient decisions taken in 1952.

One thing that is immediately clear from the table is the multi-dimensional and novel complexity of West Germany's position. Financial arrangements of this kind were unprecedented. Germany emerged by the end of 1952 as a quasi sovereign state but with an internationalized defence budget, that was making an unprecedented internal redistribution having entered into obligations to make substantial payments to a state, Israel, that had not even existed five years earlier, whilst assuming responsibility for debts contracted by the Weimar republic, which, though German, was separated from the Federal Republic by two intervening regimes—the Third Reich and the post-war occupation statute.

But the table also reveals in stark terms the real priorities of the Adenauer government. Of the three narrative strands with which we started—the politics of memory, economic reconstruction, Cold War—the Cold War trumps everything.[24] Though disarmed until the mid-1950s, West Germany was in no way disencumbered of the costs of defence. It paid large contributions first to the Allied armies of occupation and then in the form of a contribution to

[24] I disagree in this judgement with Hughes who, by adding together all forms of social expenditure whether 'new' and war-related or not, ranks welfare higher than defence; see Hughes, *Shouldering the Burdens*, 195. If our aim is to assess priorities in response in the aftermath of the war it seems better to take a more limited view of social spending.

the joint Western defensive effort.[25] These provisions weighed heavily on the budgetary process in Bonn. And their impact on the German economy was all the more pronounced because the funds were on the whole not spent, but set aside in an accumulating fiscal reserve. West Germany was required to make financial provision for heavy defence spending but the political and diplomatic log jam over the creation of German armed forces meant that rather than contributing to industrial growth through the rebuilding of the German military-industrial complex, Germany's defence contribution actually amounted to the requirement to accumulate a substantial budget surplus.

By comparison, the figures reveal the comparatively modest sums that West Germany was required to pay both in compensation for the most grievous crimes committed under Hitler and to settle the debts left unpaid since 1933. These numbers give great additional weight to the story of political balancing described by Moeller, Frei, and Clay Large. In the annual budget, the requirements of the Cold War and the needs of domestic welfare massively dwarfed any consideration for Germany's past liabilities. It is often noted that Adenauer's statement of responsibility towards Israel in the Bundestag on 27 September 1951 was hedged around by an extended commentary on the suffering of Germans expelled from the East and the need to ensure that any payments to Israel did not jeopardize the integration of Germany's own refugees. The financial accounts make clear what this meant in practice. In 1953, the funds disbursed to accommodate Germany's refugee population were 13 times greater than the payments begrudgingly conceded to Israel.

And this point is pressed further home once we consider to whom the compensation payments were made and the conditionality that was attached. Israel received payments for 8 years under the terms of the agreements reached in 1952, totalling 3 billion DM. Only a small part of this was in hard currency, pounds sterling, with which Israel procured desperately needed oil. The majority was in kind, in the form of goods chosen from a selected list of German products unlikely to compete with Germany's regular exports. But what is even more striking is the disparity between the deal done with the state of Israel and the arrangement reached with the Jewish claims conference under which the Adenauer government agreed to set up an additional compensation system for individual victims of racial persecution. This individual compensation mechanism was modest in 1952, but was ultimately

---

[25] Lutz Köllner and Hans-Erich Volkmann, 'Finanzwissenschaftliche, finanzwirtschaftliche und finanzpolitische Aspekte eines deutschen Beitrags zur EVG', in MGFA edn, *Anfänge westdeutscher Sicherheitspolitik 1945–1956* Band 2 *Die EVG-Phase* (Munich, 1990).

to emerge as a very large and long-term commitment.[26] However, the most important provision of that compensation mechanism was that it would be limited to victims of Nazism who had suffered persecution on German soil or had some connection to Germany in its boundaries of 1937. In other words the Germans agreed to compensate their 'own' victims. With the backing of the US occupation authorities, they set themselves against demands from the Jewish Claims Conference for compensation to be extended to those who had suffered persecution not only in Germany, but across occupied Europe.[27] This was a crucial limitation, of course, because the overwhelming majority of the victims of the Holocaust were neither German nor Austrian, nor did they suffer their fate on the territory of Germany.

And even more far-reaching were the implications of the London debt treaty. Under the terms of the Treaty ratified after a year of negotiations on 27 February 1953, Germany benefited from the forgiveness of more than 50 per cent of both the debts it had contracted prior to 1933 and those which had piled up since 1945. Its total liability was reduced from 30 billion DM to 14 billion. But it agreed even to these generous terms only under the provision of Article 5 (2) of the Treaty, which postponed any further reparations claims until a final peace treaty was agreed between the Allies and a reunified German state. When taken in conjunction with the Paris reparations agreement of 14 January 1946 and the transitional treaties regarding the recognition of West Germany as a sovereign state of 26 May 1952, Germany, its citizens and firms were shielded against any claims arising from their employment and mistreatment of millions of forced workers from across Eastern and Western Europe.[28] This extraordinary provision elicited violent protests from the Dutch, who had specifically raised the question of compensation for forced labour.[29] But they were over-ridden by the United States and Britain, who wanted to see the loan deal signed, and had no interest in seeing financial concessions they made to Germany diverted towards the payment of reparations to third countries.[30] The Netherlands refused to sign the Treaty. But otherwise, the Federal Republic benefited from a belated 'zero hours'. As of

---

[26] Karl Hessdörfer, 'Die finanzielle Dimension', in Herbst and Goschler, *Wiedergutmachung*, 55–9.

[27] Rudolf Huhn, 'Die Wiedergutmachungsverhandlungen in Wassenaar', in Herbst and Goschler, *Wiedergutmachung*, 145–6. This position was already established in the US occupation zone prior to 1949; see Goschler, *Schuld*, 147–8.

[28] Ulrich Herbert, 'Nicht entschädigungsfähig? Die Wiedergutmachungsansprüche der Auslaender' in Herbst and Goschler, *Wiedergutmachung*, 273–302.

[29] Rombeck-Jaschinski, *Das Londoner Schuldenabkommen*, 455–6.

[30] Goschler, *Schuld*, 154–9.

1953, West Germany's rapid economic recovery was substantially disencumbered of any outstanding liabilities from the Nazi period. It was not until the 1990s, following reunification that the issue of individual compensation for forced labourers was put back on the table by class action suits in US courts.[31] By then, of course, the sums involved were modest in relation to the wealth of corporate Germany. Furthermore, the number of potential claimants had dwindled. But even then it took the intervention of the Clinton State Department and the Red-Green coalition in Berlin to bring home to the German business community the seriousness of the issue at stake.

## III

When set against the scale of the damage done by the Nazi regime and the unresolved financial legacy of the pre-1933 period, it is hard not to conclude that the Federal Republic in 1952 managed to negotiate a remarkably favourable settlement. How do we account for this lopsided final reckoning of reconstruction?

One might suppose that one of the things that made this lopsided settlement possible was the fact that the grid of relativities described in Table 1 was not available to contemporaries. The extent of the imbalance between military spending and domestic welfare measures and payments to foreign creditors was perhaps not known. But, in fact, there is every reason to think that precisely such calculations were being done at the time, not just in Germany but abroad as well. Certainly the financial trade-offs between the competing claims on Germany were discussed insistently. When direct negotiations with Israel began in 1952 a linkage was immediately established to the London debt talks. Outside the formal negotiations, the German government made clear that only a favourable deal in the London debt talks would permit an acceptable settlement with Israel. And they also made clear that they were counting on American generosity and expected American Jews to understand this point.[32] Indeed, it was precisely the shameless fashion in which Bonn attempted to manipulate this linkage that forced the Israelis to suspend negotiations in May 1952. At the London creditors conference meanwhile, Germany's chief negotiator, the banker Hermann Abs, balanced the demands of the Western creditors for repayment, not only against the claims of Israel, but also against the demands of the US and Britain for a large German defence contribution. And, to complete the circle, in the negotiations over defence spending, Finance Minister Schäffer insisted that by far the most important contribution that he could make to Western security was to ensure that

---

[31] Ibid., 413–76.
[32] Wolfssohn, 'Globalentschädigung', 166.

Germany's population, which now found itself on the frontline of the Cold War was kept in good health and properly housed.[33] Germany's multi-billion DM refugee compensation program ought, therefore, to be weighed in the balance alongside the many international obligations to be made upon it.

Since these connections were made so openly it is hard to resist the conclusion that the outcome reflects a brutal play of political force. Indeed, some German historians do not shrink from making the self-exculpatory point that ultimately the hierarchy of priorities that determined the 1952 settlements was dictated to Germany from the outside—by their counterparts in each of the separate sets of negotiations and ultimately by the US.[34] There is no question that the priority of the Truman administration was Western defence, first and last. This required a stable West Germany capable of making a large military contribution. The sequencing of decisions in 1952 is indicative. The outline of Germany's defence budget was set in the first months of 1952 in negotiations between the Germans and their future EDC/NATO partners. These talks included an agreement on which parts of Germany's internal welfare spending could be counted towards the defence contribution.[35] The deal with Israel came next in the sequence, in May-June 1952. But its terms were defined by what was considered feasible in light of the London debt talks. The need to satisfy Germany's many foreign creditors dictated the modest parameters of the settlement with Israel. Following this train of logic, Michael Wolffsohn even manages to reach the contentious conclusion that West Germany paid compensation to Israel not because of American pressure, but despite the demands of its American, British, and other creditors.[36]

The role of the US in the settlement with Israel was certainly veiled. The US did not want to be seen to be pressuring Germany openly on Israel's behalf.[37] And Wolffsohn speculates that there would have been little sympathy for the Israeli cause, if Germany had chosen to dig in its heels so as to give full priority to the London creditors. But behind the scenes, Washington made perfectly clear to Bonn that it would tolerate no unnecessary delay in the Israel negotiations and it would certainly not allow Germany to pursue the strategy

---

[33] Henzler, *Schäffer*, 402.

[34] Joerg Fisch, *Reparationen nach dem zweiten Weltkrieg* (Munich, 1992), 117–29.

[35] Henzler, *Schäffer*, 411.

[36] Wolffsohn, 'Globalentschädigung', 171.

[37] Ibid., 165; Yeshayahu A. Jelinek, 'Die Krise der Shilumim/Wiedergutmachungs-Verhandlungen im Sommer 1952' in *VFZ* 1, 38 (1990), 121–3; Rombeck-Jaschinski, *Das Londoner Schuldenabkommen*, 253 and 256; Huhn, 'Wiedergutmachungsverhandlungen', 143–4.

favoured by Abs, of prioritizing a settlement in London. With regard to Israel, Germany must be seen to be proactive and to be conducting negotiations in good faith.[38] During the most precarious phase of the negotiations in April and May 1952, High Commissioner McCloy was under direct instructions from Secretary of State Acheson to ensure that Adenauer was in no doubt about the US position.[39] When the German cabinet first reached deadlock on 5 April McCloy agreed to raise with Washington the possibility of financial concessions to Germany, which might ease the possibility of a deal. And the pressure for talks to continue was unrelenting. When the Israelis were forced by German intransigence to break off negotiations, McCloy on 21 May arranged for Adenauer to have a personal meeting with General Julius Klein, the head of the Jewish veterans association in the US. Klein threatened that unless he has a satisfactory answer by the following day he would mobilize Taft, the leader of the Republican majority in the Senate, to block the passage of the *Deutschlandvertrag* and the EDC treaty. Faced with the unravelling of his entire strategy, Adenauer promptly raised the terms of Bonn's offer to a level that though it outraged his more cautious cabinet colleagues enabled the Israelis to return to the table.[40] Even on 26 May on the occasion of the signature of the *Deutschlandvertrag* itself Adenauer had to submit to lectures by both Acheson and Anthony Eden, the British Foreign Secretary, on the crucial importance of finalizing the Israel deal.[41]

And the trade-offs as far as Washington was concerned were real. In April 1952 the representative of the US bondholders who had lent money to the Weimar Republic had stressed to the State Department that they were not willing to make sacrifices on behalf of Israel.[42] But two months later, in mid-June, the State Department intervened decisively to signal to the London debt negotiators that the time for haggling was over. Germany had raised its offer to Israel and the American bondholders were now expected to settle.[43] Washington thus triggered the final resolution of the London debt talks. Indeed, Washington had structured the entire solution of the convoluted problem of Germany's foreign debts. A little known clause in the post-war aid agreements made Marshall Plan obligations senior to all other

---

[38] Rombeck-Jaschinski, *Das Londoner Schuldenabkommen*, 253.

[39] Ludolf Herbst 'Einleitung', in Herbst and Goschler, *Wiedergutmachung*, 24; Huhn, 'Wiedergutmachungsverhandlungen', 147–8.

[40] Ibid., 153.

[41] Ibid., 154.

[42] Rombeck-Jaschinski, *Das Londoner Schuldenabkommen*, 272.

[43] Ibid., 316.

financial claims.[44] This gave the US the power to regulate the terms of the entire settlement. Crucially the US decided which sorts of debt Germany would have to settle. The London negotiations extended only to debts contracted prior to 1933 and after 1945. They thus excluded the enormous unpaid bills run up by the Reich during the occupation of Europe. With regard to Western Europe these clearing debts came to more than 20 billion Reichsmark.[45] But, even with these debts off the table the potential German liability was enormous. To clinch the London debt agreement in July 1952, the Truman administration did what President Harding's administration had failed to do in the early 1920s. It imposed on the US taxpayer the cost of postponing the repayment of most of the Marshall loans.[46] Germany's post-1945 obligations were cut from 16 billion to only 7 billion DM, a concession of 56 per cent. The American share of the post-1945 loans was discounted by as much as 62.5 per cent. This dramatic concession limited the demands that Germany's other creditors could reasonably make to 56 per cent of the Weimar-era obligations, which as a result were reduced from 13.5 billion to 7.5 billion.[47]

Undeniably the interests of the US in the viability of the Federal Republic were decisive. But to present the outcome simply as a result of American priorities renders the Germans passive, when they were in fact full participants in the process. Having secured acceptance from the Americans for its own massively proportioned internal compensation program, Germany did not dispute the priorities set by Washington with regard to its external obligations. But at every stage the Adenauer government fought to keep the level of the claims to a minimum.[48] Finance Minister Fritz Schäffer fought stubbornly on all fronts. But no less importantly, when it seemed in May 1952 as though the entire network of deals was about to collapse, Adenauer and his key supporters in the cabinet, most notably Minister for Economic Affairs Ludwig Erhard overrode the sceptics and agreed to come to terms. Given the

---

[44] Helge Berger and Albrecht Ritschl, 'Die Rekonstruktion der Arbeitsteilung in Europa. Eine neue Sicht des Marshallplans in Deutschland 1947–1951' *Vierteljahrshefte für Zeitgeschichte*, 43, 3 (1995), 499.

[45] Hermann J. Abs, *Zeitfragen der Geld- und Wirtschaftspolitik* (Frankfurt, 1959), 19.

[46] Rombeck-Jaschinski, *Das Londoner Schuldenabkommen*, 320.

[47] Fisch, *Reparationen*, 118.

[48] Goschler criticizes the lack of any positive concept of compensation on the German side which reduced German policy to resistance; see Goschler, *Schulden*, 151–2. But with his narrow focus on compensation questions Goschler ignores the enormously far-reaching goals being pursued by Adenauer at this point, to which compensation as demanded by the US was indeed no more than a means.

fragile internal state of West Germany this was no small matter. As opinion polls revealed, despite its extremely modest scope, only 11 per cent of the German population approved the compensation agreement with Israel.[49] It is in the interplay of resistance and acceptance, both justified in economic terms, that we see the specificity of 1952 as the true moment of transition from the post-war era of crisis, to the new era of unbounded economic growth.

## IV

Viewed from the German side this was a battle they had been fighting for more than thirty years. In the 1920s the governments of the Weimar republic had had to arbitrate an only slightly less complex web of internal and external claims. So the basic terms of the argument were familiar. Some things, however, had changed. In the 1920s it had still been possible, indeed necessary to contest the basic metric of Germany's capacity to pay. Since modern economic statistics were still in their infancy in the aftermath of World War I, a whole variety of financial and industrial measures were used and argued over. In 1928, in a particularly remarkable episode, the illustrious *Verein fuer Sozialpolitik*, once the stomping ground of Schmoller, Max Weber et al., issued a two volume collection of essays denouncing in principle the very idea of measuring national economic capacity in terms of a simple macro-economic metric, such as national income.[50] By the 1950s this at least had been settled. GDP was the appropriate measure of Germany's capacity to pay. From the point of view of the history of large-scale governance the emergence of GDP as a basic metric is a non-trivial event. Ever since, GDP and its various derivatives have formed a global cognitive grid. Charles Maier has pointed to its significance as an indicator of the scope of what he calls US empire.[51] When NATO considered its options with regard to the Warsaw pact the measure of the resources at its disposal was nothing less than total societal productive capacity.

The purpose of the NATO estimates of GDP was to achieve a rough parity of contribution, an exercise in economic and political balancing act later discussed under the heading of 'burden sharing'.[52] And in this context

---

[49] Wolffsohn, 'Wiedergutmachungsabkommen', 206–7.

[50] Adam Tooze, *Statistics and the German State: The Making of Modern Economic Knowledge 1900–1945* (Cambridge, 2001).

[51] Charles S. Maier, *Among Empires: American Ascendancy and its Predecessors* (Cambridge Mass., 2006), 174–7.

[52] For a fascinating early systematic application of the concept see Irving B. Kravis and Michael W. S. Davenport, *The Journal of Political Economy*, 71: 4 (Aug. 1963), 309–30.

**Table 2.** German Government Estimate of European Tax Burden, 1950

|  | Tax and social contributions as % of national income | Post-tax disposable income ($) |
| --- | --- | --- |
| Germany | 38.92 | 265.95 |
| UK | 37.56 | 443.31 |
| France | 36.76 | 347.25 |
| Italy | 23.33 | 186.39 |

*Source*: 812-813 in Lutz Köllner and Hans-Erich Volkmann, 'Finanzwissenschaftliche, finanzwirtschaftliche und finanzpolitische Aspekte eines deutschen Beitrags zur EVG', in MGFA, *Anfänge westdeutscher Sicherheitspolitik 1945–1956*, volume 2, *Die EVG-Phase* (Munich, 1990).

particular importance attached to comparative estimates of taxation. A little noticed but important axiom of post-war international negotiations was that the Germans should pay higher taxes than any other Europeans. This moved from being simply an assumption to a manifest principle of Western international politics when in April 1950 the Adenauer government attempted to implement a tax cut. In a scandalous and open intervention in Germany's fragile sovereignty the occupying authorities suspended the law. Adenauer's cabinet did its best to rally German public opinion against this challenge.[53] But they could not escape the now accepted grid of economic knowledge. So, to defend their position, they produced data like those shown in Table 2, which proved the German point, though only by a narrow margin.

Of course, the statistics of the overall tax burden begged the question of distribution. As the SPD opposition pointed out in their attacks on Schäffer's tax reduction plans, the important question was not simply how much Germany could pay, but which Germans should bear the burden.[54] The obstinacy of Adenauer's government with regard to foreign claims was underpinned by its domestic agenda of releasing the German middle class from the burdens of a high tax regime. The Adenauer cabinet regarded the tax cut of 1950 as a crucial first step towards the realization of their vision of the social market economy. Schäffer's plans reduced the burden of income tax on the middle class, whilst retaining extremely high

See also Charles S. Maier, 'Finance and Defense: Implications of Military Integration, 1950–1952' in Frances H. Heller and John R. Gillingham (eds), *NATO. The Founding of the Atlantic Alliance and the Integration of Europe* (New York, 1992), 335–51.

[53] Henzler, *Schäffer*, 382.

[54] Henzler, *Schäffer*, 381–2.

rates for top incomes and making much smaller cuts at the lower end.[55] This was justified in terms of the overriding need to encourage saving and capital formation. And what was at stake was not merely material interest. For Schäffer, Erhard and the CDU, the high tax regime inherited by the FRG was a standing reminder of the disastrous decades of war and dictatorship. Since 1945 the occupation authorities had added further punitive layers of taxation. As of February 1946, Germans earning more than 24,000 Reichsmarks were taxed at a marginal rate of 90 per cent, those earning more than 60,000 Reichsmarks were subject to a marginal rate of 95 per cent.[56] As Fritz Schäffer liked to point out, these rates were nine times heavier than in the glory days of the *Kaisserreich*. Meanwhile, 54 per cent of the revenue was consumed by unproductive occupation costs and social expenditure.[57] In fact, the overall tax take in 1950 was closer to three times that of 1913, but the comparison was still telling. Viewed in these terms, tax reform was one more way in which Adenauer's regime sought to escape from the burdens of the past. Not that we should ignore narrower calculations of party political advantage. At the critical cabinet meeting on 15 May 1952 at which the demands of Israel and the demands of the foreign creditors were set directly against each other, Schäffer and Adenauer were agreed on one thing. There was no question of a tax increase to ease the trade-off. 1953 was an election year and the entire future of West Germany hung on the success of the Adenauer coalition against the neutralist, socialist opposition.[58]

Tax was clearly a partisan issue. But on the single largest item of domestic expenditure there was a considerable degree of convergence between the major political parties in Bonn. The principle that Germans who suffered losses as a result of the war should receive compensation was established already during the war by generous Nazi legislation. And this idea of social solidarity was not disputed after 1945 by any of the major political parties. Nor was it contested by the American occupation authorities who led the way in insisting that in the interests of political and social stability a compensation mechanism for the homeless refugees and bombed-out population should be put in place as a matter of urgency. The problem was the sheer scale of the potential claims. German figures suggested that 28 million people had suffered damage estimated at between 130 and 200 billion Deutschmarks.

[55]  Ibid., 380.

[56]  Lothar Müller, 'Fritz Schäffer—erster Finanzminister der Bundesrepublik', in Wolfgang J. Mückl, *Föderalismus und Finanzpolitik* (Schoeningh Paderborn, 1990), 99.

[57]  Henzler, *Schäffer*, 351.

[58]  Rombeck-Jaschinski, *Das Londoner Schuldenabkommen*, 280.

Nor was it obvious what principle of restitution to prioritize. To have provided full compensation and thus to have replicated the social structure of pre-war Germany in the limited confines of post-war West Germany, as the Association of the *Vertriebene* demanded, would, paradoxically, have required a massively redistributive tax. The SPD and the Americans, by contrast, favoured emergency relief for the worst affected. Everyone agreed that without economic growth the circle could not be squared.

The first opportunity for a general solution came with the monetary reform of 1948, which could have been rigged to give substantially larger holdings of the new currency to the war-damaged. But this might have compromised the chief priority, which was to restart production, saving, and investment. In the event, the American occupation authorities gave priority to economic growth and left the question of redistributive justice for the refugee population to the newly founded Republic. Desperate to avoid either a punitive wealth tax or a disruptive reallocation of tax revenue between Federal government and the member states of the Bund, Finance Minister Schäffer attempted to limit the annual compensation fund to a modest 1.5–2 billion Deutschmarks per annum.[59] But by the end of 1950, under massive political pressure he had been forced to agree to a 50 per cent wealth tax spread over 30 years and amortized at the rate of between 4 and 6 per cent. Along with Bonn's other spending commitments this raised the federal share of total public spending in West Germany from as little as 9 per cent in 1949 to over 42 per cent a year later.[60] In 1951 the increasingly complex draft law was fought through a thicket of parliamentary committees, only to emerge for final plenary debate in the spring of 1952 precisely when Adenauer was most in need of parliamentary support for his bold foreign policy. Seizing their opportunity the leader of the *Vertriebene* organized a final round of extra-parliamentary mobilization combined with the threat that he and his parliamentary clique would resign the CDU whip and join with the SPD in voting against Adenauer's critical foreign policy initiatives. The result was a series of dramatic last minute concessions, which raised the annual compensation fund to no less than 4.8 billion. The government also agreed to remove the cap on the value of assets that could be claimed for compensation and

---

[59] On the federal issues of the German fiscal constitution see Peter H. Merkl, 'The Financial Constitution of Western Germany', *The American Journal of Comparative Law* 6:2 (1957), 327–40.

[60] Gerhard Stoltenberg, 'Legislative und Finanzverfassung 1954/55' in *Vierteljahrshefte fuer Zeitgeschichte* 13:3 (1965), 243.

front-loaded the funding so that large-scale expenditure on pensions and emergency relief could begin immediately.[61] This fractured the consensus with the SPD, but not enough to jeopardize the two-thirds majority that was required for the first amendment to the West German constitution, without which Bonn could not have ensured a uniform implementation of the *Lastenausgleich* across the federation.

## V

There was a straightforward political and strategic logic that determined the basic hierarchy of spending by the Federal Republic. Defence and social coherence were the first priorities, with the United States largely setting the terms for the arrangements both with Israel and the London creditors. But this rank order was reinforced by a second logic. Apart from the desire to minimize the overall burden on the German economy, the central preoccupation of Germany's negotiating teams in 1952 was to ensure that foreign claims did not destabilize the balance of payments. Any actual transfer of payments in foreign currency had to be balanced by inflows on the current or capital account. These could take the form of net earnings from exports, official assistance such as the Marshall Plan, or private foreign loans. If the exchange parities fixed in September 1949 were not to be jeopardized, the availability of foreign currency determined what could be transferred. The welfare provisions for war damaged Germans were enormously expensive but involved transfers of DMs from one German to another. And though payments towards the European Defence Community might initially appear to be foreign transactions, in fact one of the first decisions taken in the defence spending negotiations was the all-important clause that no more than 15 per cent of European defence spending would be 'out of country'.[62] Germany could of course expect to benefit from a large inflow of dollars from spending by US troops stationed in Germany under the new NATO strategy.

Of course, the German balance of payments had been an object of economic and political argument ever since 1919. And it was in the manipulation of the balance of payments, the regulation of foreign exchange transfers and foreign indebtedness that Hitler's central banker Hjalmar Schacht had acquired his infamous reputation as the dark wizard of modern finance.

---

[61] Henzler, *Schäffer*, 347–8.

[62] Monika Dickhaus, *Die Bundesbank im Westeuropaeischen Wiederaufbau. Die internationale Waehrungspolitik der Bundesrepublik Deutschland 1948 bis 1958* (Munich, 1996), 140–1.

**Table 3.** Quarterly balance of payments position, FRG 1950–1954 (million $ US)

| | Overall net balance of trade and services | Net balance with EPU | Net balance with 'dollar zone' | Foreign aid | Compensation payments | Repayments under London debt agreement |
|---|---|---|---|---|---|---|
| I-1950 | −215 | −121 | −99 | 162 | | |
| II-1950 | −79 | −30 | −75 | 82 | | |
| III-1950 | −119 | −77 | −51 | 120 | | |
| IV-1950 | −188 | −161 | −41 | 128 | | |
| I-1951 | −143 | −86 | −69 | 123 | | |
| II-1951 | 131 | 223 | −104 | 152 | | |
| III-1951 | 85 | 158 | −90 | 114 | | |
| IV-1951 | 113 | 207 | −115 | 40 | | |
| I-1952 | 0 | 111 | −108 | 24 | 0 | |
| II-1952 | 222 | 182 | −2 | 21 | −1 | |
| III-1952 | 230 | 163 | 13 | 38 | −1 | |
| IV-1952 | 116 | −6 | 69 | 31 | −1 | |
| I-1953 | 134 | 51 | 64 | 12 | −15 | −15 |
| II-1953 | 246 | 148 | 51 | 17 | −7 | 0 |
| III-1953 | 245 | 123 | 77 | 13 | −10 | −24 |
| IV-1953 | 346 | 211 | 92 | 21 | −15 | −14 |
| I-1954 | 263 | 182 | 77 | 30 | −23 | −27 |
| II-1954 | 203 | 156 | 44 | 18 | −35 | −31 |
| III-1954 | 279 | 165 | 112 | 12 | −29 | −70 |
| IV-1954 | 213 | 161 | 71 | 10 | −34 | −23 |

*Source*: *Statistisches Handbuch der Bank Deutscher Länder 1948–1954* (Frankfurt, 1955), 256–9.

By 1945 all of Europe was enmeshed in the network of foreign exchange controls and bilateral clearing agreements which were indelibly associated with the malign influence of Schacht. Breaking out of this constraining system was the central objective of international reconstruction announced at the Bretton Woods conference of 1944. And within the Federal Republic, the Minister of Economic Affairs Ludwig Erhard had made the liberalization of the current account into the centre of his mission to establish the social market economy in Germany.[63] Encouraged by the organizations of the Marshall Plan the new West German state had made itself into a pioneer of decontrol. However, as is visible in Table 3 the results were ambiguous.

After 1949 the rapid liberalization of the German economy had sucked in massive volumes of imports. And the Korean war boom had worsened the problem by shifting the terms of trade sharply against Germany. The result

[63] Reinhard Neebe, *Weichenstellung für die Globalisierung. Deutsche Weltmarktpolitik, Europa und Amerika in der Ära Ludwig Erhard* (Cologne, 2004).

was to throw the balance of trade into deficit, jeopardizing the entire effort at trade liberalization. As reserves plunged, the German government under allied pressure was forced to raise taxes, restrict credit and restore many of the odious 'Schachtian' controls.[64] This was a profound political shock and it was this fiasco of the first phase of liberalization which set the stage for the highly pessimistic interpretation of Germany's balance of payments outlook, which in turn underpinned the extremely modest deals with Israel and the London creditors negotiated in 1952. It was these figures which underpinned the coalition between Hermann Abs the chief negotiator, the Bank deutscher Länder and the Finance Minister Fritz Schäffer who joined together to resist both the international demands on Germany and Ludwig Erhard's efforts at a rapid re-liberalization of Germany's foreign account. They did not go as far as the advocates of the so-called 'structural school' in the 1920s, who had insisted that Germany's balance of payments problems were unalterable. But Abs and the central bankers pointed insistently to the fundamental obstacles that continued to obstruct German efforts to achieve a positive balance with the dollar zone.[65]

So dogged was their resistance that it led close to the point of disaster. By April and May 1952 it seemed that there was no way of squaring the demands of Israel, the London creditors, NATO and the domestic political interest. But at this point they were overwhelmed not only by High Commissioner McCloy's direct pressure on Adenauer, but also by a decisive intervention by Economics Minister Erhard. Despite the setback of the Korean crisis Erhard never relinquished his wide-ranging liberalizing agenda. He insisted on the need to return to the programme of international expansion. He fretted at the narrowly European confines of *Westbindung* as it appeared to be emerging in the shape of France's Coal and Steel Community and the EPU. At the earliest possible opportunity he wanted a return to the global agenda of liberalization as pushed forward by Bretton Woods and GATT. And he certainly did not want to see the dark legacy of the pre-1945 period jeopardizing

---

[64] Monika Dickhaus, 'Fostering "The Bank That Rules Europe": The Bank of England, the Allied Banking Commission, and the Bank Deutscher Länder, 1948–51', *Contemporary European History*, 7:2 (1998), 161–79. Ludwig-Erhard Stiftung (ed.), *Die Korea-Krise als ordnungspolitischer Herausforderung der deutschen Wirtschaftspolitik* (Stuttgart, 1986).

[65] The importance of the difference between the German balance of payments with the dollar and EPU zones was highlighted by Christoph Buchheim, 'Das Londoner Schuldenabkommen' in Ludolf Herbst (ed.), *Westdeutschland 1945–1955* (Munich, 1986), 218–29.

Germany's relationship with its key global partners, notably the United States and Britain. Despite the shaky start made by the Federal Republic there was no option but to bank on the future. As Erhard put it to Adenauer in a truly remarkable letter on 16 May 1952:

> If we do not bank on further economic expansion, we abandon ourselves . . . from a more dynamic assessment of the situation and particularly from the political aspect it may very well serve the German interest better to acknowledge a greater amount of debt, if we thereby strengthen Germany's credit and in the end even reconcile the Jews of the world to the German past. The difficulty is that the possibilities cannot be weighed or measured and therefore also do not impress the German public . . . but either we have a future, in which case we may wager something, or we are lost, and then all agreements are without significance.[66]

What truly marks 1952 as the turning point in politics of reconstruction is the fact that it saw the conjunction of two radically different economic visions: on the one hand the rhetoric of crisis inherited from the 1920s and enjoying its last moment of credibility, and on the other hand a new vision of the limitless opportunities opened up by economic growth. Erhard's letter to Adenauer is a remarkable indicator of this liminal moment, because it acknowledged both possibilities. The early summer of 1952 was not yet a moment at which everything was certainly possible. Indeed the possibility of total disaster could not yet be ruled out. But it was no longer a moment at which one could remain fixated on the ruins of what Germany had once been and deny all responsibility for the future. In this sense 1952 marks the true end point of reconstruction.

## VI

It is speculation of course, but it was surely fortunate for West Germany that Erhard and Adenauer's vision of a daring compromise prevailed in the summer of 1952. From that moment onwards, with memories of post-war crisis dwindling in the rear view mirror, it is hard to see how the rest of the world could have been reconciled to the stark imbalance between the surging dynamic of West German economic growth and the dark legacy of unresolved political and moral issues. If a settlement had been possible at all, it would certainly have been on terms far less favourable to West Germany. And that raises unsettling counterfactual possibilities. If rather than the terms agreed in

---

[66] Author's translation from Wolfssohn, 'Globalentschädigung', 170–1. See also Neebe, *Weichenstellung.*

1952, West Germany had held out, only to face more substantial demands at a later date, would Adenauer have been able to contain the nationalist resentment that continued to boil beneath the surface? In 1952, 68 per cent of the German population either opposed compensation for Israel outright or considered the modest sum agreed to be excessive. Fourteen years later at the end of the Adenauer era in 1966, 46 per cent were still resentfully opposed to any further support for Israel, which had already 'received too much'.[67] If the 'German question' had remained unresolved, who would have anchored the process of European integration when France entered its period of mounting crisis after 1954?

The significance of the moment of consolidation in 1952 has been presented here with reference to Germany. But it had ramifications across Europe.[68] In *Postwar*, Tony Judt remarks that it was not until the early 1950s and then rather suddenly that an uneasy kind of political calm began to descend over Europe.[69] Both the timing and the substance of the 1952 settlements have much to do with this. They gave Adenauer's Germany both a major stake in the emerging international order and the economic muscle to sustain it. Having accepted what they considered to be heavy international responsibilities under the terms of the 1952 agreements, the Bank deutscher Länder insisted on a cautious approach to liberalization. Rather than Erhard's radical push for currency convertibility, the last vestige of the interwar system of controls—the separation between the dollar zone and the European Payments Union—was maintained until 1958. And within that system West Germany came increasingly to serve as a steadying anchor. After 1952 the transformation of the German balance of payments was nothing short of spectacular. Factors beyond Germany's control played a considerable part in this process. Crucially, the adverse shift in the terms of trade that had occurred as a result of the Korean war was dramatically reversed. But German economic policy choices also played their part. Operating outside the limelight and beyond the ideological contestation over the social market economy, the conservative monetary policy corset implemented by the central bank from 1951 and the tight fiscal policy imposed by Schäffer did their job. After 1952, consumption expenditure fell despite the rising level of economic activity and for the first time in two generations Germany began to

---

[67] Wolffsohn, 'Wiedergutmachungsabkommen', 211.

[68] Michael Creswell, *A Question of Balance; How France and the United States Created Cold War Europe* (Cambridge Mass., 2006).

[69] T. Judt, *Postwar*, 242.

emerge as a major export champion fully capable of meeting its foreign obligations. With its main trading partners constrained within the fixed exchange rate zone of the EPU, Germany's surplus blossomed and the Bank deutscher Länder emerged as a dominant force. Britain and France by contrast slipped into the quite unprecedented position of relying on Germany for credits. Thanks in large part to the decisions of 1952, the immediate result of reconstruction from World War II was a successful, but narrowly West European structure built around a conservative West Germany.

# Reconstruction in East-Central Europe: Clearing the Rubble of Cold War Politics

**Holly Case**

## In a word: reconstruction

There are many reasons why the term 'reconstruction' should be problematized and why East-Central Europe is a good place to look for anomalies in its usage. Consider Albania, for example. Due to the nature of Italian direct investment, Albania emerged from the Second World War with more developed infrastructure than it had in 1938.[1] What meaning does 'reconstruction'—a term broadly enough applied in Albania after the war—have under such circumstances? The other extreme is Poland, a state that lost territory in the East, acquired a comparably sized swathe of it in the West, and saw its capital city of Warsaw completely annihilated during the last months of the war, with the extent of destruction exceeding 90 per cent in some places. What does reconstruction look like in a territory that had not previously been part of the state? Or when the level of destruction is so great that the starting point is a near tabula rasa? The diversity of East-Central European states' experience of both the war and the period of reconstruction makes it difficult to speak of either in strictly regional terms.[2]

---

[1] John R. Lampe, *Balkans into Southeastern Europe: A Century of War and Transition* (New York, 2006), 154. Albania did sustain losses in mines, livestock, and housing, however. Ibid., 180. Lampe also notes that the Romanian economy 'benefited from German investment during the war'.

[2] On the diversity of experiences of post-war states during the transition to communism, there is by now an abundant and growing body of work. The work of Zbigniew Brzezinksi, *Soviet Bloc: Unity and Conflict* (Cambridge, Mass., 1960), proved influential, arguing that the communist camp was neither homogeneous, nor monolithic, nor unchanging. Since then, there has been a spate of works emphasizing national uniqueness among the states that experienced Red Army occupation and the communist takeover after World War II. Most recently Bradley Abrams, *The Struggle for the Soul of the Nation: Czech Culture and the Rise of Communism* (Lanham, Md., 2004); John Connelly, *Captive University: The Sovietization of East German, Czech, and Polish Higher Education, 1945–1956* (Chapel Hill, 2000); Charles Gati, *Hungary in the Soviet Bloc* (Durham, N.C., 1986);

*Past and Present (2011)*, Supplement 6

A similarly profound challenge is posed by the use—or avoidance—of the term 'reconstruction' during and after the immediate post-war period itself. Although references to 'reconstruction' were made repeatedly within the countries of East-Central Europe, only rarely did Western authors and exiles speak of 'reconstruction' efforts in East-Central Europe after 1947.[3] When Westerners did speak of reconstruction in the East, they were generally leftist groups and individuals who considered socialism a desirable alternative.[4] Hence the leftist Fabian Society based in London took considerable interest in the progress of East-Central European States toward state socialism.[5]

Outside leftist circles, it was often assumed that no such thing as reconstruction happened or could take place without the Marshall Plan. On the rare occasions when the word 'reconstruction' *was* used by non-leftist Westerners to describe what was happening in East-Central Europe after

Norman Naimark, *The Russians in Germany: A History of the Soviet Zone of Occupation, 1945–1949* (Cambridge, Mass., 1995), to name a few.

[3] For examples of indigenous references to reconstruction, see Tibor Vágvölgyi, *Pártépítés-országépítés a magyar dolgozók szabadságharcának tűzvonalából* (Budapest, 1946); Michał Kaczorowski, *Początki odbudowy kraju i stolicy, 1944–1949* (Warszawa, 1980); Wł. Kurkiewicz, W. Olszewski, and A. Tatomir (eds), *Odbudowa państwa polskiego w latach 1944–1946* (Warszawa, 1947); O. D. Landy (ed.), *Reconstruction in Hungary* (Budapest, 1948); *The Fulfilment of the Three-Year Plan of Economic Reconstruction in Poland* (Warszawa, 1950); Ivan Karić, *The New Yugoslavia in Reconstruction and Building Up* (Beograd, 1947); Václav Lacina, *In Czechoslovakia Now: A Year of Reconstruction* (Prague, 1946); Poland. Krajowa Rada Narodowa, *Polish National Economic Plan: Resolution of the National Council concerning the National Economic Plans and the Plan of Economic Reconstruction for the Period of January 1, 1946-December 31, 1949 (dated September 21, 1946)* (Warszawa 1946). It is also true that the word 'reconstruction' was often used in the West in reference to US-sponsored initiatives and aid. See, for example, United States Department of State, *Foreign Relations of the United States* [henceforth *FRUS*], 1946. General; the United Nations, volume I (1946), 'Formulation of a foreign financial program: policy to help war-devastated and liberated countries meet their dollar requirements pending the beginning of loan operations by the International Bank for Reconstruction and Development', 1391–1436.

[4] See, for example, Joseph Vincent Yakowicz, *Poland's Postwar Recovery: Economic Reconstruction, Nationalization, and Agrarian Reform in Poland After World War II* (Hicksville, NY, 1979); Shiela Grant Duff, John Parker, Michael Young, H. D. Hughes, James Callaghan, and Carol Johnson, *Czechoslovakia: Six Studies in Reconstruction* (London, [1946?]).

[5] Grant Duff, et al., *Czechoslovakia*, 6.

the war, the term generally assumed a negative connotation. In a 1948 article on 'Political Trends in Eastern Europe', for example, Andrew Gyorgy wrote about 'Postwar Reconstruction Politics', characterizing it as follows: 'the use of Soviet influence to put in power regimes friendly to Russia' and 'suppression of the opposition, liquidation of its leaders, and consolidation of the one-party state'.[6]

Even within the nascent communist regimes of the region the term 'reconstruction' was often used differently than in the West. Communist planners saw in the immediate post-war period an opportunity to start again and build an economy and society on completely different bases, rather than a mandate to 'reconstruct' what had once been.

The politics and historical contingency involved in the use of the word 'reconstruction' is at the root of why this period in the region's history has garnered fresh interest in the decades since the collapse of communism. Yet this interest was not revived by historians, but rather by policy-makers, bankers, economists, and political scientists. Their choice was a practical one. In the budding field of 'transitology', or the study of transitions from communism to post-communism, the problem of economic 'reconstruction' was one for which they sought precedents. A conference organized in the early 1990s thus undertook 'a reassessment' of reconstruction efforts in post-war Europe and Japan, above all of the Marshall Plan.[7] 'The extraordinary problems faced by Eastern Europe and by the former Soviet Union make us search for parallels', the organizers wrote. 'When did countries in modern history face similar problems of rebuilding their economies; how did they cope with the challenge; what lessons follow for Eastern Europe today?'[8]

The wars in Yugoslavia also inspired new interest in reconstruction and a resurrection of the term by policy-makers and social scientists dealing with the war-torn successor states.[9] The ideational (or ideological) component of reconstruction played heavily into both areas of renewed interest. Just as for

---

[6] Andrew Gyorgy, 'Political Trends in Eastern Europe', in *Foreign Policy Reports*, XXIV, no. 13 (15 November 1948) 146–56 at 146.

[7] Jacqueline T. Limberger, *Mechanisms for Rebuilding Europe: The Marshall Plan for West European Reconstruction and New Western Initiatives for East European Stabilisation* ([Nathan, Qld.], 1992); Rudiger Dornbusch, Wilhelm Nölling, and Richard Layard (eds), *Postwar Economic Reconstruction and Lessons for the East Today* (Cambridge, Mass., 1993).

[8] Dornbusch et al. (eds), *Postwar Economic Reconstruction,* vii.

[9] See, for example, Daniel Daianu and Thanos Veremes, *Balkan Reconstruction* (London, 2001); Transitions Online, *Balkan Reconstruction Report* (Prague, 2001), http://balkanreport.tol.cz; International Energy Agency, *Energy in the Western Balkans: The Path to Reform and Reconstruction* (Paris, 2008).

the post-war communist regimes, post-socialist 'reconstruction' would entail an ideational shift, an overhaul in systems of thinking and behaviour (as manifest in education, culture, and structures of governance), as much as physical rebuilding.

Despite these historical parallels, social scientists and economists have yet to seek precedents for reconstruction *within* the region, specifically during the period following the First and Second World Wars. The result is that the immediate post-World War II period in the region's economic history in particular remains obscured behind the haze of Cold War politics even as the ongoing economic crisis has lent renewed vigour to an understanding of Europe as a continent divided into East and West, particularly in terms of economics.[10]

The present haunts the history of reconstruction in this region, so much so that it remains difficult to glean what actually happened in Europe after World War II in terms of state-sponsored and competing efforts to reshape the economy and society. When scholars speak of reconstruction in the West or in Japan, they feel confident they are describing something real. But that reality is derived from a politics of comparison that depends on the existence of the East bloc, and indeed cannot be comprehended without an understanding of how the East was the perpetual foil for Western European reconstruction and the role it played in the creation of post-war (Western) Europe. Cold War historian Vojtech Mastny reinforced this perception when he argued in 1996 that the Cold War could probably have been prevented, but then the 'benefits' of the Cold War, specifically the Marshall Plan and Western Europe's unification, would never have happened.[11] This perception has fed and sustained a self-image among Western Europeans that remains deeply embedded today, one that renders the immediate post-war experience of

---

[10] See, for example, Ahto Lobjakas, 'Emergency EU Summit Puts Premium on Unity', in *Radio Free Europe Radio Liberty*, 1 March 2009, http://www.rferl.org/content/Emergency_EU_Summit_Puts_Premium_On_Unity/1501183.html, [accessed 25 June 2009]; Nicu Popescu, 'The Return of "Eastern Europe"', in euobserver.com, Thursday, 5 March 2009, http://blogs.euobserver.com/popescu/2009/03/05/the-return-of-eastern-europe/ [accessed 25 June 2009]. In a bizarre and disturbing comparison, Bank Austria made reference to the 'monetary Stalingrad' it was facing in the East. Ambrose Evans-Pritchard, 'Failure to save East Europe will lead to worldwide meltdown', in Telegraph.co.uk, 14 February 2009, http://www.telegraph.co.uk/finance/comment/ambroseevans_pritchard/4623525/Failure-to-save-East-Europe-will-lead-to-worldwide-meltdown.html [accessed 25 June 2009].

[11] Vojtech Mastny, *The Cold War and Soviet Insecurity: The Stalin Years* (New York, 1996), 195–7.

East-Central European peoples and states conceptually invisible and perpetually 'un-reconstructed'.

Meanwhile, scholars of East-Central Europe have long concerned themselves with whether or not Stalin had a small-'p' plan for the region after the war.[12] Yet we have failed to look as closely at the various big-'P' plans of the post-war period (the Two-year Plan, Three-year Plan, Five-year Plan) that were running their course in the countries of East-Central Europe just after the communists came to power. Recent works on the post-war period deal almost exclusively with politics and/or culture, for the most part ignoring the economics of the immediate post-war period, unless to reaffirm claims of Soviet economic imperialism.[13] And scholars of the region have barely explored the historical standards for what (indeed whether) reconstruction was, what its achievements and failures were, and for whom. A careful probe into this period could reveal a great deal about how Cold War politics constituted Cold War economics, rendering it impossible to speak of one without invoking the other.

In this contribution, I would like to make such a preliminary probe, investigating post-war reconstruction in East-Central Europe from a variety of

---

[12] The literature dealing with the question of whether or not Stalin had always intended the Soviet Union to assume a dominant role in East-Central Europe is vast. To name a few: Mastny, *The Cold War*; Vojtech Mastny, *Russia's Road to the Cold War: Diplomacy, Warfare, and the Politics of Communism, 1941–1945* (New York, 1979); Gati, *Hungary and the Soviet Bloc*; Peter Kenez, *Hungary from the Nazis to the Soviets: The Establishment of the Communist Regime in Hungary, 1944–1948* (New York 2006); Scott Parrish, 'The Marshall Plan, Soviet-American Relations, and the Division of Europe', in Norman Naimark and Leonid Gibianskii (eds), *The Establishment of Communist Regimes in Eastern Europe, 1944–1949*, (Boulder, Colo. and Oxford, 1997), 267–90; Jerzy Tomaszewski, *The Socialist Regimes of East Central Europe: Their Establishment and Consolidation, 1944–1967* (London, 1989); László Borhi, *Hungary in the Cold War, 1945–1956* (Budapest and New York, 2004); Aldo Agosti, 'Recasting Democracy: Communist Parties Facing Change and Reconstruction in Postwar Europe', in Padraic Kenney and Gerd-Rainer Horn (eds), *Transnational Moments of Change: Europe 1945, 1968, 1989* (Lanham, Maryland, 2004), 3–26.

[13] See, for example, Balázs Apor, Péter Apor, and E. A. Rees, *The Sovietization of Eastern Europe: New Perspectives on the Postwar Period* (Washington, DC, 2008); Joseph Rothschild and Nancy M. Wingfield, *Return to Diversity: A Political History of East Central Europe Since World War II* (New York, 2008); Mark Pittaway, *Eastern Europe 1939–2000* (Brief histories. London, 2004). One notable exception is a 1997 book by Padraic Kenny, in which he argues that economic Stalinism in Poland was not truly imposed, but rather negotiated. Padraic Kenney, *Rebuilding Poland: Workers and Communists, 1945–1950* (Ithaca, 1997).

perspectives. The analysis operates on two levels and is divided into parts accordingly. Part I considers the nature and extent of wartime destruction in the states of East-Central Europe and the various standpoints on the tasks of post-war reconstruction. There follows a section on indigenous precedents of the policies implemented after the Second World War. Part II attends to the politics behind assessments of the period of post-war reconstruction, specifically in terms of émigré groups and statistical comparisons.

# I

*1945–1950: Claims and counter-claims*

Although the scale of wartime destruction across the region varied widely, it was nowhere insignificant and in some areas total. Among the hardest hit were the Polish cities of Warsaw, Gdańsk and Wrocław, where up to ninety per cent of homes and infrastructure were destroyed during the war.[14] 'All around are ruins and more ruins. The overwhelming majority of houses are on fire and the ashes reach us, mixed with the stench of corpses', an eyewitness said of Gdańsk at the end of the war.[15] Overall, almost one third of Polish industry and retail, and one half of transport and communication systems were destroyed, while half the agricultural sector was fallow.[16] Schools and health services meanwhile sustained losses of over half their pre-war standing.[17]

Elsewhere in the region damages were substantial, but not as severe. In Czechoslovakia just over one per cent of flats were completely destroyed and another twelve per cent were damaged.[18] And in Budapest after the siege, seventy-three per cent of homes were considered habitable, sixteen per cent partly habitable, and the remaining eleven per cent uninhabitable.[19] Bulgaria, despite the Allied bombing of Sofia toward the end of the war, emerged with most of its economic infrastructure intact, while Yugoslavia sustained

---

[14] Izabella Tojanowska (ed.), *Wspomnienia z odbudowy głównego miasta* (Gdańsk, 1978), 8–9; Marek Ordyłowski, *Życie codzienne we Wrocławiu, 1945–1948* (Wrocław, 1991), 11; Michał Stryczyński, *Gdańsk w latach 1945–1948: odbudowa organizmu miejskiego* (Wrocław, Warszawa, Kraków, Gdańsk, Łódź, 1981), 10–17.

[15] These were the words of an editor for the Polish Press Agency, S. Strąbski, cited in: Stryczyński, *Gdańsk*, 10.

[16] Władysław Miś, *Od wojny do pokoju: gospodarka Polski w latach 1944–1946* (Warszawa, 1977), 10–13; *The Fulfilment of the Three-Year Plan*, 7–11; *Polska gospodarka planowa* (Warszawa, 1948), 15–17.

[17] Yakowicz, *Poland's Postwar Recovery*, 13.

[18] Grant Duff, et al., *Czechoslovakia*, 62.

[19] Krisztián Ungváry, *Battle for Budapest: 100 Days in World War II* (London, 2003), 330.

significant damage to industry and mines, as well as to transport and communication infrastructure.[20]

In speaking of the tasks of reconstruction, new state leaders emphasized the need for industrialization, nationalization, agrarian reform, currency reform, and retribution for war crimes, but also for new ways of thinking about society and economics in general. Czechoslovak president Edvard Beneš thus told the Czechoslovak parliament in 1946 that 'a new social moral is beginning to be built up amongst us. [W]e are not merely changing institutions, but we wish to, and must, create also a *new man*'.[21] And alongside that 'new man', a 'new woman' was to emerge from the processes set in motion after the war, one more active in the economy generally and in industry in particular.[22]

The emphasis on a break with the past comes through elsewhere as well. Bolesław Bierut, then the head of the State National Council in Poland, commented in 1946 on changes the new regime planned to effect in workers' housing in the city. 'We have inherited the ruins of a city that was built chaotically, a city in which the workers' districts were fantastically overpopulated and neglected, while wealthy inhabitants had luxurious residential quarters: a city in which the natural right of man to space, light and green areas was denied to the working class.'[23] All of that was to change, Bierut continued. Reconstruction was not merely to be a replacement of the old, but the creation of something new. Later assessments of the immediate post-war period stressed the theme of transformation. A 1970 book on Yugoslavia's economic development since the war opens: 'Before the Second World War, Yugoslavia was among Europe's most retrograde countries economically. Her economy had every characteristic of a backward and semi-colonial economy.'[24] Similarly, a Polish book from the 1960s mentioned the 'reconstruction—or rather the CONSTRUCTION' of the country's capital,

---

[20] On wartime damages in Yugoslavia, see Jože Moravec (ed.), *25 Years of the Yugoslav Economy* (Beograd, 1970), 7. On Bulgaria, see M. C. Kaser and E. A. Radice (eds), *The Economic History of Eastern Europe, 1919–1975, vol. II, Interwar Policy, the War, and Reconstruction* (Oxford, 1986), 502–3.

[21] Edvard Beneš, *The Opening of the Prague Parliament: Message of President Dr. Edvard Beneš to the National Assembly of the Czechoslovak Republic* (Prague, 1946), 36–7.

[22] Malgorzata Fidelis, 'The New Proletarians: Women Industrial Workers and the State in Postwar Poland, 1945–1957', Ph.D. diss., Stanford University, 2006, in Dissertations & Theses: Full Text [database online]; available from http://www.proquest.com (publication number AAT 3197429; accessed 26 June 2009), 1–2.

[23] Bolesław Bierut, *The 6-Year Plan for the Reconstruction of Warsaw* (Warszawa, 1949), 77.

[24] Moravec (ed.), *25 Years*, 7.

alluding to the 'spirit which prevails to this day in the new, changed Warsaw'.[25]

Part of that process of transformation (especially in Poland, Czechoslovakia, and to a lesser extent Yugoslavia) involved repopulating and developing newly acquired or largely vacant territories formerly inhabited by ethnic Germans or Italians. This aspect of reconstruction has been the focus of some post-communist historiography, which views the peopling and development of these territories as part of a longer term process of national homogenization. A 1991 book on the reconstruction of the city of Wrocław, for example, argues that during the period from 1945 to 1948, 'Wrocław became a new, different city, with a new Polish population'.[26] Although Poles in Wrocław had constituted a minority 'in a sea of Germans' all the way up to 1946, it did not take long, the author concluded, before the very word 'native' with respect to inhabitants of the city assumed a negative connotation.[27]

The challenge of integrating new territories was not shared by all states in the region, however. In fact several of them—Hungary, Romania, Bulgaria— lost territory they had possessed before or during the war. Yet one experience common to the region was post-war destitution, as states and peoples faced difficulties which required immediate attention more than long-term planning. Among these difficulties were food and basic supply shortages. To assess need and provide aid in the form of 'food, consumers' goods and essential rehabilitation items', UNRRA (United Nations Relief and Rehabilitation Administration) was created in 1943. Three years later, in 1946, UNRRA estimates of 'Reconstruction and Development Needs' for various European countries placed Czechoslovakia's need near that of Norway, while Yugoslavia and Greece were comparable to Denmark.[28] Up until its dissolution in 1947, UNRRA (using mostly money contributed by the US) delivered more than one billion dollars worth of aid in the form of food, clothing, medical supplies, agricultural support, and support for the industrial rehabilitation to East-Central Europe. Most of this aid went to Czechoslovakia, Poland, and Yugoslavia, since former allies of Nazi Germany (Hungary, Romania, and Bulgaria) were largely ineligible.[29]

---

[25] Adolf Ciborowski, *Warsaw: A City Destroyed and Rebuilt* (Warsaw, [1964?]), 8.

[26] Ordyłowski, *Życie codzienne*, 5.

[27] Ibid., 24, 248.

[28] *FRUS, General; the United Nations*, volume I (1946), 'Formulation of a foreign financial program', 1393.

[29] Kaser and Radice (eds), *The Economic History of Eastern Europe*, 523. Czechoslovakia received $261.3 million, Poland $477.9 million, and Yugoslavia $415.6 million in total

Although initially UNRRA supported recovery of industrial capacity, its later assessments of need did not include provisions for 'reconstruction or development'.[30] In some respects the follow-up to UNRRA aid was the Marshall Plan, which included provisions for all aspects of economic reconstruction, and was famously offered to East-Central Europe, even initially accepted by some states, but ultimately rejected at Soviet insistence. This watershed moment of the Cold War is generally cited as a, if not *the* moment when the economic and political division of Europe became manifest.

The historiography on the Marshall Plan is part of the same broad debate about whether or not Stalin had a 'plan' for the region. Scott Parrish has argued that 'the Soviet leadership came to view [the Marshall Plan] as an attempt to use economic aid not only to consolidate a West European bloc, but also to undermine recently won, and still somewhat tenuous, Soviet gains in Eastern Europe'.[31] Regardless of whether or not consolidating Western Europe and undermining Soviet interests in East-Central Europe was the objective of the US in 1947, it certainly became so by 1948, when American economic policy vis-à-vis the region was fully subordinated to its foreign policy objectives in Europe as a whole, and included 'the limitation of Eastern Europe's war potential and the recovery and development of the economies of Western Europe'. Since the overarching US foreign policy goal in the region was to 'improve the relative economic advantages of Western Europe over countries in the Soviet bloc', US policy-makers were careful not to undertake initiatives that would stimulate East-Central European economies unless the benefit to Western Europe was significantly greater.[32]

Already in 1945, the US government viewed Soviet interests in the region as primarily economic, insofar as 'Regardless of political developments in these areas, it is evident that Moscow hopes to retain dominant economic influence [. . .] If the Russians succeed in this program of economic

---

UNRRA aid. Hungary received $4.4 million in aid, which amounted to less than 0.4 per cent of the total amount of aid distributed to East-Central Europe.

[30] *FRUS, General; The United Nations*, volume I (1946), 'Formulation of a foreign financial program', 1393; *FRUS, General; The United Nations*, volume I (1947), 'The United States program for providing relief assistance to war-devastated countries, upon the termination of the United Nations Relief and Rehabilitation Administration (UNRRA)', 1029–38.

[31] Parrish, 'The Marshall Plan', 268.

[32] See *FRUS, Central and Eastern Europe; The Soviet Union*, volume IV (1950), Poland, 1044.

integration of these controlled areas with the Soviet economy, the perspective for the development of Soviet economic-military potential in the long run are immensely increased.'[33] The US leadership also feared that the tentacles of Soviet power could penetrate into Western Europe through economic channels. Thus it was a matter of concern when foreign policy experts in the US reported that Austria, Denmark, Norway, and Sweden were still heavily dependent on Polish coal in 1951.[34]

Émigré politicians were especially active in raising the spectre of Soviet economic imperialism and pushing for tougher US policy vis-à-vis the communist regimes in East-Central Europe. To this end, they cast the region as central to Soviet plans and thus key to US interests in Europe and the world. One Hungarian exile, György Bessenyey, wrote in May 1953:

> I firmly believe that without the industrial output of Eastern Germany, Poland, Czechoslovakia and even Hungary and Rumania, the present Soviet policy of developing and consolidating rather than expanding the Communist Empire, would be doomed to failure. Although the area and population of the countries behind the Iron Curtain seem to be small and insignificant when compared to the gigantic powers confronting each other in the world, it well might be that they are the weight which will tip the scales in one or the other direction and by doing so decide the outcome of the Cold War.[35]

Bessenyey sought to raise special awareness of 'the tremendous, unrelenting and ruthless effort to whip up, through the different Three- and Five-year Plans, in unprecedented manner the production of especially the heavy industry', tapping into US fears that East-Central European states' economies were being primed to produce weapons.[36] An anonymous author writing

---

[33] *FRUS: Diplomatic Papers. Europe*, volume V (1945), Union of Soviet Socialist Republics, 934–5.

[34] *FRUS: Europe: Political and Economic Developments (in two parts)*, volume IV, part 1 (1951), 'Multilateral relations', 143.

[35] Hoover Institution for War, Revolution and Peace [henceforth HIWRP], Ference Marosy collection, Box 1, Folder 'Bessenyey, György Baron, 1948–1953', Bessenyey to Marosy, May 1953.

[36] Another exile, Jan Wszelaki, wrote in 1959: 'It is now commonly accepted that—at least, until the fall of 1956—the Soviet Union had been grossly exploiting that area, though only the few who have studied the issue realize of what significant advantage this has been to the postwar recovery and subsequent expansion of Soviet economy'. HIWRP, Alexander D. Bunescu collection, Box 5, A.C.E.N. Economic Committee I, Assembly of Captive European Nations, Sixth Session, Jan Wszelaki, 'The European Captive

from Hungary in 1950 declared that reconstruction efforts in the region were commendable, 'but for reasons which are often strategic'.[37]

As politicians and exiles in the US tried to decipher the Soviet Union's long-term objectives and fashion a policy to counter them, major changes were taking place in the societies and economies of the region on a number of levels. Land reforms initiated a considerable shift in the distribution of land holdings by decreasing the number of mega-estates (100+ yokes) and increasing the number of small holdings (0–100 yokes).[38] Despite the magnitude of the reforms, their scale was actually smaller than that of the post-World War I land reforms in Bulgaria, Romania, and Yugoslavia.[39] Nevertheless, the land reforms, coupled with the emphasis on industrialization and later construction of socialist workers' cities such as Nowa Huta in Poland and Sztálinváros in Hungary, resulted in significant changes in the distribution of populations from rural to urban areas. Before the war in Poland, for example, sixty-three per cent of the population was rural. By 1957, Poland's population became more urban than rural, with only forty-seven per cent living in the countryside.[40] The dip in other countries, such as Albania, was less drastic, but nonetheless apparent.[41]

---

Countries: Soviet Economic Asset or Liability?', 28 Dec. 1959, Supporting Study (revised and updated) to A.C.E.N. doc. 147 (V) Econ., 17.

[37] In HIWRP, Štefan Osuský collection, Box 64, Folder 7, 'Liberation and Union: The Future of Danubian Federation and Atlantic Union, A Symposium', Washington D.C. (1952), 16.

[38] Kaser and Radice (eds), *The Economic History of Eastern Europe*, 505. Landed estates larger than 100 yokes amounted to over 46 per cent of the total land in Hungary in 1931, whereas in 1947 that figure was reduced to just over 21 per cent, most of which were state farms.

[39] Ibid., 593.

[40] HIWRP, Alexander D. Bunescu Papers, Box 5, A.C.E.N. Economic Committee I, Assembly of Captive European Nations, Seventh Session, 'Agriculture in Soviet Occupied European Countries', ACEN Doc. 246 (VII) Econ., 5 December 1960, 34.

[41] Albania: 1938 = 80 % rural, 1955 = 75 % rural. HIWRP, Alexander D. Bunescu Papers, Box 5, A.C.E.N. Economic Committee I, Assembly of Captive European Nations, Seventh Session, 'Agriculture in Soviet Occupied European Countries', ACEN Doc. 246 (VII) Econ., 5 December 1960, 34. Figures for the other East-Central European countries were as follows: Czechoslovakia: 1937 = 35% rural, 1958 = 20% rural; Hungary: 1939 = 62% rural, 1956 = 60% rural; Latvia: 1939 = 65% rural, 1959 = 44% rural; Lithuania 1940 = 77% rural, 1959 = 61% rural; Romania 1931 = 78% rural, 1958 = 68% rural; Estonia 1939 = 67% rural, 1959 = 44% rural.

Another important feature of reconstruction were the Two-, Three-, and Five-year Plans initiated in the various states starting in 1947.[42] Besides the Yugoslav Plan, which was especially ambitious and more a replica of the Soviet model, other economic plans in the region were centred primarily on the task of 'achieving as quickly as possible the prewar level of economic activity, with restoration of personal consumption as the prime objective'.[43] The Polish 'Resolution of the National Council concerning the Plan of Economic Reconstruction', dated 21 September 1946, gave as its 'Chief Aims' 'the raising of the standard of living of the working masses above the pre-war level [and] special emphasis on the development of those branches of industry which [. . .] will make possible the most rapid development of consumer goods production'. Priority of production was to be given to goods in the following order 'a) staple foodstuffs, b) necessary footwear, textiles and clothing, c) industrial articles for household use, d) other consumer goods'.[44]

During the process of introducing economic planning, there was also some information sharing between the states of the region, and beyond. The most prominent 'model' for economic reconstruction was that offered by the Soviet Union, which sent experts—overseen by Nikita Khrushchev—to consult with new regimes on how best to undertake the task of reconstruction and long-term economic planning.[45] During the years just after the war East Germany was considered a novice worthy of particular attention, requiring tutelage in economic planning practices from other socialist states. Hence the details of the Polish Three-year Plan were translated into German for East Germans 'to study the structure of the plan, its goals and methods to make them useful for [addressing] German economic planning tasks'.[46] Another work in the same series by Yugoslav leader Josip Broz Tito, entitled *How We*

---

[42] Yugoslavia's Five-year Plan (1947–1951); Poland's Three-year Plan (1947–1949); Hungary's Three-year Plan (1947–1949); Czechoslovakia's Two-year Plan (1947–1948); Bulgaria's Two-Year Plan (1947–1948); Albania's Two-year Plan (1949–1950); Romania's One-year Plan (1949).

[43] Kaser and Radice (eds), *The Economic History of Eastern Europe*, 610. According to the Yugoslav Plan, 'the ratio of industrial to agricultural production was in Yugoslavia to be reversed from 45:55 in 1939 to 64:36 in the horizon year, 1951, and within industry the ration of producers' goods to consumers' goods was to be exactly reversed (from 43:57 in 1939 to 57:43 in 1951)'. Ibid., 622.

[44] Poland, *Polish National Economic Plan*, 7, 17–18.

[45] Ciborowski, *Warsaw*, 67.

[46] C. A. Werner, *Der polnische Weg: Veröffentlichungen zum Dreijahresplan* (Berlin, 1948), 5.

*Do It: Report on the Path Yugoslavia is Following*, was published in German in 1947.[47]

Leftists in Western Europe also took an interest in the achievements of economic planning efforts and considered their possible applications within their own states. 'Czechoslovakia provides the British Labour Movement with an interesting comparison against which to measure our own aims and achievements since the war', Labour MP H. D. Hughes wrote in 1946.[48]

In terms of inter-state interactions, perhaps the most radical shift effected during the period of reconstruction was in the direction of trade. In 1938 import and export figures for trade with the Soviet Union throughout much of the region were around zero per cent. By 1950, however, that figure had risen to as high as sixty-three per cent for some countries and was significant for all of them.[49] Some of that trade was part of the reparations payments owed by allies of Nazi Germany—above all Hungary and Romania—to the Soviet Union according the Paris Peace Treaty. In addition, Bulgaria was required to make reparations payments to Yugoslavia and Greece, and Hungary to Czechoslovakia and Yugoslavia for damages to property in territories formerly under their control.[50]

*Origins and precedents*

How many of the policies and perceptions of the post-World War II period were rooted in earlier understandings and experiences of 'reconstruction'? A brief foray into historical uses of the term 'reconstruction' in and about this region is revealing of the extent to which earlier precedents influenced later practices and perceptions.

Beginning in the late nineteenth century, the notion of economic reconstruction in this region was tied to nationalism and state-building. The authors of an 1885 book on Ottoman South-eastern Europe thus perceived a link between 'National Resurrections' and 'Economic Reconstructions'.[51] The book's authors were themselves engaged in creating a precedent for Europe's post-war economic division by promoting Greek nationalism

---

[47]  Josip Broz Tito, *Wie wir es machen: Bericht über den Weg, den Jugoslawien geht* (Berlin, 1947).

[48]  Grant Duff, et al., *Czechoslovakia*, 6.

[49]  Lampe, *Balkans*, 223.

[50]  Joseph S. Roucek, 'The Bulgarian, Rumanian, and Hungarian Peace Treaties', in *Annals of the American Academy of Political and Social Science*, vol. 257, *Peace Settlements of World War II* (May 1948): 97–105 at 100–101.

[51]  Lucy Mary Jane Garnett and John S. Stuart-Glennie (eds), *Greek Folk-songs from the Turkish Provinces of Greece, Albania, Thessaly, (Not Yet Wholly Free,) and Macedonia* (London, 1885), xix.

over others within the region, an early fracture with later ramifications. Greece is not now considered part of 'Eastern Europe' and the politics of comparison have meant that Greece's economic health (or lack thereof) has rarely if ever been used as a standard or advanced as a reasonable point of comparison with its neighbours to the north and east. Nevertheless, similarities between Greece and other states of East-Central Europe—and particularly South-Eastern Europe—abound, especially in terms of the relationship between nationalism and integration into the broader 'European' economy.

In the aftermath of the First and Second Balkan Wars (1912–1913), some statesmen in the West began to think the order of emphasis between 'National Resurrections' and 'Economic Reconstructions' laid out in the 1885 volume should be reversed to favour the latter. Having witnessed the fall-out of a series of brutal ethnic cleansing campaigns during the Balkan Wars, in 1914 French Senator Baron d'Estournelles de Constant proclaimed the necessity to build infrastructure in the region so that the states and peoples of the Balkans could be better connected to the rest of Europe.

> [T]hese unhappy Balkan States have been up to the present, the victims of European division much more than of their own faults. If Europe had sincerely wished to help them in the past thirty years, she would have given them what makes the life in a country, that is, railways, tramways, roads, telegraphs and telephones, and in addition, schools. Once these fertile countries were linked to the rest of Europe, and connected like the rest of Europe, they would of themselves become peaceful by means of commerce and trade and industry, enriching themselves in spite of their inextricable divisions.[52]

De Constant's assessment shows that the conception of an economic division of Europe into East and West evolved well before World War II, and in fact emerged in part out of Western Europeans' anxiety about the nature and stability of East-Central European economies.

Discussions of reconstruction resurfaced again in the wake of the First World War with the emergence of a more clearly defined concept of what it meant. The specific aims of post-World War I reconstruction encompassed widespread social and economic reforms and consolidation of nation-states

---

[52] International Commission to Inquire into the Causes and Conduct of the Balkan Wars, *Report of the International Commission to Inquire into the Causes and Conduct of the Balkan Wars*. Carnegie Endowment for International Peace. Divisions of Intercourse and Education Publication, vol. 4. (Washington, DC, 1914), 8.

to replace the collapsed Habsburg, Ottoman, and Russian empires.[53] The emphasis on nation-building in the process of reconstruction after the First World War was destined to remain a central feature of the rhetoric after World War II. A Hungarian publication from 1949 thus declared that the perspective from which to approach the problem of reconstruction was that of 'Hungary, the Hungarian people, the fate of the nation, its present and future development'.[54]

These later observers felt that much of what was started during the period after World War I—most notably land reform and a kind of social revolution—remained unfinished. The Second World War saw their unintentional continuation as the war economy flattened social disparities and concentrated control and ownership of key industries in the hands of the state, even as governments within the region—many of them allied with Nazi Germany—and their exiled counterparts in London and New York spun plans for post-war economic revival.[55]

In 'selling' post-war economic reforms to legislators and the public, the region's leaders often emphasized the indigenous roots of such reforms. In a speech to the Czechoslovak parliament in 1946, Czechoslovak president Edvard Beneš told his audience that he saw the First World War, interwar period, and the Second World War as 'one single great entity of events'.

> In the history of the world and of Europe this period will present a special, great chapter swollen with the extreme ferment of revolution. [. . .] It is in the spirit of this epoch of revolution that we must solve the problems that face us in the sphere of our home policy; and in fact our policy since the 4th of April 1945—practically since the last year of our Government's domicile abroad—has been pursued in this sense. *In a word, we are reconstructing our State.*

---

[53] See, for example, Edward Rose, *The Progress of Financial Reconstruction in Poland* (Warsaw,1924); Serbian Child Welfare Association of America, *Co-operative Reconstruction: A Report of the Word Accomplished by the Serbian Child Welfare Association of America* (New York, 1924); Bedřich Štěpánek, 'Economic and Financial Reconstruction of Czechoslovakia', in *The Annals of the American Academy of Political and Social Science* (July 1922).

[54] László Gáspár and Oszkár Zsadányi (eds), *Újjáépítő magyarok: az országépítés három esztendeje* (Budapest, [1949?]), 7.

[55] On the social levelling and other economic effects of the war, see Bradley F. Abrams, 'The Second World War and the East European Revolution', in *East European Politics and Societies*, vol. 16: 3 (2002), 623–64.

The difference in the post-war transformation was thus one of degree insofar as the extent of the transformation after World War I hit up against restraints that the Second World War subsequently eliminated, and, in the process, 'revolutionized the whole world'.[56] The declared objectives of post-World War I reconstruction indeed had considerable overlap with those for after World War II. Agricultural, currency, and education reform were all contained within both sets of goals.[57] But none of these reforms had yet realized the ideal, Beneš and others argued.

In presenting the situation in this way, Beneš sought to comfort those who feared a Soviet takeover. Czechoslovakia was firmly rooted in the European, indeed global political trends of the time, he told his audience. Other authors sympathetic to the new regime followed Beneš's lead, pointing to continuities manifest in the transition. A 1947 book by Maurice Hindus outlined earlier Czechoslovak precedents for state ownership. He noted that the First Czechoslovak Republic had owned much of the country's forests, several 'highly mechanized feudal estates', hotels, health resorts, sanitariums, and had furthermore monopolized the railways, telegraph, telephone, postal service and radio, in addition to fisheries, salt, tobacco, and potato alcohol breweries. 'This history of co-operative ownership, of state and municipal proprietorship, of social ministrations and personal benefactions, did much to prepare Czechoslovakia for nationalization [...] The Czech revolution', he concluded, 'must likewise be viewed as essentially of an indigenous Czech nature'.[58] Another booklet published in Prague in 1946 asserted that the nationalization 'of mines and key industries' would have taken place 'even if the majority of the nation had not been of socialist conviction'.[59] Drawing on earlier precedents was thus a way of making the socialist reforms seem indigenous and popular, rather than imposed from the outside.

The comparison with the post-World War I period seemed an apt one for one Polish historian revisiting the theme of post-war reconstruction in 1980:

> The reconstruction of the country in the twentieth century was being organized already for the second time. The first was begun in 1918, and although the two had different goals, a different range

---

[56] Beneš, *The Opening of the Prague Parliament*, 23–5.

[57] Rose, *The Progress of Financial Reconstruction*, 20–3; Foreign Policy Association Information Service, *The Reconstruction of Poland*, 11 June 1930, vol. VI:7, 131–48, at 142; Lacina, *In Czechoslovakia Now*, 39; 'Economic Committee of the Central and Eastern European Planning Board', *Jugoslav Postwar Reconstruction Papers*, ed. Nicholas Mirkovich, vol. 1:2.

[58] Maurice Hindus, *The Bright Passage* (New York, 1947), 179–81, 183.

[59] Lacina, *In Czechoslovakia Now*, 15, 39, 42–3.

[zakres] of problems and different ranges of activity, there were certain essential convergences. In both landmark periods we undertook rebuilding [odbudowa] simultaneously with reconstruction [rekonstrukcja] of the country [. . .] And furthermore, in both cases we began the rebuilding before the recreated country's borders had been fixed.[60]

The mention of borders is significant, for the question of territory and population played a major role in determining the nature and course of reconstruction, particularly in states that gained, lost, or recovered territory. The two most notable cases are Czechoslovakia and Poland, but Yugoslavia's acquisition of parts of Istria and Dalmatia from Italy are also worth mentioning. Prior to World War I, none of the three states existed as such, and after both world wars the territorial arrangement had a profound impact on reconstruction plans. After World War II in particular, the question of what to do with the ethnic Germans (as well as with the Italians, in the the case of Yugoslavia) became bound up with that of how to pay for reconstruction.[61] The removal of the Germans, collaborators, and a number of Hungarians from Czechoslovakia, for example, made nationalization of their property much easier as 'there were no compensation problems'.[62] Indeed, in his speech to the Czechoslovak Assembly on 28 October 1945, President Beneš made it clear that

> German property is to be taken over in addition [. . .] to our reparation claims against the German Reich, which throughout seven years perpetrated so much devastation and pillage that all the German property in our country is far from adequate to make it good [. . .] The burden weighing upon our State finances must be lightened by [. . .] a realization of the assets which the State will

---

[60] Kaczorowski, *Początki odbudowy*, 15.

[61] Incidentally, Lacina referred back to the end of the First World War and the creation of the First Czechoslovak Republic when confronting the German question. It was then, he argued, that 'the nation [the Germans] had regarded as inferior assumed control of its own affairs, and left them only the share that corresponded to their numbers'. He thus cast the German question as one of the unresolved loose ends of post-World War I reconstruction. Lacina, *In Czechoslovakia Now*, 30. On the economic significance of Yugoslav acquisitions, see Kaser and Radice, (eds), *The Economic History of Eastern Europe*, 507.

[62] Grant Duff, et al., *Czechoslovakia*, 6.

receive from the confiscation of German and Hungarian property
and from the property of traitors and collaborationists.[63]

Post-World War I political fantasies of national homogenization were also
declared realized in Poland in the wake of World War II, as territorial changes
resulted in the expulsion of Germans from the western territories and the
resettlement of many Poles from other parts of Poland, including the eastern
territories (lost to the USSR), in their place.[64] As a result, the country went
from being sixty-nine per cent Polish in 1931, to being more than ninety-eight
per cent Polish by 1971.[65] Poland's post-war leadership cast the state's territorial acquisitions to the west in particular as the *sine qua non* for post-war
reconstruction. The Minister of Industry and President of the Economic
Committee of the Cabinet thus told the National Council on 21 September
1946, that 'No economic reconstruction of Poland is possible without our
holding the Western Territories. Without the Western Territories Poland
cannot exist as an economically sovereign state.'[66]

While the progress of reconstruction in Poland and Czechoslovakia was in
many respects helped along by territorial gains and the confiscation of
German and other assets, in the countries that lost territory or had to pay
reparations to the USSR following the Second World War—particularly
Hungary and Romania—there were other territorial and demographic challenges. In the case of Hungary, reconstruction efforts included a drive to
develop infrastructure in the provinces, rather than focusing on the capital
city of Budapest as previous regimes had done.[67] Furthermore, in both
Hungary and Romania confiscated Jewish property had driven parts of the
wartime economy and covered for shortfalls, providing a source of income
that was no longer available to post-war governments.[68] The new regimes also
faced having to explain why relinquishing Bessarabia to the Soviet Union or

---

[63] Beneš, *The Opening of the Prague Parliament*, 31, 33, 35. Yet Beneš also acknowledged that
the transfer of populations would mean the loss of 'some 800,000 workers at least' and
that 'the existing economic strength and capacity of the Republic will be appreciably
weakened and the State impoverished'.

[64] Yakowicz, *Poland's Postwar Recovery*, 1.

[65] Paul R. Magocsi, *Historical Atlas of Central Europe* (Seattle, 2002), 131; Norman Davies,
*God's Playground: A History of Poland*, vol. II (New York, 1982), 595.

[66] *Polska gospodarka planowa*, 20.

[67] Gáspár and Zsadányi (eds), *Újjáépítő magyarok*, 13.

[68] See Vladimir Solonari, *Purifying the Nation: Population Exchange and Ethnic Cleansing in
World War II Romania* (Baltimore, 2009); Christian Gerlach and Goütz Aly, *Das letzte
Kapitel: Realpolitik, Ideologie und der Mord an den ungarischen Juden 1944/1945*
(Stuttgart, 2002).

Transylvania to Romania did not represent a betrayal of the ideals of the nation. Exiled politicians from these countries were especially outspoken in their condemnation of 'Soviet imperialism'.

In their critiques, exiles sought indigenous precedents for reconstruction activity to bolster the legitimacy of non-communist parties and pave the way for the return of exiled statesmen. Above all they were eager to show that the positive achievements of reconstruction could not be attributed to the communist regimes, but were the product of domestic ingenuity and momentum. A Romanian Voice of America broadcast from 1955 thus accused Romanian communist officials of stealing and claiming as their own plans for expanding the electrical infrastructure of Romania that had been prepared by the wartime Romanian regime. 'Many elements of the [1949] plan (in fact the majority of them) were compiled from serious studies made before 1944 on this subject by other capable Romanian engineers', the broadcast reported.[69]

Similarly, L. D. Schweng, who served as Chief of Research for the Bank of Hungary during the interwar period, observed in 1951 that 'The purposeful interference of the state in matters of economics to ensure a more efficient utilization of the country's resources and to promote industrialization had been a standard feature of the Hungarian scene [in pre-war Hungary]'. He mentioned two 'plans proper' prior to World War II, the 'One Billion Pengő Plan of 1938 and the Ten Year Plan for Agriculture of 1942'.

> Had it not been for the war, their impact on Hungarian economic life would have been considerable, not only in increasing output and in improving the efficiency of production, but also in remolding economic organization through the extension of state controls. Several of the projects figuring in the [post-war] Three Year and the Five Year Plans were based on and are the continuation of blueprints drawn up on projects undertaken under the 1938 and 1942 plans.[70]

In the face of claims of frustrated exiles like Schweng, communist regimes adopted a very proprietary relationship to the notion of the planned economy, all the more so to efface the commonalities between wartime economies

---

[69] HIWRP, Alexander D. Bunescu collection, Box 6, Folder Electrice: R.P.R. Energia Electrică Industria Electrotehnică, United States Information Agency, (Voice of America) Daily Broadcast Content Report for Rumanian, 27 Dec. 1955, 'Electrification Program of the Romanian Communist Regime' by G. Rosu.

[70] L. D. Schweng, *Economic Planning in Hungary since 1938* (New York, 1951), 1. In terms of the projects Schweng claimed were continuations of earlier planned projects, he listed the power plant of Mátravidék and the irrigation project of the Trans-Tisza region.

(and even some of the post-war economies of Western Europe) and the planned economies of East-Central European socialist or transition states.[71]

So just as 'reconstruction' was a politicized term, so too was 'planned economy'. In the introductory essay of a 1987 volume published in Budapest on the activities of the Ministry for Reconstruction in Hungary just after the war, we read that 'During the war, but mostly thereafter in England, France, the USA and other capitalist countries there were some state interventions in the economy, but such interventions served above all the interests of big capital'.[72] Similarly, a 1948 Polish brochure on the Three-year Plan defined the term 'planned economy' as follows:

> [B]y planned economy is meant only such economy as permanently fulfills the following conditions: a) a national economic plan, comprising the productive forces of the nation in their entirety or at least in their main parts, is being periodically prepared, b) this plan aims at an all-round development of productive forces, c) at the same time it aims at the prosperity of the whole society, and not only of the propertied classes, d) it is actually obligatory, i.e., it is being carried out, e) a system of reports, regularly comparing the execution of the plan with the plan itself, is established. The foregoing terminological explanation permits, among others, a clear differentiation between planned economy and the war economy of modern capitalist States [. . .] Planned economy is possible only in certain social and economic regimes, namely in the socialist and the transitional, by the latter being meant a regime in which power is wielded by the people, a regime possessing a large socialized sector comprising at least all the key industries and the whole credit apparatus (popular democracy).[73]

The brochure defined planned economies in such narrow terms that the term could *only* apply to socialist states, which the author(s) felt the need to state explicitly, to prevent confusion of the sort stirred up by 'western propaganda'.

In general, the fact that many of these booklets and addresses were published within the region, but in English and therefore clearly meant to reach a broader international audience indicates that state leaders were acutely aware that the system was on display, and that success or failure would mean success or failure of entire ideologies. As Beneš put it, 'The whole world is looking on

---

[71] See Tony Judt, *Postwar: A History of Europe Since 1945* (New York, 2005), 67–72.

[72] Beatrix Boreczky (ed.), *Az újjáépítési minisztérium működésének válogatott dokumentumai, 1945–1946* (Budapest, 1987), xi.

[73] *Polska gospodarka planowa*, 8–9.

us [. . .] If we fail in this whole operation it is possible that we might compromise the very principle itself for years to come. Those among you who are socialists will know what that means'.[74]

The question of precedents for economic planning initiatives has come up again recently, in the wake of the economic crisis. Since 2008, the spectre of Cold War politics has loomed persistently, especially around states' economic responses to the crisis.[75] Yet even before the crisis, in considering historical precedents for reconstruction in Western Europe, Japan, and other parts of East Asia (Hong Kong, Taiwan, Singapore, South Korea), one group of economists concluded that the most 'important historical lesson' to be drawn from the aforementioned cases has been that

> their success is based upon an undogmatic recognition that markets must be governed in order to provide support for entrepreneurial initiatives undertaken at government suggestions. None of the 'economic miracles' which have been achieved in these countries could have been attained by following the short cut to capitalism mapped out for the former command economies of Eastern Europe.

In short, in Western Europe 'rational economic planning and national economic accounting were put into place, aided by the Marshall Plan, to provide for the reconstruction of the necessary infrastructure and key sectors of industry in the order they were needed to ensure balanced recovery'.[76] Planned economies were therefore *necessary* for reconstruction, the group concluded. Nevertheless, indigenous precedents of post-war economic planning have not garnered the attention of political scientists, economists and policy-makers.

There are a number of under-studied parallels between economic ideas and phenomena that emerged after the war and what has happened since 1989. The idea to create a 'Bank for Central-Eastern Europe' was voiced by Polish exile Antoni Plutyński in London in 1944. The logic behind its proposed

---

[74] Beneš, *The Opening of the Prague Parliament*, 37.

[75] These include everything from the famous *New York Times* ad depicting George W. Bush and Ben Bernanke as communists for giving $700 billion to bail out the financial markets, to renewed claims of a division of Europe in terms of economics. Andrew Clark, 'US trader attacks "trickle-down communism" of markets bail-out', guardian.co.uk, Wednesday, 24 September 2008, http://www.guardian.co.uk/business/2008/sep/24/wallstreet.useconomy [accessed 28 June 2009]. For renewed 'division of Europe' rhetoric, see footnote 10.

[76] Jan Kregel, Egon Matzner and Gernot Grabher (eds), *The Market Shock: An Agenda for the Socio-Economic Reconstruction of Central and Eastern Europe* (Vienna, 1992), 117–18.

creation mirrored the justification for the founding of the so-called European Bank for Reconstruction and Development that was created in 1991.[77]

Another example of an immediate post-World War II regional preoccupation that was buried under Cold War politics and has resonance in our time was the goal of establishing a regional federation that would eventually merge with the nascent European Union. The federation schemes of exiled statesmen were fashioned to recast the reconstruction effort in Cold War terms. As such, these plans brought the politics of the Cold War to bear on the policies of reconstruction.

## II
### Émigré federalists

Among the key players in the politicization of reconstruction were former statesmen and politicians in exile from the region, whose efforts to fashion a programme for post-war reconstruction began early, indeed in the first years of the war. The most outspoken and sophisticated of these were exiled statesmen from the occupied countries (Poland, Czechoslovakia, Yugoslavia, and Greece), who could most legitimately claim to represent the unheard voice of the people.

Plans formed within and around their own parties, governments-in-exile in London, and organizations like the New York-based Central and Eastern European Planning Board (established in 1941). The Polish Labour Group in New York, for example, published a *Program for People's Poland* in 1943, 'a result of the common work of many unknown people, all representing the underground groups of peasants, workers, and democratic intelligentsia' in Poland.[78]

For many exiled politicians and former statesmen, reconstruction would ideally entail the creation of a regional federation of states as a means to prevent Great Power neighbours from undermining the security and infiltrate the economies of states within the region. In their eyes, the vulnerability of the region's economies and governments to German domination was the result of the lack of economic cooperation between the states of the region during the interwar period. The failure of the League of Nations and regional

---

[77] Antoni Plutyński, *We are 115 Millions* (London, 1944), 110; Paul A. Menkveld, *Origin and Role of the European Bank for Reconstruction and Development* (London, Dordrecht, Boston, 1991), 96–7.

[78] *Program for People's Poland* (New York, 1943). The *Program* was also submitted to the Polish National Council and Parliament in Exile in London by Polish Socialist Party and Peasant Party representatives in exile for consideration.

agreements like the Little Entente and the Balkan Entente to effect genuine economic and political symbiosis represented to them false starts of the post-World War I period that demanded rectification in the wake of the Second World War.

Post-war governments and exile politicians thus made plans for a regional federation to reform the broken alliance between states in the region as a means of protection, both economic and geopolitical.[79] In the words of one economist writing in 1947, 'it is very questionable whether there would ever have been a Second World War if the community of the Danubian nations had been maintained and reformed instead of being destroyed'.[80] 'To the question, what is the most essential issue in postwar planning for central and eastern Europe, the only correct answer is, the problem of federation', wrote Planning Board secretary general Feliks Gross.[81] These ideas received a practical push with the cooperation agreements between Poland and Czechoslovakia, and between Yugoslavia and Greece in January of 1942. That same year, Gross laid out the mission of the Planning Board, which included 'true and close collaboration of the four nations' in the direction of forming a regional federation of states after the war.[82]

In addition to the goal of federation, the exiles affiliated with the Board outlined plans for an overhaul of the region's economy and society, which had proven vulnerable to German infiltration before and during the war. Their plans were also laid out in the pages of the New York-based journal

---

[79] There was much talk of the possibility of an alliance of Balkan states after the war, for example. Horst Haselsteiner, 'Föderationspläne in Südosteuropa', in Ferenc Glatz (ed.), *Europäische Visionen* (Budapest, 1995), 67–79, at 74–6. As Haselsteiner points out, such ideas already had a pre-war pedigree. See also K. Manchev, *Panevropa i balkanskata federatsiia: idei ili realizatsiia* (Lom, 1932); N. Khandzhiev, *Panevropa i obedinenieto na iuzhnitie slaviani* (Sofiia, 1931); Christine Galitzi, 'The Balkan Federation', in *Annals of the American Academy of Political and Social Science*, vol. 168, *American Policy in the Pacific* (July 1933), 178–82, http://www.jstor.org/stable/1019051; L. S. Stavrianos, 'The Balkan Federation Movement: A Neglected Aspect', in *The American Historical Review*, 48:1 (Oct. 1942), 30–51, http://www.jstor.org/stable/1843247.

[80] Frederick Hertz, *The Economic Problem of the Danubian States: A Study in Economic Nationalism* (London,1947), 222–3.

[81] Feliks Gross, 'Peace Planning for Central and Eastern Europe', in *Annals of the American Academy of Political and Social Science*, vol. 232, *A Challenge to Peacemakers* (Mar. 1944), 169–76 at 169.

[82] HIWRP, Central and Eastern European Planning Board collection, 'Report of the Secretary General on the Activity of the Central and Eastern European Planning Board from January 1942 to April 15, 1943'.

*New Europe*, a prominent venue for the ideals of the Board.[83] Given the considerable overlap between the leftist leanings of the Board and socialist groups, in addition to provisions for punishment of collaborators, the various plans generally included agrarian reform, some degree of nationalization of industry, and wide-ranging social reform.[84]

During the three years immediately following the war, however, exile politics underwent a radical shift. Only the goal of regional federation remained a semi-prominent feature of exile politics, as 'one by one our countries were swallowed up by the most rapacious empire the world has ever seen', the Soviet Union.[85] Interest in a federal solution spread to representatives of the states formerly allied with Nazi Germany (Hungary, Romania, and Bulgaria) and increasingly shed or deemphasized the social component of post-war planning, which came to be associated with the communist takeover. After the 'final liberation' of Eastern Europe from the 'common bond of slavery', the President of the Hungarian National Council said at a luncheon hosted by the National Committee for a Free Europe in February of 1951, the states of East-Central Europe were 'determined that the common experiences and hard-learned realizations which have united us in our sorrow, misery and exile, shall be the cement of a closer union of our nations'.[86]

Exile federalists also spoke of the region's eventual absorption into nascent European unification initiatives. Hence former political and other elites from Albania, Bulgaria, Czechoslovakia, Estonia, Hungary, Latvia, Lithuania, Poland, Romania, and Yugoslavia living in exile signed the 'Williamsburg

---

[83] To name a few, Felix Gross, 'Premises to a Draft for European Reconstruction', (May 1941), 150–1; Hubert Ripka, 'Is a Federation in the Baltic-Aegean Area Possible?' in *New Europe* (Feb. 1941), 54; Stanislas Stroński, 'First Step Towards a Better Europe', in *New Europe* (Feb. 1941), 55; Michael A. Heilperin, 'Europe's Economic Future and International Organization', (March 1941), 93–4; Feliks Gross, 'Some Trends in European Federalism', (September 1941), 263–5; Roman Michałowski, 'The Significance of Eastern Europe', (November 1941), 312–19; Stanisław Strzetelski, 'Federation in its Place', (January, 1942), 45–6; Alexander Hertz, 'The Cultural Unity of Europe', (June 1942), 198–202; Gustaw Bychowski, 'Psychological Reconstruction in Post-War Europe', (August 1942), 268–9; A Group of U.S. Military Experts, 'A Federation for Eastern Europe', (April 1941), 117–21; Felix Gross, 'Regionalism and Universalism', (January 1942), 47–50.

[84] *Program for People's Poland*, 17; *Democratic Postwar Reconstruction in Central Eastern Europe*, Antioch Reconstruction Series, No. 1 (Yellow Springs, Ohio, 1943), 6, 40–8, 72–4; Gross, 'Peace Planning for Central and Eastern Europe', 173–5.

[85] HIWRP, Stephen D. Kertesz collection, Box 27, National Committee Material, Speech of Monsignor Bela Varga, President of the Hungarian National Council.

[86] Ibid.

Declaration' of 1952, on the anniversary of the Virginia Bill of Rights. 'We know that the peoples of Central Eastern Europe are firmly resolved upon their liberation to join the Community of Free Nations, and that they are eager to take their natural place in the great movement of free peoples toward better relationships and closer union. The free peoples will establish between themselves strong regional ties and by this join in the formation of a United States of Europe'.[87]

Yet these exile groups and National Councils/Committees were often clouded in scandal and internal divisions that were heavily influenced by wartime divisions and amplified by Cold War politics. Was it acceptable to form an anti-Soviet bloc with former members of extreme right wing parties?[88] Was it possible to support economic and social reform in the region without feeding communist propaganda?

Among the individuals who felt the growing weight of Cold War politics most acutely was the Hungarian exile Rusztem Vambery, a self-declared 'old-fashioned liberal'. Vambery served briefly as the Hungarian ambassador to the US after the war, a post from which he resigned in frustration in 1948, arguing that Hungary had become 'a marionette in a diplomatic puppet show'. Despite 'diametrically disagreeing with the methods of the communists', Vambery acknowledged in an unpublished manuscript giving the reasons for his resignation that 'the rigid military discipline of the Party was instrumental in rebuilding a devastated country'.[89] But recognizing the achievements of communist-led reconstruction efforts was precisely the sort of political taboo for which Vambery was roundly criticized in Hungarian émigré circles.[90] Above all, Vambery lamented the fact that 'It is

---

[87] HIWRP, Stephen D. Kertesz collection, Box 27, National Committee Material, Williamsburg Declaration of 1952, 3.

[88] More than one national committee (whose members imagined prominent roles for themselves in future, post-communist governments in the region) underwent a crisis or split resulting from disagreement on this point. See, for example, HIWRP, Alexander D. Bunescu collection, Box 4, Corespondența Politică, 1949–1951, Letter from M. Ghica-Cantacuzino; Ibid., Corespondența Politică, 1952-, Testamentul lui Maniu by Nicolae Penescu, 5; HIWRP, George Caranfil collection, Box 1, Folder 2, Letter Addressed by Pamfil Seicaru to General Radescu, President of the Romanian National Committee, Concerning Romanian Exile Policy; HIWRP, Ferenc Marosy collection, Box 1, Bessenyey, György Baron, 1948–1953, Letter from Bakách-Bessenyey György, Baron 1948.VI.7 to Marosy; FRUS, Central and Eastern Europe; The Soviet Union, volume IV (1950), 'Poland', 1041–2.

[89] HIRWP, Rusztem Vambery collection, 'Failure of a Mission and Mission of a Failure' 1948.

[90] *Amerikai Magyar Népszava*, 31 May 1948.

a peculiarity of our tragic age that the world is divided into two camps. Anyone who refuses to join either becomes the enemy of both'.[91]

*Comparisons and Statistics*

In 1986, the second of a three-volume *Economic History of Eastern Europe* was published, covering 'Interwar Policy, the War, and Reconstruction'. In the conclusion, the author, Władysław Brus, noted that it was impossible to summarize 'the results achieved in the reconstruction of the productive capacity and in improving the material and social conditions of the population' without undertaking an 'extremely careful analysis of the differences in conditions immediately after the two World Wars, and also between those in eastern Europe and western Europe'.[92]

In large part, such an analysis has yet to be made for this period.[93] Instead, the literature and popular press dealing with reconstruction in East-Central Europe is laced with cynical comparisons, such as one from the Research and Information Department of the ex-patriot Free Europe Committee in 1957 comparing buying power indices of Hungary with those of Switzerland.[94] Similarly, a US study compared 'dollar values' of GNP in 1955 between East-Central European states, the USSR, and the US.[95]

While such comparisons can be illuminating, they do not represent comparable cases, either in terms of the size or in the historic economic performance of the countries in question. It would seem logical that to judge how being or not being a 'satellite' or receiving aid through the Marshall Plan affected economic performance in the immediate post-war period, a more realistic comparison should be undertaken between East-Central European countries and countries like Greece, Italy, Ireland, or Portugal. In comparing

[91] Ibid.

[92] Kaser and Radice (eds), *The Economic History of Eastern Europe*, 639–40.

[93] For subsequent periods, some literature exists. Indeed, an entire journal came into existence in France (*Revue d'Études Comparatives Est-Ouest*) with the express aim of making such comparisons. In fact, however, the journal contains very few actual comparisons across the Iron Curtain. A notable exception is: Septième Partie, 'Comparison entre les pays de l'Est et les pays de l'Ouest', in *Revue d'Études Comparatives Est-Ouest: Economie, Planification et Organisation*, vol. X: 1–2 (Mars-Juin 1979), 319–62. The article highlights several surprising similarities, despite structural differences in the economies of the cases under consideration (France, Italy, the USSR, and Hungary).

[94] HIWRP, Alexander D. Bunescu collection, Box 8, Folder Salarii-Prețuri: R.P.R. Salarii-Prețuri, Free Europe Committee, Inc. Research and Information Department 'Graphic Comparisons of Purchasing Power' (1957), 14–15.

[95] Frederic L. Pryor and George J. Staller, 'The Dollar Values of the Gross National Products in Eastern Europe 1955', *Economics of Planning*, vol. 6: 1 (1966).

agricultural production figures from 1938, for example, it becomes clear that Greece's economic performance was either comparable to or below that of most East-Central European countries at the time, meaning that a comparison with Greece would make more sense than one with, say, the US, Germany, Great Britain, or France.[96]

Comparison of post-war East-Central European states' economic performance with that of Greece in particular has rarely if ever been undertaken. This oversight stems in part from the fact that the struggle for the geopolitical soul of Greece was the centerpiece of the Truman Doctrine and thus a crucial starting point of the Cold War, one that played a significant role in the Cold War politics of comparison embedded in the showcasing of the 'Greek economic miracle' of the 1950s to 1970s.[97] The omission of Greece is also the result of the Greek Civil War and accompanying economic crisis which lasted throughout the first four years of the period of reconstruction.[98]

**Table 1.** Industrial production indices (1934, 1938, 1946–1949) [1937=100][99]

|      | IT  | NL  | NO  | Sp   | PL  | RO  | Gr  | HU  | YU  | BG  | CS  |
|------|-----|-----|-----|------|-----|-----|-----|-----|-----|-----|-----|
| **1934** | 80  | 90  | 75  | 94.7 | 71  | 94  | 83  | 76  | –   | –   | 69  |
| **1938** | 100 | 101 | 100 | –    | 109 | 100 | 109 | 98  | 108 | 108 | –   |
| **1946** | 71  | 77  | 97  | 96.7 | –   | –   | 62  | –   | 90  | –   | –   |
| **1947** | 91  | 98  | 115 | 95.1 | –   | –   | 78  | –   | 138 | –   | –   |
| **1948** | 99  | 116 | 128 | 99.6 | 150 | 84  | 85  | –   | 171 | 100 | 230 |
| **1949** | 109 | 129 | 137 | 97.7 | 177 | –   | 101 | 125 | 192 | 100 | 307 |

[96] Greece performed slightly worse than Poland and Romania, considerably worse than Bulgaria, Hungary, Yugoslavia, and Czechoslovkia, and a great deal worse than Great Britain, Belgium, Sweden, and Germany. Joseph S. Roucek, 'The Geopolitics of Danubia', in *American Journal of Economics and Sociology*, vol. 5:2 (Jan. 1946), 211–30, at 216.

[97] A partial exception can be found in the work of John R. Lampe, specifically, Lampe, *Balkans*, 218–23; John R. Lampe and Marvin R. Jackson, *Balkan Economic History, 1550–1950: From Imperial Borderlands to Developing Nations* (Bloomington, 1982), 579–80, 597. The comparison reveals that even as late as 1980 Yugoslavia was outperforming Greece in standard of living indices. Lampe, *Balkans*, 220.

[98] See Athanasios Lykogiannis, *Britain and the Greek Economic Crisis, 1944–1947: From Liberation to the Truman Doctrine* (Columbia, MO, 2002).

[99] B. R. Mitchell, *International Historical Statistics: Europe 1750–1993* (New York, 1998), 421–2 (post-war figures are based on statistics collected by the United Nations, compiled in its *Statistical Yearbook*).

But there are other possible points of comparison. For example, change over time within and across countries; how did the economies of various European states perform relative to their earlier performance and how do those indices compare?[100]

The comparison of figures over time reveals the extent to which post-war industrial production indices in Poland, Yugoslavia, and Czechoslovakia outstripped those in Greece, Italy, and Spain.[101] Such figures—in the area of industrial output in particular—were played up by communist regimes. A comparison chart in a Polish publication from 1950 thus showed the 'level of industrial production' in various Eastern and Western European countries since 1938 (up to 1948), revealing dramatic increases in several East-Central European states.[102]

So has anyone ever attempted to undertake comprehensive, disinterested comparisons of economic performance indices across the East-West divide? The only organization that made such comparisons regularly was the United Nations, in which representatives of both 'sides' of the Cold War participated. Yet the UN did not start publishing its *Statistical Yearbook* until 1947, and many of the early figures (for the period 1945–1950) are missing or incomplete. Furthermore, instead of producing an aura of neutrality, UN studies were often considered untrustworthy by both sides. In Romania an official in the Central Directorate of Statistics was imprisoned for providing the UN with requested data before having it 'cleared with the appropriate party forum'.[103] And in 1961, the émigré Romanian National Committee in the US published a series of 'Comments on the Study': 'Economic Development in Rumania' prepared by the Secretariat of the Economic Commission for Europe of the United Nations, complaining that the UN study was missing a chapter on 'Soviet exploitation' and had glossed over 'Russian neo-colonialism'.[104]

---

[100] Such a comparison highlights the relative extent and speed of recovery of economic capacity during the immediate post-war period.

[101] This has been observed recently in a book by Derek Aldcroft and Steven Morewood, who wrote in 1995 that 'the reconstruction and recovery of the East European economies was quite spectacular. After a slow start the overall performance stands comparison with that of most of the nations of Western Europe'. Derek Aldcroft and Steven Morewood, *Economic Change in Eastern Europe since 1918* (Aldershot, 1995), 104.

[102] *The Fulfilment of the Three-Year Plan*, 19.

[103] Egon Balas, *Will to Freedom: A Perilous Journey through Fascism and Communism* (Syracuse:, 2000), 328.

[104] HIWRP, Alexander D. Bunescu collection, Box 1, (manilla folder), Romanian National Committee, Comments on the Study: 'Economic Development in Rumania' prepared

So while the bias in Western literature was generally in the choice of cases to compare (i.e. Hungary to Switzerland), and focusing on failures of the system as well as on Soviet hegemony and exploitation,[105] the tendency of the new communist regimes was toward overemphasizing the role of Soviet assistance, exaggerating success, and, in the realm of statistics, measuring economic performance largely relative to earlier domestic indicators (generally from 1938 or 1945) rather than relative to other states. The various X-year plans were thus calibrated to achieve target growth rates using pre-war or immediate post-war levels as the baseline. Hence a book on *Poland's Postwar Recovery* included data on the accomplishments of the Three-year Plan (1947–1949) in terms of 'total value of national income' (with 100 being the 1938 level).[106]

Such internal comparisons were the target of criticism from exiles and Western economists and politicians, who complained that economic data coming from socialist states was full of contradictions and omissions. In the words of a Romanian politician in exile, 'The scarcity of statistics and the concealment with which the communist governments wrap up their activities and relationships engender suspicions'.[107] Even within the region the Stalinist era (~1947–1953) of economic data-gathering and presentation came under fire during the period of destalinization (~1954–1956) and

---

by the Secretariat of the Economic Commission for Europe of the United Nations and published in the *Economic Bulletin for Europe*, 13:2 (1961). See especially 24–6.

[105] See, for example, HIWRP, Alexander D. Bunescu collection, Box 5, A.C.E.N. Economic Committee I, A.C.E.N., 395 (VI) Sec., 16 March 1960, 'Draft Memorandum concerning the report on Soviet Economic Integration of the Captive Countries' (A.C.E.N. doc. 188 (VI) Econ.; Romanian Delegation to A.C.E.N.); Ibid., Assembly of Captive European Nations, Sixth Session, Jan Wszelaki, 'The European Captive Countries: Soviet Economic Asset or Liability?' 28 Dec. 1959, Supporting Study (Revised and updated) to A.C.E.N. doc. 147 (V) Econ.

[106] These were given as 67% in 1946, 125% in 1949, and 186% in 1952. Yakowicz, *Poland's Postwar Recovery*, 152–3. The publication boasted that non-agricultural employment had doubled over 1938 levels. 'Improvements during the Three-Year Plan raised average real wages of manual workers in 1949 approx. 7% above average rates in 1938, and more than double those of 1946.'

[107] HIWRP, Alexander D. Bunescu collection, Box 1, (manilla folder), Romanian National Committee, 'Comments on the Study: "Economic Development in Rumania" prepared by the Secretariat of the Economic Commission for Europe of the United Nations and published in the *Economic Bulletin for Europe* 13:2 (1961), see especially 25. See also ibid., Box 8, Article by Martin Hoffman 'How to Read National Income Statistics', in *East Europe*, Nov. 1962.

thereafter.[108] Of his own role as the top economic expert of the Romanian Foreign Ministry from 1949–1952, Egon Balas wrote that 'professional expertise was a rare thing in those days, and this explains how somebody with so little experience and such relatively poor training as myself could in a few months achieve the status of the ministry's top economic expert and become a man whose professional competence—unlike his devotion to the party line—nobody ever dared to question'.[109]

Indigenous comparisons between socialist states of the time—an oft-deployed strategy during the Cold War[110]—also glossed over some significant economic realities, exiles argued. The states that had joined the Axis during World War II, for example (Hungary, Romania, Bulgaria), instead of receiving material and technical aid from the Soviet Union as Poland did, had to pay reparations to the USSR equivalent to between seven and seventeen per cent of national income during the first several years after the war.[111] These states were also affected by their near exclusion from United Nations Relief and Rehabilitation Administration (UNRRA) aid, which as former allies of Nazi Germany they were not entitled to receive.[112]

Taken as a whole, the period of reconstruction has been buried under statistics of the post-reconstruction period in the West, and the statistics of the post-reconstruction period have been buried within the narrative of successful reconstruction in the East. In the case of the former, the achievements of East-Central European economies during the 1940s and early 1950s became the standard against which later performance was rated, highlighting decline in everything from average annual growth rates of gross industrial output to the share of consumer goods in the total of industrial output.[113] Meanwhile, communist regimes, especially in times of political crisis,

---

[108] Cited in J. Wilczynski, *The Economics of Socialism after World War Two: 1945–1990* (New Bunswick and London, 2008), 29.

[109] Balas, *Will to Freedom*, 215.

[110] See, for example, Kaser and Radice (eds), *The Economic History of Eastern Europe*, 564–641.

[111] Aldcroft and Morewood, *Economic Change*, 101.

[112] Lampe, *Balkans*, 181.

[113] HIWRP, Alexander D. Bunescu Papers, Box 5, Folder A.C.E.N. Economic Committee II, Stephen Fischer-Galati (ed.), 'Eastern Europe in the Sixties', 1. Bulgaria 1951–55 = 10.4 per cent growth over 1961 = 9.9 per cent; Czechoslovakia 11.2 to 8.9 per cent; East Germany 13.6 to 6.2 per cent; Hungary 14.9 to 12 per cent; Poland 19.1 to 10.5 per cent; Romania 9.8 to 15.6 per cent. See also ibid., Aleksander Kutt, 'Statement about the Output of Consumer and Producer Goods in Soviet Bloc Industry', 18 Feb. 1964, 6. Bulgaria dropped from 61.8 per cent in 1950 to 50.5 per cent in 1961; Czechoslovakia from 48.4 to 39.8 per cent; Romania from 47 to 36.1 per cent.

regularly revisited the period of post-war reconstruction as a shining example of what socialism had done for the countries of East-Central Europe.[114]

## Conclusion

When the economic crisis hit in 2008, a number of Western European political figures were quick to condemn new members for dragging down the whole of the Union, as politicians and economists spoke of a renewed 'division of Europe'. At the root of this 'division' has been the presumed *Sonderweg* of East-Central European states, who, it is often assumed, missed out on a critical aspect of post-war European experience: the process of economic reconstruction. During the era of *perestroika* and *glasnost* in the 1980s, some even speculated that there might be a second chance, another Marshall Plan forthcoming that would correct the historical detour taken by these states.[115]

But just as the economic crisis caused many to reaffirm Cold War prejudices, it has also pointed to cracks in the logic of Cold War economic truisms. At the Conference of Polish economists in 1967, a group of Polish economists condemned their Stalinist predecessors for offering 'apologetic justification of current economic policies' instead of genuine scholarship.[116] Readers of today are likely to notice the striking similarity between the economics of 'apologetic justification of current economic policies' practised by communist economists in the 1940s and 1950s, and by banks, economists and financial experts in the West prior to 2008, who were skilled at finding sound economic reasons to declare that the predatory growth of the 1990s and 2000s was sustainable.

The fallibility of neoliberal economists that has been foregrounded lately may cause us to revisit some of their earlier work and start asking some difficult questions, such as: Were there global trends at work in the immediate post-war period—in terms of economic planning ideas and practices, raw

---

[114] This was particularly true in Poland, where albums and other publications about the reconstruction of Warsaw and other cities were produced in ever more lavish editions at regular intervals throughout the communist era, especially during times of political upheaval (1970s and 1980s). See, for example, Kaczorowski, *Początki odbudowy;* Tojanowska (ed.), *Wspomnienia;* Stryczyński, *Gdańsk;* Ciborowski, *Warsaw;* Bierut, *The 6-Year Plan.* Outside Poland, see Boreczky (ed.), *Az újjáépítési minisztérium.*

[115] Henri Dunajewski, 'Le plan Marshall et les pays de l'Europe de l'Est', in *Revue d'Etudes Comparatives Est-Ouest: Economie, Planification et Organisation,* XIV:1 (Mars 1983), 47–73, at 72–3. Incidentally, Greece was about to receive 'a second Marshall Plan' in the form of $7.9 billion from the EC over the period from 1985 to 1989. Judt, *Postwar,* 528.

[116] Cited in Wilczynski, *The Economics of Socialism,* 29.

materials supply and labour issues—that could be drawn out through sustained comparison of East-Central Europe with other parts of the world, such as Latin America, for example? Was the so-called 'Western European miracle', so much a product of the Cold War conceptually that it cannot in the long term survive the Cold War's disappearance (either as an idea or as an economic phenomenon)? If Greece was the poster child of the Western model for reconstruction, what does the recent and flamboyant failure of the Greek economy reveal about the 'reality' of the economic 'division of Europe'? Accordingly, why are there so few sustained comparisons of East-Central European economic performance with states to which they were more readily comparable during the interwar period? And what would such comparisons reveal? Closer study of the period of reconstruction, and above all a careful comparison across European states for this period is long overdue and would certainly render the mechanisms by which Cold War politics have shaped our conception of European states' economies—as well as our conceptual geography of Europe as a whole—more transparent.

I do not want to suggest that we should write histories that project post-1989 European integration back onto the past. Such an undertaking would produce elisions and misleading emphases of its own. Rather, I propose that we not assume coherence of Western Europe as a category, nor of Eastern Europe, without more critical study of similarities and differences within and between individual states' economic strategies and performance and over a longer stretch of time. For only thus can we establish whether there might have been other factors *besides* the Cold War that affected the economic performance and reconstruction policies of European states during the post-war period. Factors that until now have been underemphasized as criteria for comparison include pre-war performance, levels of wartime destruction, movement of labour, demographics (such as age, urban/rural, minorities), raw materials resources, indigenous precedents, trade, and capital sources, to name a few. Consideration of these factors has been done for individual states' economies and for parts of Eastern and Western Europe *en bloc*, but the time has come to compare across blocs and seek cases that are comparable according to a variety of criteria. The point of such comparison should not be to ignore the effects of the Cold War, but rather to better grasp the extent of its impact on both post-war reconstruction and the concomitant construction of Europe.

# The Soviet Union after 1945: Economic Recovery and Political Repression

**Mark Harrison**

The story of the Soviet Union's post-war years appears almost as remarkable as the story of the war.[1] The USSR came to victory in 1945 only after first coming close to total defeat. In 1945 the Red Army occupied Tallinn, Riga, Vilnius, Warsaw, Berlin, Vienna, Prague, Budapest, and Sofia, but behind the army the country lay in ruins. Its people had suffered 25 million premature deaths. The survivors were profoundly weary. Many hoped for reconciliation and relaxation.

Despite this, in the years immediately following, the Soviet economy and polity returned quickly to their previous form. There was renewed political and economic mobilization. Economic resilience was reflected in rapid Soviet post-war economic recovery. Political resilience can be seen in Stalin's rapid consolidation of the political system: there would be no reforms for a decade. The rigid hierarchies of party and state control were not loosened up, but were reinforced while their frontiers were pushed outward to the shores of the Baltic and into Central Europe.

What gave the Stalinist political economy its post-war resurgence? I will place the Soviet recovery in a broader European context. The result is a puzzle: across most of Europe there was a clear association between post-war pros-perity and economic and social reforms, but not in the Soviet Union. A closer look at Soviet post-war institutions in the late 1940s suggests that if anything they were more centralized, militarized, secretive, and punitive than in the late 1930s. The rapid Soviet economic recovery from World War II becomes less surprising when we take into account the Soviet economy's very large backlog of unexploited potential, not all of it due to the war. Institutions are

---

[1] Earlier versions of this paper were presented to a panel at the annual meeting of the Allied Social Sciences Associations, Chicago, 5–7 January 2007, and the Balzan Conference on Post-War Reconstruction in Europe, Birkbeck College, London, 5–6 June 2008. I thank Vladimir Kontorovich and the referees for comments and advice; the University of Warwick for research leave; and the Hoover Institution for its hospitality and access to documents in its superb archive.

still important, though, because ineffective institutions can mean that unexploited potential is never realized. In one respect, unchanged Soviet institutions could operate more efficiently than before: the war gave Stalin new information about his enemies, and he could exploit this temporarily to improve the quality of repression. To summarize, a large backlog of unexploited economic potential and more efficient repression were two sources of post-war Soviet economic resilience, but their common feature was that they were both temporary.

## 1945 in perspective

On the eastern front, World War II was devastating. In four years, fought mostly on Soviet territory, the war killed one in eight Soviet citizens, and destroyed one third of their national wealth. The country was full of displaced people and torn families. Industry was struggling to restore peacetime production. In comparison, Russia's seven-year Great War and Civil War of 1914 to 1921 were only somewhat less devastating. Also fought mostly on Russian territory, the Great War and Civil War killed around one in ten citizens of the former Empire through fighting, disease, and starvation.[2] Through the 1920s, the Bolshevik leaders struggled to get the economy back to square one—the level of 1913. In this sense, the Soviet Union was itself a project of post-war reconstruction.[3] In 1929, when Stalin launched his Great Breakthrough to forced-march industrialization and the all-out collectivization of peasant farms, the Soviet economy was probably still lagging behind the pre-war benchmark of output per head of the population.[4]

Although the human losses from World War II were on a wider scale, Soviet recovery after 1945 was also more rapid. The economy was in far better shape than in 1921. Both wars were followed by harvest failure and regional famine, but the famine of 1946 killed a fraction of the numbers that died of hunger at the end of the Civil War.[5] Average Soviet incomes climbed back to their pre-war (1938) level as early as 1948. After the Civil War, in

[2] S. G. Wheatcroft and R. W. Davies, 'Population', in R. W. Davies, Mark Harrison, and S. G. Wheatcroft (eds), *The Economic Transformation of the Soviet Union, 1913–1945* (Cambridge, 1994), 63.

[3] I thank one of the referees for this highly relevant point.

[4] Paul R. Gregory, 'National Income', in R. W. Davies (ed.), *From Tsarism to the New Economic Policy: Continuity and Change in the Economy of the USSR* (Basingstoke and London, 1990) 237–47.

[5] Michael Ellman, 'The 1947 Soviet Famine and the Entitlement Approach to Famines', *Cambridge Journal of Economics*, 24:5 (2000), 603–630.

**Table 1.** War damage and reconstruction in Europe: years and per cent per year, annual average

|  | Pre-war year when GDP per head fell below 1945 | Post-war year when GDP per head exceeded 1938 | Annual growth, per cent, 1945 to year when GDP per head exceeded 1938 |
|---|---|---|---|
| Netherlands | 1869 | 1948 | 27% |
| France | 1895 | 1949 | 18% |
| Austria | c.1860 | 1950 | 17% |
| Denmark | 1928 | 1946 | 14% |
| Italy | 1904 | 1950 | 13% |
| Greece | c.1870 | 1956 | 10% |
| Norway | 1935 | 1946 | 9% |
| Soviet Union | 1935 | 1948 | 8% |
| Finland | 1937 | 1946 | 7% |
| Belgium | 1921 | 1948 | 5% |
| Germany | 1936 | 1954 | 2% |

*Source:* Calculated from Angus Maddison 'Statistics on World Population, GDP and Per Capita GDP, 1-2006 AD' (updated March 2009), available from http://www.ggdc.net/maddison/. For the Soviet Union, GDP per head in 1945 is assumed the same as in 1946. In six countries not shown in the table, average wartime incomes did not fall below the pre-war level: the United Kingdom, and neutral Portugal, Spain, Sweden, Switzerland, and Ireland.

contrast, it took seven to ten years of peace for average Soviet incomes to struggle back to the 1913 level.

In the Soviet Union, as elsewhere, the restoration of pre-World War II output turned out to be the prelude to a prolonged post-war acceleration of growth that persisted long after this moment. Across Europe, there was a 'Golden Age' of economic growth and rising living standards that continued through the 1950s and 1960s.[6] Despite restricted East-West trade, heavier burdens of defence and investment, and a lower average starting point, Soviet consumers also experienced gains comparable with those of Western Europeans.

One would scarcely have predicted the rapid recovery of the Soviet economy after 1945 from the dismal precedent of the 1920s; it becomes less remarkable in the contemporary European context. Table 1 places the USSR in this setting. For each country, the first column measures the depth of the wartime shock by considering how far back one would have to go to find a year that was worse than 1945, measured by average incomes. (A defect of this measure is that it is influenced by the rapidity of pre-war growth.) The second

[6] Nicholas Crafts and Gianni Toniolo, 'Post-war Growth: An Overview', in Nicholas Crafts and Gianni Toniolo (eds), *Economic Growth in Europe Since 1945* (Cambridge, 1996), 1–37.

Table 2. Political regime and economic development in Europe across World War II: numbers of countries

|  | With GDP per head: | |
| --- | --- | --- |
|  | **Above median** | **Median or below** |
| Polity 2 index, 1938: | | |
| Above zero | 9 | 2 |
| Zero or below | 2 | 9 |
| Polity 2 index, 1950: | | |
| Above zero | 11 | 3 |
| Zero or below | 1 | 10 |

*Notes*: Countries are Albania (1950 only), Austria (1950 only), Belgium, Bulgaria, Czechoslovakia (1950 only), Denmark, Finland, France, Germany, Greece, Hungary, Ireland, Italy, Netherlands, Norway, Poland, Portugal, Romania, USSR, Yugoslavia, Spain, Sweden, Switzerland, Turkey, and UK. The Polity 2 index subtracts autocracy scores from democracy scores, and also fixes standardized scores, to create a composite index of the political regime suitable for time series analysis, with values ranging from +10 (strongly democratic) to −10 (strongly autocratic).
*Source*: Jari Eloranta and Mark Harrison, 'War and Disintegration, 1914–1945', in Stephen Broadberry and Kevin O'Rourke (eds), *Unifying the European Experience: An Economic History of Modern Europe*, vol. 2: 1870–2000 (Cambridge, forthcoming).

column measures the speed of recovery by the year in which incomes returned to 1938, taken as the pre-war benchmark. The third column measures the rate of expansion from 1945 to the recovery benchmark. In the face of various difficulties our source omits Soviet GDP per head in 1945, but the harvest failure of 1946 and other difficulties of Soviet reconversion to peacetime production make it realistic to assume that Soviet GDP per head in 1945 was around the same level as in 1946.

Table 1 shows that, by the standards of other European countries, the Soviet economy of 1945 was not especially depressed. Its growth had been knocked back by ten years; some other countries had lost decades. Soviet recovery was swift, but some others were swifter. Having lost half a century or more, Austria, France, and the Netherlands experienced double-digit growth during their recoveries.

The consolidation of Stalin's rule was also broadly representative of continental trends. The war against the dictators made surprisingly little difference to Europe's constitutional make-up. As Table 2 shows, by the end of the Great Depression, democracy (indicated by a positive 'Polity 2' score) was confined to the rich margins of Western Europe; virtually every poor country on the continent had fallen under more or less authoritarian rule. By 1950, a few of the hotel guests had changed rooms. West Germany and Italy were now democracies, for example, while Poland and Czechoslovakia had become one-party states. In net terms the distribution was more or less unchanged. The gross turnover was largely a product of military defeat. Since the Soviet Union had survived the war undefeated, its political continuity does not look out of line.

If Soviet economic recovery and political continuity were unexceptional, what then is there to explain? The puzzles appear only when we look more closely at the fine grain of these things. For one thing, the determinants of rapid recovery across Europe varied from West to East. In Western Europe, common commitments to market institutions and the sharing of American resources through Marshall aid are acknowledged as important catalysts for recovery.[7] These conditions did not apply across Eastern Europe, and specifically not in the Soviet Union.

The grain of post-war political transitions is also confusing. Because they lost the war, and because of which other countries beat them, some countries passed directly from fascism to democracy, from fascism to communism, or from democracy to communism. The only other European country to join in the war and survive with its constitution intact was the United Kingdom. Despite winning the war, the UK saw the electoral defeat of its war leader and a passage from liberal to social democracy. In fact, every European country that was caught up in the war underwent significant economic, social, or political change immediately afterwards—except the Soviet Union.

### The Post-war Soviet Political Economy

The Soviet Union was the only warlike power to emerge from the war with its pre-war regime intact and, if anything, reinforced. In the post-war years Stalin's rule remained harsh and intransigent, Stalin becoming less active only because of age.[8] Managing the legacy of wartime conflict at home, Stalin preferred vengeance over reconciliation. While the Germans retreated he selected entire national minorities suspected of collaboration for mass exile. The renegade Vlasov officers were executed and the men imprisoned. No one returned from forced labour in Germany or from prisoner-of-war camp without being 'filtered' by the NKVD. Those party members that

---

[7] J. Bradford De Long and Barry Eichengreen, 'The Marshall Plan: History's Most Successful Structural Adjustment Program', in Rudiger Dornbusch, Wilhelm Nölling, and Richard Layard (eds), *Post-war Economic Reconstruction and Lessons for the East Today* (Cambridge Mass., 1993), 189–230; Barry Eichengreen, 'Institutions and Economic Growth: Europe after World War II', in Crafts amd Toniolo (eds), *Economic Growth*, 38–70.

[8] Yoram Gorlizki and Oleg Khlevnyuk, *Cold Peace: Stalin and the Soviet Ruling Circle, 1945–1953* (New York, 2004).

survived German occupation had to account for their wartime conduct and show that they had resisted actively, if they were to avoid discrimination and repression.[9]

As for the economic system, it is implausible to suppose that it was entirely unchanged by the war, and natural to ask whether the lessons and innovations arising from the war made some contribution to post-war recovery. The problem is, however, that Soviet economic institutions of the late 1940s differed from those of the late 1930s only in ways that exaggerated their previous defects.

The post-war economy was more militarized than before. In 1941 a surprise attack had devastated the country. After 1945 the Soviet economy carried a permanently heavier military burden in order to be ready for the next war, which was likely to be nuclear, within days or hours. Since the Soviet economy remained smaller than that of its likely adversaries, this meant a burden heavier in proportion to GDP than that carried by the United States, for example. After a difficult demobilization, the Soviet defence industry began to grow again with major boosts from programs for atomic weapons, rockets, jets, and radar.[10] The outbreak of the Korean War saw a return to the mass production of conventional weapons.[11]

The dispersal of the population into the remote interior of the Urals and Siberia, conducted before the war by mass deportations and the metastasis of the Gulag archipelago, was continued by wartime evacuation. Until World War II, the Soviet defence industry was concentrated in the established industrial regions of the European USSR. Wartime evacuation shifted its centre of gravity hundreds of kilometres to the east. After the war, many defence factories were kept back from the return to the west, and remained in their wartime locations. New atomic and missile industry complexes were added to them, the construction work often being subcontracted to the forced labourers of the Gulag. The result was a proliferation of closed, secret 'mono-towns', often in bleak, inhospitable locations.[12] The militarization of the interior was

---

[9] Amir Weiner, *Making Sense of War: The Second World War and the Fate of the Bolshevik Revolution* (Princeton, 2001).

[10] See relevant chapters in John Barber and Mark Harrison (eds), *The Soviet Defence-Industry Complex from Stalin to Khrushchev* (Basingstoke, 2000).

[11] Mark Harrison, 'Industrial Expansion under Late Stalinism (1945–1955): the Short-Run Dynamic of Civilian Output from Demobilisation to Rearmament', *Journal of European Economic History*, 17:2 (1989), 359–78, and 18:3 (1990), 601–3.

[12] Gregory Brock, 'Public Finance in the ZATO Archipelago', *Europe-Asia Studies*, 50:6 (1998), 1065–81. ZATO (*zakrytye administrativno-territorial'nye obrazovaniia*) is translated as 'closed administrative-territorial formations'.

matched by the garrisoning of the borders. Stalin waged a protracted war of occupation in order to reabsorb the Baltic region and Eastern Poland.[13] Beyond the borders, Eastern Europe was politically and economically sovietized.[14]

It has been reasonably suggested that, amid the disruptions of war, soldiers, regional leaders, managers, and farmers must have learned how to direct their activities with greater self-reliance, more independently of the centre's instructions.[15] Did such wartime experiences not carry over into the post-war period? Possibly, yes; but, to the extent that they did, this legacy was firmly rejected as soon as possible. 'Normal' centralization of the economy, temporarily disrupted by invasion and war mobilization, was restored well before the war ended; in fact, wartime planning for the post-war period was one of the instruments that reinstated the pre-war command system.[16] From 1946, Stalin embarked on a blunt reassertion of the party's authority over management, the regions, and cultural life.[17] The legal priority of state over private property was reinforced and its enforcement became more punitive.[18] Wartime tendencies to creeping privatization on the collective farm were sharply reversed.[19] Stalin kept in place the uniquely harsh regimentation of

---

[13] For example, George Reklaitis, *Cold War Lithuania : National Armed Resistance and Soviet Counterinsurgency,* the Carl Beck Papers in Russian & East European Studies no. 1806, (Pittsburgh, 2007).

[14] Włodzimerz Brus, '1950–1953: The Peak of Stalinism', in M. C. Kaser (ed.), *The Economic History of Eastern Europe, 1919–1975,* vol. 3: *Institutional Change within a Planned Economy,* (Oxford, 1986) 3–39.

[15] It is wrong, however, to think of the late 1940s as a particular time of reformist ideas about market socialism or planned decentralization. Enrico Barone's proposal for market-like allocation within an economy based on public ownership, first published before World War I, was translated into English and published before World War II as 'The Ministry of Production in the Collectivist State,' in F. A. Hayek (ed.), *Collectivist Economic Planning* (London, 1935), 245–90. The first practical proposals to decentralize management within the Soviet economy to be advanced (unsuccessfully) by a powerful leader rather than a scholar or critic were those of the Minister of Industry Sergo Ordzhonikidze in 1931, as R. W. Davies has shown in *The Industrialisation of Soviet Russia,* vol. 4: *Crisis and Progress in the Soviet Economy, 1931–1933* (Basingstoke, 1996).

[16] Harrison, *Soviet Planning,* 192–7.

[17] Gorlizki and Khlevnyuk, *Cold Peace.*

[18] Yoram Gorlizki, 'Theft Under Stalin: A Property Rights Analysis', PERSA Working Paper no. 10 (28 June 2001), University of Warwick, Department of Economics, available from http://www.warwick.ac.uk/go/persa.

[19] Alec Nove, 'Soviet Peasantry in World War II', in Susan J. Linz (ed.), *The Impact of World War II on the Soviet Union* (Totowa NJ, 1985), 71–90.

civilian workers introduced just before and during the war; the scale and scope of forced labour were expanded, despite growing concerns about the damage being done to the economy and society.[20] Secretiveness rose to new heights.[21] The first test of whether the Soviet Union had learned to manage its resources more humanely in a crisis, and delegate decisions more effectively, came with the harvest failure of 1946. The outcome was a regional famine in which one and a half million people died.[22] On the positive side, perhaps it is 'only' one and a half million; as already mentioned, this figure was a marked improvement on 1921.

Finally, the war selected a new generation of leaders that would eventually provide Stalin's successors. All of them—Bulganin, Khrushchev, Malenkov, Mikoian, and others—had dipped their hands in the blood of Stalin's victims, not all with enthusiasm. Some of them would eventually face up to the necessity of reform, but the steps that seemed to them, at the time, like giant leaps of faith and courage were timid and faltering by 'normal' standards. While scholars have scoured the decade of late Stalinism for precursors and standard-bearers of reform, it is astonishing how thin the evidence remains, and how heartless are the 'heroes' that emerge: Lavrentii Beriia, Stalin's wartime security chief, who came to see the forced labour system of the Gulag as damaging and wanted to scale it down; and Nikolai Voznesenskii, Stalin's wartime economic planner, who was interested in the merits of rules over discretion in making policy.[23]

To summarize, the Soviet economy faced the tasks of post-war reconstruction with economic institutions that, if not completely unchanged by the war, were changed in all significant respects for the worse. This makes explanation of the speed of post-war recovery more difficult.

---

[20] Don Filtzer, *Soviet Workers and Late Stalinism: Labour and the Restoration of the Stalinist System after World War II* (Cambridge, 2002); Andrei Sokolov, 'Forced Labor in Soviet Industry: The End of the 1930s to the Mid-1950s, An Overview', in Paul R. Gregory and Valery Lazarev (eds), *The Economics of Forced Labor: The Soviet Gulag* (Stanford, 2003), 23–42.

[21] Mark Harrison, 'Secrecy', in Mark Harrison (ed.), *Guns and Rubles: the Defense Industry in the Stalinist State* (New Haven, 2008), 230–54; Gorlizki and Khlevnyuk, *Cold Peace*.

[22] Ellman, 'The 1947 Soviet Famine'.

[23] Aleksei Tikhonov, 'The End of the Gulag', in Gregory and Lazarev (eds), *The Economics of Forced Labor*, 67–74; Mark Harrison, *Soviet Planning in Peace and War, 1938–1945* (Cambridge, 1985), 230–5.

## Explaining Soviet recovery

It would be a solution if we could persuade ourselves that 'worse' was better: that the rapid Soviet post-war recovery should be simply credited to the command system, which mobilized resources all the more effectively with every increase in centralization and repression. When contemporary Western observers tried to get perspective on Soviet post-war economic growth, and began to calculate just when the Soviet economy would overtake the United States, that is more or less what they concluded. A relatively sober assessment was that of Abram Bergson. Reviewing Soviet economic performance in the 1950s, Bergson emphasized 'the political control over the rate of investment' as a feature of the Soviet system without an American counterpart, and concluded: 'Khrushchev is seeking, as Stalin did, to "overtake and surpass" the United States economically. . . Khrushchev's plans for the future may often be overoptimistic, but they have some basis in fact.'[24]

An alternative approach sets the Soviet post-war recovery in a longer-run context. It starts with the observation that the scope for recovery is created by the depth of the adverse shock that precedes it. This view takes its inspiration from the Hungarian economist Ferenc Jánossy, who first proposed the idea that the great European post-war boom was largely a return to the 'trend-line'—the path marked out by extrapolating each country's pre-war growth.[25] Slower growth in the 1960s, Jánossy argued, was merely the end of a prolonged post-war recovery phase. The failure to understand this point, he believed, had led policy-makers in both socialist and market economies to make mistakes. Many believed that post-war recovery was already complete when the pre-war level of output had been restored, or when damaged facilities had been rebuilt. These became pessimistic about subsequent growth prospects because they did not perceive the opportunities represented by the remaining gap between actual output and the trendline. By the 1950s the trendline, Jánossy believed, rising with the passage of time, was already well above the pre-war maximum. Conversely, others supposed that the

---

[24] Abram Bergson, *The Real National Income of Soviet Russia Since 1928* (Cambridge, Mass., 1961), 295 and 297–8.

[25] Ferenc Jánossy, *The End of the Economic Miracle: Appearance and Reality in Economic Development* (New York, 1971). For further evaluation see Nicholas Crafts and Terence C. Mills, 'Europe's Golden Age: an Econometric Investigation of Changing Trend Rates of Growth,' in Bart van Ark and Nicholas Crafts (eds), *Quantitative Aspects of Europe's Post-war Growth* (Cambridge, 1996), 415–31; Nicholas Crafts and Terence C. Mills, 'After the Golden Age: A Long-Run Perspective on Growth Rates That Speeded up, Slowed Down and Still Differ', *Manchester School* 68:1 (2000), 68–91.

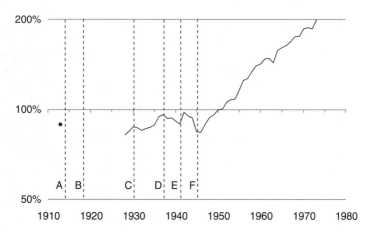

**Fig. 1.** Soviet GDP per head, 1913 and 1928, and per worker, 1928 to 1973, showing six key
dates: per cent of 1950 on a logarithmic scale
*Key:* **A** (1914) World War I. **B** (1918) Civil War. **C** (1930) Collectivization. **D** (1937) The
Great Terror. **E** (1941) World War II. **F** (1945) Post-war period.
*Sources:* The series from 1928 to 1973 are from Mark Harrison, 'Trends in Soviet Labour
Productivity, 1928-1985: War, Post-war Recovery, and Slowdown', *European Review of
Economic History* 2:2, 171-200. To get a long view we must chain two sets of primary data,
one for 1928 to 1966 based on the constant 'adjusted' factor costs of 1937, and another for
1950 to 1985 based on adjusted factor costs of 1982. The two series are inconsistent, however. Inspection of the overlap in the series suggests a strong Gerschenkron effect, the change
in weights from 1937 to 1982 reducing the growth rate of GDP by about a quarter. This
suggests a way of adjusting the measured output of the early period, prior to the overlap, to
late prices. The result is a series for the whole period, 1928 to 1985, based on a consistent
standard of valuation. The data point for 1913 is found from the ratio of GDP per head in
1913 to 1928 in Maddison, 'Statistics'.

acceleration was a new permanent peacetime trend, and so fell into the trap of
'new era' optimism. Consequently their long-range plans became overambi-
tious; they failed to anticipate the inevitable slowdown when the trendline
was finally regained, and then met it with an exaggerated sense of failure.

The argument is easily applied to Soviet data. It is an argument about
productivity rather than living standards, so in Figure 1 we look at real
Soviet GDP per worker. Our first observation is 1913. After a break, the
observations resume in 1928 and then follow continuously to 1973, the
year that ended the 'Golden Age.'

On the same chart we see six shocks. World War I (A) and the Civil War (B)
together left Soviet incomes in 1928 still somewhat below the 1913 level; not
all the ground had been made up when Stalin launched the country onto a
course of forced rapid industrialization. The third shock (C) is the collectivization of agriculture launched at the end of 1929, which brought farm

surpluses under state control at the cost of destroying millions of lives and a significant fraction of the country's agricultural and social capital.[26] Under gathering war clouds the economy suffered a fourth shock when Stalin carried out his Great Terror (D) in 1937, which paralysed industry and the economy.[27] The economy had not recovered from the Great Terror, let alone collectivization and even the relatively distant traumas of 1914 to 1921 when Hitler attacked, bringing World War II (E) to the Soviet Union in 1941. Notably, if we consider aggregate labour productivity, the war itself was not a negative disturbance. It was the two transitions, from peace to war, and then from war to peace again, that damaged productivity, and the transition to peace (F) in 1945 was more damaging than the preceding transition to war.

How should we evaluate Soviet post-war recovery in this context? Figure 2 shows our options. A restricted focus on the 1940s and 1950s, that ignores what happened before and after, gives us (A) rapid recovery from 1946, merging into impressive peacetime growth to 1961, at an annual average growth rate of GDP per worker of 3.8 per cent over 15 years.

Taking the data back to 1928 and forward to 1973 suggests a more cautious view: in 1941 the economy still had a hangover from 1937 and perhaps even a headache from 1930. The sources of Soviet rapid growth after 1946 are partly those of recovery from war, but in addition the economy was still catching up on an accumulated pre-war backlog of unexploited opportunities. Associated with this view is a more prudent estimate (B) of the underlying trend of productivity growth: not 3.8 per cent, but a mere 2.0 per cent per year over the 45 years from 1928 to 1973.

But this may not be a long enough perspective. In 1928, the economy had not fully recovered from Russia's Great War and Revolution. Taking into account all the data available, including 1913, gives us a still more cautious figure of 1.3 per cent annual growth as the Soviet productivity trend over 60 years—a trend that would *never* allow it to 'catch up and overtake' Western Europe or the United States. Against that background, the rapid growth of the

---

[26] R. W. Davies, *The Industrialisation of Soviet Russia*, vol. 1: *The Socialist Offensive: the Collectivisation of Soviet Agriculture, 1929–1930* (Basingstoke, 1980); R. W. Davies and S. G. Wheatcroft, *The Industrialisation of Soviet Russia*, vol. 5: *The Years of Hunger: Soviet Agriculture, 1931–1933* (Basingstoke, 2004).

[27] Barbara G. Katz, 'Purges and Production: Soviet Economic Growth, 1928–1940', *Journal of Economic History* 35:3 (1975), 567–90; R. W. Davies. 'The Soviet Economy and the Launching of the Great Terror', in Melanie Ilič (ed.), *Stalin's Terror Revisited* (London and New York, 2006), 11–37.

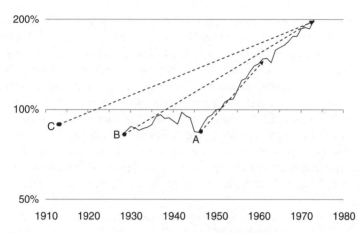

**Fig. 2.** Soviet GDP per head, 1913 and 1928, and per worker, 1928 to 1973, showing
alternative underlying trends: per cent of 1950 on a logarithmic scale
*Key:* **A** (1946 to 1961): 3.8% per year. **B** (1928 to 1973): 2.0% per year.
**C** (1913 to 1973): 1.3% per year.
*Sources:* as Fig. 1.

post-war years appears as a transient spurt that would inevitably exhaust itself
within 30 years after the war.

In this perspective, the 'resilience' of the post-war Soviet economy is explained by the size of the backlog of unrealized growth potential arising from
preceding disasters. Because this backlog existed and was so large, the economy could spend thirty years making it up and, while it did so, put on the
appearance of dynamism. However, the backlog alone does not explain what
we see. Many countries have backlogs of unrealized potential that they never
realize. When they fail in this way, institutions that are faulty or ineffective are
often the cause: power is unrestrained, the rule of law is weak, enterprise and
initiative are taxed or punished, and so on. Thus, we come back to institutions. I will point to another aspect of the war that renewed the temporary
lease of the Soviet dictatorship and command system on life: the war dramatically improved the efficiency with which Stalin could manage his domestic enemies.

### The quality of repression

As the war ended, millions of ordinary Soviet people were intoxicated with joy
at the announcement of the victory and celebrated it wildly in city squares and
village streets. Feeling that the war had shown the people to be deserving of

their leaders' trust, many hoped that the enemy's defeat could be followed by relaxation and reconciliation. Later, Il'ia Ehrenburg recalled:

> I firmly believed that after victory everything would suddenly change. . . When I recall conversations at the front and at the rear, when I re-read letters, it is clear that everybody expected that once victory had been won, people would know real happiness. We realized, of course, that the country had been devastated, impoverished, that we would have to work hard, and we did not have fantasies about mountains of gold. But we believed that victory would bring justice, that human dignity would triumph.[28]

Despite such hopes ten years would pass, and Stalin himself would leave the scene, before Khrushchev opened up social and historical discourse in a way that was radical and shocking in contrast to the stuffy conformity of Stalinism, although pathetically limited by the standards of the wider world.

Research in Stalin's archives has made clear (not that there was much doubt) the murderous attributes of his regime.[29] Stalin's rule was built on repression. Not repression alone, since repression must be implemented and those who carry it out must consent to do so. Nonetheless, repression was Stalin's primary instrument. The war saw a striking change in its quality. Before the war, terror was indiscriminate, sweeping up the loyal and disloyal alike. In contrast, post-war repression was selective, focused, and efficient.

The climax of pre-war repression was the Great Terror. In 1937 Stalin set out to exterminate all his enemies, including those he designated as 'objective' or 'unconscious' enemies.[30] Under a public spotlight, show trials rid the party and state of thousands of servants, most of them innocent of any truly seditious action or even intention. Beneath the surface, secret executive mandates ordered the deaths of hundreds of thousands that had found their way by one route or another into the files of the security organs.

---

[28] Cited by Jerry F. Hough, 'Debates About the Post-war World,' in Susan J. Linz (ed.) *The Impact of World War II*, 255.

[29] Robert Conquest, *The Great Terror: A Reassessment* (40th Anniversary edn), (Oxford, 2008); Gorlizki and Khlevniuk, *Cold Peace*; Oleg V. Khlevniuk, *Master of the House: Stalin and his Inner Circle* (New Haven, 2009); David R. Shearer, *Policing Stalin's Socialism: Repression and Social Order in the Soviet Union, 1924–1953* (New Haven, 2009); Paul R. Gregory, *Terror by Quota: State Security from Lenin to Stalin (an Archival Study)* (New Haven, 2009).

[30] Mark Harrison, 'The Dictator and Defense', in Mark Harrison (ed.), *Guns and Rubles: the Defense Industry in the Stalinist State* (New Haven, 2008), 1–30.

The changing tenor of repression can be studied in the files of the ruling party's 'control commission', Stalin's watchdog on the party members.[31] As the 1930s wore on, the slightest suspicion of compromising circumstances—including not only misconduct but past association with others about whom doubts had been raised—led to censure and dismissal, followed increasingly by transfer of the case to the security services, detention, interrogation, torture, and imprisonment or execution. During 1937, as the number of those that could be found guilty by association exploded, the work of the control commission was paralysed by suspicion of its own members and employees.

Ten years later, the quality of repression was very different. There was still suspicion; every allegation of guilty association or misconduct was still investigated. The control commission's investigations were meticulous and exact. A party member's past association with 'enemies of the people' and 'traitors' living abroad, including family relationships, was no longer an issue, provided it had been confessed to the party, so there was no deception, and provided it had been discarded, so that contact was broken. Bad associations and social origins were no longer an irreparable stigma; they could be wiped away by patriotic behaviour during the war. No one was presumed innocent, but many were exonerated after investigation, and even sharply adverse judgments often led to nothing worse than a slap on the wrist. What could not be repaired was wartime treachery or passivity; it was intolerable for a party member, for example, to have lived under German occupation without engaging actively in resistance or the partisan movement.

The sharp change in the quality of repression from the late 1930s to the late 1940s can be explained in more than one way. Most obviously, Stalin learned that indiscriminate bloodletting was costly; he could not afford to lose tens or hundreds of thousands on suspicion alone. As early as 1938 and 1939, Stalin permitted limited effort to go to rehabilitating some of the more obviously unjust sentences that fell short of execution. But for many it was too late; he

---

[31] The Archive of the Hoover Institution, Stanford University, contains thousands of files of the party control commission from 1934 to the 1960s in its 'Archives of the Soviet Communist Party and Soviet State' microfilm collection, based on the holdings of the Russian State Archive of Contemporary History (RGANI). My study of these files has focused on two collections, *opis* 1 (minutes of the party control commission, February 1934 to June 1939) and *opis* 6 (reports, references, verbatim accounts, protocols, June 1939 to October 1966). On the history and operations of the party control commission see Arch Getty, 'Pragmatists and Puritans: The Rise and Fall of the Party Control Commission', The Carl Beck Papers in Russian and East European Studies no. 1208, (Pittsburgh, 1997); Andrei Markevich, 'How Much Control is Enough? Monitoring and Enforcement under Stalin', PERSA Working Paper no. 53, (Warwick, 2007).

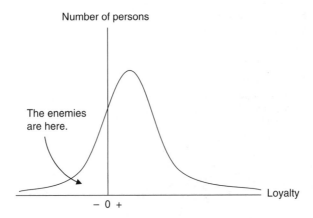

**Fig. 3.** The distribution of loyalty

had already executed tens of thousands of talented managers, engineers, artists, and military leaders.

To set this in context, consider the Great Terror as Paul Gregory has modelled it.[32] In this view Stalin ruled subject to a revolution constraint set by the maximum number of 'enemies' that could be at liberty in society without triggering his overthrow. In 1937 Stalin became convinced that the number and potency of his enemies was greater than he had previously thought. In number, he saw a large and growing stratum of embittered citizens, previously dispossessed or disenfranchised, that would never be reconciled to the Soviet regime, and many others with uncertain political or ethnic loyalties. In potency he saw that the growing risk of war would soon give them the chance to turn traitor, even if this was an opportunity that the 'potential' enemies did not yet foresee or appreciate.

Figure 3 illustrates this perception. The dotted line shows the true distribution of the Soviet population over loyalty and disloyalty. Stalin defined those with negative loyalty (shown to the left of the vertical axis) as his enemies. When he feared that their number (shown as the area under the distribution in the negative loyalty sector) and potency might breach his revolution constraint, he wanted to kill them.

This was only the start of Stalin's problem, however. Before he could kill his enemies, he had to identify them. Under a dictator, people do not disclose their true loyalties; whatever they feel, everyone tries to look loyal. As a result, the more powerful the dictator, the less he can trust what people tell him,

---

[32] Gregory, *Terror by Quota*, 166–71 and 293–4.

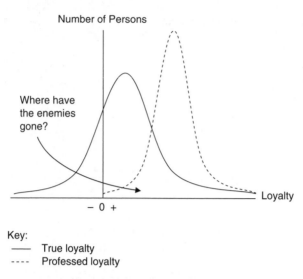

Key:
—— True loyalty
- - - - Professed loyalty

**Fig. 4.** The distribution of loyalty: where have the enemies gone?

a paradox that Ronald Wintrobe has called 'the dictator's dilemma'.[33] Stalin could not observe the true distribution of loyalty, shown in Figure 4 as the solid line; he could see only the professed distribution (the dotted line), which seems to show no enemies. He knew his enemies existed, but where had they gone?

The problem was that they had scattered and gone to hide among the loyal. After two decades of increasingly repressive dictatorship, all citizens looked alike and could be told apart only by such imperfect markers as class origins and past political and social affiliations. Given that, according to Gregory, Stalin's solution was to impose excess repression. He decided to kill all those in the left tail of the professed loyalty distribution, despite the fact that all claimed to be loyal—and despite the fact that many of them truly were loyal. He killed many more than his estimate of the true number of enemies in the hope that, at the cost of killing many of the truly loyal, he would also catch a high proportion of those that were only simulating loyalty.

This stratagem was extraordinarily costly. It also encountered diminishing returns. By the end of the Great Terror Stalin's security service had exhausted the low-grade information it held on the potentially disloyal strata. But then,

---

[33] Ronald Wintrobe, *The Political Economy of Dictatorship* (Cambridge, 1998), 20–36.

a stroke of luck: the war opened a new window for Stalin to peer into the souls of his subjects! Hitler's invasion gave millions of Soviet citizens the freedom to choose, for the first time in twenty years, whose side they were on. The phase in which the Red Army was retreating allowed many to lose their fear of Stalin's regime or to replace it with a greater one—fear of the consequences of *not* switching allegiance to the invader at the opportune moment. Under these conditions, some revealed previously latent preferences for disloyalty by accepting surrender or collaboration, or by adopting an attitude of wait-and-see, where Stalin had ordered patriotic resistance.

His subjects' wartime behaviour gave Stalin a flood of new information. He found that it was no longer necessary to sort and classify people on the basis of historical political allegiance and social origin. He did not throw away the historical accounts, but he closed them and opened a new set of books based on the war.

In a study of post-war Ukraine, Amir Weiner found that after the war the regime began systematically to sort and regrade people by new criteria: wartime conduct and ethnicity.[34] The cultural mechanism that regraded them was a pervasive idea—that the war had healed the divisions in the nation and provided the opportunity for redemption. The people that carried this idea in their heads and acted on it were the soldiers returning from the front.

Weiner shows how many people perceived war service as removing the stigmas of adverse social origin and forgiving pre-war sins. Life could begin again. This integrated the wartime experience into the repeated purification of Soviet society, and changed the cleansing process by making social origin redeemable. Those that behaved badly in the war, in contrast, could not redeem themselves. The post-war era began, as a result, with a new secret party purge amid the shattered ruins of the Ukraine, and this purge took precedence over the other pressing tasks of reconstruction.

The break with the past was not complete. The post-war years also saw Stalin stirring up vicious intrigues against potential rivals distinguished by their war service—Marshal Georgii Zhukov, for example, and the Leningrad leadership, which was showing signs of excessive independence—and he had some of these killed. More widely in society, ethnicity became relatively important as an indirect marker of loyalty because the Soviet state found itself still at war with resurgent nationalisms from the Baltic to the Ukraine; the creation of the state of Israel also caused Stalin to suspect Soviet Jews of divided loyalties. These countervailing changes moderate the trend we observe, but we still observe it.

---

[34] Weiner, *Making Sense of War.*

To summarize, the war tended to collapse the distribution of professed loyalty into the true one. As a result, Stalin could identify his enemies and deal with them person by person, not *en masse*. Selective terror became a better choice than mass terror, at least for a few years. Eventually, the natural tendency to conformism under a dictator would again blur the distinguishing marks of the 'enemy'. Rather than return to mass terror, Stalin's successors would try to dispense with terror altogether.

We asked how it was that the Soviet command system effectively mobilized resources into post-war recovery. The increased efficiency with which Stalin managed his enemies after 1945 was an enabling factor in the Soviet post-war economic recovery. Strong political authority was at the core of the command economy; this would be revealed vividly, forty years later, by the economic collapse that accompanied the disintegration of Soviet political authority under Gorbachev.

## Conclusions

We started from the post-war resilience of the Soviet political and economic system, with rapid economic recovery from the war accompanied by political consolidation and an absence of post-war reforms. On close inspection we find that the war contributed to two factors that between them explain both the pace of recovery and the resilience of Stalin's dictatorship.

The rapid growth of the Soviet economy from 1946 was part of a long rebound from a series of disasters of which the war contributed the most recent instalment. The long-run trajectory of the Soviet economy was scarcely dynamic. In 1945, however, it was far below this trajectory; there was great scope for catching up on the backlog of unrealized potential, and this helps to explain the rapidity of Soviet economic development from the late 1940s to the 1960s.

Soviet post-war recovery and growth was organized within the framework of a centralized command system for mobilizing resources. The working arrangements of this mobilization system also benefited from the increased efficiency of Stalin's post-war rule. The war greatly increased Stalin's information about the distribution of loyalty in Soviet society. This explains how Stalin could manage his enemies without incurring the costs of mass terror, and so rule as Soviet dictator more efficiently than before the war.

# Stalin and the European Communists after World War Two (1943–1948)

## Silvio Pons

Two basic differences in the Soviet attitude to Europe can be discerned in the years following the Second World War as compared with the aftermath of the First. On the one hand, although conflicts between imperialist interests, state rivalries over hegemony, economic crises and social turmoil were expected to reappear, it was no longer possible to see revolution in its original sense as the answer. On the other, Soviet Russia was no longer marginal to international politics, indeed its role appeared central to Europe's future. Furthermore, Soviet influence in post-war Europe was amplified by the formation of communist parties whose activities in anti-fascist movements and in the resistance had made them stronger and more legitimate than they had ever been.

In 1944–45, Stalin saw the reconstruction of Europe as a process based on the geopolitical division of the continent between Soviet Russia and Great Britain. Sooner or later conflict between the Soviet and the capitalist worlds would arise, but it was not on the immediate agenda. Moscow encouraged both Eastern and Western communists to follow the line of national unity—which reflected the prospect of post-war collaboration with the Western powers—and to avoid any revolutionary uprising. In principle, all communists were given the chance to articulate their own national policy, which was supposed to be consistent with Soviet interests. Radical pressures towards insurrection and civil war were contained, although not entirely marginalized.

Much earlier than expected, when the Marshall Plan was launched in 1947, all this came to an end. Moscow re-established control over European communists by founding a new international organization, the Informburo (Cominform), four years after the dissolution of the Comintern. The 'two camps' doctrine proclaimed a new challenge against the West. Radical elements were on the rise in the international movement, as well as in particular parties. The political objectives of European communists diverged. Eastern communists were called upon to establish a definitive monopoly of power, Western communists to start mass mobilization against the formation of a bloc under US hegemony. Nevertheless, while the new turn was to produce the definitive shift towards sovietization in East Central Europe, it did not herald any revolutionary thrust beyond the Soviet sphere of influence. On the contrary, promotion of revolution from above in the East and avoidance of revolution from below in the West went hand in hand, and led to the excommunication of the Yugoslav Communist Party, breaking the unity of the 'Socialist camp'.

This article aims to reassess the relationship between Soviet policy and European Communism in the aftermath of World War Two. In the post-Cold War historiography, the central issue has obviously been the establishment of communist regimes in East Central Europe. Nevertheless, although a considerable amount of new evidence (especially archival) has been produced and even published over the past twenty years, a comprehensive approach in the post-war international history of the communist movement has yet to be developed. Traditional accounts have become obsolete in too many respects, while recent studies have usually been limited to single, albeit crucial, questions.[1]

## The National Fronts: moderates and radicals

From June 1941, the communist parties were called upon to follow a national-unity policy against Nazism. Comintern's dissolution in June 1943 was seen by Stalin as a decisive step forward in applying that policy. As Djilas notes, Stalin attributed real political significance to the thesis of the growing national character of the communist parties.[2] Stalin had always

---

[1] For accounts of the post-war international communist movement from before the archives were opened, see Fernando Claudin, *The Communist movement: from Comintern to Cominform* (New York, 1975); Paolo Spriano, *Stalin and the European Communists* (London, 1985). For seminal archive-based studies, see the essays published in Giuliano Procacci et al. (eds), *The Cominform. Minutes of the Three Conferences 1947/ 1948/1949*, Fondazione Feltrinelli, *Annali*, vol. 30 (Milan, 1994). For some more recent case studies, see in particular: Eduard Mark, *Revolution by Degrees. Stalin's National-Front Strategy for Europe, 1941–1947*, CWIHP, Working Paper 31, (Washington DC, February 2001); Silvio Pons, 'Stalin, Togliatti, and the Origins of the Cold War in Europe', *Journal of Cold War Studies* 3 (Spring 2001); Martin Mevius, *Agents of Moscow: the Hungarian Communist Party and the Origins of Socialist Patriotism, 1941– 1953* (Oxford, 2005). John O. Iatrides, 'Revolution or Self-Defense? Communist Goals, Strategy, and Tactics in the Greek Civil War', *Journal of Cold War Studies* 7 (Summer 2005).

[2] Milovan Djilas, *Conversations with Stalin*, (New York, 1962); Italian translation, M. Gilas, *Conversazioni con Stalin*, (Milano, 1962), 88–9. Cf. Georgi Dimitrov, *Diario. Gli anni di Mosca (1934–1945)*, edited by Silvio Pons (Torino, 2002), 611–12 (8 and 11 May 1943), 618 (21 May 1943), 629 (8 June 1943). See also N. Lebedeva and M. Narinskii (eds),

considered the Comintern a cumbersome vehicle for the Soviet state's policy. In conditions of war, he thought the time had come for a solution aimed at liquidating the dual institutional nature of Soviet international policy.[3] In his view, effective Soviet leadership of the communist movement required a network of bilateral relationships established between the Soviet state, incorporating Comintern's former apparatuses, and the individual parties. In other words, dissolution of the Comintern did not herald a 'normalization' of the Soviet state, but neither was it simply cosmetic. Stalin truly intended to modify the communist movement's *modus operandi* and to seek ways to strengthen the national parties in their respective societies. The problem, both in Moscow and outside the USSR, was how to achieve such aims.

The theory was first put into practice in Italy, following the Anglo-American landing in July 1943, the fall of Mussolini's regime and the armistice reached on 8 September 1943 between the Allies and the military government which had been installed in the South with Marshal Badoglio at its head. Moscow considered the possibility of lending its support to the anti-Fascists' intransigent positions against any form of collaboration with the monarchy or with the post-Fascist forces. This would mean opening a conflict with the Allies and promoting the political and social radicalization which was already developing in northern Italy with the efforts of the resistance against the Nazi occupiers and against Fascists faithful to Mussolini. The alternative was to reach a diplomatic agreement with the Badoglio government, thus encouraging the communists to collaborate in the name of moderation and 'national unity'. These two options were formulated by Togliatti in late 1943 and early 1944. At that point the radical alternative—which had the support of Dimitrov, head of the International Department, and of Molotov, the Foreign Minister—seemed likely to be chosen. However, Stalin eventually decided in favour of the moderate solution. In his meeting with Togliatti on the eve of the Italian leaders' departure from Moscow on 4 March 1944, the core of the policy to be followed by the PCI (Italian Communist Party) was established.[4]

---

*Komintern i vtoraia mirovaia voina* (hereafter KVMV), 2 vols (Moscow, 1994–1998), vol. I, docs 134, 136, 137, 142, 143; *Dimitrov and Stalin 1934–1943*. Alexander Dallin and Fridrich I. Firsov (eds), *Letters from the Soviet Archives*, (New Haven and London, 2000), 233–53.

[3] Stalin had privately revealed his intention to dissolve the Comintern already in April 1941, before the Nazi attack on the Soviet Union. See Dimitrov, *Diario*, 302–3 (20 and 21 April 1941).

[4] Russian State Archive for Social and Political History (RGASPI), Moscow, f. 82, d. 1231, ll. 1–2; Dimitrov, *Diario*, 691–3 (4 and 5 March 1944); KVMV, docs 168, 174.

With this decision a precedent was set for the other European parties, based on three founding elements: the rejection of civil war as a political prospect for the communists; the choice to take part in governments of national co-alition; and the pre-eminence of communist leaders back from Muscovite exile rather than those involved in the resistance movements. In addition to establishing the first boundaries for spheres of influence, the famous agree-ment between Stalin and Churchill of October 1944 set limits to communist action in areas of Western interest. Stalin gave Churchill the necessary assur-ances regarding Italy, suggestively noting that Togliatti would avoid embark-ing upon an 'adventure'. At the same time, Togliatti reaffirmed his own leadership in the PCI, by containing the party's more intransigent elements.[5] The PCF (French Communist Party) was led to follow the Italian precedent, even though France presented a conflictual situation and the local commun-ists rather expected a rendering of accounts with General De Gaulle. The turning point came after Stalin's meeting with Thorez in November 1944, on the eve of Thorez's return to France. In his talk with Thorez Stalin insisted on the need to prevent the communists from becoming isolated and to build political alliances.[6]

The line indicated by Stalin did not distinguish between Western and Eastern Europe, but placed emphasis on the 'nationalization' of the com-munist parties, co-ordinated with the guidance of Moscow. While planning Europe's partition into spheres of influence, the Soviets were not interested in a divided continent.[7] In the autumn and winter of 1944, the 'national fronts'

See Francesca Gori and Silvio Pons (eds), *Dagli archivi di Mosca. L'Urss, il Cominform e il Pci (1943–1951)*, Fondazione Istituto Gramsci, *Annali*, VII (Roma, 1998), docs 1–9.

[5] RGASPI, f. 558, op. 11, d. 283, l. 12–13. On the relationship between Stalin and Togliatti in 1944, see Pons, 'Stalin, Togliatti, and the Origins'. For more details, Silvio Pons, *L'impossibile egemonia. L'Urss, il Pci e le origini della guerra fredda (1943–1948)* (Roma, 1999), 155–74. See also Elena Aga-Rossi and Victor Zaslavsky, *Togliatti e Stalin. Il PCI e la politica estera staliniana negli archivi di Mosca*, 2nd edn (Bologna, 2007).

[6] Dimitrov, *Diario*, 769–70 (19 November 1944). See *Istochnik* 4 (1995), 152–8. On the strategy of PCF in 1944, see Philippe Buton, *Les lendemains qui déchantent. Le Parti communiste français à la Libération* (Paris, 1993).

[7] Norman M. Naimark, 'Stalin and Europe in the Post-war Period, 1945–53: Issues and Problems', *Journal of Modern European History* 2 (2004), 32. On Soviet plans for post-war spheres of influence, see Silvio Pons, *In the Aftermath of the Age of Wars: the Impact of World War II on Soviet Security Policy*, in Silvio Pons and Andrea Romano (eds), *Russia in the Age of Wars 1914–1945*, Fondazione Feltrinelli, *Annali*, XXXIV (Milan, 2000), 277–307.

line was also followed in East Central Europe, where the advance of the Red Army and the fall of the pro-Hitler regimes put the refounding of states and the creation of coalition governments on the agenda. In these countries, unlike those of the Western sphere such as France and Italy, the communists could count on the Soviet military presence and therefore aim to seize decisive levers of power. But the political line was formulated in virtually identical terms. In truth, the Czechoslovakian communists were the only ones whose cards were already in order on the 'national fronts' line. They could boast primacy in East Central Europe, consolidated at the time of the December 1943 agreements between Stalin and Beneš and founded upon their role in the resistance movement.[8] All the others had difficult adjustments to make. Already in Moscow's sights for having ignored the 'national fronts' line, the Polish communists could not even claim a major role in the resistance movement. They were called on to adopt the image of a national party as an alternative power to the government in exile in London.[9] Stalin himself dictated a moderate line to the Hungarian communists, starting with the composition and programme of the new national unity government. In adopting Moscow's directives the Hungarian leadership adopted the French communists' national party model.[10] The Bulgarian communists had played a leading role in the anti-Nazi resistance and, with Moscow's assent, had insisted on strong representation in the National Liberation Committee. However, Dimitrov asked them to strengthen their positions while not thinking of the party as 'the only decisive factor in the country and dictating our will to the Allies'.[11] The Romanian communists were instructed along the same lines.[12]

The 'national fronts' line and its implications were not accepted by all communists. In the world of European Communism, radical tendencies cut across every party. The Soviet representatives in Europe themselves did not always hinder these tendencies and at times even supported them, as did Aleksandr Bogomolov—the chief Soviet diplomatic representative in

---

[8] Vojtech Mastny, *Russia's Road to the Cold War. Diplomacy, Warfare, and the Politics of Communism, 1941–1945* (New York, 1979), 143.

[9] Krystyna Kersten, *The Establishment of Communist Rule in Poland, 1943–1948* (Berkeley and Los Angeles, 1991).

[10] Peter Kenez, *Hungary from the Nazis to the Soviets. The Establishment of the Communist Regime in Hungary, 1944–1948* (New York, 2006), 25–7.

[11] Vesselin Dimitrov, *Stalin's Cold War: Soviet Foreign Policy, Democracy and Communism in Bulgaria 1941–48* (London, 2008), 69 ff. Dimitrov, *Diario*, 777–8 (13 December 1944).

[12] Mark, *Revolution by Degrees*; Dimitrov, *Diario*, 790 (4 January 1945).

Europe—by harshly criticizing Togliatti's moderation in Italy in September 1944.[13] Some parties proved recalcitrant, unwilling to renounce the opportunity for revolution in a war context. The epicentre of the radical tendencies was the Yugoslav Communist Party, which stood out for a tendency to develop its own strategy without paying too much attention to advice from Moscow.[14] As early as 1942, Dimitrov had criticized the absence of a 'general national character' in Tito's political propaganda, along with the Yugoslav communists' lack of dedication to creating a 'national front' against the Nazi-Fascist occupiers.[15] This friction survived after the creation of the Yugoslav Liberation Committee. In April 1944, Molotov explained to Djilas Moscow's opposition to the sovietization of Yugoslavia, and set out the national unity line chosen for Italy in a political lesson that was to be ignored by the Yugoslav communists.[16]

Euphoric with victory, Tito and his comrades saw themselves as the vanguard of the expanding Socialist world. In a way they embodied the new pride instilled in the communist movement by the successful anti-Fascist struggle, after the defeat and terror of the pre-war years. It was the Yugoslavs who fanned the flames of civil war in Greece, Albania and Italy, besides preparing their own hegemony in a future confederation of Balkan states. The most sensational case of insubordination was that of Greece, where the limits of Moscow's control were made clear. The Greek Communist Party, in complete contrast to the Italians, took up arms in response to the alliance between London and the monarchy in a country assigned to Great Britain by the agreements between Stalin and Churchill.[17] In December 1944, the partisan movement led by the communists launched a mass mobilization that transformed rapidly into an armed uprising in Athens. Stalin was confronted with a fait accompli, and his disapproval was total. 'I had advised that this struggle should not be undertaken in Greece', he confided to Dimitrov; the Greek

---

[13] Foreign Policy Archive of the Russian Federation (AVPRF), Moscow, f. 098, op. 27, p. 159, d. 11, l. 103–08. See also Pons, 'Stalin, Togliatti, and the Origins'.

[14] Geoffrey Swain, *Tito and the Twilight of the Comintern*, in Tim Rees and Andrew Thorpe (eds), *International Communism and the Communist International*, (Manchester and New York, 1998).

[15] *KVMV*, II, doc. 68, pp. 216–17. Dimitrov, *Diario*, 422, 494–95 (10 March and 10 August 1942).

[16] *Vostochnaia Evropa v dokumentakh rossiiskikh arkhivov 1944–1953* (hereafter VEDRA), 2 vols (Moscow-Novosibirsk, 1997–98), vol. I, doc. 2, 28–35.

[17] KVMV, doc. 198, 474. See also Iatrides, 'Revolution or Self-Defense?'; André Gerolymatos, *Red Acropolis, Black Terror. The Greek Civil War and the Origins of Soviet-American Rivalry, 1943–1949* (New York, 2004), 122–8.

communists had committed an 'act of idiocy'.[18] Shortly after the Greek communist insurrection had failed, Stalin expressed to the Yugoslav communist Hebrang his strong annoyance at the *hubris* of the Belgrade leadership.[19] A few months later, the Yugoslav occupation of Trieste provoked the first crisis among the Allied powers. Although Tito's move had not initially been discouraged in Moscow, Stalin insisted on a retreat after the Western reaction. Tensions between Moscow and Belgrade ran so high that the Italian communists still in August 1945 feared war between Yugoslavia and the USSR.[20]

### The ambiguities of popular democracy

In the final months of the war, Moscow took steps to rein in the radicalism widespread in the European communist parties. The doctrine of a 'peaceful road' to Socialism based on anti-Fascist democracy—invented at the time of Popular Fronts in the mid-thirties—was now adopted as an alternative to revolutionary insurrection. In East Central Europe this idea held particular importance, as the communists were called upon to play a decisive role in the formation of the social and political arrangements in the USSR's sphere of influence. As the economic and political bases of society had already been sufficiently disrupted by the war, the ground for a revolution 'from above' was largely set.[21] The monopoly of force achieved by the USSR in the eastern portion of Europe was called on to strengthen the new ruling classes formed by the progressive forces and the communists. As early as January 1945, in a meeting with Dimitrov and Yugoslav and Bulgarian leaders, Stalin illustrated his openness to possibilities for the post-war period: 'perhaps we are making a mistake when we think that the Soviet form is the only one leading to Socialism. The facts show that the Soviet one is the best, but it is absolutely not the only one'.[22] In April 1945, Stalin expressed this concept to Tito, the

---

[18] Dimitrov, *Diario*, 793–4 (10 January 1945).

[19] VEDRA, I, doc. 37, p. 130.

[20] Fondazione Istituto Gramsci, Archivio del Partito comunista italiano (APC), Roma, Direzione Nord, Verbali, 5 agosto 1945. Dimitrov, *Diario*, 834, 838 (17 and 28 May 1945). Gori and Pons (eds), *Dagli archivi di Mosca*, docs 9–10. Milovan Djilas, *Rise and Fall* (New York, 1985); Italian translation M. Gilas, *Se la memoria non m'inganna. Ricordi di un uomo scomodo 1943–1962* (Bologna, 1987), 106. On the relations between Stalin, Togliatti, and Tito in early 1945, see Pons, *L'impossibile egemonia*, 175–82.

[21] Ian Gross, *War as Revolution*, in Norman Naimark and Leonid Gibianskii (eds), *The Establishment of Communist Regimes in Eastern Europe, 1944–1949*, (Boulder, 1997), 17–40.

[22] Dimitrov, *Diario*, 802 (28 January 1945).

European communist leader most reluctant to adopt it.[23] Two months later, in a meeting with the German communists, Stalin declared the inappropriateness of the Soviet model for Germany and pointed to the prospect of an 'anti-Fascist parliamentary democratic regime'.[24] One of the major episodes in the imposition of the 'popular democracies' doctrine in the parties of East Central Europe involved opposing and alienating the generation of Hungarian communists who were veterans of 1919 and nostalgic for the Republic of Councils.[25] In Germany, too, the militants of a communist Left that preserved the memory of the first post-war period and longed for Bolshevik-style revolutionary action were relegated to the margins by the occupation authorities and displaced by the leaders returning from Muscovite exile.[26] Outside the range of the Red Army, the leaderships of the Italian and French Communist parties also moved along that same wavelength. From the final phase of the war onwards, rejection of the 'Greek model' was a point of strategic dissent within the PCI and the PCF, as well as between the Western leaderships and the Yugoslavs.

In the context of tensions between moderates and radicals, as well as between centre and periphery (especially if China is taken into account),[27] the 'popular democracy' formula, however nebulous, raised crucial questions for the communists. As the Second World War had also been a civil war, did its conclusion put an end to a whole era? Or, on the contrary, was the time of 'international civil war', as the Bolsheviks had called the inter-war period, not really over? Was civil war itself still the obvious road to power, or was the brake being imposed by Soviet interests not a contingent aspect, but the opening of a new strategy? Stalin provided no real answers to such questions. The moderation preached by Moscow was not a clear choice of cultural and political revision. In East Central Europe the objective of sovietization was advised against because it would risk provoking the reaction of enemy forces both at home and abroad. In Western Europe the possibility of insurrection was blocked by invoking the supreme interests of the USSR's foreign policy. The idea of promoting 'popular democracy' was an attempt to provide a

---

[23] Djilas, *Conversations with Stalin*; Italian translation, 120.

[24] Dimitrov, *Diario*, 841 (7 June 1945). See *Istoricheskii Arkhiv* 4 (1996). Wilfried Loth, *Figliastri di Stalin. Mosca, Berlino e la formazione della Rdt* (Urbino, 1997), 26–7.

[25] Mevius, *Agents of Moscow*, 82–6.

[26] Norman Naimark, *The Russians in Germany. A History of the Soviet Zone of Occupation, 1945–1949* (Cambridge, Mass., 1995), 257–8, 271.

[27] Dieter Heinzig, *The Soviet Union and Communist China 1945–1950. The Arduous Road to the Alliance* (Armonk, 2004).

communist response to Europe's post-war arrangements. But it was a pro-visional and reversible response.[28]

Stalin took spheres of influence more seriously than anti-Fascist democracy. He offered his contemporaries no grand design comparable to Roosevelt's. The dichotomy between Lenin and Wilson, which in the final year of the First World War had attracted hopes for peace, was not to be repeated after the Second. In Stalin's vision, state-building, power policy and imperial rivalry were the key concepts. In the long run, he saw post-war Europe as the setting for a new conflict between the Soviet and capitalist worlds, as he confessed privately at the time of the Yalta Conference.[29] His famous prophecy to Djilas about the prospect of each great power establishing its own system in their respective spheres of influence was consistent with that scenario.[30] However, there was no 'road map' in Stalin's thinking.[31] More than in a preordained design, the premises for the sovietization of East Central Europe lay in a political culture incapable of conceiving the exercise of power as anything but domination, conflict, and total security.

In the aftermath of the struggle against Fascism in Europe, several communist parties were building a mass base and in many European countries, including Western ones, they were participating in government.[32] But in the Soviet sphere the rise of the European communist movement revealed areas of shadow. Far from homogeneous, the region showed manifest diversity, socially and politically.[33] Only in Yugoslavia was a communist party firmly in power. Elsewhere, except for Czechoslovakia, growth in party membership did not translate into winning major social consensus and national legitimation. The fragility of the communist presence, and the perception of a strong anti-communist tradition, made the Soviets more ready to adopt methods of preventive repression especially in countries like Poland and Romania, where

[28] Fabio Bettanin, *Stalin e l'Europa. La formazione dell'impero esterno sovietico (1941–1953)* (Roma, 2006), 161–81.

[29] Dimitrov, *Diario*, 802 (28 January 1945). See also *Sto sorok besed s Molotovym. Iz dnevnika F.Cueva* (Moscow, 1991), 78. On the roots of Stalin's thinking in international policy, see Silvio Pons, *Conceptualising Stalin's Foreign Policy: On the Legacy of the Ideology/Realism Duality*, in *Stalin. His Times and Ours*, ed. Geoffrey Roberts (IAREES, 2005), 175–90.

[30] Djilas, *Conversations with Stalin*; Italian translation, 121.

[31] Naimark, 'Stalin and Europe in the Post-war Period', 36. See also Norman Naimark, *The Sovietization of Eastern Europe, 1944–1953*, in Melvyn P. Leffler and Odd Arne Westad (eds), *The Cambridge History of the Cold War*, vol. I, *Origins*, (Cambridge, 2010), 175–97.

[32] Geoff Eley, *Forging Democracy. The History of the Left in Europe, 1850–2000* (Oxford, 2002), 289–91. Aldo Agosti, *Bandiere rosse. Un profilo storico dei comunismi europei* (Roma, 1999), 146.

[33] Zbigniew Brzezinski, *The Soviet Bloc. Unity and Conflict* (Cambridge Mass., 1967).

security interests were given high priority. While advancing reservations and objections, as Gomulka did in Poland, the local communists adapted.[34] They saw Soviet bodies as their institutions of reference in refounding their own states and national governments, and Soviet protection as something to be taken for granted. The alienation of broad sectors of society was considered inevitable in a process experienced as revolutionary. For the communists, although dependence on the Soviet Union was an insoluble contradiction as far as their national legitimacy was concerned, it was the very cornerstone of their political culture. This led them to go along with the Soviets' conduct even when its rationality left a lot to object to, or to play the role of zealous followers, anticipating real or presumed moves. It was not a well judged strategy, but a culturally motivated practice aimed at the incapacitation of democratic society and the systematic destructuring of political life.[35] The interaction between Moscow and the communist parties of East Central Europe thus produced a dynamic discernible even before international tensions had reached a point of no return. While the first post-war year was coming to a close, the USSR's sphere was not sovietized, but was increasingly characterized by authoritarian or semi-authoritarian regimes.

By the summer of 1946, key decisions had been made in Moscow about post-war reconstruction and foreign policy priorities. The Soviet model for reconstruction was based on autarchy and rearmament, while the perceived threat from the United States was increasingly emphasized.[36] In the USSR the rise of Zhdanov reflected the growing role of the party apparatus and greater importance of inter-party relations in international affairs.[37] From the same period comes the first evidence that the possibility of setting up a new international organization of communist parties was being discussed. It was raised at some of Stalin's meetings with Rakosi, Tito, Dimitrov, and other Yugoslav and Bulgarian leaders. Rakosi reported to his party on the need to create a 'new International', with no organizational functions, after having met Stalin

---

[34] *SSSR-Polska. Mekhanizmy podchineniya. 1944–1949 gg. Sbornik dokumentov* (Moscow: Airo-XX, 1995), doc. 30, p. 120; I. Yazhborovskaia, *The Gomulka Alternative: The Untravelled Road*, in Naimark and Gibianskii (eds), *The Establishment of Communist Regimes in Eastern Europe*, 135. Kersten, *The Establishment of Communist Rule in Poland*, 137.

[35] Gross, *War as Revolution*, 32–3.

[36] Vladimir O. Pechatnov, *The Soviet Union and the World, 1944–1953*, in Leffler and Westad (eds), *The Cambridge History of the Cold War*, vol. I, 103.

[37] G. Adibekov, *Kominform i poslevoennaia Evropa*, (Moskva, 1994), 15 ff. Nataliia Egorova, *Stalin's Foreign Policy and the Cominform, 1947–1953*, in Francesca Gori and Silvio Pons (eds), *The Soviet Union and Europe in the Cold War 1943–53* (London, 1996), 197–207.

and Molotov on 1 April 1946, though he specified that the time was not yet ripe.[38] When Tito and Stalin met in late May, Stalin claimed that re-establishing the Comintern was 'not even being discussed'.[39] But shortly thereafter, at a joint meeting with the Yugoslavs and Bulgarians, though Stalin mentioned the liquidation of the Comintern as a positive decision that had 'untied the hands' of the communist parties, he also discussed the possibility of creating a new international communist organization.[40] It is not clear whether the issue was brought up by the East European leaders or by Stalin himself. In any case, the restoration of an international system of links between the communist parties was on the agenda in top-level talks. The British Pollitt and the Italian Secchia also came out in favour of a new organization, in response to the reinstatement of the Socialist International. It is quite possible that such talk was a trial balloon launched by leaders of the more radical elements of European Communism, starting with the Yugoslavs.[41]

Apparently Stalin continued to lend credence to national articulation of the parties. As he had already done a number of times at the end of the war, he explained to the German communist Ulbricht the essential elements of a 'democratic way' to Socialism.[42] In May 1946 he stressed to a Polish delegation that dictatorship of the proletariat and sovietization of the country were not necessary, because the presence of the Red Army was a guarantee against any return to the past. He portrayed Poland as a 'new kind of democracy' destined to be a model for the Western democracies as well.[43] At a meeting with Polish Socialist leaders on 19 August 1946, he declared that in the countries of East Central Europe the war had opened 'a different, easier way of development, which requires less blood, the way of socioeconomic reforms', and had given rise to a 'new democracy', one 'more complex' than the pre-war experiences.[44] He spoke in similar terms during the same period to a delegation of English Labour Party members and the Czech communist leader

---

[38] Csaba Békés, 'Soviet Plans to Establish the Cominform in Early 1946: New Evidence from the Hungarian Archives', *Cold War International History Project Bulletin* 10 (1998), 135–6.

[39] *Istoricheskii Arkhiv* 2 (1993), 28.

[40] Leonid Gibianskii, 'The Soviet Bloc and the Initial Stage of the Cold War: Archival Documents on Stalin's Meetings with Communist Leaders of Yugoslavia and Bulgaria, 1946–1948', *Cold War International History Project Bulletin* 10 (1998), 113–15, 127.

[41] RGASPI, f. 82, op. 2, d. 1353; Pons, *L'impossibile egemonia*, 90–2; Geoffrey Swain, 'The Cominform: Tito's International?', *Historical Journal* 35 (1992), 641–63.

[42] Wilfried Loth, *Stalin's Plans for Post-War Germany*, in Gori and Pons (eds), *The Soviet Union and Europe in the Cold War*, 26.

[43] VEDRA, I, doc. 151, p. 457.

[44] VEDRA, I, doc. 169, p. 511.

Gottwald.[45] The Bulgarian communists too, who were by now in power, received word to set aside the objective of the dictatorship of the proletariat.[46] Stalin's statements appeared to authorize a vision of substantial continuity with the policies launched in the final period of the war, which implied abandonment of the Soviet model as the only way. The notion of 'national roads' echoed in the public political discourse of the main European communist leaders, East and West, during 1946.

However, the policy of the communist parties in East Central Europe was already changing as a consequence of the exercise of power. The objective of establishing 'popular democracies', based on the centrality of communists, proved to be intrinsically authoritarian and impossible to reconcile with being a credible national party.[47] Between the second half of 1946 and early 1947 the authoritarian regimes in Poland and Romania took definitive shape, with strict control exercised by the communists over the key ministries and the apparatus of control, the more or less forced fusion with Socialists on the model already adopted in Germany, the false pluralism of the 'national fronts', the holding of elections in a police-state climate, and the persecution, intimidation, and arrest of leading anti-communists.[48] They thus joined Bulgaria and Yugoslavia. National communists were taking on the features of peripheral rulers of the Soviet 'external empire'. It is no accident that Stalin continued to treat their national leaders as junior partners and party functionaries, rather than as statesmen. The political difference between the two parts of Europe was growing. In Western Europe, the communists continued to cling to coalition governments, even neglecting the signs of an emerging bloc policy. In much of East Central Europe the policy of the 'national fronts' was increasingly losing credibility. However, we should not understand this as simply the end to a tactical pretence made necessary by the deteriorating international situation.[49] The discourse of 'popular democracy' was

---

[45] Georgi Dimitrov, *Dnevnik 9 mart 1933- 6 februari 1949* (Sofiia: Universitetsko izdatelstvo 'Sv. Kliment Okhridski', 1997), 533–5 (2 September 1946); G. P. Murashko, A. F. Noskova, *Sovetskii faktor v poslevoennoi Vostochnoi Evrope (1945–1948)*, in *Sovetskaya vnesnyaya politika v gody 'cholodnoi voiny' (1945–1985). Novoe prochtenie* (Moscow, 1995), 90.

[46] Vesselin Dimitrov, 'Revolution Released: Stalin, the Bulgarian Communist Party and the Establishment of the Cominform', in Gori and Pons (eds), *The Soviet Union and Europe in the Cold War*, 284.

[47] Walter A. Kemp, *Nationalism and Communism in Eastern Europe and the Soviet Union. A Basic Contradiction?* (London, 1999), 100–1.

[48] On the case of Poland, see Kersten, *The Establishment of Communist Rule in Poland*, 315–41.

[49] For such a view, see Mark, *Revolution by Degrees*.

obviously instrumental to a large extent—as sovietization remained the basic idea and a permanent option. Nevertheless, to the communists' mind, 'nationalization', still a significant policy, did not fail because of incompatibility between the anti-Fascist transition and the Soviet model. Its lack of success was due to the persistent influence of cultural and political archetypes, combined with the mounting pressure of Soviet security imperatives.

### The Cominform: a failed challenge

When the Marshall Plan was launched, in June 1947, the Soviets were worried about the capacity of some East European parties to maintain power in their own countries and were already trying to strengthen their control of the major West European parties. Moscow saw Hungary and still more Czechoslovakia as the weak links in the Soviet sphere.[50] Very soon after the Paris conference on the Marshall Plan, Stalin forced the Czechs to give up their intention to participate. Reconstruction in East Central Europe was thus to be dependent on the Soviet Union.[51] On the other side, the French and Italian Communist parties were almost simultaneously removed from the coalition governments, in May 1947, and the Soviet leaders did not hide their dissatisfaction. Zhdanov wrote an angry letter to Thorez, which was forwarded to the communist leaders of Eastern Europe and to Pollitt.[52] The need for control over the Western parties to be re-established was evident during the Paris talks in late June 1947, when Molotov expressed his dismay to Djilas, complaining that the Western communists were not co-ordinating their national policies with Moscow.[53] The Western communists had hoped to remain cautiously positive about the Marshall Plan in order to avoid alienating public opinion and maintain their chances of winning elections.[54] They were forced to abandon this possibility once Moscow rejected the Plan.[55] Even so, in a meeting with Dimitrov on 8 August 1947, Stalin reiterated his displeasure with the behaviour of the French and the Italian communists.[56]

[50]  VEDRA, I, docs. 209, 219.

[51]  VEDRA, I, cit., doc. 227, p. 673.

[52]  RGASPI, f. 77, op. 3, d. 89.

[53]  Djilas, *Rise and Fall*; Italian translation, 144.

[54]  AVPRF, f. 098, op. 30, p. 170, d. 13. R. Martinelli and M. L. Righi *La politica del partito comunista italiano nel periodo costituente. I verbali della direzione tra il V e il VI Congresso, 1946–1948*, Fondazione Istituto Gramsci, *Annali* II (Roma, 1992), 431–2, 450.

[55]  APC, Comitato Centrale, *Verbali*, 1947, riunione dell'1–4 luglio 1947.

[56]  Dimitrov, *Dnevnik*, 556.

The American plan for the reconstruction of Europe took Stalin by surprise, as did the positive responses from Western Europe. Stalin aimed to prevent the formation of a Western bloc by mobilizing the two major Western communist parties, while tightening control over East Central Europe. Under Stalin's hidden direction, harsh criticism of 'parliamentarian illusions' was expressed by Zhdanov to the PCI and PCF delegates at the founding conference of the Cominform in Poland in late September 1947.[57] Moscow stepped back from supporting their national political line. International Communism was now taking a new turn, towards centralization and radicalism. Under the pressure of the Cold War divide, the communist parties had to abandon collaboration with other political forces, moving essentially to social mobilization and even extra-legal action. Four years after the dissolution of the Comintern, Stalin seemed ready for a new challenge, based on a 'two camps' thesis.

However, there was still ambiguity in his plans. Zhdanov called for mass mobilization against the Marshall Plan, without openly indicating the path of civil war. He made no mention of the civil war carried on by the communists in Greece, now backed by Moscow's material aid though not by open political support.[58] Full alignment with the foreign policy theses formulated by Zhdanov did not necessarily entail an insurrectionist thrust in the domestic context. But the parties were called on to promote mass agitation and strikes that might serve as a prologue to insurrection. The Yugoslavs openly pushed for such an outcome, by reaffirming the 'Greek model'. After the conference, both French and Italian leaders sought clarification directly from Stalin. In November-December 1947, Stalin advised Thorez and Secchia to avoid extreme consequences, though he maintained that the parties should be kept ready for any event.[59] It was quite soon to be clear that the step taken with the foundation of the Cominform was conceived by Stalin more as a necessary recovery of leadership over the leading European communist parties than as

---

[57] *The Cominform*, 453–60. Stalin was in daily contact with Zhdanov and Malenkov, Moscow's delegates, during the founding Conference of the Cominform. See the documentation in *Sovescaniia Kominforma. 1947, 1948, 1949. Dokumenty i materialy* (Moscow, 1998).

[58] Artiom Ulunian, *The Soviet Union and the Greek Question, 1946–1953: Problems and Appraisals*, in Gori and Pons (eds), *The Soviet Union and Europe in the Cold War*, 150–1.

[59] *Istoricheskii Arkhiv* 1 (1996), 9–10, 14. Gori and Pons (eds), *Dagli archivi di Mosca*, doc. 20.

the complete enunciation of an offensive design against the 'Western camp'. The strategy of discipline prevailed over the strategy of mobilization.[60]

In East Central Europe, the Soviets' apprehension over the weakest link in their sphere of influence inspired Zorin's mission to Prague, which lay at the origin of the communist coup in late February 1948.[61] The Prague coup was destined to sharpen perceptions in Europe of Soviet expansionism following the foundation of the Cominform.[62] But in Western Europe Soviet policy was quite different. The case of Italy is particularly revealing. Despite their criticisms of the PCI, Soviet policy-making on Italy was extremely cautious. In early 1948 Italy, unlike France, was not yet fully included in the Western system. Nevertheless, Stalin made no serious move to shift the country's international status. In March 1948, while tensions were mounting, Togliatti sent a secret message to Moscow stating that the Communist Party was prepared for an armed insurrection in northern Italy. But he also made clear that, even if Moscow should ask them to unleash civil war, the Italian communists would act only in extreme circumstances, and stressed moreover that such a step could lead to another world war. Stalin and Molotov quickly endorsed Togliatti's view. They recommended armed conflict only in the case of a military attack by reactionary forces, while warning against the Yugoslavs' advice.[63] Subsequently, the landslide defeat of the left in the Italian elections of April 1948 demonstrated the resilience of the forces making up the Western sphere. Thoughts of a communist mobilization aiming to inhibit the formation of the Western bloc had largely melted away. Indirectly, the lesson learned from Italian affairs confirmed the Soviet choice to retreat to a focus on the USSR's security objectives in East Central Europe.

The role of the Cominform thus became definitively much more crucial for the building of an anti-Western 'bloc'. In this setting, Yugoslavia represented an increasingly awkward partner in Stalin's eyes. His choice to downsize the militant impact of the Cominform had already dissolved the apparent accordance between Moscow and Belgrade, allowing the old rust to re-emerge. Stalin's determination to consolidate the ranks of the 'Socialist camp' did the

[60] Silvio Pons, *A Challenge Let Drop: Soviet Foreign Policy, the Cominform, and the Italian Communist Party, 1947–48*, in Gori and Pons (eds), *The Soviet Union and Europe in the Cold War*, 246–63.

[61] G. P. Murashko, 'Fevralskii krizis 1948g. v Chekhoslovakii i sovetskoe rukovodstvo. Po novym materialam rossiiskikh arkhivov', *Novaia i noveishaia istoriia* 3 (1998).

[62] Vojtech Mastny, *The Cold War and Soviet Insecurity. The Stalin Years* (Oxford, 1996), 43–4.

[63] Pons, *A Challenge Let Drop*, 259.

rest. The decision to denounce Belgrade was taken in Moscow in March 1948, after the coup in Prague and after Stalin had made clear to the Yugoslavs and Bulgarians that any militant challenge in the Balkans was out of the question.[64] However, in the accusations made against Tito Stalin preferred to avoid posing the real question—that of international policy—and employed the well-worn *leitmotiv* of 'deviationism'. The paradox here was that the Yugoslavs had been more consistent advocates of sovietization than Stalin himself. But their radicalism fuelled autonomy and insubordination. By outlining a distinct regional role, they might supply a reference point for other countries of East Central Europe. The second Cominform Conference, held in Bucharest on 19–23 June 1948, was the excommunication tribunal. The most interesting aspect of Zhdanov's report was what it omitted. He avoided any significant reference to foreign policy issues, thus making clear that they pertained to Moscow exclusively. The delegates from East Central Europe, intimidated by the obvious implications of Tito's condemnation, kept a low profile on the very notion of 'popular democracies'.[65]

The break between Stalin and Tito held a dual significance: the end of 'national ways' in the East, and the abandonment of the cominformist challenge in the West. Historians have almost invariably emphasized the motive of Tito's independence behind the break, underestimating the motive of his radicalism. But the two points were strictly connected. Consequently, the Cominform did not mark any change in the bedrock Stalinist conceptions of international policy, which for twenty years had contained the communists' revolutionary impetus within the confines of Soviet state interests. By mid-1948, when the Berlin crisis delineated the division of Germany, the call to mobilize against American imperialism sounded like an expedient of Soviet foreign policy, aimed at tightening the Soviet bloc. A differentiation was now established between the parties of Eastern Europe, subject to a harsh regime of limited sovereignty, and the parties of Western Europe, led to

[64] 'Na poroge pervogo raskola v socialisticheskom lagere. Peregovory rukovodjashchikh dejatelej SSSR, Bolgarii i Jugoslavii, 1948g.', *Istoricheskii Arkhiv* 4 (1998), 92–123. Dimitrov, *Dnevnik*, 596–603 (10 February 1948). Djilas, *Rise and Fall*; Italian translation, 182–3. Gibianskii, *The Soviet Bloc and the Initial Stage of the Cold War*, 115–17, 128–34.

[65] On the break between Stalin and Tito in 1948, see particularly Leonid Gibianskii, 'The Soviet-Yugoslav Conflict and the Soviet Bloc', in Gori and Pons (eds), *The Soviet Union and Europe in the Cold War*, 222–45; Leonid Gibianskii, The *Origins of the Soviet-Yugoslav Split*, in Gibianskii and Naimark (eds), *The Establishment of Communist Regimes in Eastern Europe*, 291–312; Leonid Gibianskii, The *1948 Soviet-Yugoslav Clash: Historiographic Versions and New Archival Sources*, in Jasna Fischer et al. (eds), *Jugoslavija v hladni vojni—Yugoslavia in the Cold War* (Ljubljana, 2004), 49–70.

exercise the uncomfortable role of systemic opposition, in the name of defending national sovereignty against the United States. The Cominform's main activity became the struggle against Tito and the witch-hunting of his followers, which set the stage for the purges of Eastern Europe's communist elites.[66]

Our conclusions can be made in three points. First, traditional leftist criticism of Stalin's policies cannot be dismissed in the light of what we now know. In fact, Soviet state interests were given absolute priority in determining the fate of the communist movement, whether by establishing new communist-led regimes in East Central Europe or by using Western communist parties to consolidate the line of national and international collaboration and, later, to fight against the establishment of a Western bloc. Revolution in the original sense was never on the agenda. Second, however, the primacy of the Soviet state was fully accepted by all communists, as they largely identified their own cause with its existence and strength. The new prestige of the Soviet Union was a source of legitimacy for all European communist parties, even more so after victory in the war. In its turn, the communist movement was an essential vehicle for spreading Soviet influence abroad, to an extent not comparable with the inter-war years. While in East Central Europe the communists, however interlaced with Moscow's agencies, were a crucial force for establishing Soviet rule, in Western Europe they provided the main channel for Soviet foreign policy and for dissemination of the myth. Third, the relationship between the Soviet state and the communist movement was nevertheless more contradictory than historians have usually assumed. The definition of Soviet interests was by no means obvious. All communists pretended to follow Soviet interests, but they actually put forward their own interpretations. Apparent tensions between centre and periphery overlapped with oblique opposition between moderate and radical elements. Although this did not undermine the movement's cultural and political unity under Soviet leadership at the end of the war, that risk was not really prevented. The legacy of the Second World War was diversity, no less than unity.

The strategy of 'national fronts' and the doctrine of 'popular democracy' proved to be scarcely consistent as a moderate scenario for post-war Europe, in the light of Soviet security imperatives and because of the basic assumptions of communist political culture. But the reversal of that strategy at the founding conference of the Cominform did not herald the alternative scenario dreamed by the radicals. Instead, the ambition to challenge the West

[66] T. V. Volokitina, G. P. Murashko, A. F. Noskova, T. A. Pokivailova, *Moskva i vostochnaia Evropa. Stanovlenie politicheskikh rezhimov sovetskogo tipa 1949–1953. Ocherki istorii* (Moscow, 2002).

came into conflict with the need to establish Soviet control over the new states of East Central Europe. Discipline and uniformity prevailed over mobilization and insurrection. This was the real source of the break between the Soviet Union and its main ally in Europe, Yugoslavia. Perceived at that time as a marginal, albeit astonishing, episode in the great game of the Cold War, such a break was a crucial passage. It shattered the monolithic image of international communism, weakening the 'Socialist camp' and affecting the stabilization of regimes in East Central Europe. Furthermore, it signalled that the birth of new communist states, while representing a key achievement in terms of power, also created dramatic contradictions in the structure, influence, and development of the communist movement. The emergence of the Soviet state as a world power had not been more crucial to the wartime growth of the communist parties and to the authoritarian revolution from above in East Central Europe than it was to be for creating the stalemate—and later decline—of the communist movement in Europe.

# Establishing Order in Post-war Eastern Germany

**Richard Bessel**

Germans are often associated, and often associate themselves, with order. Theirs, it seems, is a culture in which people expect the state, society and economy to function. Yet at the end of the Second World War Germany experienced the most extreme disorder imaginable; then, to the surprise of many contemporaries, order was re-established very quickly. Indeed, Germany's transition in 1945—from war to peace, from extreme violence to the beginning of a long march towards settled conditions—is one of the most remarkable in modern history.[1]

In 1945 Germany became the first country in modern history to achieve total defeat. Germans were confronted with the disintegration of their world at every turn: as a result of the enormous eruption of violence during the last months of the war, the massive destruction of the country's infrastructure, the collapse of public administration, the plummeting of economic activity, the breakdown of law and order, the detention of millions of German prisoners of war, and the arrival of millions of foreign occupation troops determined to tolerate no opposition from the defeated population. When the war ended, a quarter of the entire German population was homeless and half the German population had lost at least one family member.[2] Basic services that

---

[1] See Konrad Jarausch, *Die Umkehr. Deutsche Wandlungen 1945–1955* (Munich, 2004); Richard Bessel, 'The War to End All Wars. The Shock of Violence in 1945 and its Aftermath in Germany', in Alf Lüdtke and Bernd Weisbrod (eds), *No Man's Land of Violence. Extreme Wars in the 20th Century* (Göttingen, 2006), 71–99; Richard Bessel, *Germany 1945. From War to Peace* (London and New York, 2009).

[2] In a survey conducted in 1952 by the Allensbach Institute for Opinion Research, of 535 young German men asked about their experiences during the war, 51 per cent had lost family members. See Elisabeth Noelle and Erich P. Neumann (eds), *Jahrbuch der öffentlichen Meinung 1947–1955* (2nd edn, Allensbach, 1956), 23; quoted in Alice Förster and Birgit Beck, 'Post-Traumatic Stress Disorder and World War II. Can a Psychiatric Concept Help Us Understand Post-war Society?', in Richard Bessel and Dirk Schumann (eds), *Life after Death. Approaches to a Cultural and Social History of Europe during the 1940s and 1950s* (Cambridge, 2003), 30.

people had come to take for granted in a developed industrial society, such as the transport system, the postal service, hospitals, running water, gas and electricity supply, food distribution, largely had ceased to function. A severe food crisis, anticipated by officials within the Reich Agriculture Ministry in early 1945,[3] loomed—although in effect it was postponed until late 1945, due not least to massive theft from Wehrmacht and other stores at the end of the war as the Nazi regime collapsed. The collapse of the Nazi police state, welcome though it was, opened the floodgates to an upsurge in crime committed in part by former forced labourers, in part by occupation soldiers, and in part by Germans themselves. Germans found themselves in a country where the black market was ubiquitous, bombed-out buildings offered considerable opportunities for looting, millions of firearms remained in circulation, youth was assumed to be running wild, and normative constraints to orderly and lawful behaviour had crumbled, the consequence of what the leading judge of the district court in Magdeburg referred to in March 1946 as 'the sunken morality of a people after the war'.[4] In almost every respect, it seemed that (in the words of Victor Klemperer) 'everything is uncertain, everything is in suspense', that there was 'nothing solid under one's feet, in one's hands'.[5]

While the obstacles to establishing order were enormous in all four occupation zones, Germans in the Soviet Zone faced particularly difficult challenges. During the final weeks of the war, as the Red Army closed in on Berlin, the fighting and, with it, the damage to housing and infrastructure had been especially intense in what was to become the Soviet Zone. Although soldiers of all the victorious Allied armies committed crimes including theft, assault, rape, and murder against German civilians, it was troops of the Red Army that engaged in the most widespread and sustained violence against the conquered members of the erstwhile 'master race'. The mass rapes by Soviet soldiers in Berlin at the end of April and early May 1945 form the most notorious example, but such behaviour was not limited to the German capital.[6]

---

[3] It had been calculated in February 1945 that if significant cuts were made to food rations, Germans could be fed into the summer but that for the period thereafter the prospects were 'considerably more unfavourable'. See Bundesarchiv-Militärarchiv Freiburg, RW 4, Nr. 712, ff. 4–7: [WFSt], 14 Feb. 1945.

[4] Landeshauptarchiv Sachsen-Anhalt, Magdeburg (= LHA-SA), Nr. 309, ff. 60–1: The Präsident des Bezirksgerichts, 'Bericht über das Gefängniswesen im Regierungsbezirk Magdeburg', Magdeburg, 25 March 1946.

[5] Victor Klemperer, *The Lesser Evil. The Diaries of Victor Klemperer 1945–1959* (translated by Martin Chalmers) (London, 2003), 11, (23 June 1945).

[6] The literature on this subject is now considerable. See Erich Kuby, *Die Russen in Berlin 1945* (Munich, 1945); Erika M. Hoerning, 'Frauen als Kriegsbeute. Der Zwei-Fronten-Krieg. Beispiele aus Berlin', in Lutz Niethammer and Alexander von

The arrival of Soviet troops in eastern Germany frequently was accompanied by terrible violence against the civilian population and the burning of towns and villages to the ground.

What is more, it was the Soviet Occupation Zone that bore the heaviest burden of accommodating the German refugees and expellees from east of the Oder-Neiße and from elsewhere in eastern Europe.[7] As the Soviet Zone was the first part of occupied Germany encountered by most Germans streaming westwards in 1945 and 1946, and as the northern parts of the Soviet Zone were among occupied Germany's most rural regions and thus deemed capable of absorbing a particularly large number of Germans from further east, the proportion of refugees and expellees among the population was higher in the Soviet Zone than in any of the western zones. Altogether, roughly 4.3 million of the total of nearly twelve million German refugees and expellees landed in the Soviet Occupation Zone/German Democratic Republic; at the birth of the GDR in 1949 they comprised about a quarter of its entire population. This put enormous strains on what was left of the infrastructure and housing stock, as well as on what might be termed community cohesion: the newcomers made demands on scarce resources, were not necessarily welcomed with open arms, were regarded by the 'natives' as something of a foreign intrusion for years and often were blamed for the post-war increase in crime—something that the police in the Baltic sea resort of Kühlingsborn, for example, attributed at the end of 1945 to the 'overcrowding of the community with refugees'.[8] The massive influx meant that millions of people uprooted and settled against their will in the Soviet Zone were profoundly disoriented and uncertain whether their new home was permanent and worth commitment, and this formed a huge obstacle to their social integration and thus to the social cohesion of the Zone.

---

Platow (eds), *'Wir Kriegen jetzt andere Zeiten'. Auf der Suche nach der Erfahrung des Volkes in nachfaschistischen Ländern* (Bonn, 1985), 327–44; Norman M. Naimark, *The Russians in Germany. A History of the Soviet Zone of Occupation 1945–1949* (Cambridge, Mass., and London, 1995), 68–140, esp. 78–83; Ingrid Schmidt-Harzbach, 'Eine Woche in April. Berlin 1945', in Helke Sander and Barbara Johr (eds), *BeFreier und Befreite. Krieg, Vergewaltigung, Kinder* (Frankfurt am Main, 2005), 21–6; Bessel, *Germany 1945*, 116–18.

[7] See Michael Schwartz, *Vertiebene und 'Umsiedlerpolitik'. Integrationskonflikte in den deutschen Nachkriegs-Gesellschaften und die Assimilationsstrategien in der SBZ/DDR 1945–1961* (Munich, 2004).

[8] Mecklenburgisches Landeshauptarchiv Schwerin (= MLHA), LBdVP, Nr. 400, f. 110: The Bürgermeister des Ostseebad Kühlingsborn, Ortspolizeibehörde, to the Landrat des Kreises Rostock, Abt. Polizei, Kühlingsborn, 18 Dec. 1945.

No less an issue with regard to post-war stabilization was the re-establishment of political life. Although German political parties were permitted to operate in the Soviet Zone in June 1945, just two months after the German surrender and well before such activity was allowed in the western zones, it soon became apparent that the new 'anti-fascist, democratic' politics favoured by the Soviet occupation authorities and their handmaidens in the Communist (and then Socialist Unity) Party created new challenges. Although one should not underestimate the genuine support for a new, democratic beginning after Nazism and war, the tactics and behaviour of both the Soviet occupiers and their German communist allies aroused fear and hostility. Making arbitrary arrests, setting up Soviet 'special camps' for real and imagined Nazis and opponents of 'progress', and hauling off civilians (particularly youths accused of underground 'werewolf' resistance) to perform forced labour, did not endear Germans in the Soviet Zone to their new masters. Consequently, many people fled to the West, which in turn undermined efforts at reconstruction and made more difficult the building of stable and well-functioning administrative structures.

Reconstruction, and thus the attractiveness of the Soviet Occupation Zone as a place to build one's future, was damaged further by the campaign of the Soviet occupation administration—determined to gain compensation for at least some of the enormous damage caused by the German invasion of the USSR—to remove goods and productive capacity from the defeated enemy. While reparations were extracted, the operations of factories and businesses interfered with and industrial plant dismantled in the western zones as well, the reparations campaign was most extensive and disruptive in the Soviet Zone (and it crippled the economy of the GDR for decades).[9] In effect, the Soviet Zone underwent a process of de-industrialization after the war, as Soviet dismantling teams removed plant and machinery, railway rolling stock and track, as well as current production. According to contemporary estimates, by the end of 1946 nearly half of the industrial capacity in the Zone had been dismantled.[10] Furthermore, even where dismantling had not (yet) taken place, the threat of it inhibited economic activity: as the Economic Ministry in Mecklenburg reported in November 1945, 'at the moment everyone is afraid of drawing attention to themselves by an increase in production and thereby [provoking] dismantling'.[11] Although post-war economic

---

[9] See Bessel, *Germany 1945*, 342, 377–80.

[10] G. W. Harmssen, *Reparations Sozialprodukt Lebensstandard. Versuch einer Wirtschaftsbilanz. Heft 1 A. Allgemeiner Teil* (Bremen, 1948), 70.

[11] Quoted in Kathrin Möller, 'Industrialisierung in Mecklenburg-Vorpommern. Zur Entstehung der ostdeutschen Werftindustrie von 1945 bis 1953', in Damian van Melis

recovery appears initially to have been fastest in the Soviet Zone,[12] soon the processes of dismantling, expropriations, and politically motivated interference in the economy undermined that recovery—and accelerated the stream of people westwards.

The consequence of all this was disorder the like of which Germans had not seen since the Thirty Years' War. Speaking at a rally in June 1946, Dr. Rudolf Paul, Minister President of Thuringia, described 'the collapse of 9 November 1918' as 'a storm in a teacup compared with the typhoon of the year 1945'.[13] Paul, who had been a member of the German Democratic Party during the Weimar Republic and headed the Thuringian government from July 1945 to July 1946 (and fled to West Berlin in September 1947), voiced an opinion which was widely held, and for good reason. In this sense, the reluctance of some historians to give credence to the term notwithstanding,[14] Germans really did experience what they regarded as a 'zero hour' at the end of the Second World War. Of course, their experiences were loaded with contradictions; continuities overlapped with the most abrupt and traumatic breaks, such as the loss of homes, the death of family members and friends, loss of employment, arrival in a new landscape with new opportunities. Therefore it

---

(ed.), *Sozialismus auf dem platten Land. Tradition und Transformation in Mecklenburg-Vorpommern von 1945 bis 1952* (Schwerin, 1999), 346.

[12] See the table in Werner Abelshauser, 'Wirtschaft und Besatzungspolitik in der Französischen Zone 1945–1949', in Claus Scharf and Hans-Jürgen Schröder (eds), *Die Deutschlandpolitik Frankreichs und die französische Zone 1945–1949* (Wiesbaden, 1983), 122.

[13] Bundesarchiv-Berlin (= BAB), SAPMO-DDR, NL 182, Nr. 1084, ff. 85–90: Willi Barth, 'Entwicklung und Tätigkeit der Beratenden Versammlung des Landes Thüringen', Berlin, 18 July 1946.

[14] Thus Lutz Niethammer has referred to 'the so-called "zero hour"' as the 'wishful thinking of the Germans' that consisted of the idea that 'everything was over and forgotten'. See Lutz Niethammer, 'Privat-Wirtschaft. Erinnerungsfragmente einer anderen Umerziehung', in Lutz Niethammer (ed.), *'Hinterher merkt man, daß es richtig war, daß es schiefgegangen ist'. Nachkriegserfahrungen im Ruhrgebiet* (Berlin and Bonn, 1983), 28. Similarly, Konrad Jarausch has written critically of the 'somewhat exculpatory concept of the "zero hour"'. See Konrad H. Jarausch, '1945 and the Continuities of German History: Reflections on Memory, Historiography and Politics', in Geoffrey J. Giles (ed.), *Stunde Null: The End and the Beginning Fifty Years Ago* (Washington, 1997), 13–14. And Harold James has referred to 'the mythical view [that] is summed up in one phrase, the designation of 2300 hours on May 8, 1945 as the "Stunde Null"—the zero hour at which the clock of German history started ticking afresh'. See Harold James, 'The Prehistory of the Federal Republic', *The Journal of Modern History*, 63:1 (March 1991), 99.

is difficult to disagree with Christoph Kleßmann's observation that Brecht's ironic comment that 'the house was built with the stones that were available' described the new beginning in 1945 very well.[15] Yet while many historians understandably prefer to emphasize continuities—as though to speak of a 'zero hour' might allow Germans to get off the hook of responsibility for Nazism—there can be little doubt that the end of the war meant a profound break in the biographies of millions of Germans, who perceived this as a personal 'zero hour'.

The extent of the challenge that faced the Germans who were charged with rebuilding administrative structures in the Soviet Occupation Zone may be gauged from the 'activity report' for the period May–November 1945 filed by the *Landrat* of the District of Demmin, in Pomerania (not far from the new border with Poland):

> On 15 May 1945, after the Red Army had marched in on 30 April 1945, I was confirmed [as *Landrat*] by the [Soviet] war commandant. The district, above all the town of Demmin, had suffered particularly heavy damage. 365 houses, roughly 70 per cent of the town, lay in ruins, over 700 inhabitants had ended their lives by suicide. Everywhere there was rubble and debris. As any coordinated direction of the regional government and of government authorities was lacking, I had to take charge in all areas and in all branches of the administration, naturally in agreement with the commandant.

> All branches of the district administration had to be reconstructed, and new office space had to be found and furnished, as most of the [government] records had been destroyed. At first it was necessary to provide the population, especially the inhabitants of the three towns [of the district], including the many refugees, with food and to accommodate the homeless. Accordingly, the greatest concern involved agriculture, in order to ensure that the fields were cultivated and the harvest brought in. [. . .]

> While at first a few former members of the Nazi Party had to be taken on as skilled workers, they nevertheless soon were removed

---

[15] Christoph Kleßmann, 'Die deutsche Gesellschaft im Zusammenbruch 1945', in Roland G. Foerster (ed.), *Seelower Höhen 1945* (Hamburg, 1998), 172. See also Christoph Kleßmann, '"Das Haus wurde gebaut aus den Steinen, die vorhanden waren", Zur kulturgeschichtlichen Kontinuitätsdiskussion nach 1945', *Tel Aviver Jahrbuch für deutsche Geschichte*, 19 (1990), 159–77.

from all public offices and from leading positions in the economy and replaced by anti-fascists. In order to get economic life moving again, I restored the three branch railway lines in the district. Unfortunately they were dismantled after a short period. [. . .]

Great difficulties arose with the industrial enterprises, as these had been either largely destroyed or dismantled by commandos of the Red Army. [. . .] One attempted to get all production started again by the most elementary means.

Bringing in the harvest and threshing the grain gave us great difficulties, as most of the machines had been confiscated and most of the horses had been driven away. By calling up all available labour the work nevertheless was accomplished, and the delivery quota was met, despite all the damage caused us by what the Red Army took without payment and without receipt, for example from 72 communities: 1,767 cattle, 896 pigs, 4,106 sheep, 32 calves, 2,221 chickens, 100,997 eggs, 282 geese and 142,200 kilograms of grain. [. . .]

The spread of typhus is due primarily to the insufficient nourishment and [resulting] debilitation. [. . .] An examination of all inhabitants between 15 and 45 years of age for venereal disease has been ordered and will be carried out with the help of police control points. [. . .]

The mood of the population is for the most part solemn and depressed. There are complaints about insufficient distribution of food. In addition the lack of clothing and footwear, especially among the resettlers [i.e. refugees], is especially noticeable with the onset of the cold weather. We have not yet received any of the promised allocations.

The accommodation of the resettlers creates particular difficulties. To the roughly 53,000 inhabitants of the district 54,000 resettlers have been added already. They were put up [first] in transit camps in the district and then distributed among the villages, since the commandant has prohibited migration into the towns.[16]

---

[16] MLHA, Kreistag/Rat des Kreises Demmin, Nr. 46, ff. 62–4: [The Landrat des Kreises Demmin] to the Präsident des Landes Mecklenburg-Vorpommern, Abteilung Innere

In this description of the terrible conditions in Demmin in 1945, the police were mentioned only once: they were expected to help carry out checks on adults for venereal disease. This is not because policing was unimportant, at a time characterized by extreme social upheaval and disorder and by high levels of crime. According to one general, internal report about the development of the 'new democratic police' (in this case, in Saxony during the period 1945–1948), there had been 'an increase in criminality of four to five times the [level of] pre-war criminality'.[17] Yet in the immediate aftermath of the German defeat, the new East German 'People's Police' comprised a small, mostly unarmed and largely ineffective force.[18] Initially the task of imposing order, of a sort, fell to the Red Army—whose soldiers, of course, also caused widespread fear and disorder by assaulting, raping, and stealing from the Germans under their control.

It is hardly surprising that, initially, the Soviet military authorities were unprepared to trust a German police force very far. Nevertheless, bit by bit Germans were given responsibility for public order and security. Local officials—mayors and *Landräte* put into their posts by the Russians and usually veterans of the German labour movement or exiled communists who had returned to Germany with the Red Army—were assigned the task of setting up local police forces.[19] Members of the new police were drawn as far as was possible from among 'proven anti-fascists'—veterans of the labour movement, workers who had supported the communists; those known to have worked in police formations under the Nazi regime were removed. This opened the profession, charged with establishing order in such difficult circumstances, to people who had never been in police uniform before. Internal statistics compiled with obsessive energy during the post-war years confirm that, as the German Administration of the Interior (the *Deutsche Verwaltung des Innern*, set up under the Soviet Administration to operate the German internal security formations) asserted in its 'Annual Report for 1946–1947',

---

Verwaltung, [Demmin], 21 Nov. 1945, 'Tätigkeitsbericht über die Verwaltung des Kreises Demmin vom Mai bis November 1945'.

[17] BAB, DO-I-7, Nr. 23, ff. 23–70 (here ff. 34–5): 'Entwicklungspolitischer Bericht der neuen demokratischen Polizei des Landes Sachsen (1945–1948)'.

[18] Richard Bessel, 'Grenzen des Polizeistaates. Polizei und Gesellschaft in der SBZ und frühen DDR, 1945–1953', in Richard Bessel and Ralph Jessen (eds), *Die Grenzen der Diktatur. Staat und Gesellschaft in der DDR* (Göttingen, 1996), 224–8.

[19] See, for example, the informative account by the II. Bürgermeister of the Pomeranian town of Anklam, who was installed in office in May 1945. MLHA, Kreistag/Rat des Kreises Anklam, Nr. 39, ff. 29–33: II. Bürgermeister, 'Tätigkeitsbericht für die Zeit vom 7. Mai bis zum 16. Juli 1945', Anklam, 16 July 1945.

'over 90 per cent of the members of the police in the Soviet Occupation Zone are people from outside the profession [*berufsfremde Menschen*]'.[20]

The size of this new East German police force initially was quite modest: in January 1946 the total personnel (both male and female, including clerical staff) of the German police in the Soviet Occupation Zone was a mere 21,973, slightly more than one member of the police per one thousand inhabitants.[21] The new police were almost completely inexperienced and untrained, often having been chosen more for their political reliability than for professional competence or previous service in police formations. Since trusted 'anti-fascists' generally were either Social Democrats or communists from the Weimar period or people who had had some experience of underground or trade-union activity, initially the new police tended to be older than the sorts of people normally recruited into a police force. Many were underweight and they were prone to illness.[22]

They also were remarkably poorly equipped. It was not until 1946 that the Soviet occupation authorities permitted the bulk of the German police in their zone to carry firearms.[23] Even in late 1946 only 30 per cent of the

---

[20] For example, statistics compiled by the German Administration of the Interior for June 1947 show that of the 39,683 recorded members of the police in the Soviet Zone, 2101 (6.0%) had worked in the police before 1945 and a further 940 (2.7%) before 1933. See BAB, DO-1-7, Nr. 138, f. 66: 'Personalstruktur. Monat: Juni 1947'. The highest percentage of those who had been employed in the police before 1945, 15.2%, was among the Administrative Police. The Administrative Police also employed by far the highest percentage of women (46.0%, as compared with 12.1% for the police as a whole); it is possible therefore, that a disproportionate number of those who had worked for the police under the Nazis were female clerical staff. On women in the early 'People's Police', see Richard Bessel, ' "Besonders schwierig . . . weltanschaulich zu schulen". Volkspolizistinnen in der SBZ und frühen DDR, 1945–1952', in Gerhard Fürmetz, Herbert Reinke and Klaus Weinhaupt (eds), *Nachkriegspolizei. Sicherheit und Ordnung in Ost- und Westdeutschland 1945–1969* (Hamburg, 2001), 155–67.

[21] See Rüdiger Wenzke, 'Auf dem Wege zur Kaderarmee. Aspekte der Rekrutierung, Sozialstruktur und personellen Entwicklung des entstehenden Militärs in der SBZ/ DDR bis 1952/53', in Bruno Thoß (ed.), *Volksarmee schaffen - ohne Geschrei! Studien zu den Anfangen einer 'verdeckten' Aufrüstung in der SBZ/DDR 1947–1952* (Munich, 1994), 237.

[22] See LHA S-A, LBdVP, Nr. 309, f. 178: Kommando der Schutzpolizei, 'Einrichtungen und Maßnahmen zum Schutze der Gesundheit von Polizeiangehörigen', Magdeburg, 3 March 1947.

[23] For example, for the 950 members of the Schutzpolizei in Magdeburg in November 1945 there were only thirteen 7.65 mm pistols available - one for the Commander, eight for the Section Chiefs ('Reviervorsteher'), two for 'keeping watch on the bank', one for 'purposes

personnel of many police units were armed, which made it impossible for them effectively to confront armed criminals (at a time when there were huge numbers of illegal arms in circulation) and generated 'a passivity within the police that can have catastrophic consequences for public order and security'.[24] They possessed few if any motor vehicles and even bicycles were a rarity, making the idea of police mobility little more than a joke.[25] They lacked working telecommunications equipment, as the telephone network had been damaged in large sections of the country during the war and the Soviet authorities initially did not permit the German police radio communication (allowing the 'People's Police' their own telex network only in 1947).[26] Consequently, during the first couple of years after the war it was virtually impossible for police stations to communicate quickly with one another or for local commanders to remain in constant contact with their superiors or subordinates. Almost none of the new police had any police training; and even after police training schools had been set up in all the east German *Länder*, following the opening of the first police training school in Saxony in March 1946, only a small proportion could be trained for their new profession quickly.[27] Many of the new police recruits proved ill-disciplined and/or corrupt, as many had joined the organization neither out of political conviction nor out of an idealistic desire to serve the public but

---

of training', and one for prisoner transports. See LHA S-A, LBdVP, Nr. 290, ff. 14–15: The Polizeipräsident to the Bezirkspräsidenten, Magdeburg, 8. Nov. 1945.

[24] BAB, DO-1-7, Nr. 364, f. 23: Deutsche Verwaltung des Innern (Reschke und Wagner) to the Sowjetische Militäradministration Deutschlands, Abt. für innere Angelegenheiten, Oberstleutnant Smirnow, Berlin-Wilhelmsruh, [?] November 1946.

[25] As late as October 1948 the Landesbehörde der Volkspolizei in Sachsen-Anhalt complained that, because the police lacked bicycles and bicycle tyres, they were in no position to protect farmers' fields effectively from thieves who used bicycles and therefore were 'far better equipped than the police officers chasing them'. See LHA S-A, MdI, Nr. 4161, f. 129: Landesbehörde to the Minister des Innern, Halle (Saale), 4 Oct. 1948.

[26] The Volkspolizei were granted permission to set up a telex network in January 1947, but this was not in place and functioning until August of that year. See BAB, DO-1-7, Nr. 19, ff. 42–117 (here f. 74): 'Jahresbericht. Deutsche Verwaltung des Innern in der sowjetischen Besatzungszone, 1946–1947'.

[27] In April 1947 Walter Mickinn, Head of the Personnel Section of the German Administration of the Interior, reported that in Thuringia 'roughly 65%' of the police still had not received training, in Brandenburg 70%, and in Sachsen-Anhalt and Mecklenburg the figure was 94% and 95% respectively. See BAB, DO-1-7, Nr. 138, ff. 76–86: Landespolizei Thüringen; ibid., ff. 89–94: Landespolizei Sachsen-Anhalt; DO-1-7, Nr. 138, ff. 99–109: Landespolizei Mecklenburg; DO-1-7, Nr. 138, ff. 112–15: Landespolizei Brandenburg.

primarily in order to gain food (ration cards), clothing (uniforms, boots) and shelter (police barracks); cases of drunkenness and theft among the People's Police were common.[28]

Despite the intense concern of the Socialist Unity Party leadership and of the German Administration of the Interior that the new police attract and retain politically reliable recruits, this often proved difficult to realize in practice. Not only was discipline a major problem—perhaps to be expected in an organization composed largely of inexperienced and poorly trained men in a chaotic environment—but the Volkspolizei also experienced considerable turnover during its early years. During 1946 alone some 20 per cent of police members in Saxony and Saxony-Anhalt left the force; in Thuringia the figure was 30 per cent and in Brandenburg it stood at 57 per cent.[29] The causes were not necessarily political in the first instance, although there were internal complaints that poor hiring practices had allowed 'politically unreliable elements into the police'. Rather, they more often were a response to long hours, poor working conditions and relatively low pay, as well as a general 'unsuitability' for the police profession. (For example, in Saxony only 7.9 per cent of the police who left the force in 1946 were removed because of their supposed 'political unreliability'; in 1947 the figure was 14.9 per cent.)[30] In other words: due to the relatively poor working conditions it was not easy for the Volkspolizei to recruit and retain the competent and politically reliable personnel that its leaders regarded as a precondition for sucess. No doubt such problems had their parallels within other professions in East Germany after the war, but they held particular significance for an organization that bore major responsibility for bringing order to the Soviet Occupation Zone.

Although its beginnings were modest, and despite the continued difficulties it experienced in hiring and retaining suitable personnel, the new 'anti-fascist-democratic' People's Police did not remain small and ill-equipped

---

[28] Norman Naimark, ' "To Know Everything and to Report Everything Worth Knowing": Building the East German Police State, 1945–1949' (Working Paper No. 10, Cold War International History Project, Woodrow Wilson International Center for Scholars, August 1994), 4–5; LHA S-A, LBdVP, Nr. 27, ff. 87–103: 'Protokoll der Konferenz der Polizeiführer der Schutz- und Landespolizei des Bezirks Merseburg am 26.10.1946 10.00 Uhr, in der Provizialverwaltung, Halle' (here the comments by Colonel Stachanowsky, ff. 87–8).

[29] BAP, DO-1-7, Nr. 19, ff. 2–18 (here f. 10): Der Leiter, Abt. P. [Personal], Mickinn, 'Jahresbericht des Leiters der Abt. P. über die Tätigkeit der Personalabteilung', Berlin, 5 Jan. 1947.

[30] BAP, DO-1-7, Nr. 23, ff. 3–17 (here f. 17): Landespolizeibehörde Sachsen, 'Die Entwicklung der Volkspolizei in Sachsen', Dresden, 5. Jan. 1949.

for very long. Already in 1946 a process of rapid expansion had begun: the total number of German police in the Soviet Occupation Zone rose from 21,973 in January 1946 to 38,767 in July 1947, 54,729 in April 1948, 68,148 in September 1948 and to 83,178 (including the 18,229 members of the Border Police and the paramilitary *Bereitschaften*) in March 1949.[31] This explosive growth was motivated first and foremost by a determination to ensure political control, as the 'anti-fascist, democratic' transformation of the immediate post-war period was followed by the imposition of a Stalinist system from 1947/48 onwards. The vastly expanded Volkspolizei—whose size by 1949 was greater than that of the police of the entire German Empire before the First World War—saw its task increasingly as political: to suppress real and imagined political opposition and be ever vigilant against alleged saboteurs and reactionary elements, as well as to provide the kernel of a future East German military force. The ethos of the 'People's Police' in the new Stalinist system coming into being was reflected in the 'Political Culture' sections established within all levels of the organization in 1948, and was expressed succinctly in September 1949 by Heinz Hoffmann (then Vice-President of the German Administration of the Interior and later the long-serving Minister of Defence in the German Democratic Republic): there was to be 'no separation between political and police work. Every police task is simultaneously a political task, just as every political task in the People's Police is simultaneously a police task.'[32] No doubt this new ethos also contributed to the establishment of order in the late 1940s, as overtly political policing contributed to the intimidation of the population (as well as to the decision of many potential trouble-makers and otherwise dissatisfied people to leave for the West).

The extreme politicization of the police paralleled a substantial reduction in crime. Indeed, it appears that the post-war crime wave peaked in late

---

[31] These figures are not exactly comparable with one another; for example, the 5–6,000 members of the railway police are not included in the figures for 1946–1948. However, the general trend is quite clear. Figures taken from statistics compiled by the German Administration of the Interior, are published in Wenzke, 'Auf dem Wege zur Kaderarmee', 237. See Thomas Lindenberger, 'Die deutsche Volkspolizei (1945–1990)', in Torsten Dietrich, Hans Ehlert and Rüdiger Wenzke (eds), *Im Dienste der Partei. Handbuch der bewaffneten Organe der DDR* (Berlin, 1998), 99.

[32] BAB, DO-1-7, Nr. 101, f. 4: Report by Vice President Hoffmann, 'Die Aufgaben der PK-Abteilung im Kampf um die ideologische Festigung der Volkspolizei', at the 2. PK-Leiter Konferenz in Berlin on 8 and 9 September 1949. See also Richard Bessel, 'Police of a "New Type"? Police and Society in Eastern Germany after 1945', *German History*, 10:3 (1992), 290–301.

1946/early 1947, and during 1947 and 1948 crime diminished in the Soviet Zone.[33] Not only had the police become far more numerous; they also appeared to be far more effective, as clear-up rates for offences reached levels of which most police forces today would be very proud.[34] Yet the growth of the police was not a reflection of the demands of policing in the conventional sense of a fight against crime, nor was it necessarily the primary cause of the consolidation of order. The reduction in crime and the progress made towards establishing social order were not due simply to the effectiveness of the police. They also were consequences of a general improvement in conditions as occupied Germany began to emerge from the administrative and economic paralysis that accompanied military defeat. According to the Saxon *Volkspolizei*:

> The so-called lawless period that makes its presence felt in every country after a war is confirmed by the high incidence of these offences [i.e. murder attended with robbery]. However, the expected decline in these offences came about due to the improvement of general living standards (secure social conditions, etc.). Whereas murder attended with robbery dominated the field of capital crimes in 1945 and 1946, during 1947 and 1948 it has become a rarity. Its place has been taken by quite natural murder due to hatred, revenge and jealousy.[35]

While it may sound odd, the predominance of 'quite natural murder due to hatred, revenge and jealousy' was taken as a sign that the period of disorder—'the so-called lawless period that makes its presence felt in every country after

---

[33] For example, in Mecklenburg in March 1947 7,293 offences were reported, in March 1948 the figure had declined to 4,700. See the 'Activity Reports' of the Mecklenburg Criminal Police for 1947 and 1948, in BAB, DO-1–7, Nr. 366 and 367. By contrast, in the first three months of 1952 altogether only 2,715 offences were reported. See BAB, DO-1–11, Nr. 703: HV Deutsche Volkspolizei, Hauptabteilung K, 'Bericht der Hauptabteilung K über die Tätigkeit der Kriminalpolizei der Deutschen Demokratischen Republik im I. Quartal 1952', Berlin, 15 Apr. 1952. Generally, see Ministerium des Innern, Kommission zur Erforschung und Ausarbeitung der Geschichte der Deutschen Volkspolizei (ed.), *Geschichte der Deutschen Volkspolizei, Band 1 1945–1961* (2nd edn, Berlin, 1987], 115–16; Thomas Lindenberger, *Volkspolizei. Herrschaftspraxis und öffentliche Meinung im SED-Staat 1952–1968* (Cologne, 2003), 47–8.

[34] In 1947 and 1948, clear-up rates in Mecklenburg, for example, generally were well over 60%. See the 'Tätigkeitsberichte' and the 'Berichte über die Kriminalität' in BAB, DO-1–7, Nr. 366, and the 'Kriminalstatistik' in BAB, DO-1–7, Nr. 367.

[35] BAB, DO-I-7, Nr. 23, ff. 33–70 (here f. 50): 'Entwicklungspolitischer Bericht der neuen demokratischen Polizei des Landes Sachsen (1945–1948)'.

a war'—was running its course and that normal times and a sense of order were returning. The main features of the extreme disorder of the immediate post-war years, administrative chaos, economic dislocation, severe food shortages, the arrival of millions of homeless refugees and expellees, and the ill-disciplined behaviour of Soviet troops, had diminished. More specifically, the main categories of crime—the vast amount of property crime that arose from the desperate conditions of the immediate post-war period and that comprised the overwhelming majority of offences, and the violent and property crime by Soviet soldiers—fell as conditions improved generally and as the numbers of Soviet troops in Germany were reduced and control over their behaviour was tightened. After a period during which there had been 'nothing solid under one's feet, in one's hands', an environment was taking shape in which post-war order could be established, in which administrative structures again functioned (and could be expected to function), and in which the state's monopoly of legitimate force again could be imposed.

This was a remarkable transformation, but one which was probably due less to the efforts of a greatly expanded police force to establish and maintain order than to a number of contextual factors. The ebbing of the 'so-called lawless period' after the Second World War, the growing effectiveness of the police (their increasingly heavy political role notwithstanding) in combatting ordinary crime, and the establishment of order in the devastated landscape of the Soviet Occupation Zone may be explained with reference to six general themes:

1. *Violence.* The violence with which the war ended in Germany was of such an intensity and on such a scale that it left little scope for continued resistance to the new order imposed by the Allies.[36] It should be remembered that the last months of the Second World War were the bloodiest: in the first five months of 1945 alone, German military losses were greater than in 1942 and 1943 put together.[37] Indeed, in January 1945 the number of German military casualties reached its absolute maximum, with over 450,000 dead in a single month; in each of the three months which followed, the number of German dead remained above 280,000, far above the roughly 185,000 members of the Wehrmacht who died in January 1943, the month of the defeat at Stalingrad. The numbers of seriously wounded and injured were even greater, at a time when German medical facilities were in a state of collapse. Furthermore, the

---

[36] This argument is developed in Bessel, 'The War to End All Wars'.

[37] Rüdiger Overmans, *Deutsche militärische Verluste im Zweiten Weltkrieg* (Munich, 1999), 265–6.

violence did not suddenly come to an end when Nazi Germany surrendered. With millions of heavily armed foreign troops, and with foreign labourers no longer tightly controlled by the Nazi police state, occupied Germany remained a violent and dangerous place during the early months of occupation. All this left the German population beaten in more ways than one after the war.

2. *Fear.* A corollary of the extraordinary violence in 1945 was fear. As the war reached its end, the Nazi police state (which had terrorized others so effectively) increasingly was turned against the German people in the effort to throttle 'defeatism' and to prevent a repetition of the collapse in November 1918. In the west, in early 1945 Germans often had more to fear from their own regime than from the Allied invaders;[38] in the east, however, they had much more to fear from the Russians, and the fear did not evaporate immediately once the Wehrmacht had surrendered. When the occupation forces arrived, they were determined to crack down hard on a German population that was assumed to have been thoroughly indoctrinated by the Nazi regime. Accordingly, they were determined to crush any resistance to Allied military rule. Anyone who stepped out of line during the early months of occupation was dealt with severely in all four zones, but especially in the French and Soviet zones. Germans had to fear harsh and often arbitrary action by Allied occupiers who assumed that the defeated population would be hostile and dangerous and who instituted programmes of 'automatic arrest', by which hundreds of thousands of Germans were taken into custody after the Allies arrived. This meant the very real threat of internment for anyone who stepped out of line (and many who were just unlucky), and a significant minority of those in Soviet internment camps did not survive their captivity. (In the Soviet Zone, according to figures released in 1990, 122,671 Germans were interned, of whom 42,889 died in the camps and 756 were sentenced to death and executed).[39] More than that—and this is where the 'People's

---

[38] The intelligence staff of the US Sixth Army Group, which had occupied large portions of Baden, Württemberg, and Western Bavaria, observed at the end of April 1945 that German civilians had to protect their homes and property not so much against the Allies as against Nazi fanatics unwilling to accept defeat. Sixth Army Group, G-2, Weekly Intelligence Summary Nr. 32, from 28 April 1945, NA, RG 407, Operations Reports, Box 1742. Quoted in Klaus-Dietmar Henke, *Die amerikanische Besetzung Deutschlands* (Munich, 1995), 853.

[39] Lutz Niethammer, 'Alliierte Internierungslager in Deutschland nach 1945. Vergleich und offene Fragen', in Christian Jansen, Lutz Niethammer, and Bernd Weisbrod (eds), *Von der Aufgabe der Freiheit. Politische Verantwortung und bürgerliche Gesellschaft im 19. und*

Police' come in—with the expansion of an increasingly effective police apparatus and the imposition of a Stalinist political and economic system, there grew a paranoid and extensive police repression of real and imagined dissent. Altogether, the German population had a great deal to be afraid of, especially in the Soviet Occupation Zone, where the fear did not dissipate as it did in the western zones with the relaxation of the occupation regime.

3. *Exhaustion.* Germans generally greeted the end of the war and beginning of peace less with jubilation than with relief and exhaustion. The war years, and particularly the last violence-soaked months of war, had taken such an emotional as well as physical toll on Germans that their main reaction once the conflict ended was one of weary resignation and a preoccupation with their own tribulations and sorrows. Most retreated into their own private, everyday concerns. The daily struggle to find enough to eat, to negotiate life often in a rubble-strewn, bombed-out landscape, to find adequate housing at a time when roughly a quarter of the German population were homeless, to set up a functioning household in a country where half of all families had lost someone during the war, dominated all else. This often left little energy for public engagement, which in turn meant that Germany's new rulers were met by a surprisingly passive population, not the fanaticized Nazi 'Volk' that many had imagined would greet them. Rather than resist the occupiers, the German population bowed to superior force, generally did what they were told, and tried as best they could to get on with their daily lives in extremely difficult circumstances. This passivity helped pave the way for a surprisingly rapid establishment of order in post-war Germany.

4. *Population Structure:* After the Second World War ended, what remained of German society consisted disproportionally of women, the very young and the old. With over four million German soldiers dead and millions more in Allied prisoner-of-war camps, there were rather few German

---

*20. Jahrhundert. Festschrift für Hans Mommsen zum 5.11.1995* (Berlin, 1995), 474; Heiner Wember, *Umerziehung im Lager. Internierung und Bestrafung von Nationalsozialisten in der britischen Besatzungszone Deutschlands (Essen, 1991)*, 31–2, 38; Alexander von Plato, 'Sowjetische Speziallager in Deutschland 1945 bis 1950. Ergebnisse eines deutsch-russischen Kooperationsprojektes', in Peter Reif-Spirek and Bodo Ritscher (eds), *Speziallager in der SBZ. Gedenkstätten mit 'doppelter Vergangenheit'* (Berlin, 1999), 125–32. See also Christof Straub, 'Zwischen Apathie und Selbstrechtfertigung: Die Internierung NS-belasteter Personen in Württemberg-Baden', in Paul Hoser and Reinhard Baumann (eds), *Kriegsende und Neubeginn. Die Besatzungszeit im Schwäbisch-alemannischen Raum* (Konstanz, 2003), 288.

men in their twenties and thirties present during the immediate post-war years (and the sex imbalance among the birth cohorts of the 1920s, the main military casualties of the war, would shape the German demographic pyramid for decades to come). As Lutz Niethammer has observed, together with Belarus the German Democratic Republic comprised the 'most female society of Europe'.[40] And if this was true for the GDR after 1949, it was even more the case for the Soviet Zone immediately after the war when millions of German men were in prisoner-of-war camps. Never in modern German history has a society been so female as that in the Soviet Occupation Zone. On 29 October 1946 there were 7,379,546 men and 9,934,188 women in the Soviet Zone—that is 73,330 fewer men and 2,229,941 more women than on the same territory in 1939;[41] put another way, during the autumn of 1946 for every 1000 males in the Soviet Zone there were 1346 females, a differential even greater than in the western occupation zones. The disproportion was particularly striking with regard to Germans in their twenties: in 1946 the number of women in the Soviet Zone between the ages of 20 and 29 was 126% higher than the number of men, and the number of women between 20 and 39 was 87% higher.[42] Thus the society in which order was to be established was a disproportionally female one, while those establishing order were almost entirely male.

5. *Integration.* Germans had little choice but to adapt to their new circumstances. The country's defeat was so overwhelming, the force displayed by the occupation armies was so massive and the possibilities for resisting the new order so small that most people had little alternative but to adapt to the new system that was emerging. This often meant seeking and finding employment in the new civil administrations that took shape during the late 1940s - and in many cases working directly for the Soviet Joint Stock Companies that had been set up in the Zone in

---

[40] Lutz Niethammer, 'Erfahrungen und Strukturen. Prolegomena zu einer Geschichte der Gesellschaft der DDR', in Hartmut Kaelble, Jürgen Kocka and Hartmut Zwahr (eds), *Sozialgeschichte der DDR* (Stuttgart, 1994), 100.

[41] See Günter Braun, 'Daten zur demographischen und sozialen Struktur der Bevölkerung', in Martin Broszat and Hermann Weber (eds), *SBZ Handbuch. Staatliche Verwaltungen, Parteien, gesellschaftliche Organisationen und ihre Führungskräfte in der Sowjetischen Besatzungszone Deutschlands 1945–1949* (Munich, 1990), 1070–1.

[42] In 1950 the number of women between 20 and 29 in the German Democratic Republic was 42% higher than the number of men of the same age, and the number of women between 30 and 39 was 61% greater than the number of men of the same age. See the tables in Wolfgang Zank, *Wirtschaft und Arbeit in Ostdeutschland 1945–1949. Probleme des Wiederaufbaus in der sowjetischen Besatzungszone Deutschlands* (Munich, 1987), 35.

order to extract reparations payments from the Germans. It meant joining political parties, which Germans did in their hundreds of thousands in the years immediately after the war.[43] It meant acceptance, perhaps willing, perhaps grudging, that the new circumstances were not temporary, that there was little one could do to change things, and that one therefore had to come to terms with the new order that was taking shape.

6. *Mobility:* For those unable or unwilling to integrate themselves into the new order or to accept the new circumstances in the Soviet Zone/German Democratic Republic, there was—at least until the East-West border finally was sealed completely in August 1961—the option of leaving for the West. This meant that many of those most hostile towards the changes taking place around them or most dissatisfied with their prospects for social and economic advancement left rather than remain and cause trouble. Thus the open border with the West, and the fact that Germans in the East had the right of abode in Western Germany, provided an escape valve for the disaffected. This was put in a nutshell by one particularly outspoken member of the Volkspolizei in Mecklenburg who in March 1951 bragged that 'it does not matter to me how many punishments are entered into my service record, since the more I have in it the more likely I am to be recognised in the west as politically persecuted if I go there'. (Soon after making this statement he deserted.)[44] In addition to the physical mobility available to the disaffected there was a consequent social, economic, and political mobility for those who stayed put. The fact that until the construction of the Berlin Wall millions of people left Eastern Germany created the prospect of rapid career advancement for many of those who stayed.[45]

---

[43] By the autumn of 1945, the Communist Party had a quarter of a million members in the Soviet Zone and the Social Democratic Party over 300,000. The Christian Democratic Union, which was licensed in the Soviet Zone on 10 July 1945, had roughly 190,000 members in the Zone by the end of 1946; and the Liberal Democratic Party saw its membership rise from roughly 90,000 in 1945 to 200,000 in 1948. See Klaus Schroeder, *Der SED-Staat. Partei, Staat und Gesellschaft 1949–1990* (Munich, 1998), 32.

[44] MLHA, LBdVP, Nr. 24, ff. 20–21: Landesbehörde der Volkspolizei Mecklenburg, Abteilung Personal, 'Gründe der Desertierungen in Altentreptow', Schwerin, 2 Apr. 1951.

[45] The opportunities for career advancement for those who remained in the GDR during the 1950s can be seen in the accounts published in Lutz Niethammer, Alexander von Plato and Dorothee Wierling, *Die volkseigene Erfahrung. Eine Archäologie des Lebens in der Industrieprovinz der DDR* (Berlin, 1991).

In conclusion, it would probably be mistaken to see the imposition of order in the Soviet Occupation Zone and early German Democratic Republic as a consequence in the first instance of the vast expansion of the German police. That expansion had other causes, as did the establishment of order in post-war Eastern Germany. This is not to say that the People's Police had no effect in this regard whatsoever. In an environment in which the apparatuses of the state grew enormously, in which the sources of much criminal behaviour in the conventional sense diminished, and in which an increasingly numerous police force became more effective in clearing up criminal cases, the presence of the Volkspolizei no doubt contributed to a post-war consolidation and a normalization of public life (albeit in very abnormal circumstances). However, the main causes of that normalization on the one hand, and the main focus of the activities of the Volkspolizei on the other, lay elsewhere.

In the event, this did not provide a foolproof or irreversible recipe for success, as the explosion in the GDR in June 1953 testifies. The 'People's Police' may have become rather effective at combatting ordinary crime and maintaining public order after the chaos of the immediate post-war years had diminished, but they failed completely to suppress the uprising in 1953.[46] Nevertheless, the combination of violence, fear, exhaustion, integration, and mobility in an overwhelmingly female society did provide a basis during the late 1940s for reestablishing order, however fragile, after the extreme disorder of 1945, and for regaining a monopoly of force by state organs after the Second World War. The order established in the Soviet Occupation Zone in the wake of the war may have had a fundamentally unstable basis, resting as it did not just on the exhaustion of the German population after the manic, failed mobilization of the Nazi years but also on the overwhelming force of the Soviet occupier and political repression. Nevertheless, it did provide a start to what proved a remarkable exit from the chaos left behind by Nazism and war.

---

[46] This can be seen clearly in the telex reports sent from around the GDR to the Hauptverwaltung der Deutschen Volkspolizei, in BAB, DO-I/11/44. See also Heidi Roth, *Der 17. Juni 1953 in Sachsen* (Cologne, 1999), 58. In many places police were disarmed by the demonstrators, and in some cases members of the police expressed solidarity with the strikers.

# At the Borders of Force: Violence, Refugees, and the Reconfiguration of the Yugoslav and Italian States

**Pamela Ballinger**

> The first task of the new authorities was to assert a monopoly of force, legitimacy and the institutions of justice ... If there were to be trials, they should take place under the rule of law. If there was to be bloodletting, then this was the exclusive affair of the state. This transition took place as soon as the new powers felt strong enough to disarm the erstwhile partisans, impose the authority of their own police and damp down popular demands for harsh penalties and collective punishment.[1]

In *Post war*, his account of Europe's emergence out of World War II and its reconstruction, Tony Judt nicely summarizes one of the greatest challenges faced by the leaders of European states and regimes at the immediate conclusion of the Second World War: how to re-establish the monopoly over (legitimate) violence after the breakdown of state authority? Judt highlights how the experience of occupation, whether by Nazi or Soviet armies, had encouraged a culture of violence and cynicism in which authority became 'a function of force alone, deployed without inhibition'. He adds, 'Curiously enough, it was precisely in these circumstances that the state *lost* its monopoly of violence'.[2] In this article, I examine such issues for the Yugoslav case, exploring how the Yugoslav state regained its monopoly on the legitimate use of violence after the confused situation of foreign occupation and civil war that shattered the first Yugoslav state and created multiple, competing agents of violence. Focusing on the situation in the Istrian peninsula between 1945 and 1954 and even more specifically on the precipitating factors resulting in the mass migration of approximately 200,000 individuals out of the area when it passed from Italian to Yugoslav control, I use this example as a window onto the broader dynamics of regime consolidation in Tito's socialist Yugoslavia. At the same time, analysis of Yugoslav efforts to control and

[1] Tony Judt, *Post war: A History of Europe since 1945* (New York, 2005), 44.

[2] Judt, *Post war*, 37.

monopolize violence can also benefit from a broader perspective on state power, as well as a comparative approach.[3] Examining how the fledgling post-war Italian state sought to establish control over violence after the fractures created by civil war in the north and dual occupations (by the Germans and the Allies), for example, can throw into relief some of the specificities of the Yugoslav case.

Indeed, Judt's comments on the 'curious' loss of control over violence by the German and Soviet occupiers also frequently held true in those zones controlled by the Western Allies, if we are to judge by accounts such as Norman Lewis' searing memoir of life in Naples under the Allies.[4] Italy was simultaneously victor and vanquished, an ambivalent position embodied by its status after September 1943 as 'co-belligerent' and the extent of the authority exercised by its pro-Allied government vis à vis its new allies often proved unclear. 'New' state authorities in both Italy and Yugoslavia not only confronted troublesome issues of how to bring former partisans and their fascist opponents to heel but also the larger imperative of securing borders around national territory, as well as redefining the communities of belonging within such territory. The nine-year Italo-Yugoslav territorial dispute (1945–1954) over where to redraw the political border between the two countries, for example, played an important role in the ideological legitimation of the respective regimes and illuminates many of the techniques employed by the new socialist authorities of Yugoslavia in attaining a monopoly on violence. Whether an intentional consequence or not of the Yugoslav authorities' efforts to consolidate their control over force, the refugee flows generated by this process created new challenges to public order in Yugoslavia and in the states to which they migrated, particularly Italy. Examining briefly the actions of the Yugoslav regime that produced refugees and the responses of the displaced themselves complicates our understanding of what 'regaining the monopoly of force' entailed along the contested Italo-Yugoslav border and, perhaps, in post-1945 Europe more generally.

### Reconfiguring states in practice and theory

The guiding question that informs this essay—that posed by Judt about how authorities claiming legitimacy as state actors curtailed other agents of violence in the immediate post-war period—may at first seem an obvious one that flows naturally out of the exigencies created by the confused situation at

---

[3] For an example of such a comparative exercise, see Norman Naimark and Leonid Gibianskii (eds), *The Establishment of Communist Regimes in Eastern Europe, 1944–1949*, (Boulder, 1997).

[4] Norman Lewis, *Naples '44* (New York, 1978).

war's end in 1945. The phrasing of the question and the renewed interest in the bases of state power after World War II, however, reflect broader debates about that reified abstraction known as 'the state' together with methodological challenges in analysing 'state effects' and the state *as* effect (and affect).[5] In my analysis here of the Istrian case, I take my theoretical cues from recent anthropological analyses of the state that focus on the agency (and agents) of power together with capacities. This perspective echoes that of scholars in other fields who have similarly redirected attention to power, seeking to go beyond restrictive realist understandings. Political scientists Barnett and Duvall, for example, conceptualize power as 'the production, in and through social relations, of effects that shape the capacities of actors to determine their circumstances and fate'.[6] In light of this, after more than a decade in which observers (too hastily) proclaimed that the state was 'losing control' and relevance in the era of globalization, some scholars struggling to capture the ethnographic complexities of states past and present have now focused on what they deem de facto sovereignty, 'the ability to kill, punish, and discipline with impunity wherever it [sovereignty] is found and practiced'.[7]

The current analytical retreat from a position that states are losing sovereignty in a globalizing world replicates, at least in some aspects, earlier debates about the nature of the post-1945 (West) European nation-state. In his well-known and controversial thesis, for example, Alan Milward argued that European integration actually facilitated the 'rescue' of the nation-state rather than its weakening.[8] Scholars of the contemporary state would do well to look more closely at transformations in European states after World War II in order to rethink their understandings of state power and capacities, just as debates about how to understand the present moment help us reframe our understandings of the decades immediately following World War II.

Within the discipline of anthropology, a refocusing of the analytical lens on key capacities of state power and on power's *verticality* reflects, in part, a growing frustration in the discipline with some of the limitations inherent in a Foucauldian view of power as diffused and weblike. At the same time, however, many anthropologists seeking to go 'beyond Foucault' have seized

---

[5] For a useful discussion, see Begoña Aretxaga, 'Maddening States,' *Annual Review of Anthropology* 32 (2003), 393–410 at 400.

[6] Michael Barnett and Raymond Duvall, 'Power in International Politics,' *International Organizations* 59 (2005), 39–75 at 42.

[7] Thomas Blom Hansen and Finn Steppuatt, 'Sovereignty Revisited,' *Annual Review of Anthropology* 35 (2006), 295–315 at 296.

[8] Alan S. Milward, *The European Rescue of the Nation-State* (Berkeley, 1992), 44–5.

upon the writings of philosopher Giorgio Agamben, whose concept of 'bare life' remains indebted in key ways to Foucault, as well as to Hannah Arendt. It is the experience of the camp and the refugee that haunts the work of both Arendt and Agamben, the empirical realities of World War II and its aftermath serving as the philosophical and ontological foundations of a model of sovereign power in the West.[9] In Agamben's formulation, 'bare life' exists as something other than mere natural or biological life; rather, bare life is life stripped of basic humanity, reduced to the biological condition. The product of a political exclusion, bare life becomes literally embodied by the bodies of individuals on the borders between life and death such as refugees and 'neomorts' (or 'living cadavers').[10] Agamben's ideas have proven productive for scholars examining the effects of power on the body. As Hansen and Stepputat put it, 'the body is always the site of performance of sovereign power, which becomes most visible in states of war, extreme conditions, fragmentation, and marginality'.[11]

Anthropologist Katherine Verdery's ethnographic studies of the socialist state offer one model for how scholars might empirically (and productively) focus on the body as the site of sovereign power. Adapting a term from Romanian writer Norman Manea [*etatizare* (literally, 'the process of statizing')],[12] Verdery writes of the efforts of the Ceausescu regime to seize control of time and people's use of it. 'To "mark time" in a particular way', she contends, 'is to propose a particular use or deployment of bodies that subtracts them from other possible uses. Alternative deployments of bodies in time reveal for us the seizure of time by power'.[13] Although Verdery's analysis does not explicitly draw on Agamben,[14] it does reflect the growing sophistication of anthropologists and others trying to pin down the ethnographic realities of state power—particularly the lived realities of power under state socialism. In her analysis of communist rule in Romania, Verdery uses a Gramscian frame that examines the relative weight of consent and coercion and the role of each in the regime's deployment of bodies and individuals' resistance to this 'etatization'. This enables Verdery to focus on the attempts

---

[9] On this point for Arendt, see Aristide R. Zolberg, 'The Formation of New States as a Refugee-Generating Process,' *Annals of the American Society of Political and Social Science* 467 (1983), 27–8.

[10] Giorgio Agamben, *Homo Sacer: Sovereign Power and Bare Life*, (Stanford, 1998).

[11] Hansen and Stepputat, 'Sovereignty Revisited', 297.

[12] Katherine Verdery, *What was Socialism and What Comes Next?* (Princeton, 1996), 40.

[13] Verdery, *What was Socialism and What Comes Next?*, 40.

[14] Agamben's *Homo Sacer* first appeared in its original Italian in 1995. An English translation of Agamben's influential work came out in 1998.

of both state actors and citizens to 'shape the capacities' that 'determine their circumstances and fate'[15] in the negotiation of sovereignty on the ground.

A focus on vulnerable bodies in Istria between 1945 and 1954 offers a productive perspective on not only the practices of power deployed by the new socialist authorities in Yugoslavia but also their effects as lived experience. These techniques included not only forms of outright intimidation and coercion but also more subtle assertions of power, including seizures of individuals' time. How to interpret the role played by violence of various types lies at the heart of historical debates surrounding the Istrian exodus.

### Gaining the monopoly of force in Yugoslavia

What is essential in Communism, regardless of its national base, is power. Power builds a new Communist society. In the actions and aspirations of every authentic Communist leader there is constant drive. A Communist leader, particularly a dictator, is shaped in the long and harsh national struggle . . . The concrete and the possible, clarity and simplicity—Tito recognized in those qualities means of power, I would even say pure power. On balance, he was less attracted to, or sustained by, the kind of power that subjugates all to itself, that meddles in everything, than he was to the power of the Party, the secret police, and the army.[16]

Although Yugoslavia enjoyed a reputation in the 1960s and 1970s for offering a 'Third Way' that combined limited market practices and relative freedoms (such as freedom to travel abroad) with 'unique' socialist principles (such as workers' self-management), the state born out of the partisan war was modelled on the Soviet Union and Stalinist principles. In November 1943, the Anti-Fascist Liberation Movement for Yugoslavia (AVNOJ) declared the creation of a new, provisional state, to be organized as a federation and headed by Marshal Josip Broz ('Tito'). Despite this confident move, at this point the outcome of the war in Yugoslavia was in no way assured. Although the British had given their exclusive military support to the communists directed by Tito (after initially providing aid and support to both the communists and the Serbian royalists headed by Draža Mihailović), there remained a welter of armed groups claiming authority, among them Mihailović's Chetniks, the Croatian Ustaša, and Slovene domobranci (home guards). As the defeat of the

---

[15] Barnett and Duvall, 'Power in International Politics', 42.

[16] Milovan Djilas, *Tito: The Story from Inside*, trans. Vasilije Kojić and Richard Hayes (New York, 1980), 59, 68.

Germans became imminent in 1944 and 1945, disarming and, in many cases, physically liquidating these domestic rivals assumed priority.[17]

For the Yugoslav situation, then, it proves more accurate to speak of *gaining* the monopoly on force, since the language of *regaining* suggests a kind of continuity of state forms and capacity that does not hold. Furthermore, Royal Yugoslavia never exercised sovereignty over the areas of Juliskja Krajina or Venezia Giulia that came under Yugoslav control after World War II; thus, in the most literal sense, the new socialist regime had to gain the monopoly over force in that territory. Although the image of a new regime struggling to gain the monopoly over violence also characterizes neighbouring Italy, in Yugoslavia the transformation of state was much more radical. Relatively few vestiges of royal Yugoslavia survived the transition to Tito's version of state socialism. The Italian transition from fascist dictatorship to democratic republic likewise implied dramatic shifts but nonetheless more bureaucratic structures, legislation, and personnel remained in place than in Yugoslavia.

In both Italy and Yugoslavia, the new governments that emerged after 1943 confronted the challenge of how to deal with collaborators and pro-fascist elements after the war's conclusion. In Italy, however, attempts at 'popular justice' or the 'justice of the piazza' largely occurred outside the framework of governmental control. As the war concluded, a wave of retribution killings occurred in northern and central Italy. Notes Domenico, 'How random or organized was this popular justice remains debatable'.[18] In some instances, particularly in the final months of the war, resistance organizations in the north established 'insurrectional tribunals' or popular tribunals to try fascists. In other cases, blackshirts (or presumed fascists or collaborators) were summarily executed without even the pretence of a trial.[19]

These killings posed direct challenges to the ability of the Italian government and the Anglo-American military commanders to contain and control violence. Together, the Anglo-Americans and the Italian leaders in Rome sought to bring fascists to justice by means such as special legal tribunals (Extraordinary Assize Courts), purges of the factories, and epuration proceedings, a process that sparked a fierce debate in Italy's legal community about the form sanctions should take.[20] By contrast, in Yugoslavia it was the new authorities who used such retributive killings as a means for instating their power. The communist authorities brooked no criticism of their

---

[17] John Lampe, *Yugoslavia as History: Twice there was a Country* (Cambridge, 2000), 228.

[18] Roy Palmer Domenico, *Italian Fascists on Trial, 1943–1948* (Chapel Hill, 1991), 141.

[19] Ibid., 146–9.

[20] Ibid., 168–84.

methods nor did a serious nationwide debate ever take place about how to come to terms with the war's losers.

Historian John Lampe has argued that executions of political rivals in Yugoslavia proved instrumental to the new regime in several ways, not only eliminating potential opposition (particularly armed opposition) but also providing ideological justification for the expansion of the state security apparatus (the Organization for People's Defence or OZNA). In consolidating power, the Yugoslav communists 'adopted a ruthlessly Stalinist and centralizing set of tactics . . . Even then, such tactics might not have succeeded but for the justification that settling wartime accounts and repairing wartime devastation provided'.[21] Among those targeted for expulsion or death were Yugoslavia's Germans (many of whom fled as the defeat of Germany became inevitable), Chetniks, White Russians, Croatian Ustasa, and Slovene domobranci. These retributions proved among the harshest meted out at war's end among the new socialist states of Eastern Europe.[22]

While such acts of retribution diminished the possibility of serious armed challenges to the new Yugoslav authorities, they likely also helped consolidate the authority of the command within the partisan ranks. Yugoslav Vice President turned dissident Milovan Djilas claims that in August 1944 the communists actually had extended an olive branch to various domestic opponents. Though it is not clear how sincere the invitation was,[23] the communists invited their enemies at home 'to join us by September 15, with the guarantee that their collaboration with the occupation would be forgiven'.[24] Some among the partisans, suggests Djilas, might have challenged this policy of amnesty, had any of the collaborators taken them up on it. As Djilas contended, 'the flame of revolution still blazed, and people were still waging a war of survival and vision. *The revolution could not be anyone's monopoly,* [Author's italics] for there were still plenty of revolutionaries who were truly and totally revolutionary, who pondered every turn of events with their own minds. They were the ones who asked themselves and their friends: how can our soldiers take in those who killed and tortured their comrades?'[25] Indulging the desire for vengeance thus probably consolidated the communist leadership's position among its own faithful. This use of large-scale

---

[21] Lampe, *Yugoslavia as History*, 226.

[22] Ivo Banac, *With Stalin against Tito: Cominformist Splits in Yugoslav Communism* (Ithaca, 1989), 19.

[23] Djilas, *Tito*, 404.

[24] Ibid., 403.

[25] Ibid.

retributive violence helped the communist leadership make a more exclusive claim (even a monopoly) on the revolution.

In considering this monopoly on the revolution and revolutionary force, Ivo Banac has stressed the similarity between the early socialist state in Yugoslavia and that of Stalin's Soviet Union. Socialist Yugoslavia's first constitution, for instance, was modelled on the USSR's 1936 constitution. The initial five-year plan adopted focused on industrialization and laid out plans for collectivized agriculture (later abandoned).[26] After the 1948 split with the USSR and Yugoslavia's expulsion from the Cominform, the Yugoslav regime ruthlessly sought out real and imagined enemies within the country, engaging in what Banac deems 'Stalinist anti-Stalinism'.[27] Thousands of *ibeovci* or 'Cominformists', accused of siding with Stalin against Tito, ended up in prison camps. The most notorious of these camps, Goli Otok (variously translated as the 'Naked Isle' or the 'Marble Isle'), employed physically and psychologically crushing techniques to break prisoners' spirits and aid in their political 'reeducation'.[28] Eighty-seven Italian communists from Venezia Giulia who had fought with their Slavic brothers to defeat fascism but then sided with Stalin (or so the charge ran) numbered among the prisoners at Goli Otok.[29]

While disarming any potential opposition (and indeed, the threat posed by *ibeovci* was not merely a phantasm), the assault on Cominformists also underwrote the regime's ideological legitimacy by rallying Yugoslavs against the Soviet threat. In the Yugoslav case, then, the functions of coercion and consent remained tightly bound up together, particularly in the first two decades of the state's existence. The partisan war provided the 'charter myth' for the first generations of Yugoslavs,[30] thereby buttressing the legitimacy of the Yugoslav military and justifying the attacks on enemies carried

[26] Banac, *With Stalin against Tito*, 17, 19–22. See also Melissa Bokovoy, 'Peasants and Partisans: A Dubious Alliance,' in Naimark and Gibianskii (eds), *The Establishment of Communist Regimes in Eastern Europe, 1944–1949*, 167–190.

[27] Banac, *With Stalin against Tito*, 244. Banac estimates that up to one-fifth of the Yugoslav party membership supported Stalin over Tito.

[28] Venko Markovski, *Goli Otok. The Island of Death. A Diary in Letters* (Boulder, 1984); Oskar Gruenwald, 'Yugoslav Camp Literature: Rediscovering the Ghost of a Nation's Past-Present-Future,' *Slavic Review* 46:3 (1987), 513–28.

[29] These included both natives of the areas of Venezia Giulia ceded to Yugoslavia and Italian communists from Monfalcone invited to replace (in what became known as the 'counter exodus') Italian workers migrating out of Yugoslavia. Mila Orlic, 'Poteri popolari e migrazioni forzate in Istria,' in Guido Crainz, Raoul Pupo and Silvia Salvatici (eds), *Naufraghi della Pace: Il 1945, I profughi e le memorie divise d'Europe*, (Roma, 2008), 38–9.

[30] Lampe, *Yugoslavia as History*, 236.

out by military and the secret police and, in turn, enabling the further expansion of the security apparatus.

In early post-war Yugoslavia, efforts to establish a monopoly over the use of (legitimate) violence brought about bloodshed and population movements (regardless of whether the latter was intentional or not). These actions would also leave a legacy of bitterness that helped fuel the rise of nationalist movements after Tito's death in 1980. The question remains, however, to what degree events in the Istrian peninsula and the broader territory claimed by both Yugoslavia and Italy mirrored these broader processes, as well as how populations in Istria experienced the Yugoslav authorities' efforts to consolidate power.

## The view from the Julian March

Between 1943 and 1945, Italian fascist and German Nazi forces (both regular military units and local militias) struggled to retain control over the area I call the Julian March, that is, the former Italian region of Venezia Giulia that included the cities of Trieste and Gorizia, as well as the Istrian peninsula. Challenging them were left-wing anti-fascist partisans of various stripes (Italian and Slovene communists owing specific loyalties to various underground communist parties but united by the international fight against fascism), the Yugoslav military (IX Corpus of the IV Yugoslav Army), non-communist partisans (including members of Catholic Action), and—in the last days of April and early May 1945—the Allied forces of New Zealand, Britain, and the US.

The confused situation at the end of April and the beginning of May 1945 as Yugoslav forces rushed to enter Trieste before the Western Allied troops (with whom, of course, they were allies) and the declaration of an uprising by the local anti-fascist Committee for National Liberation (CLN) meant that no one party could have claimed to have 'liberated' the city from the Germans nor did any one group hold the monopoly on force. During the forty days of Yugoslav military presence in the city of Trieste, both regular troops and local partisan bands enacted summary justice by executing military personnel and civilians in the *foibe*, grottoes or pits in the karstic terrain above the city. British and American interviewers at the time determined that the 'hunt for fascists' (*caccia ai fascisti*) had led to summary trials and executions, as well as deportations to Yugoslavia.[31] Rumours circulated that OZNA was seizing individuals and spiriting them off to Ljubljana.[32]

---

[31] Glenda Sluga, *The Problem of Trieste and the Italo-Yugoslav Border: Difference, Identity, and Sovereignty in Twentieth-Century Europe* (Albany, 2001), 90.

[32] Sluga, *The Problem of Trieste and the Italo-Yugoslav Border*, 90.

Similar episodes of violence occurred in Istria after the Italian army's capitulation in September 1943 and again at war's end. The work of historians like Giampaolo Valdevit and Raoul Pupo has demonstrated that in contrast to the more spontaneous outbursts of *foibe* violence in 1943, the 1945 killings proved much more organized and were orchestrated by both regular and irregular military forces. This violence proved part of an effort to eliminate potential rivals for power rather than efforts at 'popular justice' so common to other parts of Italy. According to Pupo, the Yugoslavs aimed at a 'preventive epuration' (*epurazione preventativa*) to disarm its opposition; for this reason, CLN activists were targeted much more than officials of the RSI (the fascist state established at Salò after the armistice in the south in September 1943), who had already lost legitimacy.[33]

The violence of the *foibe* in Istria and Trieste in 1945 thus represented a programmatic effort to eliminate all that represented the Italian state. The apparent indiscriminateness of such violence and deportations, claims Valdevit, was designed to send a chilling message to the Italians of Venezia Giulia that they must assume a subaltern position in the projected 'Seventh Republic' of Yugoslavia.[34] Here, fear rested on not only the summary deportation or execution of vulnerable bodies but also the particularly grisly manner in which individuals met their deaths, frequently having their hands bound with barbed wire and being shot or pushed alive into the deep karstic abysses. Those who survived the fall would die an agonizing death, surrounded by the corpses of other victims.[35]

In spite of the fear created in the populace by both these killings and the rumours that spread about them, the Yugoslav military ultimately failed to consolidate its power in Trieste as a result of the larger geopolitical dynamics within which the 'crisis' unfolded. Yielding to Anglo-American and Soviet pressure, Yugoslav forces withdrew from the city on 12 June 1945. The disputed territory was then divided into a Zone A (including Trieste and the Istrian city of Pula/Pola) administered by an Anglo-American Allied Military Government (AMG) and a Zone B under the control of Yugoslav military authorities. This arrangement was intended to be temporary until Italy and Yugoslavia could reach an agreement over the territory. Ultimately, the territorial contest over Zones A and B proved as much a propaganda war as

---

[33] Raoul Pupo, 'Violenza politica tra guerra e dopoguerra: il caso delle *foibe* giuliane, 1943–1945,' in *Foibe: Il Peso del Passato*, ed. Giampaolo Valdevit (Venice, 1997), 47–8.

[34] Giampaolo Valdevit, 'Foibe: l'eredità della sconfitta,' in Giampaolo Valdevit (ed.), *Foibe: Il peso del passato*, (Venice, 1997).

[35] For details, see Roberto Spazzali, *Foibe: un dibattito ancora aperto* (Trieste, 1990).

a military confrontation, underscoring the issues of ideological force at play here. The audiences for this propaganda included both the international community and the populations resident in the region, whose bodies were mobilized by proponents on both sides in numerous rallies and protests in favour of annexation to either Italy or Yugoslavia. In contrast to the AMG, which saw itself largely as a placeholder (particularly after the 1948 Cominform split made clear that Trieste would not come within the Soviet orbit), the Yugoslavs treated their administration of Zone B as a prelude to permanent rule, seeking to establish their hegemony by means of both coercion and consent.

After the 1947 Peace Treaty with Italy definitively awarded to Yugoslavia southern Istria (including Pula/Pola), Zones A and B were redrawn.[36] As the Yugoslavs consolidated control over the areas of Istria now incorporated into the Yugoslav state, large-scale migrations out of the area took place. In contrast to earlier movements, these were largely organized, as individuals who 'opted' for Italian citizenship by the Treaty's terms (Article 19) were required to move to Italy. The subsequent 1954 Memorandum of Understanding that gave the cities of Trieste and Gorizia to Italy and the remainder of Istria to Yugoslavia likewise prompted large-scale migrations from the former Zone B. In total, an estimated 220,000 individuals left the original Zone B and the cities of Pula/Pola, Rijeka/Fiume, Zadar/Zara, many (though not all) of them coming to Trieste either in transit or as a site for resettlement.

As a result of political transformations in Italy and (the former) Yugoslavia in the 1990s, this mass migration from the Istrian peninsula between 1943 and 1955 has re-emerged into public and scholarly consciousness in Italy, Slovenia, Croatia, and beyond. Italian commentators on the 'Istrian exodus' have tended to focus on the more spectacular forms of violence that accompanied the installation of Yugoslav authority in that territory (which had officially become part of Italy as a result of the 1920 Treaty of Rapallo)—in particular the violence of the *foibe*. Finding persuasive the claims of former refugees to have suffered an ethnic cleansing in Yugoslavia *avant la lettre*, some Italian scholars and journalists have interpreted the mass migration as

---

[36] According to the Peace Treaty, the city of Trieste and its surroundings would become an international territory (the Free Territory of Trieste or FTT) under the protection of United Nations. The Great Powers (and in particular the US and the USSR), however, could not agree upon a candidate for governor and thus the FTT existed as an idea more than a reality. Allied Military Government continued in the city until the settlement of the territorial question in 1954.

the consequence of a concerted campaign to ethnically cleanse Istria of its Italian population.[37]

In work I have done elsewhere,[38] I have tried to challenge this simplistic reading, which flattens out the complexities of both the regime's actions and the issue of who left Istria (as well as who remained) after World War II and why. A number of Italian historians have similarly subjected the 'ethnic cleansing' thesis to critical scrutiny. Pupo has conducted perhaps the most extensive empirical examinations of this interpretation, rejecting the notion of an organized plan to rid Istria of its Italians.[39] Pupo contends that many observers have misunderstood the nature of the Yugoslav targeting of individuals in the Julian March after the war, failing to distinguish between the authorities' persecution of those who identified as Italian in *political* rather than cultural or ethnic terms. The real target of the communists were 'people who wanted (favoured) Italy (coloro che volevano l'Italia)' that is, so-called 'reactionaries', not Italians per se.[40] Orlic seconds this interpretation, stating forcefully that at no level of authority (from the local up to the federal) does one find evidence of a plan to cleanse Istria of Italians. Rather, there existed a determined effort to root out those labelled as 'enemies of the people',[41] a policy that hit Italians in Istria in a disproportionate manner.

In Istria, ethno-national identity tended to coincide with economic class and political power, a pattern that dated back to the Venetian period in which elites speaking Italian dialects dominated. Although the Habsburg era witnessed the growth of a Slovene and Croatian rural bourgeoisie centred in towns like Kastav/Castua, Pazin/Pisino, and the Kvarner Islands, this nascent Slavic middle class was subjected to intense assimilation pressures during the period of fascist control over Istria.[42] Many of these Slovene and Croat elites

---

[37] For a few examples, see Lampe, *Yugoslavia as History*, 232; Arrigo Petacco, *L'esodo: la tragedia negata degli italiani d'Istria, Dalmazia e Venezia Giulia* (Milan, 1999); Gianni Oliva, *Foibe* (Milan, 2003); Guido Rumici, *Fratelli d'Istria*, 1945–2000 (Venice, 2001), Guido Rumici, *Infoibati* (Venice, 2002).

[38] Pamela Ballinger, *History in Exile: Memory and Identity at the Borders of the Balkans* (Princeton, 2003); Pamela Ballinger, 'Cleansed of Experience? Genocide, Ethnic Cleansing, and the Challenges of Anthropological Representation,' in Alex Hinton and Kevin O'Neill (eds), *Genocide: Truth, Memory, and Representation* (Durham, 2009).

[39] Raoul Pupo, 'Gli esodi nell'Adriatico orientale: Problemi interpretative,' in Guido Crainz, Raoul Pupo, and Silvia Salvatici *Naufraghi della Pace: Il 1945, I profughi e le memorie divise d'Europe* (Roma, 2008), 14.

[40] Raoul Pupo and Roberto Spazzali, *Foibe* (Milan, 2003), 113.

[41] Orlic, 'Poteri popolari e migrazioni forzate in Istria,' 29–31.

[42] Egidio Ivetić, 'On Croatian Nation-Building in Istria (1900–1914),' *JGKS [Jahrbücher für Geschichte und kultur Südosteuropas]* 8, 61–71 at 65.

immigrated to neighbouring Yugoslavia. As a result, a significant percentage (though certainly not all) of the class enemies targeted by the socialist regime were identified as 'Italians' or seen as connected with an Italian political class and project. Even Italians with solid anti-fascist credentials sometimes became the objects of persecution, suggesting that in Istria as in other parts of Yugoslavia the new socialist authorities sought to neutralize any potential political rivals.[43]

The approximately 800 surviving statements of refugees from Zone B collected by the Comitato di Liberazione Nazionale dell'Istria (CLN) between 1948 and 1954 document clearly how many individuals there perceived the imposition of a socialist system as particularly hostile to Italians. Individuals reported the expropriation of their houses, for example, on the pretext of providing lodging for needy families.[44] This policy obviously impacted most on those with desirable lodgings and concentrated in cities and towns, that is, the politically and economically dominant class, rather than landless peasants. Likewise, teachers in Italian language schools appear to have come under particular pressure,[45] as did clergy identified as Italian.[46] In addition, the economic hardship caused by the creation of a special border currency, the Jugolira, devastated the savings of many wealthier Istrians and disadvantaged those residents of Zone B who worked in Zone A.[47] The authorities in Zone B required such workers to convert a part of their salary into Jugolire. The authorities also created numerous physical impediments to those commuting to Zone A for work, periodically closing the border or blocking maritime traffic.[48]

The statement given to the CLN in September 1949 by Anna* (pseud.), a woman living near Izola/Isola in Zone B, indicates how the pressures created

---

[43] On this, see Antonio Budicin, *Nemico del Popolo* (Trieste, 1995).

[44] See for example, Dichiarazioni Politiche (DPs) no. 122, 273, 628 and 629 on deposit at the Istituto Regionale per la Cultura Istriana (IRCI) (Trieste). For the decree regarding lodging, see DP 216, IRCI (Trieste).

[45] Consult, for instance, DPs 274, 280, 889 and 890, IRCI (Trieste).

[46] On this, see Orlic, 'Poteri popolari e migrazioni forzate in Istria,' 31–4. Alexander offers a detailed discussion on the complex relationship between the socialist regime in Yugoslavia and religious authorities. In Istria, ethno-national divisions within the Catholic clergy rendered the situation perhaps even more complicated. For details, consult Stella Alexander, *Church and State in Yugoslavia since 1945* (Cambridge, 1979), 133–6.

[47] On the issuing of the Jugolira, see DP 220, IRCI (Trieste).

[48] Pamela Ballinger, 'La frantumazione dello spazio adriatico,' in Emilio Cocco and Everardo Minardi (eds), *Immaginare l'Adriatico* (Milan, 2007).

by such actions could converge and reinforce one another, prompting affected individuals to depart the territory:

> My husband is a sailor by profession and has never worked in the Yugoslav Zone of the Free Territory of Trieste [i.e. Zone B] where, however, he has always maintained his residence. On the 5th of August 1949 I received a written communication from the Housing Section of the Citizen People's Committee of Isola stating that I had to vacate my apartment within 24 hours for the following reason: 'This order follows as a result of the non-payment of contributions [i.e. taxes on the salary from Zone A].'
>
> I declared that I had not been allotted other housing and that I wasn't permitted any recourse. Called before the People's Committee to ask for clarification, I was told that I should make a request to immigrate to Trieste.
>
> In regards to the 'non-payment of contributions' I stated that I had never received any notification in regards to the ordinance of the People's District Committee of Capodistria concerning the obligation for those working in Zone A to convert partially their salaries . . . On the 12th of September 1949 I left for Trieste together with my three children.

Whether this woman exercised a 'choice' in going to Trieste, given that she was ordered to migrate after non-payment and threatened expropriation of her lodgings raises the question of constraint and agency in post-war Istria.

With its claim that Italians were targeted indiscriminately on the basis of their ethno-national identity and thus had little choice but to leave, the ethnic cleansing thesis erases the agency of individuals like Anna. Acknowledging that some elements of choice existed, however, should not lead us instead to classify the Istrian exodus as a voluntary migration, thereby risking a simplification as problematic as that of the ethnic cleansing explanation. Perhaps the very question of whether what occurred in Istria qualifies as ethnic cleansing or not is a scholarly dead end. As Orlic suggests, 'Instead of continuing to ask ourselves: was the exodus ethnic cleansing or a spontaneous phenomenon, we can try to understand what were the problems that the self-proclaimed People's Authority had to confront with the establishment and consolidation of power in the territory of the former Venezia Giulia'.[49]

---

[49] Orlic, 'Poteri popolari e migrazioni forzate in Istria', 27.

Orlic underlines the complex nature of efforts by the new rulers of Istria to incorporate into the Yugoslav state its Italian populations, including those who supported the anti-fascist struggle. She thus locates in the process of establishing a socialist state a range of causal factors motivating the Istrian exodus, as well as shaping the forms and directions it took.

In consolidating their hold over force, authorities waged these struggles through and on vulnerable bodies, at times aiming to mobilize bodies in labour and at other points seeking to halt or even immobilize bodies seeking flight. The sometimes contradictory nature of these struggles emerges quite clearly in the responses of Yugoslav authorities to the citizenship option laid out in the 1947 Peace Treaty with Italy that ceded southern Istria to Yugoslavia. A prerequisite for opting for Italian citizenship was Italian as language of customary use (*lingua d'uso*); the Treaty obligated successful optants to move from the ceded territory to Italy. At first glance, the re-opening of the option process in 1952 to accommodate unmet demands to migrate suggests that the socialist authorities used this as a means to rid themselves of restive local populations who might challenge their authority. In reality, however, local People's Committees overseeing the option process from the Yugoslav side frequently *rejected* requests to opt on the grounds that the applicants were not 'genuine' Italians as judged either by linguistic usage or their ethnic surnames. This reflected the regime's pressing need for skilled labour and the desire to prevent the departure of such workers (who tended to identify as Italian) en masse.

In April 1948, for example, Giancarlo* from Oprtalj/Portole complained to the CLN that the Yugoslav authorities were not honouring the terms of the Peace Treaty. He asserted:

> The operation of the option process at Portole is in open contra-diction with the Peace Treaty in that citizens whose language of customary use is Italian but whose surnames are of Slavic origin are not permitted to exercise their right to opt. Such is the case of my cousin, doctor S.D., whose language of customary use is Italian but who cannot exercise his right to opt because he is considered a Croatian citizen.
>
> In this way, many young people whose language of use is Italian but who have not been granted their options have been called to arms and sent to Susak, to Dalmatia and Serbia, as letters from their family members reveal. Having been accused of disseminating propaganda encouraging young people not to present themselves when called up by the military and of carrying out espionage for the

Italian military, I was sure to be arrested. Thus I fled clandestinely from Portole on the 4th of April 1948 and took refuge in Trieste.[50]

Here, an individual resisted the attempt to mobilize his body (in the truest sense of the term, military mobilization) and instead turned his body into an instrument of flight.

For the period between the first and second options (1948 and 1952), the CLN documents evidence the regime's diverse efforts to mobilize bodies for the purposes of both politics and labour. Statements taken in 1950, for example, reveal individuals resisting efforts to be conscripted into 'voluntary' labour brigades. Betta*, a woman who migrated from the island of Susak/Sansego recounted,

> On Monday October 16, 1950, fifty or so young people . . . who were doing premilitary service and who were stationed in the elementary school [at Sansego] were taken to Fiume for so-called voluntary labour . . .

> I can attest that at Sansego scores of people have been taken by force to Fiume for work . . . In raising these brigades, the communists and police went around and everyone was afraid. Some people tried to flee and to hide but in general people were terrified because last year two sailors from Sansego were killed.[51]

Individuals testified to similar actions occurring on the nearby island of Lošinj/Lussino, many of whose residents were forced to go to work in Rijeka/Fiume, along the railway line of Lupogliano-Stallie, and in the mine at Raša/Arsia.[52] Some Istrians resisted this mobilization of their bodies by hiding (when possible) or fleeing. Called up on Palm Sunday, for example, 37-year-old Vittorio* from Buje/Buie refused to go on religious grounds; the intervention of an uncle with the authorities spared him that day, though he was not so fortunate a few days later.[53]

Precisely because they recount incidents that usually ended in flight, the CLN documents illustrate some of the most dramatic situations in which the authorities employed heavy-handed tactics. Yet even in examples like those of the labour brigades where coercion sometimes proved quite explicit,

---

[50] DP 113, IRCI (Trieste).

[51] DP 600, IRCI (Trieste).

[52] DP 601, 603, 611, IRCI (Trieste).

[53] DP 111, IRCI (Trieste). For similar cases, consult DP 603, IRCI (Trieste), DP 610, IRCI (Trieste), and DP 598, IRCI (Trieste).

elements of consent are not absent. In the Yugoslav case, questions of coercion and consent remain tightly bound up together. Some of my informants who remained in Istria and participated in communist youth activities, for example, instead recalled their spontaneous participation in such brigades, which were intended to rebuild a new, socialist society founded on brotherhood and equality. Thus while it would be easy to read the brigades or elections as merely examples of coercion, it is more productive to think of them in Verdery's terms: examples of etatization that seek to direct bodies to certain ends and divert them from others. Employing individuals on work brigades is not only about demonstrating the state's power to do things (move bodies, build railways, and so on) but also its ability to prevent those bodies from doing other things by monopolizing their time. In her research on Romania, Verdery notes how individuals alternately acquiesced and struggled to resist these top-down deployments of their bodies and time. Such a viewpoint restores agency to the individuals subjected to state power, focusing attention on the capacities of state actors in tandem with the capacities of state subjects.

Even as the Yugoslav authorities used the threat of force both implicitly and explicitly to establish rule over Istria and integrate it into a Yugoslav polity, then, individuals on the ground engaged their bodies in response to these measures. The Istrian case highlights the need to problematize more profoundly the issue of force and 'bodily politics' instead of relying upon a false dichotomy of voluntary/forced migration (or ethnic cleansing)[54] that rests, in turn, on an overly simplified model of power. A theoretical perspective that focuses on the many faces of power—coercion and consent together with the agency of those responding to efforts to inscribe sovereignty onto bodies— may help us go beyond the conceptual impasses that have plagued studies of the Istrian exodus, as well as debates about violence and displacement more generally. Likewise, an empirically comparative approach may prove productive in rethinking how states (re-)established the monopoly over force in the aftermath of World War II.

## Concluding thoughts

Efforts by the Yugoslav state to establish a monopoly over the use of force in Istria reflect and refract the larger processes by which power was consolidated in Yugoslavia after 1945. The historical specificities of class and political position in the Istrian peninsula meant that those targeted as enemies of the people often were identified (through either self-ascription or external

---

[54] For a thoughtful analysis of the problems created by the forced migration paradigm, see Rogers Brubaker, 'Migrations of Ethnic Unmixing in the "New Europe"', *International Migration Review* 32:4 (1998): 1049.

ascription) with the former ethno-national majority: Italians. Although scholars like Pupo have refuted the notion that the Istrian exodus is a *sui generis* event, they have nonetheless insisted on the difference between the migrations from Istria and the contemporaneous expulsions of Germans that took place in other parts of Eastern Europe.[55] While the Istrian case lacks the systematicity or clear intent that characterizes the German case, I would nonetheless venture to suggest that there exist many instructive parallels with other population movements out of states characterized by nascent socialist regimes. Even in the case of the Germans, we find interesting exceptions like the Masurians, German-speaking Poles who the Polish government sought to retain within its borders even as it pushed out other individuals identified as German. Just how exceptional were the Masurians?[56] Might a new picture of the German expulsion or other post-war displacements emerge if we reconceptualize the issue of force in forced migration? What might this tell us about post-war reconstruction and the monopoly over force more generally?

Likewise, if we focus on one of the most visible consequences of the Yugoslav efforts to consolidate power in Istria—large-scale population movements—how might this shift our understanding of state capacities in not only Yugoslavia but also Italy during the early post-war period? The presence of Allied Military Government in Trieste from 1945–1954 underscores the ways in which key aspects of Italian sovereignty were constrained by Italy's ambiguous position as defeated power, co-belligerent, and emerging Cold War bulwark. The terms of the 1947 Peace Treaty were largely dictated by the Great Powers, as was the 1954 settlement of the Italo-Yugoslav dispute. Events along that border and beyond created flows of refugees from Istria and Central and Eastern Europe more broadly that threatened to overwhelm the economically devastated and politically fragile post-fascist republic of Italy. Although the operation of international bodies like the United Nations Relief and Rehabilitation Administration and the International Refugee Organization is a story for another day, it points to the important role in early post-war Italy played by inter-governmental organizations. What does it mean to gain the monopoly on force, then, when a state does not even fully control the movement of peoples in and out of its

---

[55] Pupo, 'Gli esodi nell'Adriatico orientale: Problemi interpretative,' 14.

[56] R. Blanke, 'Polish-speaking Germans and the Ethnic Cleansing of Germany East of Oder-Neisse,' in Béla Várdy, S., T. Hunt Tooley, and Huszár Várdy (eds), *Ethnic Cleansing in Twentieth-Century Europe*, (Boulder, 2003); J. J. Kulczycki, 'Who is a Pole? Polish Nationality Criteria in the "Recovered Lands", 1945–1951,' *Canadian Review of Studies in Nationalism* XXVIII (2001), 107–118.

territory? Anthropologists and historians attuned to both the high politics that produce refugee flows and the choices of individuals on the ground about migration are particularly well positioned to answer these questions about de facto sovereignty, as bodies become the sites at which power is performed and negotiated by states, agencies, and individuals.

# Regaining the Monopoly of Force: Agents of the State Shooting Fugitives in and around Belgium, 1940–1950

## Pieter Lagrou

World War II is widely seen as having eroded the relatively well-established principle that force in modern nation-states can only legitimately be used by the agents of those states.[1] First of all, the years 1943–48 in particular arguably witnessed a legitimacy crisis, caused by the competing claims of the occupier and the post-war government, and, especially, by the development of forms of 'private' violence claiming legitimacy, such as the paramilitary forces of the collaboration and the resistance. Post-war governments faced an arbitration problem. On the one hand, there was the formal legitimacy of police forces and judiciary, be they national or belonging to the occupation forces, in their repression of resistance activities for the sake of the maintenance of public order and safety. On the other there was the claimed legitimacy of resistance actions, for instance when attacking and looting postal offices to feed individuals sought by the occupation forces or when eliminating denouncers and infiltrators.[2] In the case of Belgium, the national judiciary decided in 1942 no longer to pursue any cases involving the use of firearms, in order to avoid becoming part of the struggle of the occupier against the resistance.[3] As a result, the German military judiciary saw an explosion in the number of cases it treated, with an expeditiousness and severity unknown in the history of

---

[1] The author thanks Koen Aerts, Jean-Marc Berlière, Jonas Campion, David Feldman, Benoît Majerus, Insa Meinen, Jessica Reinisch, and Antoon Vrints for their critical comments and suggestions on earlier versions of this article.

[2] See Pieter Lagrou,'La guerra irregolare e le norme della violenza legittima nell'Europa del novecento' in Luca Baldissara e Paolo Pezzino (dir.) *Crimini e memorie di guerra* (Napoli, 2004) 89–102 and Pieter Lagrou, 'Guerre honorable sur le front de l'Ouest : crime, punition et reconciliation', in Gaël Eismann et Stefan Martens, *Occupation et répression militaire allemandes* (Paris, 2007) 201–20.

[3] See Antoon Vrints, 'Patronen van polarisatie. Homicide in België tijdens de Tweede Wereldoorlog', in *Bijdragen tot de Geschiedenis van de Eigentijdse Geschiedenis*, 15 (2005), 183.

*Past and Present (2011)*, Supplement 6

Belgian penal law. In June 1945, a special law was adopted for the amnesty of resistance acts judged as criminal offences and no less than 3,000 wartime crimes were recategorized as patriotic acts.[4]

Secondly, the same years seem to have created a considerable increase in both crimes against private property and violent crime in Belgium. The huge surge in black market activity, shortages of food and fuel, a modified circulation of firearms (first a severe reduction through the confiscation policy of the occupier, then a considerable increase) and the development of highly mobile and extremely violent forms of banditry all contributed to a sense of urgency and crisis. The years 1942–46 form a spectacular exception in the long term very low average of homicide in twentieth-century Belgian history, jumping from the still average 109 cases in 1941 to 216 in 1942, over 700 in 1943 and 1,852 in 1944. The figures for 1945 and 1946 remain above the level of 1942 and only in 1947 do homicide figures drop to pre-war levels, to continue a downward trend to the historical lows of the 1950s and 1960s.[5] In this context, the national police forces were ordered to make increased use of their firearms, and to ensure 'that every shot should be a hit'.[6] After the liberation, the military tribunals who dealt with collaboration charges also handled 30,000 cases of theft committed during the blackout (maintained after the liberation in September 1944 until the end of the war out of fear of German bombing) and no less than 50,000 cases of offences committed to the detriment of the Allied occupation forces, whose bulging storehouses invited the covetousness of the local population.[7] Nor was it always easy to distinguish between ordinary crime on the rise and the heroic fight of the resistance. In Oostakker, for instance, where post-war commemorations and a monument honoured the memory of eighty-nine patriots executed by the occupier after judgement by German military field courts, recent research identified among them the seven members of an infamous gang that had terrorized the

---

[4] Mathieu Syx, *L'arrêté-loi du 22 juin 1945 octroyant l'amnistie pour des infractions commises pendant l'occupation en vue de soutenir l'action de la résistance, et certains aspects de son application à Bruxelles.* unpublished MA thesis directed by P. Lagrou, Université Libre de Bruxelles, 2007.

[5] Vrints, 'Patronen van polarisatie', 177–87.

[6] Circular 2405 by commander Van Coppenolle to the gendarmerie, 6 August 1943, quoted by Jonas Campion, *Le rétablissement de la légalité policière après la Seconde Guerre mondiale. Les Gendarmeries belge, française et la Koninklijke Marechaussee néerlandaise,* unpublished PhD thesis, Paris IV-Université Catholique de Louvain (2009), 93.

[7] John Gilissen, 'Étude statistique sur la répression de l'incivisme', *Revue de droit pénal et de criminologie,* 31:5 (1951), 513–628.

region in the autumn of 1942 and five German soldiers sentenced and executed for capital offences.[8]

At the same time, and quite paradoxically, 1945 is also often presented as a new dawn of human rights, born out of the aversion to the abuse by state agents of their monopoly of force. The excesses of Nazism would in this version have engendered a normative change, much more restrictive when it comes to legitimizing the use of force, even by those invested with legal monopoly. Notably, post-war trials would for the first time seriously challenge obedience to superior order by agents of the State as an argument in the defence of war criminals.[9] The challenge for the post-war state then becomes daunting, if the monopoly of force had to be simultaneously both curtailed and reconquered, as it faced quite unprecedented competing claims from rival forces during the occupation years and an undeniable surge of private violence against property, against individuals, and against the—contested—agents of the state. As the British ambassador cabled to the Foreign Office in London in September 1944: 'What is the authority of a government when only one out every 5 armed men in the street is answerable to it?'[10] Could post-war governments conduct the purge of their national police forces, beg allied occupation forces for firearms to equip them to control banditry and communist resistance forces, while pleading restraint in the use that could be made of those arms?

Let us therefore first recall the norms as they existed at the time of the German invasion. The Hague Convention of 1907, in its third section on 'military authority over the territory of the hostile State' stipulates the simple transfer of the monopoly of force to the occupying army.

Art. 43.

The authority of the legitimate power having in fact passed into the hands of the occupant, the latter shall take all the measures in his power to restore, and ensure, as far as possible, public order and

---

[8] Tim De Craene, *Terechgesteld. Duitse executies in Oost- en West-Vlaanderen, 1941–1944* (Erembodegem, 2009).

[9] See Pieter Lagrou, 'Eine Frage der moralischen Überlegenheit? Die Ahndung deutscher Kriegsverbrechen in Belgiën', in Norbert Frei (dir.) *Transnationale Vergangenheitspolitik. Der Umgang mit deutschen Kriegsverbrechern in Europa nach dem Zweiten Weltkrieg* (Göttingen, 2006), 326–350.

[10] Pieter Lagrou 'U.S. Politics of Stabilization in Liberated Europe. The View from the American Embassy in Brussels, 1944–1946' *European History Quarterly*, 25 (1995), 209–46.

safety, while respecting, unless absolutely prevented, the laws in force in the country.[11]

The transfer of legal competence also implied a transfer of authority over nationals in charge of public order and safety and implied a duty of obedience of police officers and civil servants to their new masters. This duty was formally inscribed in national legislation, especially after the precedent of the First World War. In Belgium, for instance, a *livret de mobilisation civile* was created by decree in March 1936, containing concrete instructions for civil servants in case of foreign occupation.

> Taken by surprise by the invasion, civil servants will not oppose any resistance to the invader. [. . .] If the occupier requests so, they will be allowed to take a formal and written engagement to continue to exercise conscientiously and loyally their function and undertake nothing, nor omit anything which might be harmful to the enemy administration of the occupied parts of the Belgian territory. [. . .] They will not be authorised to invoke their refusal to sign such an engagement, which does only concern the exercise of their functions, to justify their departure from the invaded territories. But they should abstain to exercise their functions if the occupier wants to impose them to execute acts incompatible with their duty of loyalty to the Fatherland.[12]

In theory, thus, the monopoly of force is a technical competence, transferable to whoever controls a given territory, as long as the national laws are respected. I have argued elsewhere that, *grosso modo*, this theory was accepted in Western Europe under German occupation during World War II.[13] The exercise of the monopoly of force was considered legitimate if performed by the German army and its military police and by national police units under their command (municipal police, judiciary police, *gendarmerie*). It was contested when exercised by German political police (the SIPO-SD, whose competency was not the maintaining of public order, but the fight against enemies

---

[11]  http://www.icrc.org/ihl.nsf/FULL/195, consulted on 17 May 2007.

[12]  Jules Gérard-Libois and José Gotovitch, *L'an 40. La Belgique occupée* (Brussels, CRISP, 1971), 80. Translation PL.

[13]  P. Lagrou, 'Irregular Warfare and the Norms of Legitimate Violence in Twentieth Century Europe', in Jost Dülffer et Robert Frank (eds), *War, Peace and Violence in International Relations* (Essen, 2009); P. Lagrou, '1945–1955. The Age of Total War' in Frank Biess and Robert Moeller (eds) *Histories of the Aftermath* (New York and Oxford, 2010), 287–96, and P. Lagrou, 'Belgium' in Bob Moore (ed.) *Resistance in Western Europe* (Oxford, 2000) 27–63.

of the *Reich*), by national auxiliary forces (*Milice, Légion Wallonne* and the various security units of collaborationist parties). It was also contested when exercised by resistance movements, especially when they targeted German military. As a striking example, one might cite the court decision in the trial of the head of the *Militärverwaltung* in Belgium, general von Falkenhausen, which estimated that the execution of hostages in retaliation for the killing of German soldiers was not as such incompatible with international law, but that the general had no business protecting Belgian collaborationists and that his signature under the orders to execute hostages in retaliation for the shooting of Belgian fascists constituted a crime.

In addition to being an abstract principle, the monopoly of force also translates into concrete acts of violence by state agents on individuals, regulated by law, but also by administrative procedures, professional traditions, cultural norms. I therefore propose in this contribution to take out one test case probing the limits of the monopoly of force, namely, the authority to shoot a fugitive ignoring a command to stop. It might be recalled that in most European countries, this authority is a distinctive prerogative of the *gendarmerie* or military police (*Feldpolizei, Marechaussee*), whereas most 'ordinary' or civilian police forces (national police, municipal police, judiciary policy) can only use their firearms in cases of legitimate defence.[14] In France, the rampant climate of violence motivated the Vichy Authorities in October 1943 to extend this prerogative to the civilian police, a prerogative revoked at the liberation, but again under consideration in the tense years 1958–62, when the police saw its *modus operandi* vastly extended.[15]

A first case takes us to the Demarcation line near Châlon sur Saône on 20 August 1942.[16] Customs officer Heinrich B. and his assistant were cycling down the country road from Sassagny to Cersot when, shortly after 6 p.m.,

---

[14] In 2008, for instance, of 80 reported cases of the use of firearms by the *gendarmerie nationale* in France, only 20 involved cases of self-defence. The combined effect of the controversial shooting of a gypsy inmate in Draguignan on 23 May 2008 and the transfer of the *gendarmerie nationale* from the Ministry of Defence to the Ministry of the Interior stirred substantial debate on the issue in France in the Spring of 2008. See 'L'affaire de Draguignan ravive la grogne des gendarmes', *Le Monde*, (28 May 2008) and 'La loi va sanctuariser l'existence d'une police militaire', *Le Monde*, (4 June 2008).

[15] See Jean-Marc Berlière, *Policiers Français sous l'occupation*, (Paris, 2009) ; and Jean-Marc Berlière, 'Un maintien de l'ordre entre naufrage des principes démocratiques et faillite de l'Etat?', in Serge Berstein and Jean-François Sirinelli (eds), *Michel Debré, premier ministre* (PUF, 2005) 539–652.

[16] Alrich Meyer and Insa Meinen, 'Transitland Belgien. Jüdische Flüchtlinge in Westeuropa während der Zeit der Deportationen 1942', *Theresienstädter Studien und Dokumente*, vol. 14 (2007), 378–431. See also Insa Meinen, *Die Shoah in Belgiën* (Darmstatt, 2009).

they saw a group of individuals heading towards the unoccupied zone. When his order 'Halt! Stop! Grenzbeamte!' was ignored by the group, who started to run in the opposite direction, Heinrich B. pulled his pistol and fired from about 25 metres on the leader of the group, Mojzesz Grunberger. The bullet hit the two-year-old daughter the latter carried in his arms in the head. Esther Grunberger was carried by ambulance to the hospital of Chalon-sur-Saône, but died the same evening. While some individuals succeeded in escaping in the confusion following the fatal shot, fourteen were arrested. Among them were the parents of the victim, diamond cutters from Antwerp, who left the city at the time of the first major razzias deporting the Jewish population. Identified as Jews, all were transferred into the custody of the SIPO-SD, transported to Drancy on 29 August and put on a transport to Auschwitz two days later, where they arrived on 2 September.

This episode is narrated by Ahlrich Meyer and Insa Meien in a fascinating recent article in which they very convincingly show, first, that the number of Jews who tried to escape, but were arrested at border crossings, railroad stations, and random control points, is much higher than usually admitted, since most disappear in overall deportation statistics. Secondly, they also show that the agents involved in the arrest of Jews are much more numerous and diversified, involving crucially customs officers and agents of the *Devisenschutz* (foreign currency control). In the case of *Zollsekretär* (custom officer) Heinrich B., a circumstantial report was submitted to the Minister of Finance (where Meinen and Meyer discovered it) on '*Waffengebrauch mit Todesfolge*' (use of firearms with lethal effect), invoking a '*unbeabsichtigter Zufallstreffer*' (unintentional and coincidental hit). The archives do not contain any trace of further procedural steps, suggesting the ministry estimated Heinrich B. had acted according to rules and regulations of the customs service.

A second episode takes us to Zepperen, in the Belgian province of Limburg, near the Dutch border, on Christmas Eve, 24 December 1943.[17] Around 11 a.m., Willy Hirschfeld, *Feldwebel* (gendarme or member of the military police), presented himself at the house of Maurice Joseph Driesmans in order to arrest him. Driesmans ran out through the back door of his house and into the fields. Hirschfeld summoned him to stop and surrender and then fired from about 150 metres in the direction of the fugitive. Hit in the head, Driesmans died instantly. The ballistic expertise revealed that in fact,

---

[17] Isabelle Cupers, 'Le procès de HIRSCHFELD, Willy Otto, feldgendarme à Saint-Trond de 1942 à 1944', unedited research paper, history research seminar directed by P. Lagrou, Université Libre de Bruxelles (2006).

the bullet entered through the forehead, thereby confirming witness accounts that Driesmans had turned around and raised his arms in sign of surrender.

Driesmans had several reasons to fear the German authorities. He was previously employed on the German airbase in Florenne and had broken his contract unilaterally at the end of November. He was however also suspected of theft of cows and calves, illegal slaughter and black market activities, which was why the *Feldgendarmerie* wanted to question him. Hirschfeld figured on the list of suspects for whom the Belgian judiciary asked extradition through the United Nations War Crimes Commission, as part of a list of *Feldgendarmen* accused mainly of torturing members of the resistance.[18] The prosecutors soon had to admit that torture did not figure as a criminal charge in the penal code and that its qualification as 'blows and injuries' carried insufficient penalties to warrant a war crimes trial. The vast majority of extradited *Feldgendarme* (primarily *Geheime Feldpolizisten*) were thus released without trial. Belgium asked for 4,400 extraditions, obtained 523 and put 103 individuals on trial. Among these figured Hirschfeld, because he could be charged with manslaughter. The court refused Hirschfeld's defence that he had acted in accordance with the field instructions of the *Feldgendarmerie*. The arrest of a meat trafficker does not warrant the use of firearms. It did recognise that, from a distance of 150 metres, it was difficult to ascertain the premeditation of the manslaughter, admitting that even if Hirschfeld had aimed at the fugitive's legs, the trajectory of the bullet was unpredictable. Hirschfeld was condemned to a prison sentence of three years, which meant that, after deduction of his preventive detention, he walked free.

There is of course a bitter irony in the fact that the Belgian judiciary failed to sentence the Gestapo—or *Geheime Feldpolizei*—agents responsible for the torture and deportation of the heroes and martyrs of the resistance because of the absence of adequate penal categories in their legal arsenal and were thus forced to fall back on rather dubious cases, such as Hirschfeld's, where the victim was an economic collaborator working on an enemy military airfield, a cattle thief and black marketeer.

In a similar case, an agent of the *Devisenschutz*, the same unit whose role in the deportation of Jews has remained unknown until the research of Meinen

---

[18] See Pieter Lagrou, 'Eine Frage der moralischen Überlegenheit? Die Ahndung deutscher Kriegsverbrechen in Belgien', in Norbert Frei (ed.) *Transnationale Vergangenheitspolitik. Der Umgang mit deutschen Kriegsverbrechern in Europa nach dem Zweiten Weltkrieg* (Göttingen, 2006), 326–50.

and Meyer, was sentenced for the killing of a fugitive currency trafficker.[19] The agent, Anton Sommer, was part of a group of four agents that had set up an ambush in the fancy Café Métropole on the Place de Brouckère in the heart of Brussels on 16 July 1943. The stool pigeon of the *Devisenschutz*, a certain Zigrand, had a rendez-vous for a deal exchanging Marks against Belgian Francs with three traffickers. The three were arrested and conducted to the billiard room at the back of the café for a body search and interrogation. During a moment of inattention, one of the traffickers, Oscar Chaballe, a 38-year-old resident of Verviers, tried to escape, crossing the large café while overthrowing all the chairs behind him to hinder his pursuers, as he must have seen in the movies. Sommer, who had just celebrated his fortieth birthday, before the war a locksmith from a suburb of Cologne without any known party affiliation, was posted at the entrance of the café, however, and he shot Chaballe in the forehead at gunpoint.[20] At his trial in July 1949, Sommer pleaded self-defence, arguing Chaballe might have been armed, and invoked the ordinance of 7 September 1942 of the *Militärbefehlshaber* for Belgium and the North of France, authorizing the use of firearms to stop a fugitive. The military court rejected the thesis of self-defence and argued that the ordinance gave the right of, but did not impose, the use of firearms when alternatives (such as, argued the military judge, throwing chairs to defeat Chaballe with his own tactics) were available. Sommer was sentenced to 10 years of forced labour, appealed against the judgement and was sentenced to 15 years in his second trial, which, considering his lengthy preventive detention, did not matter much, since he could be set free after having served one third of his term. Chaballe's behaviour remained a mystery, since he was no longer there to comment. Did he overestimate the severity of the occupier's courts (his accomplices were sentenced to one and three months in prison) or underestimate the resolve of his arrestors?

The cases of Hirschfeld and Sommer were in a way as crystal clear as the profile of their victims was murky. The length of their prison sentence seemed mainly inversely proportional to the distance the bullet travelled; three years for a stray bullet at 150 metres; fifteen for a shot at gunpoint. Because of the imperative to identify cases of manslaughter or murder, the issue of the

---

[19] Affaire Sommer Anton (Köln, 1/07/1903), Conseil de Guerre de Bruxelles du 16/05/1949, Cour Militaire de Bruxelles du 16/11/1949. Unpublished research paper by Alla Nozhenko, history seminar directed by P. Lagrou, Université Libre de Bruxelles (2006).

[20] Sommer's non-affiliation to the Nazi party was mentioned in the trial as a mitigating circumstance, but Insa Meinen was able to trace back Sommer's affiliation to the NSDAP as early as 1 March 1933 in the Bundesarchif. Communication by Meinen to author, December 2009.

legality of the shooting of fugitives also occupied centre stage in symbolically much more important cases. The Belgian war crimes trial programme had the central ambition to demonstrate its capacity to apply a limited form of extra-territorial justice, namely to judge the suspected authors of crimes committed outside the national territory, but whose victims were Belgian nationals, or nationals of states allied to Belgium during the war. At the core of this project lay the determination to participate in the judgement of atrocities committed in German concentration camps. Since it had been a systematic policy of the German occupier to deport tens of thousands of Belgian citizens and residents to Germany and occupied Poland and to commit most of the crimes and atrocities outside of the national borders, impunity could only be defeated if the extra-territoriality of the crimes was answered by the extra-territoriality of the exercise of justice. As the trial of a dozen camp guards of Wolfenbüttel—one of the numerous camps 'forgotten' by the allied courts—and prison guard Ernst Köppelmann showed, however, it proved again very difficult to qualify systematic abuse, torture, and starvation in terms of individual penal responsibility. In Germany no less than in Belgium, the court needed a corpse and a suspected author of manslaughter or murder.

Richard Winter's case presented just that. Winter, like most of our suspects, was a middle-aged worker, too old for front service and first drafted in 1939 in the *Landesschutzenbatallion* in Pomerania, later as *Unterscharfuhrer* or sergeant mainly in charge of guarding prisoner-of-war camps of Polish, French, Russian, and Italian captives.[21] In August 1944, Winter was sent to Misburg, a 'commando' of the Neuengamme concentration camp in the Hamburg region and thus effectively enrolled the SS. Summary executions were very common in the concentration camp regime, as a form of punishment and to set frightening examples and enforce discipline. Even in concentration camps, however, the personnel had not completely lost some legalistic reflexes and most summary executions were staged as the shooting of fugitives in escape attempts. Winter had participated in at least two of those executions, one, which resulted in the death of two Russian inmates in October 1944, and another resulting in the death of a French and a Belgian inmate in February 1945. Winter argued that his instructions regarding high security prisoners ordered him to shoot fugitives at gunpoint without summation. In his account, camp guards at Misburg were reminded every

---

[21] See Maxime Brebant, *L'affaire Winter*, unpublished research paper in the history seminar directed by P. Lagrou, Université Libre de Bruxelles (2006). Brebant is currently preparing a PhD thesis at the University of Reading on the Allies' cooperation in war crime trial programmes.

morning that any prisoner at a five-metre distance from his platoon should be considered a fugitive and shot. However, in both cases, the shooting had been preceded by beatings and in the last case, the court even considered that Winter had ordered a *Kapo* to beat the victims with a spade to force them to seek refuge. The investigation proved arduous, depending crucially on the witness account of a former Yugoslav inmate now in British detention for reasons unmentioned. The court even failed to correctly identify the Belgian victim because of a spelling mistake.[22] The flimsy travesty of a summary execution into an interrupted flight attempt was however unquestionably unmasked and Winter was sentenced to death by execution. The sentence was commuted into life imprisonment, and like all his fellow *Kriegsverurteilte*, diplomatic pressure from Bonn assured his premature release in the early 1950s.

One last of these cases carries us into the dark heart of Nazi criminality in Belgium, with the trial of Otto Siegburg.[23] Siegburg, a 50-year-old professional policeman, served in the *Kriegsmarine* during World War I, entered the criminal police after he retired from the Navy in 1925 and took his NSDAP membership in 1933. Gestapo agent in Lodz and Posen from 1939, he arrived in Brussels in March 1943 as a member of the *Judenabteilung* of the SIPO-SD, in charge of stalking Jewish clandestines. Siegburg was sentenced to death and later on appeal to fifteen years of forced labour, for his central role in the brutal assassination of Erner Hillel on the night of 11 -12 June 1943, in the apartment in the Brussels suburb of Wemmel where he was hiding. Siegburg and his accomplices wanted to force Hillel, a stateless Jew of Polish origin, but resident in Belgium since 1927, to give them the addresses of other clandestines. After he was beaten to death, the SIPO-SD squad threw his corpse in the trunk of their car and carried him off. The Hillel murder could be considered a professional error, since it was the central mission of the SIPO-SD to arrest and deport the Jews of Western Europe as discretely as possible, and not to commit bloody murders in the process. Siegburg's line of defence again illustrates the legalistic reflex, even with a central agent of the Final Solution. Siegburg denied that his role had been to stalk and arrest Jews to send them off to their deaths in the East. He was just a regular policeman in charge of arresting individuals whose residence permits had expired or were falsified. In this job, he always carried an automatic rifle, of course, to dissuade potential fugitives, as the instructions of his unit required him to do.

---

[22] Brebant quite triumphantly succeeded in identifying the victim 60 years later; cf. note 21.

[23] Bouchra El Aïssati, *Le procès de Otto Siegburg*, unpublished research paper in the history seminar directed by P. Lagrou, Université Libre de Bruxelles (2006).

The lawfulness of the shooting of fugitives was obviously not only an issue of retrospective arbitration for the military judiciary after 1945. Walter Ganshof van der Meersch, head of the military justice (*auditeur général*) had to dispense legal advice both to his prosecutors in charge of investigating the cases of *Feldgendarme* who had killed during the occupation (who thus happened to be the only ones that could be given acceptable sentences, contrary to the professional torturers, expert enough to avoid the death of their suspects), and to his own *gendarmes* guarding German prisoners-of-war. He thus happened to be writing recommendations on the doctrine to be implemented and jurisprudence to be applied retrospectively, obviously a most delicate exercise. Between 1945 and 1947, 60,000 German prisoners-of-war were put to work in Belgian mines.[24] The social climate down in the pits was quite violent. One German prisoner-of-war died of his injuries after a brawl in September 1945. Two Belgian foremen were severely beaten up and had their hair shorn at 1000 metres underground one year later in September 1946. The most serious security problem was quite pacific, however. Almost 4,000 German prisoners-of-war simply walked home in the course of a mere two years—that is an average of almost six a day, or put another way, more than six times the number of Belgian prisoners-of-war who deserted German captivity in five full years, for a comparable overall figure of captives. Consulted by the commander of the *gendarmerie*, Ganshof van der Meersch instructed in January 1947 that officers should uphold the field manual of 1911 and the law of August 1913, which both ordered the shooting of fugitives; he argued that it was not incompatible with the Geneva Convention of 1929—which requested that prisoners-of-war be treated humanely—as long as two formal summons had been issued and when there was good reason to suspect the fugitives disposed of a lethal weapon. Ganshof also recommended shooting fugitives in the legs, except at night.

Van der Meersch's recommendations simply confirmed the *Instruction sur le service de garde, de planton et d'escorte* (instructions on the guard, platoon and escort service) that had been applied since May 1946 and which even instructed officers to shoot without warning after sunset. In the course of the two years of their captivity, no less than twenty German prisoners-of-war were shot dead by camp guards during attempted escapes—admittedly far less than the eighty prisoners-of-war who died during mining accidents, but

---

[24] See Rik Verwaest, 'Gevangen tussen de mazen van de wet: de behandeling van de Duitse krijgsgevangenen in België na 1944 en de toepassing van de Conventie van Genève door België', unpublished research paper communicated by courtesy of the author, CEGESOMA, 2008.

still a powerful proof that the instructions were there to be applied.[25] Seventeen strikes were also brutally repressed and on several occasions prisoners-of-war refusing to return to the pits were forced to do so, literally at the point of the bayonet. During one single incident on 23 November 1946, between a Belgian foreman and rebellious German prisoners-of-war, a Belgian soldier in charge of surveillance in the pits shot seven of the latter in the legs.

It would be erroneous, however, to suppose Belgian camp guards were trigger-happy, or used their field instructions to vent their thirst for revenge on hapless homesick German soldiers. Crossing the Belgian-German border was a dangerous undertaking in the immediate post-war years and German custom officers killed more of their compatriots between 1946 and 1952 than Belgian military police.[26] The smuggling of coffee in particular was both a highly rewarding and a perilous trade. The resale price of a kilo of coffee on the German side of the border was worth twice the price of purchase on the Belgian side. The smuggling was sometimes occasional and amateurish, with women and youngsters crossing the woods with a few kilos on their backs, sometimes large-scale and professional, as in the case of the gang that stole an armoured vehicle in a Belgian Army depot and crossed the border unhindered by the bullets of the border guards. The repression was consistently severe, with the systematic use of firearms when summons remained unanswered. Local historian Wolfgang Trees registered no less than thirty-one smugglers shot to death on the border crossing between 1946 and 1952 and more than one hundred serious injuries. Among the dead were a 16-year-old boy, shot in 1946, a woman of 36 shot by accident in 1951 (the customs officers failed to find any illegal goods on the victim) and an 18-year-old groom shot in the head while carrying 60 Marks-worth of coffee. As in all similar cases examined above, notably the case on the Demarcation line in August 1942 by his colleague Heinrich B., the customs officer who fired the

---

[25] Hermann Jung, *Die deutschen Kriegsgefangenen im Gewahrsam Belgiens, der Niederlande und Luxemburgs.* (*Zur Geschichte der deutschen Kriegsgefangenen des Zweiten Weltkrieges*, vol. 12) (Bielefeld, 1966), quoted by Verwaest, 'Gevangen tussen de mazen'.

[26] See Wolfgang Trees, Schmuggler, *Zöllner und die Kaffeepanzer : die wilden Nachkriegsjahre an der deutschen Westgrenze* (Aachen, 2002). See also the exhibit in the *Zollmuseum Friedrichs* in Aachen-Horbach (www.zollmuseum-friedrichs.de) and Kurt Cremer, 'Kaffeepanzer im Bohnenkampf' on http://einestages.spiegel.de; [accessed 14 October 2009]. Many thanks to Cyrille Fijnaut, author of an excellent *History of the Dutch Police* (Amsterdam, 2008) and editor of a volume *The Impact of World War II on Policing in North-West Europe* (Leuven, 2004) for having drawn my attention to this singular episode.

fatal shot was acquitted, having acted '*nach Dienstvorschrift*' (according to the service instructions). The behaviour and routines of East German border guards, almost 400 of whom have been brought to trial since 1989 for their deadly shots at fugitives trying to make it across the Iron Curtain, are thus not just the acts of unthinking executioners of a ruthless regime, but very much part of a post-war history and a professional ethos on the respective western borders of both German states.[27] 1989 and the end of the Cold War might in that regard have been much more of a watershed than 1945 and the end of the Second World War.

One last and quite fuzzy case allows us to shed a slightly different light on the use of firearms by agents of the state in the long and violent twentieth century. On 16 July 1944 Nicolas Mombach, aged 59, wearing a *Wehrmacht* uniform and rifle, shot a bartender on the sunny terrace of a Brussels café in Molenbeek, after the latter had refused to serve him more drinks because of his advanced state of drunkenness.[28] Evacuated by the *Feldgendarmerie*—exclusively competent for the arrest and interrogation of German military personnel—the deroute of the German army the following month saved Mombach from a German court marshal, that might very well have resulted in a death penalty and instant execution. He was thus brought to trial before a Belgian military court in May 1949. Mombach's was a hopeless case. Two German *Feldgendarme* confirmed in court that no single German field manual or operational guidelines for the German Army in Belgium could possibly justify his completely unwarranted lethal use of his rifle, under the condition he was in (in uniform and drunk). Still, Mombach benefited from the relative clemency of the Belgian judicial system and was sentenced to fifteen years of forced labour. Mombach's case, straightforward as it was in terms of the circumstances of the crime, was still a most interesting case of jurisprudence for two reasons.

First of all, most of the procedure dwelled on his uncertain nationality. It was quite crucial for the verdict to ascertain whether or not Mombach was a Belgian national—in order to establish whether he could be convicted of treason, more specifically 'carrying weapons in the service of the enemy', which was punishable by the death penalty, independent of what the suspect

---

[27] See Roman Grafe, *Deutsche Gerechtigkeit. Prozesse gegen DDR-Grenzschütze und ihre Befehlsgeber* (Munchen, 2004) and http://www.grenzer.com/BGmain.htm, [accessed 30 October 2009]. See also Guillaume Mouralis, *Une épuration allemande. La RDA en procès, 1949–2004* (Paris, 2008).

[28] See Tanja Steinmetz, *La répression des criminels de guerre après la Deuxième Guerre Mondiale en Belgique. Le cas de Nicolas Mombach*, unpublished research paper in the history seminar directed by P. Lagrou, Université Libre de Bruxelles (2006).

had or had not done with those weapons.[29] As a native from Luxembourg, his ancestors had had Belgian, Dutch, French, and Luxembourg citizenship, but Mombach himself had never spent much time as a Luxembourg resident.[30] In the absence of a firmly established citizenship, he could be considered as a peculiar sort of *Staatenlose*. The German occupation in the summer of 1940 found him in Brussels, unemployed and alcoholic. Because of his Luxembourg ancestry, and because of the *Eingliederung* of Luxembourg in the *Reich*, the occupier considered Mombach as a *Volksdeutsche* eligible for German social welfare. From welfare, Mombach went to a job in the military post service (*Feldpost*)—a militarized service, whence the uniform and the rifle. Mombach's lawyers of course pleaded he was a Luxembourg national, to spare him from the death penalty as a traitor of the Belgian nation.

There were also some good reasons to consider Mombach as a Belgian, especially his long spells in the service of the Belgian army. His related extensive criminal record, mostly episodes of violence and public drunkenness are a second aspect that make his case remarkable. Born in 1885, Mombach served in the Belgian army from the age of 16 and left for the Congo Free State after three years, on a contract with the Katanga Mining Committee. Between 1905 and 1908 he had been commander for the Tanganyika Lake district of what was then the Congo Free State, private property of Belgian king Leopold II. In 1908, the territory fell under the control of the Belgian state as a regular colony, after an international campaign against the violent abuse of the local population and their ruthless exploitation by forced labour. Mombach fell victim to the clean-up efforts of the Belgian state. Arrested in Belgium in 1911, he was sent back to the Congo and condemned to twelve years of prison at a trial in Elizabethville in 1912. The extracts of the 1912 trial documents in the 1949 trial file are incomplete, but broadly outline the following. In 1906, Mombach had directed a punitive campaign with his

---

[29] It is only in the examination of the requests for pardon addressed to the head of state by convicts sentenced to the death penalty that the effective use of firearms was taken into consideration. Carrying arms without known lethal effect was routinely pardoned and the sentence commuted to life imprisonment. Where manslaughter was involved, premeditation and legitimate self-defence were taken into account. See Koen Aerts, *Persona non grata. Genadeverlening bij ter dood veroordeelden tijdens de repressie na de Tweede Wereldoorlog (1944–1950)*, unpublished Masters Thesis, University of Gent (2005).

[30] On the late sedimentation of a precise notion of Luxembourg citizenship, see Denis Scuto, *La construction de la nationalité luxembourgeoise. Une histoire sous influence française, belge et allemande (1839–1940)/The construction of the Luxembourgish nationality (1839–1940)*, unpublished PhD thesis, Université Libre de Bruxelles (2009); and Denis Scuto, 'Qu'est-ce qu'un Luxembourgeois ? Histoire de la nationalité luxembourgeoise du Code Napoléon à nos jours', *Hémecht*, 58 : 1 (2006).

indigenous troops against three villages, which were burned down. Three men and two women were summarily executed in the operation and countless were injured. Mombach served only two years of his prison sentence and was again employed in the colonial service, as an agent for the Katanga railways, in 1914. In 1921, he came back to Belgium to live a precarious existence; until the German occupier in May 1940 discovered some German ancestry for him and gave him a job, a uniform, and a rifle.

What sense can one make of the chaotic trajectory of Mombach, a man of uncertain nationality, sentenced twice for war crimes in an interval of 37 years, serving different masters, in the Belgian army, the Colonial *Force Publique* and the Nazi *Wehrmacht*? Certainly Mombach's trajectory is one of brutalization throughout a life spent wandering through army barracks and prisons, a life of colonial brutality, unemployment, and alcohol. Mombach did not shoot a bartender in the summer of 1944 because he developed a habit in the Congo Free State between 1905 and 1908, but, compared to the snapshots cited above, where conscientious agents of the state act according to their instructions and pull the trigger on a fatal instant, Mombach's case shows the intense circulation of personnel and experience in soldiering and policing, between the colony and the metropole, between Belgium, Germany, and even tiny Luxembourg.

Through rather haphazardly chosen examples, this contribution has tried to go beyond treating the monopoly of force as an abstraction of social scientists and historians. The boundaries of what constitutes legitimate and criminal use of the monopoly of force can only be delineated through concrete forms of violence—in this case, the use of firearms by agents of the state. World War II was a time of exceptional violence, which might lead to a perception of a totally normless Nazi state—or at least a state practising incommensurable norms in its orgy of violence—set against the well-established rules and limited use of violence by the liberal state. Some of the links established between regulated violence and the boundless violence of the Nazi state are simply a matter of discourses of legitimization, strong and atavistic reflexes even for soldiers and civil servants of a nation such as Germany without an established tradition of a liberal state. Richard Winter and Otto Siegburg, respectively active in the concentration camp system and in the Final Solution, exterminating European Jewry, attempted a travesty of their heinous crimes and arbitrary killings. There was, however, also a tremendous amount of ordinary violence going on, for which there was a common frame of reference for Belgian and German police and customs officers facing prioners-of-war, cattle thieves, smugglers, and Jewish fugitives. Yet, as the case of customs officer Heinrich B. shows, the extraordinary violence of the Nazi racial dystopia also percolated into the apparent 'normality' of the routine exercise of the monopoly of violence. Heinrich B., cycling down the Demarcation line, behaved as a customs officer was supposed to behave and he was probably quite appalled by the horrific outcome when he discovered the bloody remains of the baby girl. This was occupied France in the summer of 1942 and not the killing fields of Riga or Minsk. Heinrich B. was however also an agent of the Final Solution and handing over his detainees to the SIPO-SD for instant shipment to Auschwitz was apparently also part of his professional routines. Willy Hirschfeld too shot at his fugitive, and probably did not expect to hit his suspect in the forehead from a distance of 150 metres. The fight against cattle thieves was however quite uncontroversially part of the mandate of the occupier to maintain public order and the Belgian post-war court was rather hesitant in its condemnation. Anton Sommer shot his victim in cold blood and at gunpoint, but his act was still part of a police routine, even if applied more ruthlessly than his victim apparently expected. As to the fifty-one German nationals—twenty prisoners-of-war and thirty-one smugglers—shot dead when trying to cross the border from Belgium into Germany, they show that Europe's post-war was not only enlightened by the noble principles of the spirit of San Francisco 1945, the new dawn of the Universal Declaration of Human Rights of 1948 or the refounding of the Geneva Conventions in 1949, in an attempt to turn the dark page of the war. They are very much part of the grim picture of post-war states taking full responsibility for their actions, unshrinking in their recourse to force to impose the stark priorities of the nation-state, continuing, in many ways, the brutal era Nicolas Mombach had lived through.

The particular irony of the project of post-war justice, exemplified by the case of Belgium in this text, is that it failed to prosecute the exceptional and extraordinary crimes committed, notably deportation, torture, and genocide, since its legal arsenal was not equipped to deal with them, nor even to define them (with the ephemeral exception of the International Military Tribunal in Nuremberg and its recourse to retroactive qualification). Forced to fall back on 'ordinary cases', notably some haphazard *Feldgendarme* killing fugitives, they ended up blurring the qualitative, substantial difference between the routines, norms, and praxis of the German police forces and their own.

Still, in trying to test the validity of the idea that the experience of occupation had challenged the monopoly of force, a certain degree of deliberate dispersion of cases seems rather rewarding: regular German military police and Nazi political police facing a foreign, occupied population; German camp guards in Nazi concentration camps; German border guards facing German smugglers in 1950 and regular Belgian military police facing German prisoners-of-war in 1946. It tends to show, first, that even the extreme violence of eliminating the ideological enemies of the Nazi state does not entirely dispense with the rules of engagement of police forces of liberal states, they on the contrary mobilize these rules to make some of this violence more 'acceptable'. It suggests, secondly, that the excessive and arbitrary use of the monopoly of violence did not delegitimate the very idea of it, but that post-war states were faced with permanent arbitration, on what they deemed unacceptable in the past behaviour of their enemy and what they deemed vital as prerogatives for their own police and military in the present and future challenges of imposing order at home and abroad. The procedural scrutiny of the judicial process shows that 1944 and 1946 were not worlds apart and that the decision not to use double standards for policemen constituted a redoubtable challenge.

Does that then mean that nothing happened in 1944–45, apart from a changing of the guard, and even that only partially? 1945 had been a conflict over who could exercise the monopoly of force, much more than what this monopoly actually allowed the authority to do to private individuals (for instance, arrest, and, in case of attempts to escape, shoot them).

This brings us back to the question of normative change. Governments and police forces were preoccupied with reaffirming the monopoly of force and certainly not with curtailing it. This was especially true for the *gendarmerie*, a militarized apparatus to maintain public order and control social protest, the main instrument post-war governments disposed of to re-establish their control of liberated societies. Which does not mean, of course, that normative change was not what part of the social corpus claimed, after four years of occupation and brutal repression. In February 1945, the representatives of the Belgian miners from the coal-mining region of the Centre, around La Louvière, addressed the following petition to the Minister of the Interior:

> We protest energetically against the attitude of the gendarmes in the service of the bosses of the mines of Bracquegnies, because of their draconian way of acting against the striking miners. The latter have been hit with truncheons, with automatic rifle butts, in addition to having used their hands and feet [sic]. We draw your attention to the fact that this manner of behaviour resembles the one practised by the Krauts [Boches] during the occupation. We regret that the representatives of the law insult us as a fifth column. Facing this situation and for the sake of public order, we request we be treated with more respect for the Belgian national sentiment.[31]

---

[31] Lettre de la régionale des mineurs du centre au ministre de l'Intérieur, 03/02/1945, quoted by Jonas Campion, *Le rétablissement de la légalité policière après la Seconde Guerre mondiale. Les Gendarmeries belge, française et la Koninklijke Marechaussee*

The right and the praxis to shoot fugitives is only a minor test case to probe changing norms and praxis of policing in West European societies after 1945. The repression of social protest and crowd control, as illustrated above, would be an even more challenging test case, even if it left fewer judicial traces.[32] On 30 July 1950, four protesters would be shot dead by the *gendarmerie* in Grâce-Berleur, a mining town near Liège, during a protest march against the return from exile of King Leopold III, accused of complicity with the occupier. This was a very violent clash indeed over legitimacy, of a compromised king, of protesters claiming to incarnate the legacy of the resistance and of a *gendarmerie* implementing routines of policing that had remained relatively unchanged since the nineteenth century, notwithstanding their relative delegitimization during the German occupation and the general repudiation of the methods of the despised *Feldgrau*.[33] A decade later, on 17 October 1961, the police repression of a demonstration in favour of Algerian independence in Paris would kill more than one hundred victims.[34] The biography of the man who directed the operations, Maurice Papon, secretary general of the *préfecture de la Gironde* during the German occupation and co-responsible for the deportation of the Jews from the Bordeaux region, could hardly better underline the continuities of repressive policies during and after the German occupation, into the 1960s. The death toll of 17 October 1961 was also comparable to that of the repression of the protest march in East Berlin on 17 June 1953, which was later turned into a national holiday in the Federal Republic, pointing to altogether similar, geographical, continuities in European history.[35]

---

*néerlandaise*, unpublished PhD thesis, Paris IV-Université Catholique de Louvain (2009), 162–3.

[32] For an excellent introduction on policing and crowd control in Belgium, see Benoît Majerus, *Occupations et logiques policières : la police bruxelloise en 1914–1918 et 1940–1944* (Brussels, 2007).

[33] See Jules Gérard-Libois and José Gotovitch, *Léopold III, de l'an '40 à l'effacement* (Brussels, 1991) and Thierry Gossens 'Comment sont morts les morts de Grâce Berleur', in *La Revue Toudi. Culture et Société*, Centre d'Études Wallonnes et République, 1, (February 2007), online on http://www.larevuetoudi.org/fr/story/comment-sont-morts-les-morts-de-gr%C3%A2ce-berleur-i-et-ii/, [accessed 2 November 2009].

[34] See Jean-Luc Einaudi, *Octobre 1961, un massacre à Paris* (Paris, 2001) and Jean-Paul Brunet, *Charonne. Lumières sur une tragédie* (Paris, 2003).

[35] See http://en.wikipedia.org/wiki/Uprising_of_1953_in_East_Germany [accessed 5 November 2009].

The norms and accepted practice of policing would not fundamentally be challenged in 1945, but—as so many other social norms and praxis—only a good two decades later, when the isolated protest of the miners of the La Louvière Region would receive a very wide echo and when their assimilation of the methods of their national police and those of the Nazi German occupier would become the slogan of a generation, coined in Paris in May 1968 as 'CRS-SS' (*Compagnie Républicaine de Sécurité—Schutzstaffeln*). Even then, however, their slogan would be met with incomprehension and indignation by the police force itself and a large part of the population which still very much adhered to the principle of the legitimate exercise of the monopoly of power by the agents of the state, fundamentally unchallenged as it had remained all through a century of war and occupation.

# Reconstructing Empire in British and French Africa

## Frederick Cooper

It was indeed empire that European leaders at the end of World War II needed to reconstruct. They had come very close to losing a struggle with another form of empire, the Nazi Reich, and in South East Asia they had lost valued territories to a country that had dared to play the empire-game with them— Japan. At the same time, both British and French leaders felt, with some reason, that they had been saved by their empires: by the resources in men and material contributed by the dominions and colonies of Great Britain and by the symbolic importance of French Equatorial Africa's refusal to follow Vichy, followed by the contributions of North African territories and diverse African people to the reconquest of European France from the Mediterranean. Both post-war governments acknowledged the dilemma they faced: their physical and moral weakness at war's end meant they had to find new bases to relegitimate empire, and their economic weakness meant they needed the production of empire all the more. Both were acutely conscious that another war might make them dependent on empire yet again. Leaders of political movements in the colonies were aware of exactly these points too.

This chapter is a sketch—an attempt to lay out a way of thinking about the post-war era, a reflection on research by myself and others on a period that is only beginning to be explored. I want to avoid the common weakness of accounts of decolonization, that read history backwards from the 1960s, when the territorial nation-state emerged as the modal end-point of the evolution of colonial empires.[1] In 1945, a clash among imperial powers of different sorts had just ended. In Dakar or Lagos as much as London or Paris, turning colonies into nation-states was only one possibility, and not necessarily the most desirable.

---

[1] On methodological and theoretical issues in the study of colonization and decolonization, see Frederick Cooper, *Colonialism in Question: Theory, Knowledge, History* (Berkeley, 2005).

In this chapter I will look in turn at five points: first, the viability of the empire-form after World War I; secondly, what happened in 1945, considering the Asian roots of an African dilemma; then I will discuss political reconstruction and the building of an inclusive empire; economic reconstruction; and finally the alternatives for Africa after the war.

## What hadn't happened earlier: the viability of the empire-form after World War I

World War I is sometimes seen as a blow against empire, the advent of a world of self-determining nation-states. But only if one reads history backwards. The empires of the losers were dismantled, but various pieces were distributed to the winners. Japan's plea for a statement condemning racism was turned down. To be sure, people in India, China, Korea, and elsewhere read Wilson's words as if they applied to them, but at Paris they found that they did not.[2] There were disturbances in 1919 in Egypt, China, Korea, and India, but the powers-that-be were at the time able to stuff the genii of self-determination back into imperial bottles. Violent conflict in Iraq, Syria, and Egypt and tension in India and Indochina continued, but imperial powers had every reason to believe they could hang on to most of their colonies, in Africa for instance, and elsewhere, as in Egypt or Iraq, working through cooperative elites whose room for manoeuvre was limited. In Africa, the claims of soldiers to have paid the blood tax to France or Britain and therefore to be entitled to some of the respect and rights of the citizen were pushed back. Indeed, the 1920s were a period of assertion of a tribal model for Africa, when Africans' claims to citizenship were rejected, when indirect rule was given a name, when officials' ideas for pushing development plans were considered and set aside, when colonial rulers asserted their genius for maintaining the distinct cultures of their subjects rather than bringing them along a road toward European models of civilization and politics.[3]

A new empire-building project arose in Nazi Germany, while Japan claimed its place at an imperial table. The USSR insisted that it was a multinational polity, providing parallel structures within the Communist party and government for elites within each national group (the definitions of which frequently shifted) to advance. The United States did not establish a conception of itself as a colonial power—it did not have a Colonial Office or

---

[2] Erez Manela, *The Wilsonian Moment: Self-determination and the International Origins of Anticolonial Nationalism* (New York, 2007); Margaret Macmillan, *Paris 1919: Six Months that Changed the World* (New York, 2003).

[3] Alice Conklin, *A Mission to Civilize: The Republican Idea of Empire in France and West Africa, 1895–1930* (Stanford, 1997).

Ministry—but it had its own repertoire of power at a distance, including the maintenance of a small number of colonies and a wider area where periodic invasions and occupations disciplined local elites when they did not cooperate with American interests or when revolution threatened. And American power was based on a century and a half of continental expansion, which produced a relatively self-conscious national population mainly because of the radical exclusion from the polity of people who were different, such as Indians and the descendants of slaves. These were all variants of imperial polities, some explicit in their embrace of an imperial mantle, some claiming to be something else. The exercise of power around the world, for all the talk of nation and of self-determination, was still exercised by a small number of powers, whose main worry was each other.[4]

The League of Nations provided a forum at which the conduct of colonial powers could at times be examined, but it left the judgement of what to do to those powers to themselves. The mandate system indeed expanded the imperial reach of Britain and France, which made German and Ottoman territories into yet another part of a varied imperial repertoire, alongside colonies, protectorates, dominions, and spheres of influence. The League, in the end, underscored the normality of colonial empire even while suggesting that there were international standards which colonial powers should meet.[5]

In the colonial world, the 1930s deepened the involuted nature of colonial regimes: the problems of depression could be sloughed off onto a countryside that could be deemed backward rather than impoverished, and in any case was less visible than capital cities. Then, in the late 1930s, when recovering production created new social strains without measures to relieve them, waves of strikes broke out in parts of the British empire: in the West Indies, in Northern Rhodesia, and in some port cities in West and East Africa. The confluence of strikes and riots in the former plantation colonies and in the parts of Africa most integrated into a wage economy led top officials to realize that by 'tribalizing' Africans they had deprived themselves of the means to think about and act on social issues in labour and in urban life that were slowly emerging as empire-wide issues.[6] The illusion that Africans

---

[4] On inter-empire conflict as a framework for history in the first half of the twentieth century, see Jane Burbank and Frederick Cooper, *Empires in World History: Power and the Politics of Difference* (Princeton, 2010).

[5] For the new wave of scholarship on the League, see Susan Pedersen, 'Back to the League of Nations: Review Essay', *American Historical Review*, 112 (2007), 1091–1117.

[6] Frederick Cooper, *Decolonization and African Society: The Labour Question in French and British Africa* (Cambridge, 1996).

lived in tribal cages and could be pushed back into them whenever authority was challenged began to fall apart as people migrated, entered new economic positions in cities and mines, and at times developed long-distance connections to other people elsewhere in the empires who in their own ways were confronting imperial authority.

## What happened in 1945: the Asian roots of an African dilemma

There are many aspects of World War II that shook empire more profoundly than the previous phase of conflagration: Hitler's giving racism a bad name, economic collapse and indebtedness to the US that limited options for reacting to problems in the colonies, and the credibility given to the alternative model of Soviet politics by its success in the war. But none was more telling than what happened in South East Asia. Dutch Indonesia, French Indochina, and British Malaya and Burma were taken over by Japan. Japan's invasions had much to do with a fear that it could be cut off from resources by other empires—it was very much an inter-empire view of the world. Japan's post-conquest relationships with local political actors were ambiguous, but some, notably Sukarno, established a modus vivendi with Japanese officials. When Japan fell, both Sukarno in Indonesia and Ho Chi Minh in Indochina were in a position to claim the state; it would take weeks before any European troops could challenge them. That meant, in effect, that these territories would have to be recolonized. Neither France nor the Netherlands was able to do that, despite bloody wars. Britain was able to reimpose its will on Malaya, but at a high cost and not for very long. Indian independence in 1947 was equally profound in its effects. When Indonesia and India entered the world of nations, the normality of empire was no longer a given. Political leaders in ex-colonies moved to make the most of this political and discursive opening.[7]

But did this mean that France and Britain saw the writing on the empire's wall? Quite the contrary. Both reacted to threats and losses in Asia by looking more to Africa. As Frederick Pedler, bright young star of Britain's Colonial Office put it 'Africa is now the core of our colonial position; the only continental space from which we can still hope to draw reserves of economic and military strength'.[8] French thinking was similar: African colonies were vital to reconstituting the economy.

[7] C. A. Bayly and T. N. Harper, *Forgotten Armies: The Fall of British Asia, 1941–1945* (Cambridge, Mass., 2006); Clive Christie, *A Modern History of South East Asia: Decolonization, Nationalism and Separatism* (London, 1996).

[8] Pedler, Minute, 1 November 1946, CO 847/35/47234/1/1947, British National Archives.

The flip side of the vulnerability of Britain and France was that other states did not have to fear efforts on their part to secure a hegemonic position or exclusive access to resources across the globe. The former imperial giants, like other states, *had* to sell commodities from their empires. That freed everyone else from the dangers of being cut off from vital supplies by policies of empire preference or monopolies. Not least of the countries liberated from fear of someone else's empire were Germany and Japan. The inter-empire rivalries that had led to two world wars would not lead to a third.

## Political reconstruction: building an inclusive empire, but not quite of equals

The tendency among scholars to put all colonial territories on the train to the nation-state gets in the way of understanding the actual give-and-take of the post-war years. The French case is the most striking, and the most frequently dismissed. If one thinks of France as a very French nation-state presiding over very subordinate colonies, the long and intense debates over how to recon-stitute a complex political entity make sense only as a smokescreen for stub-born maintenance of the status quo. But the archives make clear the acute uncertainty in official circles about what sort of polity France was and could become.[9]

The French Empire was renamed French Union; colonies became *terri-toires d'outre-mer*. They were part of a multiplex, not dualistic, polity con-sisting of old colonies in the Caribbean, new colonies in Africa, Algeria, protectorates like Morocco, and mandates like Cameroon, each of which had a distinct juridical status debated at length in French assemblies. Government leaders agreed that representatives from the colonies would have to help write a new constitution, but their numbers would not be pro-portional to population. But even a few Africans in the assembly, which also acted as a legislature, was enough to drive such durable, oppressive institu-tions as forced labour and the *indigénat*, separate administrative justice, out of existence. Senegalese deputies Léopold Senghor and Lamine Guèye helped draft and argued for constitutional articles concerning the French Union, and after colonial delegates briefly walked out, the majority realized that the con-stitution would have no legitimacy without their consent.

In the end, the 1946 Constitution proclaimed that inhabitants of all these entities would now have the 'qualities' of French citizens. This provision did

---

[9] The discussion of France and French Africa in the following pages is based on my current research. For an early version, see my 'Alternatives to Empire: France and Africa after World War II,' in Douglas Howland and Luise White (eds), *The State of Sovereignty: Territories, Laws, Populations* (Bloomington, 2009), 94–123.

not translate into universal suffrage for another decade nor did it say precisely whether people in overseas France were citizens of the French Union or of the French Republic. But it conveyed the rights of the constitution to people in the empire, and its language of equivalence quickly proved a springboard for claims to give substance to that language. The new constitution no longer made citizenship contingent on the subject's submitting to the French civil code instead of Islamic or customary law in private legal matters, such as marriage and inheritance. In the Overseas Ministry's own interpretation, 'the legislature wanted to mark the perfect equality of all in public life, but not the perfect identity of the French of the metropole and the overseas French'.[10] In principle, the new French Union would be multicultural as well as egalitarian.

Here we arrive at the basic dilemma of post-war empire: could an imperial regime adopt a more democratic form of governance, a more nuanced view of sovereignty, and still remain imperial? Unlike empires of the past, which from Rome to the Austro-Hungarians had incorporated people of different ethnicities, civilizations, or nationalities into gradations of status within an inclusive—albeit coercive—polity, citizenship in a European empire now entailed economic and social rights as well as political ones. The consolidation of the welfare state after the war implied growing expectations that the state would guarantee, in some form, citizens' access to pensions, family allowances, health care, and education. If older empires had emphasized hierarchical social order, the French republic proclaimed norms of equivalence of all citizens. Bringing millions of impoverished subjects into citizenship in the 1940s could thus entail high costs, if claims based on contemporary standards of citizenship were made good.[11] And it was not clear that citizens of either European or African France could quickly set aside habits and expectations of privilege and authority, of discrimination and denigration, built up in decades of colonial rule.

These dilemmas help to explain the schizophrenic character of post-war French colonialism—at times integrative, capable of calm debate with African or Asian political activists, at times brutally violent against an entire category of people perceived to be a collective threat. Africans could sit in the French legislature, and African labour unions could organize, strike, and claim equal pay and benefits for equal work. At the same time, anything that fell into the category of 'insurrection' received the full colonial treatment. During the repression of the revolt in Madagascar in 1947 and the Algerian

---

[10] Afrique Occidentale Française, Directeur Général des Affaires Politiques, Administratives et Sociales (Berlan), note, July 46, 17G 152, Archives du Sénégal.

[11] On the social dimensions of citizenship, see Cooper, *Decolonization and African Society*.

war of 1954–62—as well as the Vietnam war up to the French defeat in 1954–French forces used collective terror against categories of people among whom rebels were supposed to lurk, and they used torture.

But even in Algeria, French governments tried at the same time pro-grammes of '*promotion musulmane*'—what Americans would call affirmative action—to get Muslim Algerians to see the benefits of inclusion in the French polity. By the mid-1950s, French governments were aware that they were caught in a trap between following through on the logic of citizenship—which was costly—and a cycle of rebellion and repression, now taking place under the gaze of international institutions and observers increasingly sceptical of the normality of colonial rule. The media, as well as government officials, began to consider openly whether preserving an empire of citizens might be less in the interest of France than devolving power and renouncing responsibility.[12]

The more decentralized colonial structure of Great Britain did not foster such a debate over equivalence of all subjects of the Queen. But Britain couldn't escape the problem of preserving empire when the very terms by which the imperial state was trying to relegitimize itself—development and political participation—were leading to an escalation of demands for social and economic resources. Attempts to get educated Africans to focus their ambitions on local government quickly failed. The focus was not London, but it was not the local council either; it was the centre of each territory. Political parties in colony after colony demanded full participation in each territory's legislative and executive institutions, while social movements demanded better wages, fairer crop prices, and more educational facilities.

British policy was at first glance quite unlike French. What was held out before Africans was, it seemed, the possibility that in some unclear time, maybe a generation or more, the Gold Coast could become Canada. Colonial Secretaries in the 1940s even claimed that such a trajectory had long been British policy. But Britain also recognized how important the em-pire's dominions and colonies had been in World War II, and the Nationalities Act of 1948 created something of an echo of what the French were doing—a second tier Commonwealth citizenship, derivative of the pri-mary citizenship of the Dominions, but applied to colonies as well. Not least

---

[12] Todd Shepard, *The Invention of Decolonization: The Algerian War and the Remaking of France* (Ithaca, 2006); Matthew Connelly, *A Diplomatic Revolution: Algeria's Fight for Independence and the Origins of the Post-Cold War Era* (New York, 2002); Raphaëlle Branche, *La torture et l'armée pendant la guerre d'Algérie 1954–1962* (Paris, 2001); Cooper, *Decolonization*.

of its significance was that it gave colonials the right to enter the British Isles. In that way, British Africans were also becoming citizens of empire.[13]

When political movements strayed beyond certain (not entirely clear) lines, as in Kenya in 1952, the colonial government, like that of France, responded with massive detentions and confinements in prison camps, interrogations under torture, capital punishment with minimal judicial oversight, and forced relocations of entire villages.[14] Yet Britain in 1952 had already accepted that the Gold Coast was being governed internally by elected African politicians and that it was en route to independence, a status it obtained in 1957. The excess of repression may well have reflected the self-perceived openness to political reform: that some Africans rejected the political inclusion and economic development that was being offered them now struck officials as an affront, not the backward inclinations inherent in the nature of the African.

Beneath this split vision of modernizing and dangerous Africans lay thinking about the nature of African society and culture that had not made, in its substratum, as sharp a break with the past as it had on the surface. Reading speeches and archival documents from the late 1940s, one comes to realize that a work of imagination was developing in the official minds of French and British imperialism. If indirect rule and the work of interwar anthropology were on the same page in recognizing both the specificity and the backwardness of African societies, the post-war leap of faith was both an embrace of potential equality and a refusal of particularity. The African worker or farmer would be like a worker or farmer anywhere. The African who could sit in the legislative council in a British colony or in the legislature in Paris was fine as an abstraction, but likely to be labelled a demagogue in practice—Nkrumah, Kenyatta, and Azikiwe all suffered this fate until they became such political necessities that they had to be remade to fit the image of the respectable African leader.[15]

### Economic reconstruction: the delicate balance of exploitation and development

The post-war dilemma for France and Britain was that they needed empire more than ever and had fewer means to enforce their power over it. With the destruction of manufacturing plant in Europe and with revolution and

---

[13] Kathleen Paul, *Whitewashing Britain: Race and Citizenship in the Postwar Era* (Ithaca, 1997).

[14] David Anderson, *Histories of the Hanged: Britain's Dirty War and the End of Empire* (New York, 2005).

[15] These themes are developed in Cooper, *Decolonization*.

uncertainty in Asian colonies, Africa loomed large in post-war planning, the most promising source of primary products, which was about all that either empire was able to sell for hard currency. Sir Stafford Cripps, the Labour Government's Minister for Economic Affairs, told the conference of African Governors in 1947, 'the whole future of the sterling area and its ability to survive depends in my view upon a quick and extensive development of our African resources'.[16] The Foreign Secretary, Ernest Bevin, fantasized, 'If only we pushed on & developed Africa we could have U.S. dependent on us, & eating out of our hand in four or five years.'[17]

This was fantasy, but it did mean that French and British governments had to take expanding the productive capacity of Africa more seriously than they had before. The Labour Government was also sensitive to accusations that it was merely interested in exploiting Africa more intensely. The Colonial Development and Welfare Act of 1940, passed in the aftermath of waves of strikes and disorders in the West Indies and central Africa in the late 1930s, provided the ideal conceptual basis for asserting that economic development would be a win-win situation. The French came up with their own develop-ment funding legislation in 1946. Both these acts repudiated, for the first time, the colonial doctrine that each colony had to pay for itself. Unlike any pre-vious effort, an explicit goal of these acts was to raise the standard of living of colonized people.[18]

The ministries in both Paris and London set about planning development for their African colonies, and both exhibited a sensibility also evident in their thinking about political change. 'African systems of land tenure and the cul-tural routines associated with them', said the head of the Colonial Office's economic division, 'if maintained to the full in their traditional form, would effectively prevent any rapid technical change, possibly any change at all'. His French equivalents believed Africans were 'frozen in anachronistic and ar-chaic concepts and do not see the necessity to participate by a voluntary and reasoned effort in the progress of their country. *On the whole the masses are*

---

[16] Transcript of African Governors' Conference, 12 November 1947, 37–40.

[17] Bevin quoted in Hugh Dalton diaries, 15 October 1948, cited in R. D. Pearce, *The Turning Point in Africa: British Colonial Policy 1938–1948* (London, 1982), 95–6.

[18] The history of 'development' is a burgeoning field. For a collection of recent contribu-tions, see *Journal of Modern European History* 8:1 (2010). For an earlier take on the subject, see Frederick Cooper and Randall Packard (eds), *International Development and the Social Sciences: Essays on the History and Politics of Knowledge* (Berkeley, 1997). One of the best recent studies of development as an on-the-ground, contested process is Monica Van Beusekom, *Negotiating Development: African Farmers and Colonial Experts at the Office du Niger, 1920–1960* (Portsmouth NH, 2002).

*not yet socially ready to adapt to the norms of a renovated life.*[19] But change they must, and so planners talked about the need for an 'agricultural revolution'. Other elements of the colonial establishment were well aware—and even boasted about the accomplishment—that Africans, without a lot of help, were producing cocoa, coffee, and other export crops, and indeed a boom in such exports was beginning, but the top planners felt they were starting at zero. Having at last admitted that Africans could be made into modern farmers and workers, they felt that only they knew how to make them fit the role.[20]

But even that conceit was a dynamic factor, for development was now clearly articulated as an imperial responsibility, and the standard of living of African rural farmers and urban workers was on the agenda. Like citizenship in French Africa, the fiction that the African was, or potentially was, a worker or farmer just like any other, soon became a claim-making construct. Trade unions were in a particularly good position to make such claims, and the post-war years in both French and British Africa witnessed a series of major strikes. The unions not only had the strategic possibility of withholding labour at a time when Africa's productive capacities were vital to empire, but they had a rhetoric with which to make claims. As early as the Dakar general strike of January 1946, the slogan 'equal pay for equal work' had become the labour movement's theme. It went on to demand a labour code that would treat workers of all origins equally, a goal achieved in 1952, and family allowances equivalent to those received by workers in France, a goal achieved by civil servants in 1950 and (in part) by private sector workers in 1956. In British Africa, such as in Mombasa's general strike of 1947, the theme of equality surfaced as well, although without the same appeal to empire-wide citizenship and its norms of equivalence that animated unions in French Africa.[21]

Getting a handle on the social struggles in Africa brought French and British governments into a spiral of escalating demands, as concessions encouraged trade union leaders and workers to make further demands and made them desirable allies of political leaders. Both governments responded by deploying the knowledge they thought they had: the experience of

[19] Sydney Caine, Minute, 23 April 1946, CO 852/1003/3, British National Archives; 'Observations et conclusions personnelles du Gouverneur Roland Pré, Président de la Commission d'Etude et de Coordination des Plans de Modernisation et d'Equipement des Territoires d'Outre-Mer', May 1954, Archives d'Outre-Mer, emphasis in original.

[20] Joseph Morgan Hodge, *Triumph of the Expert: Agrarian Doctrines of Development and the Legacies of British Colonialism* (Athens OH, 2007); Joanna Lewis, *Empire State-Building: War and Welfare in Kenya, 1925–52* (Oxford, 2000).

[21] Frederick Cooper, *On the African Waterfront: Urban Disorder and the Transformation of Work in Colonial Mombasa* (New Haven, 1987).

managing class conflict at home. They began to articulate a vision of a stable workforce, socialized into industrial discipline and urban life, breaking ties with backward rural villages and settling permanently, with wives and children, in cities, minetowns, and commercial centres. They envisioned a new gender order based on the ideal of the male breadwinner, as much as a new system of organizing labour. Not surprisingly, the vision stood at an oblique angle to the reality of daily life in post-war cities, as Africans faced not only difficult conditions of life, but also sought to create forms of family life and urban association that differed considerably from the Eurocentric models of the labour officers.[22] Nonetheless, even the imaginary possibility of a new order of class relations in Africa—and fear not only of radical movements, but of social chaos—confronted colonial governments with the high costs of meeting wage demands and providing the social services necessary to give their new visions even a semblance of reality.

### African alternatives: claim-making between empire and nations

We assume, from the way things ended up in the 1960s, that every African politician was or should have been claiming the right to have an independent nation-state. Such claims were present at the start, but the constellation was, at war's end, much wider than that. The Pan-African Congress of Manchester of October 1945 proclaimed the common struggle of the African diaspora against colonialism, but it was vague on what would replace it—territorial autonomy was not foremost on the agenda.[23] In the autumn of 1945, political activists in French Africa began a series of campaigns for seats in the assembly in Paris. The most important claim made by practically all the political activists in French Africa was for citizenship to be extended as widely as possible and to convey the fullest set of rights that could be wrung from the assembly. After the constitution enshrined a generalized citizenship for French Africans, political elites continued to battle to correct the flaws in the document and to insist that not just full political rights, but social and economic

---

[22] Cooper, *Decolonization*. The pioneering research of Georges Balandier began in the mid-1950s to expose the complex realities of African urban life. *Sociologie des Brazzavilles noires*, 2nd edn (Paris, 1985 [1955]). For a recent study of family life and gender relations, see Lisa Lindsay, *Working with Gender: Men, Women, and Wage Labour in Southwest Nigeria* (Portsmouth, NH, 2003). On gender and politics, see Lynn Thomas, *Politics of the Womb: Women, Reproduction, and the State in Kenya* (Berkeley, 2003).

[23] Another possibility that seemed viable at war's end but was soon marginalized was that of a single anti-imperial project embracing both Africans and African-Americans. See Penny von Eschen, *Race against Empire: Black Americans and Anticolonialism, 1937–1957* (Ithaca, 1997).

rights, including the benefits of the new welfare state, would go to all Africans. A group of political activists founded in 1946 a political party, the Rassemblement Démocratique Africaine intended to take on French power across all of Africa, and until its leaders divided in 1958 over the issue of claiming immediate independence, it focused on demands for social and economic equality and more political voice and autonomy within the French Union.[24]

There were blockages along this route, but major milestones too, such as the Labour Code of 1952 that brought the 40-hour week, paid vacations, organizing rights, and other benefits of the French worker to all wage workers in the colonies. Union leaders were well aware that their arguments depended on the French connection and on the French Union being considered a meaningful unit of belonging and activity. But Léopold Senghor made it clear that he wanted that Union to be about political and civil equality, not about conformity to a French way of life. As he put it in regard to the Senegalese who had elected him, 'If they are politically French, they are not culturally French.'[25]

We know, in retrospect, that citizenship was too little, too late in Algeria, but in 1946 it was not such a sure thing. For Ferhat Abbas, a leading Algerian political leader, the point was to acquire a citizenship without giving up the sense of a distinct Algerian nationality. As he put it, 'For us, the problem is to find a form that permits us to integrate Muslim nationalism into French politics, and the best form seems to us to be federalism.'[26] What Abbas and Senghor meant by federalism was not exactly what most politicians from European France had in mind—the latter were thinking more of a devolution of specified political functions, with strong, French, institutions at the federal level. But a leading centre-right politician, Paul Coste-Floret, could say in

---

[24] Politicians in post-war Senegal, Côte d'Ivoire, and Dahomey, most notably, were emerging from a relatively lively activist milieu and organizing themselves effectively. Where education and associational life was more curtailed, especially in French Equatorial Africa, the first politicians came out of government service and missions, with less autonomy, and access to office-produced politics, rather than politics leading to office. See Florence Bernault, *Démocraties ambiguës en Afrique Centrale: Congo-Brazzaville, Gabon: 1940–1965* (Paris, 1996). See also Joseph Roger de Benoist, *L'Afrique Occidentale Française de 1944 à 1960* (Dakar, 1982), Ruth Schachter Morgenthau, *Political Parties in French-Speaking West Africa* (Oxford, 1964), and Tony Chafer, *The End of Empire in French West Africa: France's Successful Decolonization?* (Oxford, 2002).

[25] Senghor, Assemblée Nationale Constituante, Commission de la Constitution, *Comptes Rendus*, 12 February 1946, 443.

[26] Ferhat Abbas, ibid., 19 September 1946, 577.

1946 what would be astounding from the Left as much as the Right today: 'We are today partisans of a pluralist democracy, that is a democracy of groups.'[27]

We are thus talking about a framework for political debate in France around federalism, which could be pushed in a direction more like an old empire, with a strong centre presiding over components marked by difference, or toward equality, with European France alongside African France in a wider political structure. The 1946 Constitution was a compromise, more like the former, but in generalizing citizenship, while allowing Muslims and others overseas to keep their civil status, it met the minimal demands of most African deputies. They regarded their defence of the citizenship provisions against attempts to dilute them as a triumph. They had put on the table alternatives that were neither continuation of colonialism nor the break-up of empire into territorial nation states. They were arguing that sovereignty was not all-or-nothing, that it could be shared among embedded territorial units or even embedded states.

In 1958, what had once been called colonies, later overseas territories, acquired the more ponderous name of 'Member States'. A few years later, Mamadou Dia of Senegal put his goal this way: 'It is necessary in the final analysis that the imperialist conception of the Nation-State give way to the modern conception of a multinational state.'[28]

The politics of citizenship—imperial, national, or federal—was far from the only dimension of African politics in the post-war years. Historians have begun to analyse a variety of forms of political discourse and organization, some located in particular spaces, others spreading out over larger networks. Political discourse took place in local languages, in lingua franca (like KiSwahili), and in European languages. By the mid-1950s, political parties were proving skilful in coopting some of these strains of political activism into their cause. They presented not only a set of grievances against colonial regimes, but a possibility of accomplishing goals as colonial states made one concession after another to elected African politicians, allowing them to promise schools, roads, and other services to constituents and distribute patronage to supporters.[29]

---

[27] Coste-Floret, Assemblée Nationale Constituante, *Débats*, 9 April 1946, 1640.

[28] Mamadou Dia in *La Condition Humaine*, August 29, 1955. See also ibid., 29 November 1951, 31 May 1956.

[29] For an example both of political mobilization in local idioms and its relation to national political organization, see Steven Feierman, *Peasant Intellectuals: Anthropology and History in Tanzania* (Madison WI, 1990); Bruce Berman and John Lonsdale, *Unhappy Valley: Conflict in Kenya and Africa* (Athens OH, 1992); and Derek Peterson, *Creative*

Political movements in the 1950s did not all focus on the individual territorial state—on Senegal, Nigeria, or the Gold Coast. Regional movements proved hard for African politicians to tame in 1950s Africa. Alternative forms of political imagination appeared at an international level: the possibility of world revolution led by the recently victorious Soviet Union and especially after the 1955 Bandung conference, the possibility of an ex-colonial bloc working collectively against imperialism.[30] Indeed, the importance of subnational and supranational alternatives may well have focused the attention of elites in both Africa and Europe on a terrain they thought they could manage in their own interests—or at least a terrain they thought they could understand.[31]

The territorial alternative seemed to be a focus of political organization in British Africa at an earlier date than it did in French Africa, and its importance grew as African politicians refused to confine themselves to local government and pressured governments to give more and more scope to elected legislative bodies in each colony. Especially after the Gold Coast riots of 1948, officials had to undertake a series of constitutional reforms in each territory.

British Africans adapted to the territorial framework in which they saw increasing possibilities for power. Kwame Nkrumah had set out after the war to work for pan-Africanist organizations in London, but when he found himself in the Gold Coast, stopping in Liberia and Sierra Leone for a bit of pan-African organizing, he recognized quickly the opportunities which the minimal degree of political participation at the territorial level allowed. With a few stops in detention, he found that those openings could be pushed wider. In 1951, he became the 'Leader of Government Business' in the Gold Coast, a kind of junior prime minister. London knew that the Gold Coast was on the road from self-government to independence, and that the other colonies were well aware of the possibilities opening up to them. In assuming his new role, Nkrumah confronted another complexity in defining a new nation-state, the fear that such a state would be used by some of its members against others who regarded themselves as a distinct collectivity, with their own cultural and

*Writing: Translation, Bookkeeping, and the Work of Imagination in Colonial Kenya* (Portsmouth NH, 2004). On politics and religion in regional perspective, see Karen Fields, *Revival and Rebellion in Colonial Central Africa* (Princeton, 1985).

[30] For more on the international context, see Odd Arne Westad, *The Global Cold War: Third World Interventions and the Making of Our Times* (Cambridge, 2005). On Bandung, see Christopher Lee (ed.), *Making a World after Empire: The Bandung Moment and Its Political Afterlives* (Athens OH, 2010).

[31] For an overall interpretation of African independence and its consequences, see Frederick Cooper, *Africa since 1940: The Past of the Present* (Cambridge, 2002).

economic interests. He put down a movement in the relatively wealthy cocoa-producing region of the Gold Coast that used his own language of nationalism to claim an Asante, rather than a Gold-Coast nation. As he consolidated power, he attempted to prevent cocoa-generated wealth from financing opposition politics, making the state into the focus of aspirations for economic development and social advancement.[32] But when Nkrumah achieved in 1957 his promise of turning the colony of the Gold Coast into the state of Ghana, he saw beyond it, hoping to create what he called a 'United States of Africa'.[33]

That is to get beyond the scope of this paper. Whatever Nkrumah, Senghor, and others wanted in 1945, by the late 1950s, it was becoming clear that what they could get was the nation-state. Nkrumah wanted more, and Senghor wanted something better. Even as governments elected under universal suffrage were gaining real power within French Africa, Senghor expressed his disappointment. Africa was being balkanized he said, invoking by his reference to an earlier imperial breakup—that of the Ottoman and Austro-Hungarian empires, the danger the nation-states would be too small, too weak, too disunited to exercise real power in the world. To him, federation had offered the possibility not only of connections with France, but of connections within Africa, of sovereignty shared both horizontally and vertically. The failure of the one would turn out to be the failure of the other.

What we are left with, looking from the vantage point of 1945, was that as France and Britain tried to reconstruct empire, African political activists, aware that empire could not be constructed as it had been before, saw uncertain but open possibilities to make claims not just for autonomy and expression of an African personality, but for forms of political inclusion and access to resources as a right open to members of a supranational polity. Out of differing but overlapping agendas at war's end came a dynamic of politics more diverse and uncertain than national narratives today allow us to see.

---

[32] Jean Marie Allman, *The Quills of the Porcupine: Asante Nationalism in an Emergent Ghana* (Madison, 1993). See also Richard Rathbone, *Nkrumah and the Chiefs: The Politics of Chieftaincy in Ghana, 1951–1960* (Athens OH, 1999).
[33] Kwame Nkrumah, *Africa Must Unite* (New York, 1963).

# Reconstructing Europe through Rejuvenating Empire: the British, French, and Dutch Experiences Compared

**Nicholas J. White**

In November 1947, Stafford Cripps, the UK's Minister for Economic Affairs, told a conference of Britain's governors in Africa that with the sterling area's dollar deficit running at £600 to £700 million a year 'we should increase out of all recognition the tempo of African economic development', boosting production of anything that 'will save dollars or will sell in a dollar market'.[1] Here was evidence that in the UK's post-war reconstruction crisis 'more completely than ever before economics and empire had come together'.[2] The same applied for Europe's next two largest maritime empires. 'One of the assumptions underlying policy in the Fourth Republic was that the French Empire [albeit restyled 'Union'] ... could be developed economically in order to strengthen France's position in the postwar world.'[3] Meanwhile, in The Netherlands where 'total regeneration was the order of the day, as to the Dutch East Indies [Indonesia] there was only one thought: restoration of the ties between mother country and the colonies, and restoration of the triangle of commerce, Netherlands-Indonesia-America, which according to the experts was essential for the revival of the Dutch economy.'[4] Although the post-war 'second colonial occupation' was partly concerned with issues of international prestige (particularly for France and Holland), a prime focus of this chapter is the relationship between the development drive overseas and the most pressing international economic issue shared by London, Paris, and The Hague, namely the dollar shortage. In the short term, at least, it will be argued that these were largely successful strategies. But, at the same time, the

[1] The National Archives of the United Kingdom (hereafter TNA), CO 847/36/2, 12 November 1947 in Ronald Hyam (ed.), *The Labour Government and the End of Empire, 1945–51*,(London, 1992), vol. 1, 299, 300.

[2] John Darwin, *The End of the British Empire: The Historical Debate* (Oxford, 1991), 197.

[3] Frances M. B. Lynch, *France and the International Economy: From Vichy to the Treaty of Rome* (London, 1997), 186.

[4] H. L. Wesseling, 'Post-Imperial Holland', *Journal of Contemporary History*, 15 (1980), 126.

latter part of this chapter demonstrates how the 'new imperialism' of the immediate post-war period exacerbated problems of colonial political management. Moreover, imperial policies and their unwitting consequences provoked new tensions within European imperial and colonial elites, and especially alienated and disillusioned key metropolitan business leaders.

## I

As secure markets for British goods, wartime and immediate post-war planning in London had viewed the colonies as vital for offsetting declining British industrial competitiveness, especially if a post-war depression, along the lines of that prevailing after 1918, induced the US to retreat into protectionism. Intensified colonial development would boost overseas purchasing power, compensating British industry for markets lost during the Second World War. Britain could also beat global depression by drawing upon colonial primary production in a situation where food and raw material shortages were expected to be far more prolonged than proved the reality.[5]

Vichy planners shared this fear of global depression and a determination to preserve imperial preferences in the post-war world. The latter would enable metropolitan France to revive and expand its production (of steel, mechanical engineering goods, and automobiles in particular) through captive export markets in Overseas France.[6] The Free French at their grand planning conference for the post-war empire in January-February 1944 at Brazzaville (the capital of French Equatorial Africa, *l'Afrique équatoriale française*: AEF) were more sensitive towards nationalist aspirations and Rooseveltian anti-colonialism. They chose to make 'the object of our colonial policy...the development of the productive potential of the overseas territories and the growth of their wealth as to assure the Africans of a better life by raising their purchasing power and improving their standards of living'.[7] In this, a more liberal tariff regime (reducing the cost of imported goods and boosting the competiveness of exports) would have to prevail. Nevertheless, from the summer of 1944, American policy-makers were to find the Free French hostile

---

[5] R. F. Holland, 'The Imperial Factor in British Strategies from Attlee to Macmillan, 1945–63', *Journal of Imperial and Commonwealth History*, 12, 1 (January 1984), 166–7; Frank Heinlein, *British Government Policy and Decolonisation, 1945–1963: Scrutinising the Official Mind*, (London, 2002), 77 n. 5.

[6] Lynch, *International Economy*, 188.

[7] Ministère des Colonies, Paris, *La Conférence africaine française, 1945* in R. C. Bridges et al. (eds), *Nations & Empires: Documents on the History of Europe and on its Relations with the World since 1648* (London, 1969), 309.

towards any opening up of North African trade to the American market and stockpiling goods for the liberation of the metropole.

Subsequently in September 1945 France's planning supremo Jean Monnet advised the Paris government against inviting American capitalists to finance colonial development, for fear of France losing economic control over its treasured resource base. In the 'spirit of Brazzaville', the desire of the Ministry for France Overseas after 1946 was to revoke the imperial preference system dating back to 1928; the Ministry of National Economy overruled, however, arguing that the severe shortage of foreign exchange demanded protected markets in the colonies for French manufactures, and a reverse supply of raw materials.[8] Moreover, in July 1946, Minister of Food Yves Farge had even gone so far as to seek control over the Ministry of Colonies 'to ensure that the empire was entirely subordinated to France's immediate supply requirements'.[9] Meanwhile, as part of Monnet's initial reconstruction programme, the Indochina states would play an integral part through an ambitious industrialization project which would not only solve Vietnam's demographic crisis through revitalizing agriculture but also develop new trade and investment opportunities for French business, and fill the vacuum in East and South East Asia left by Japan's collapse.[10]

Before the Japanese Occupation, some 8 per cent of Dutch imports had been derived from Indonesia and 10 per cent of Dutch exports flowed in the opposite direction. As well as the massive transfers of invisible earnings to Holland, the Netherlands East Indies (NEI) was believed to have accounted for 14 per cent of Dutch GNP in 1938.[11] To resurrect these benefits, following

[8] Lynch, *International Economy*, 189, 197–8.

[9] Martin Thomas, 'The Roots of French Decolonization: Ideas, Economics and Reform, 1900–1946' in Martin Thomas, Bob Moore, and L. J. Butler, *Crises of Empire: Decolonization and Europe's Imperial States, 1918–1975*, (London, 2008), 140.

[10] Andrew Hardy, 'The Economics of French Rule in Indochina: A Biography of Paul Bernard (1892–1960)', *Modern Asian Studies*, 32, 4 (1998), 824–8; Hugues Tertrais, 'France and the Associated States of Indochina, 1945–1955' in Marc Frey, Ronald W. Pruessen, and Tan Tai Yong (eds), *The Transformation of Southeast Asia: International Perspectives on Decolonization*, (Armonk NY, 2003), 73–4.

[11] Pierre van der Eng, 'Marshall Aid as a Catalyst in the Decolonization of Indonesia, 1947–9', *Journal of Southeast Asian Studies*, 19, 2 (September 1988), 336; Marc Frey, 'Dutch Elites and Decolonization', paper presented at the 'Trajectories of Decolonisation' conference, University of Cologne (October 2008), 3. I am grateful to Professor Frey for permitting me to cite his paper, which has subsequently been published in German as 'Niederländische Eliten und die Dekolonisierung Indonesiens' in *Jahrbuch Zentrum für Niederlande-Studien*, 18 (2008). Thanks are also due to Professor Frey for kindly commenting on this chapter.

the establishment of Dutch control in the 'outer islands', as well as bridge-heads on Java and Sumatra by the end of 1946, the Dutch drew up a development plan for Indonesian rehabilitation. A reconstruction bank would underpin the swift re-establishment of road, rail, and power supplies as well as the European-dominated mineral extraction and plantation industries. In this, Dutch private capital would once again play a leading role, supplemented by some $300m per annum from the United States. At the same time, 'inducement goods'—textiles especially—would be imported to draw the Indonesian population away from the Republic which had been declared by Sukarno on Japan's sudden surrender in August 1945.[12]

But, on top of their roles as markets and raw material suppliers for metropolitan production, as well as fields of investment for European capital, the real attraction of the colonial empires in the era of reconstruction lay in the contribution they could make to relieving acute balance of payment deficits, and especially plugging the US dollar gap. Britain, France, and The Netherlands shared a desperate need for foreign exchange (and especially dollar) earnings from colonial exports to purchase food and goods vital for metropolitan reconstruction but which were extremely scarce in Western Europe.

Through the sterling-area system, the UK was able to pool dollar earnings from colonial exports, the big four in 1949–50 being rubber (mainly from Malaya), tin (mainly from Malaya), cocoa (mainly from the Gold Coast), and bauxite (mainly from British Guiana).[13] As the premiere dollar earner of the pre-war colonial empire, the reoccupation and reconstruction of Malaya was a key priority. To ensure the swift despatch of industrial inspection schemes to reoccupied Malaya, the Supreme Allied Commander in South East Asia, Lord Louis Mountbatten, was reminded by the War Office that 'Importance of early rehabilitation of industry is therefore far reaching and not confined to well being of Territory'.[14] The War Damage Commission in the UK, meanwhile, gave priority to the rebuilding of key infrastructure likely to stimulate South East Asian trade, notably India Buildings in Liverpool, the headquarters of the leading British shipping line to the region, the Ocean Steam Ship

---

[12] Marc Frey, 'Control, Legitimacy, and the Securing of Interests: European Development Policy in South-East Asia from the Late Colonial Period to the Early 1960s', *Contemporary European History*, 12, 4 (November 2003), 399.

[13] *The Sterling Area: An American Analysis*, London: Economic Cooperation Administration Special Mission to the United Kingdom (1951), 79–83.

[14] Nicholas J. White, *Business, Government, and the End of Empire: Malaya, 1942–57*, (Kuala Lumpur, 1996), 65.

Company, which had been severely damaged by German bombing.[15] Malaya's surplus with the dollar area increased from $170m in 1948 to $350 million in 1952.[16] In a BBC radio broadcast on 22 June 1948, four days after the declaration of the Emergency—a euphemism for the 12-year shooting war against the Malayan Communist Party (MCP)—the leading rubber estate owner, Sir John Hay, declared that:

> Malaya's rubber production . . . produces dollars to an amount that exceeds in total value all domestic exports from Britain to the US . . . if, for any reason, the operations of the great rubber industry are interrupted or seriously impaired, Britain's dollar situation would be rendered more acute than ever. This country would then have less food, less clothes, and there would be fewer dollars with which to buy raw materials—and that would mean unemployment. All of us are thus deeply concerned in what is happening in Malaya.[17]

Concurrently, colonial exports to the UK achieved even greater significance as dollar savers. The great success story here was the growth of the Northern Rhodesian copper industry from the 1930s. Pre-war, Britain received less than a quarter of its supplies from what would become Zambia and the quantities destined for the US were miniscule. In 1949–50, by contrast, Northern Rhodesia supplied nearly half of Britain's requirements in addition to one-eighth of the copper imported by the US.[18] Meanwhile, Britain's maze of protectorates and client states in the Middle East also came under the sterling-area umbrella, meaning that oil exports could be paid for in sterling. In 1947, 60 per cent of Britain's oil was extracted from the region, and in 1949 a Cabinet committee hoped that by 1951 this would increase to 82 per cent, representing the 'largest single factor in balancing British overseas payments'.[19] Loss of oil production in Iran following the nationalization of the

---

[15] Malcolm Falkus, *The Blue Funnel Legend: A History of the Ocean Steam Ship Company, 1865–1973*, (London, 1990), 273–4. Stafford Cripps's brother, Leonard, and his cousin, Sir John Hobhouse, were leading directors of Blue Funnel.

[16] A. J. Stockwell, 'British Imperial Policy and Decolonization in Malaya, 1942–52', *Journal of Imperial & Commonwealth History*, 13 (1984), 78.

[17] White, *Business, Government, and the End of Empire*, 99.

[18] *Sterling Area: An American Analysis*, 85–6; L. J. Butler, *Copper Empire: Mining and the Colonial State in Northern Rhodesia, c. 1930–64*, (London, 2007), 111.

[19] Ronald Hyam, *Britain's Declining Empire: The Road to Decolonisation*, (Cambridge, 2006), 124; Ritchie Ovendale, *Britain, the United States and the Transfer of Power in the Middle East, 1945–62*, (Leicester, 1996), 18.

Abadan refinery in 1951 was more than compensated for by the growth of output from the British-protected states on the other side of the Persian Gulf, especially Kuwait.[20] The defence of the Middle East also took on new urgency to protect Africa's dollar-earning and dollar-saving potential from Soviet expansionism.[21]

As well as maintaining the value of the pound (and thus making US imports cheaper), the sterling-area system acted as a 'counter-inflationary cushion' at a time when nationalization of the commanding heights was under way and the welfare state was being established alongside reconstruction in metropolitan Britain.[22] Krozewski and Hinds have both argued, therefore, that it became highly unlikely that the Attlee government would grant wholesale independence for the colonial empire because it was here that political control allowed the UK to maintain a grip on monetary and financial policy (and especially prevent colonial governments from freely spending their dollar earnings). Independent members of the sterling area (such as Australia) were increasingly unwilling to submit to Bank of England diktats after 1945. There was also a fear that a transfer of power to irresponsible radical nationalists would lead to the rapid running down of colonial sterling balances, resulting in massive destabilization and inflation at home.[23]

In this attempt at imperial rejuvenation, independence for India and Palestine in the course of 1947–48, and at the cost of partition in both cases, might appear contradictory. But these withdrawals can actually be seen as part of an imperial rationalization 'cutting adrift from dependencies which were net liabilities'.[24] India 'had ceased to be an imperial asset. As far as visible trade was concerned India was now in deficit with the US and was no longer a net contributor to the Sterling Area's dollar pool'.[25] The same applied to Burma whose India-bound exports, in contrast to Malaya's massive US rubber and tin trades, did not make the troubled territory a significant dollar earner.[26] Meanwhile, Foreign Secretary Ernest Bevin told the Cabinet

---

[20] Simon C. Smith, *Kuwait, 1950–1965: Britain, the Al-Sabah, and Oil*, (Oxford, 2000).

[21] Wm. Roger Louis, *The British Empire in the Middle East, 1945–1951*, (Oxford, 1984).

[22] Holland, 'Imperial Factor', 168.

[23] Gerold Krozewski, *Money and the End of Empire: British International Economic Policy and the Colonies, 1947–58*, (London, 2001); Allister Hinds, *Britain's Sterling Colonial Policy and Decolonization, 1939–1958*, (Westport CT and London, 2001).

[24] Holland, 'Imperial Factor', 169.

[25] P. J. Cain and A. G. Hopkins, *British Imperialism: Crisis and Reconstruction, 1914–1990*, (Harlow, 1993), 196.

[26] Smith, R. B., 'Some Contrasts Between Burma and Malaya in British Policy in South-East Asia, 1942–6' in R. B. Smith and A. J. Stockwell (eds), *British Policy and the Transfer of Power in Asia: Documentary Perspectives*, (London, 1988), 46–8, 68–72.

in September 1947, Britain's withdrawal from Palestine would have the advantages of no longer expending scarce British resources in the suppression of 'one Palestinian community for the advantage of the other', while avoiding 'pursuing a policy destructive' of Britain's relationship with the oil-producing Arab states.[27] In contrast, the Treasury in London became increasingly attracted to colonial economic development in Africa, especially after the convertibility crisis of August 1947. Solving the post-war dollar shortage by stimulating colonial exports was also a key element in the September 1949 decision to devalue the pound by 30 per cent. Heightened interest in the economic potentialities of the rump empire beyond South Asia was also emphasized by the creation of the Cabinet's Colonial Development Committee at the end of 1948.

In post-war France imperial autarky was to be combined with an increasing stress on the dollar-earning potentialities of the overseas territories of the French Union. The revised Monnet Plan for 1948–52 (the first combined plan for the French empire as a whole) downgraded concerns over the living standards of colonial peoples in an overarching demand for an escalation of colonial exports beyond the Francophone world (to North America, Western Europe and the Far East especially) in an attempt to rectify the Franc Zone's overall foreign exchange deficit, and particularly that of European France. At the same time, the colonial territories would save on hard currency through supplying metropolitan France with edible oils, cotton, sisal, wool, rubber, timber, and minerals.[28] Moreover, as France, like Britain, faced a balance of payments crisis during 1947, colonial governments were increasingly compelled to restrict imports from outside the French Union: in Gabon, despite promises of decentralization, the British merchant house, John Holt & Co. (Liverpool) Ltd, found import licences and foreign currency allocations tightly controlled from the AEF capital in Brazzaville.[29] Indeed, the cement of an even more integrated post-war imperial economic system was to be the Franc Zone, co-ordinated by the Banque de France. Very much akin to the Sterling Area, the foreign exchange proceeds of the French overseas territories were paid into a common pot, and the colonies were given hard currency allowances (usually far less than their contributions to the central pool) to purchase imports from outside

---

[27] TNA, CAB 129/21, CP (47) 259, 18 September 1947 in Hyam (ed.), *Labour Government*, 75.

[28] Lynch, *International Economy*, 190–1.

[29] Bodleian Library of Commonwealth and African Studies at Rhodes House, John Holt & Company (Liverpool) Ltd Records, MSS Afr. s 825 [hereafter JH], 470a (ii), Libreville Administration Reports, June and Sept. 1947.

the Zone.[30] The stress on dollar earning, as well as the direct supply of commodities for French reconstruction, increased the importance of Black Africa, especially as Vietnam descended into war after 1946 and North Africa, particularly Algeria, began to experience violent political unrest as well. An intensification of cash crop production was particularly focused upon but after 1950 there was also an upsurge in mining activity—iron ore in Mauritania, bauxite in Guinea, manganese in Gabon, phosphates in Senegal and Togo and uranium in Niger, as well as aluminium smelting in Cameroon drawing upon the hydroelectric power of the Sanaga River.[31] The French Pacific took on added value too, not least because New Caledonia's nickel was a precious dollar earner.[32]

In The Hague, the popular phrase 'Indië verloren, rampspoed geboren' ('The Indies lost, misfortune born') was underlined from the spring of 1947 as the Dutch cabinet came to appreciate that The Netherlands lacked foreign exchange to continue financing its own, let alone Indonesian, economic recovery. Indeed, during the 1920s and 1930s, Indonesia's export trade had diversified away from the metropole as new export products such as rubber, copra, and fuel oil came on stream and were sold on world markets. Particularly significant here was the rubber trade with the United States, and the Dutch 'home' economy was able to sustain a major dollar deficit in the interwar years thanks to the NEI's dollar surplus.[33] It was decided, therefore, to launch an all-out military offensive against the Republic to revitalize these pre-war benefits. A full-blown reoccupation of Java and Sumatra would permit stocks of export products to be seized and for export producing industries to be reactivated to earn foreign exchange. Moreover, it would convince the Americans to release funds for the rejuvenation of Indonesia's infrastructure as part of Holland's development plan (but which were being held back by Washington's doubts about the ability of the colonial

---

[30] Jean Suret-Canale, 'From Colonization to Independence in French Tropical Africa: The Economic Background' in Prosser Gifford and Wm. Roger Louis (eds), *The Transfer of Power in Africa: Decolonization, 1940–1960*, (New Haven, 1982), 461.

[31] Martin Thomas, 'Decolonizing the French African Federations after 1945' in Thomas, Moore, and Butler, *Crises of Empire*, 160; Suret-Canale, 'Tropical Africa', 453–4.

[32] Martin Thomas, 'Territories Apart: Madagascar, the Togo Trusteeship and French Island Territories' in Thomas, Moore, and Butler, *Crises of Empire*, 325.

[33] J. Thomas Lindblad, 'The Economic Relationship between the Netherlands and Colonial Indonesia, 1870–1940' in Jan Luiten van Zanden (ed.), *The Economic Development of the Netherlands since 1870*, (Cheltenham, 1996), 113; Anne Booth, 'Growth and Stagnation in an Era of Nation-Building: Indonesian Economic Performance from 1950 to 1965' in J. Thomas Lindblad (ed.), *Historical Foundations of a National Economy in Indonesia, 1890s to 1990s*, (Amsterdam, 1996), 402.

administration to maintain law and order throughout much of Java and Sumatra). The first 'police action' which began on 20 July 1947 was revealingly code-named 'Operation Produce'.[34] The offensive was terminated after two weeks through pressure from the UN, and, given international sympathy for the Republic, the US continued to refuse to disburse the Export-Import Bank loan. But the Dutch were now in control of much of the export-crop-producing areas of Java in addition to the tea, rubber, oil palm, and tobacco plantation belt along the east coast of Sumatra and the fuel oil and coal resources around Palembang.[35] Concurrently, the Dutch successfully resisted American proposals in the Marshall Aid programme to cancel the dollars earned by Dutch oil refineries in the Netherlands Antilles—which processed Venezuela's output—against Indonesia's dollar deficit.[36]

Indeed, much of this Dutch, French, and British effort at rejuvenating empire was tolerated by the United States, anxious to stabilize political conditions in Western Europe.[37] By 1949, on top of improving 'the livelihood and general welfare of the population of dependent areas', US officials justified including the colonies in the European Recovery Programme (ERP) because this would improve the balance of payments position of Western Europe vis-à-vis the United States and increase production of commodities of strategic value to the West in the emerging Cold War.[38] The Americans, like the European colonials, had come to accept that the material prosperity of Africa and Asia and the economic recovery of Europe were mutually compatible. There would be 10 billion francs of Marshall Aid spending in French West Africa (*l'Afrique occidentale française*: AOF) between 1948 and 1952, the bulk of which was allocated to railway construction and port and road

---

[34] Van der Eng, 'Marshall Aid', 336–7; Frey, 'Dutch Elites', 1, 3; Marc Frey, 'The Indonesian Revolution and the Fall of the Dutch Empire: Actors, Factors, Strategies' in Frey, Pruessen, and Yong, *Transformation of Southeast Asia*, 94.

[35] Bob Moore, 'Indonesia: The Realities of Diplomacy' in Thomas, Moore, and Butler, *Crises of Empire*, 324. British engineering interests looked forward to booming sales of small power units for plantations and coastal shipping since 'the Dutch . . . *must* devote all their energy and available hard currency to re-establishing their export trade', which 'would be carried out at the expense of the full rehabilitation of the major public and utility services' (emphasis in original). Harrisons & Crosfield Archive, Guildhall Library, London, Ms. 37663, report by J. N. Rofe and M. I. Prichard, 22 August 1947.

[36] van der Eng, 'Marshall Aid', 341–2.

[37] Ibid., 338, 340; Lynch, *International Economy*, 198; Wm. Roger Louis and Ronald Robinson, 'The Imperialism of Decolonization', *Journal of Imperial & Commonwealth History*, 22, 3 (1994), 467–73.

[38] Frey, 'European Development Policy', 403.

development to assist in the export of colonial production.[39] As we have seen, the Dutch set great score on attracting US aid to the rejuvenation of the Indonesian economy. After the temporary US-brokered *Renville* rapprochement between the Dutch and the Indonesian Republic of January 1948, Washington doled out $506 million in Marshall Aid to the Netherlands, including $84 million for reconstruction of the Indies. At this stage (i.e. before the Republic's purging of its communist element after the latter's abortive coup in December 1948) the Dutch were still regarded as 'the best guarantee of stability and strategic war materials supply'.[40] Such largesse was rarely publicly articulated because explicit support for the revival of European colonialism sat uncomfortably with the rhetoric of the Atlantic Charter or the Truman Doctrine. But, as Washington appreciated in the late 1940s and early 1950s, 'Rapid decolonization might both undermine the European economies, and cause instability in the Third World, which could only benefit Moscow', not least because the 'dollar gap forced European powers to increasingly earn dollars through their colonial possessions'.[41] Intra-imperial exchange controls and trade preferences, despite the global free trade crusade in Washington, were also accepted in the short term as a *quid pro quo* for enhanced US security: for example, 68 per cent of the US's cobalt (crucial for jet engine manufacture) was derived from European colonial territories in 1950.[42]

## II

Relieved of pressure from the United States for immediate decolonization, the British in tropical Africa continued the more intrusive economic imperialism of the war years, including bulk purchasing by state-run commodity boards at fixed prices below world market rates. For example, early in the war, the UK government had established the West African Produce Control Board to buy export crops (notably cocoa) and regulate exports. In 1947, two specific Cocoa Marketing Boards were established, one in Ghana and one in Nigeria. The crop was bought from African peasant farmers and cooperatives through licensed buying agents from whom the marketing boards took over

---

[39] Thomas, 'French African Federations', 160–1.

[40] Moore 'Realities of Diplomacy', 327; see also R. J. McMahon, *Colonialism and Cold War: The United States and the Struggle for Indonesian Independence*, (Ithaca, NY, 1981).

[41] David Ryan, 'By Way of Introduction: The United States, Decolonization and the World System' in David Ryan and Victor Pungong (eds), *The United States and Decolonization: Power and Freedom*, (Basingstoke, 2000), 17.

[42] H. S. Wilson, *African Decolonization*, (London, 1994), 86–7.

the raw cocoa at the ports.[43] Bulk buying of copper, which had been suspended in 1944, was actually reintroduced by the Ministry of Supply in 1947 and continued until 1953.[44] At the same time, there were grandiose plans for the development of new export industries in Africa, designed to deal with the twin problems of food and raw material scarcities and the shortage of hard currency to purchase imports. The classic example here was the East African Groundnuts Scheme as a means of relieving the metropolitan shortage of edible oils and fats. The scheme came under the control of the Ministry of Food's Overseas Food Corporation after April 1948. It was a disaster. In 1949 the proposals of a working party sent to the Tanganyika mandate were accepted and the whole venture closed down, save for experimental work. The vast majority of the £40 million budget was spent on clearing a mere 1.4 per cent of the planned total area of 3.2 million acres, and more groundnuts were planted than were ever produced for export to the UK. But, as with other British colonial development debacles, such as plans for the mass production of eggs in the Gambia, Groundnuts clearly illustrates the new imperial spirit in London. Indeed, the principal failing was the lack of a feasibility study to ascertain whether the envisaged large-scale mechanized production of crops—never tried in British tropical Africa before—would actually work. But it was precisely 'the urgency to produce' which meant that there was insufficient time for preliminary surveys and pilot projects.[45]

Although initiated in the 1920s, French Sudan's Office du Niger rice and cotton irrigation scheme was vastly expanded after 1945 with the intention of providing dollar-saving cotton for the French textile industry and rice for Senegal, which in turn produced dollar-saving peanuts for the French vegetable oils industry. The post-war era witnessed the Office engaged in a frenzied push to open up new areas, upgrade irrigation, level fields, and introduce mechanization. By 1961 the scheme came to rival Groundnuts for wastefulness and lack of productivity, sucking up over half of the AOF's collective agricultural budget and producing a miserable 0.3 per cent of the anticipated 300,000 tons of raw cotton.[46] Mechanized agricultural projects in French

[43] *Sterling Area: An American Analysis*, 474. Similar boards followed for groundnuts, oil palm, oil seeds, and cotton in the British West African territories.

[44] Butler, *Copper Empire*, 112–15.

[45] Joseph Morgan Hodge, *Triumph of the Expert: Agrarian Doctrines of Development and the Legacies of British Colonialism* (Athens, 2007), 209–13.

[46] Monica M. van Beusekom, 'Disjunctures in Theory and Practice: Making Sense of Change in Agricultural Development at the Office du Niger, 1920–60', *Journal of African History*, 41, 1 (2000), 80–1; D. K. Fieldhouse, *Black Africa, 1945–1980: Economic Decolonization and Arrested Development* (London, 1986), 13–14.

West Africa generally ended as 'fiascos' and most new growth in production was achieved by extending the area cultivated rather than through technical innovation.[47] But, like copper production in British Africa, there were success stories in late-colonial French Africa. In Ivory Coast, the opening of the port of Abidjan after 1951, combined with the growth of new roads, the mechanized clearing of forests, and the mass immigration of labour from Upper Volta, allowed Ivorian coffee production to rise by over 14 times from 10,000 tons in 1937 to 144,000 in 1960.[48]

Such development efforts in the late colonial world entailed a vastly enhanced role for the state. In 1945, the UK's Colonial Office succeeded in securing from the Treasury £120 million over a decade for the colonies through a new Colonial Development and Welfare Act, which greatly expanded upon the previous provisions of 1929 and 1940, and colonies were now requested to draw up 10-year development plans. To facilitate economic development throughout the colonial empire, the Colonial Development Corporation (CDC), with borrowing powers of up to £100 million, was formed in London in 1948. Colonial Secretary, Arthur Creech Jones, informed Prime Minister Attlee that the CDC would 'promote in every possible way increased colonial production on an economic and self-supporting basis with an eye to the production of foodstuffs, raw materials and manufactures whose supply to the UK or sale overseas will assist our balance of payments'.[49] Between 1945 and 1949 alone, the British pumped £86 million in grants and loans into Malaya's reconstruction, 'a huge amount in view of the Labour Government's scarce resources'.[50]

Recognizing that French private capital could not be relied upon to create a modernized colonial infrastructure, the state took on even more of a role in the French overseas empire. The *Fonds d'Investissement et de Développement Economique et Social des Territoires d'Outre Mer* (FIDES) was formed in 1946, followed by a specialist public fund for Indochina two years later. This represented a colonial investment fund some seven times larger than the UK's projected expenditures on its empire.[51] It also represented a remarkable reversal in French colonial practice, since after 1900 the *Loi de finances* had

---

[47] Suret-Canale, 'French Tropical Africa', 453.

[48] Ibid., 462.

[49] John Kent, *British Imperial Strategy and the Origins of the Cold War, 1944–49* (Leicester, 1993), 132.

[50] Wm. Roger Louis, 'The Dissolution of the British Empire in the Era of Vietnam' in Wm. Roger Louis, *The End of British Imperialism: The Scramble for Empire, Suez and Decolonization* (London, 2006), 563.

[51] Hardy, 'Paul Bernard', 827.

prohibited any drawing upon the metropole's budget for colonial needs—economic development had thus been funded by local taxation plus the efforts of the private sector.[52] Over the period 1949–55 France invested 1,340,000 million francs from public funds in the empire as against 100,000 million francs from private (principally French) investors from 1947–55.[53] According to Marseille for the 1940–58 era the private/government sector ratio of investment for the French empire was 1:5, as against 1:1.23 before 1914, 7:1 for 1915–29 and 1.48:1 for 1930–39.[54]

Within the FIDES framework ten-year development plans for individual territories and federations were drawn up in Paris for the period 1947–56. Revealingly, in AOF and AEF more than 60 per cent of credits were allocated to infrastructure development. There were other channels of French public funds for the empire as well, such as the Overseas France Bureau of Mines, the Atomic Energy Commission and the Petroleum Research Bureau, which took on responsibility for prospecting, capitalization of enterprises, and infrastructure development in mineral extraction. There was also a massive rise in equity participation and loans by the *Caisse Centrale de la France d'Outre-Mer* in colonial mining enterprises. In the AEF High Commissioner Bernard Cornut-Gentille (1947–51) declared that economic development was the 'essential activity' of his government, and impressed this upon the local assemblies of the Union in an effort to depoliticize them.[55]

To oversee the new development drive, the British Colonial Office's staffing strength increased by 45 per cent between 1945 and 1954. Wartime demands for production, marketing, and supplies as well as post-war development had already boosted the role of the Economic Department, and when it became a separate division in 1949 the development specialists accounted for a third of Colonial Office personnel.[56] In the colonies themselves, local bureaucracies were significantly expanded, especially new technical departments, such as labour, agriculture, forestry, and surveying, demanding more specialist skills sets from British and Dominion personnel than the pre-war transferable generalists. A full-scale recruitment drive was

---

[52] Suret-Canale, 'French Tropical Africa', 451.

[53] Lynch, *International Economy*, 200.

[54] J. Marseille, *Empire colonial et capitalisme française. Histoire d'un divorce*, (Paris, 1984), 105 cited in Fieldhouse, *Black Africa*, 13.

[55] Elikia M'Bokolo, 'French Colonial Policy in Equatorial Africa in the 1940s and 1950s' in Gifford and Louis, *Transfer of Power in Africa*, 196–7; Suret-Canale, 'French Tropical Africa', 452, 453–4.

[56] Ronald Hyam, 'Introduction' in Hyam (ed.), *Labour Government*, xlv; Hodge, *Triumph of the Expert*, 199.

launched in June 1945, attracting over 11,000 new recruits by 1953.[57] This 'second colonial occupation' (as the phenomenon has been famously termed for East Africa)[58] extended into British South East Asia as well. Pre-war Malayan Civil Service 'generalists' were now joined by an army of techno-crats, including economic advisers, trade union advisers, and organization and methods advisers and it has been estimated that the post-war Malayan Union/Federation of Malaya secretariat was six to seven times as large as the pre-war Federated Malay States equivalent.[59] On top of this, was the 'mini-ature Whitehall'—including representatives of the metropolitan Treasury, Board of Trade, Ministry of Transport, and Ministry of Labour–which sur-rounded the Commissioner General's Office in Singapore after 1948, as the island colony replaced New Delhi as UK headquarters in Asia.

This extension of bureaucracy was mirrored in the French empire with a significant increase in personnel and administrative capacity, particularly in agriculture and forestry departments. In Guinea, for example, decommis-sioned French soldiers swelled the ranks of the *Service des Eaux et Forêts*.[60] In western Cameroon, John Holt & Co's representatives complained that the 'local governments are delving more and more into commerce (and less and less, it seems, into their own work) and, unfortunately, with their limited experience in that sphere quite often demand and expect a degree of cooper-ation from the Firms ... far beyond the realms of commercial reason'.[61] In the Netherlands East Indies, commodity marketing boards and even a crash pro-gramme of industrialization supervised by the Department of Economic Affairs had preceded the Japanese Occupation. This statist tendency in the economy would be expanded post-war with the regulation of exports and imports, and a general penchant for planning, epitomized by the *Herstelbank* (Rehabilitation Bank) established in May 1948. The Department of Finance and its quangoes increased staffing levels from 900 to 1500 between 1947 and 1948 alone.[62] From the end of 1947 reformist lieutenant-governor Hubertus

---

[57] Ibid., 204–5.
[58] D. A. Low and J. M. Lonsdale, 'Introduction: Towards the New Order, 1945–63' in D. A. Low and Alison Smith (eds), *History of East Africa*, vol. 3 (Oxford, 1976), 13.
[59] J. M. Gullick, 'Prelude to Merdeka: Public Administration in Malaya, 1945–57', *South East Asia Research*, 5, 2 (1997), 158, 163.
[60] James Fairhead and Melissa Leach, 'Desiccation and Domination: Science and Struggles over Environment and Development in Colonial Guinea', *Journal of African History*, 41, 1 (2000), 44.
[61] JH, 470a (ii), quarterly report from N'kongsamba Agent, 6 June 1947.
[62] Howard Dick, 'Formation of the Nation-State, 1930s–1966' in Howard Dick et al., *The Emergence of a National Economy: An Economic History of Indonesia, 1800–2000*, (Crows Nest, New South Wales, 2002), 162, 180, 183; J. Thomas Lindblad, *Bridges to New*

van Mook declared that the rejuvenated Indonesia would stop recruiting metropolitan Indologists, traditionally educated at the Universities of Leiden and Utrecht for colonial administration. However, van Mook did believe that there remained plenty of scope for a new wave of Dutch experts in sociology, law, and economics who in the new 'developmentalist empire' could 'help transform the country and demonstrate . . . the need for a continuing partnership between the Netherlands and Indonesia'. Many of these social scientists, engineers and agricultural experts would serve subsequently in West New Guinea (Holland's colonial outpost in South East Asia after the transfer of power in the rest of the NEI between 1949 and 1950).[63]

These new colonials were not necessarily rapacious imperialists but were attracted to overseas service by a genuine desire to 'do good', seeking to raise colonial living standards in rejuvenated empires in which both Europeans and colonial peoples would benefit from overseas development. Yet, as the metropole's reconstruction crisis deepened, especially after 1947, the British Colonial Office's vision of colony-centred, welfarist development as a prelude to eventual self-government gave way to the Treasury's penchant for maximum primary production for export to the dollar area and the Board of Trade's desire to uphold markets for British manufactures in the colonies. Necessarily, therefore, the development of secondary industry overseas was held back.[64] At Brazzaville, industrialization of the colonial territories was to be encouraged but this would 'have to take place by stages, with prudence and method, *within the strict limits imposed by the general plan for production*' (emphasis added).[65] For the AOF metropolitan industrialists vetoed processing designed to increase the exportable value of commodities, and where manufacturing plant did develop this was largely of the import substitution rather than export orientated variety, designed to cut down on import requirements from outside the Franc Zone.[66]

At the same time, expatriate private enterprise continued to predominate. Plans for nationalizing the Northern Rhodesian copper-mining industry, discussed intermittently in the Colonial Office during wartime and between 1945 and 1951, were shelved: 'the practical counter-arguments were compelling: maximum production, designed to save Britain precious dollars and

*Business: The Economic Decolonization of Indonesia* (Leiden, 2008), 67, 68; Booth, 'Growth and Stagnation', 403.

[63]  Frey, 'Dutch Elites', 11–13.

[64]  L. J. Butler, *Industrialisation and the British Colonial State: West Africa, 1939–1951* (London, 1997).

[65]  *La Conférence africaine française*, 309.

[66]  Suret-Canale, 'French Tropical Africa', 453, 458; Lynch, *International Economy*, 191.

to fuel the recovery of metropolitan industries, required minimal state interference in the Copperbelt's day-to-day operations'.[67] Indeed, generally the ongoing metropolitan need to earn and save dollars meant that Labour's brief flirtation with the colonial state as a chief agent of economic growth gave way to a renewed emphasis on a partnership between public and private capital. Thus by the time the Conservatives returned to office in 1951, the CDC was confirmed as merely complementing the role of the British private sector.[68] As Fieldhouse argued, socialist principles were sacrificed to metropolitan self-interest in Labour's colonial polices of 1945–51.[69]

Despite the arrival of the big colonial state in French tropical Africa, the new development drive was a boon for French businesses. French firms picked up lucrative contracts for port and road development, such as the *Sociétié Française d'Enterprises de Dragages et de Travaux Publics*, which had been denied opportunities in Indochina. The group assets of the *Société Financière Française et Coloniale* (SFFC), the French and Colonial Finance Company, leapt from 26 million francs in 1935 to 155 million in 1949, and expansion in Africa, such as the development of air transport, increasingly compensated for the insecurities of Indochina as well.[70] The sprawling import-export firms in Black Africa, the *Société Commerciale de l'Ouest Africain* and the *Compagnie Française de l'Afrique Occidentale* reached their zenith in the post-war reconstruction era. They handled the upsurge in French African exports to France and beyond, underpinned by the absence of marketing boards of the British variety and the presence of huge subsidies which guaranteed colonial commodity sales on the French market at preferential prices. The surcharges for French goods flowing the other way to fulfil publicly-funded development projects were even higher.[71] Much FIDES and other funding—possibly the vast majority—actually flowed back to metropolitan France as repatriated profits, salaries for European personnel or the cost of training schemes conducted in France. This was all facilitated by unrestricted transfers within the Franc Zone and after 1948 by the pegging

---

[67] Butler, *Copper Empire*, 192–3.

[68] Nicholas J. White, 'Decolonisation in the 1950s: The Version According to British Business' in Martin Lynn (ed.), *The British Empire in the 1950s: Retreat or Revival?* (London, 2006), 101.

[69] D. K. Fieldhouse, 'The Labour Governments and the Empire-Commonwealth, 1945–51' in Ritchie Ovendale (ed.), *The Foreign Policies of the British Labour Governments, 1945–51* (Leicester, 1984).

[70] Thomas, 'French African Federations', 161; Hardy, 'Paul Bernard', 835–7.

[71] Fieldhouse, *Black Africa*, 19; Suret-Canale, 'French Tropical Africa', 461–2.

and free convertibility of local currencies, such as the franc CFA created in 1945 in French Africa, with the 'métro' Franc.[72]

At the same time, social and political developments initiated by the European imperial powers in the post-war era were designed to streamline, rationalize, and consolidate empire, to rejuvenate colonialism by making colonial peoples partners in their own economic exploitation. In the British Empire this involved, inter alia, the Africanization of local government leading on to *eventual* independence within the Commonwealth, and the development of cooperatives and apolitical 'responsible' trade unionism.[73] In *la plus grande France,* running alongside the development push as epitomized by FIDES, was the formation of the Union itself, enshrined in the constitution of the Fourth Republic of October 1946 and 'founded on equality of rights and duties, without distinction of race or religion'. Arising from the Brazzaville powwow was a belief amongst French officialdom that excessive coercion was holding back the development potential of the empire: hence 1946 would also witness the abolition of the arbitrary legal system, the much despised *code de l'indigénat,* as well as forced labour in the overseas territories. It was hoped, meanwhile, that nationalist discontents could be productively channelled into development partnerships with metropolitan France by providing *évolué* politicians with seats in the French parliament as well as the new supra-assembly of the French Union. Colonial subjects now became citizens of the French Union, and elections (albeit on a gradually widening franchise) were held throughout French Africa from late 1945 for direct representation in the Paris legislature. Added to this after 1946 was the Inspection du Travail, employing metropolitan industrial relations machinery to try and promote colonial labour 'stabilization'.[74]

In June 1942, Dr. van Mook, as minister for the colonies in the Dutch government-in-exile and at that stage lieutenant-governor of the provisional

---

[72] Ibid., 454–5, 461.

[73] Ronald Hyam, 'Africa and the Labour Government, 1945–51', *Journal of Imperial & Commonwealth History,* 16 (1988), 150; Timothy Oberst, 'Transport Workers, Strikes and the "Imperial Response": Africa and the Post World War Two Conjuncture', *African Studies Review,* 31, 1 (April 1988),128–9; Paul Kelemen, 'Modernising Colonialism: The British Labour Movement and Africa', *Journal of Imperial & Commonwealth History,* 34, 2 (2006), 223–44.

[74] Frederick Cooper, 'The Senegalese General Strike of 1946 and the Labor Question in Post-War French Africa', *Canadian Journal of African Studies,* 24, 2 (1990), 166, 168; Frederick Cooper, '"Our Strike": Equality, Anticolonial Politics and the 1947–48 Railway Strike in French West Africa', *Journal of African History,* 37, 1 (1996), 83–4.

government of the NEI, called upon Britain's colonial secretary, Lord Cranborne. Van Mook confided that 'the present relationship' between Holland and the NEI 'could not be recreated after the war'; he 'had in mind the possibility of some kind of federation'. There 'would be a Netherlands Government and a Government of the NEI, which would have equal status, and above them, responsible for defence and foreign policy and matters of general interest, an Imperial Government'. Such a political strategy would provide an 'attractive alternative to the propaganda which was daily pumped into [the peoples of Indonesia] by the Japanese'. It would also 'counter the vigorous propaganda which was going on in the United States and China to the effect that recent events [i.e. the fall of South East Asia to Japan] had shown the Dutch—and the British—not only to have been Imperialists but bungling Imperialists at that'.[75] After 1946, the Dutch political strategy for Indonesia had evolved even further to envisage the creation of several semi-independent Indonesian states outside Republican territory, and the establishment of a federal government dominated by pro-Dutch Indonesian politicians. It was hoped that the Republic itself would be enticed into this federal structure in a union between The Netherlands and the United States of Indonesia in which the influence of the Republic would be diluted and a Dutch supervisory role assured as necessarily would 'economic cooperation between Holland and Indonesia'.[76]

## III

To what extent did this development push pay off for the Europeans? As the Colonial Office often warned in the British case it was all hopelessly optimistic, ignorant of local conditions, and downright exploitative (as epitomized by Groundnuts). Indeed, the Economic Policy Committee informed the Cabinet in March 1951 that there was limited prospect of a large-scale increase in colonial production, and lacking basic infrastructure there was limited attraction for external investors.[77] Correlli Barnett argues that the 'second colonial occupation' was 'inevitably at the expense of the United Kingdom herself as an industrial society' 'on behalf of the pululating [sic] and poverty-stricken'.[78] But these liabilities in the post-war balance sheet of

---

[75] TNA, CO 825/35/4, 12 June 1942 in A. J. Stockwell (ed.), *Malaya*, Part I (London, 1995), 8.

[76] van der Eng, 'Marshall Aid', 342.

[77] Heinlein, *Government Policy*, 30–1.

[78] Correlli Barnett, *The Lost Victory: British Dreams, British Realities, 1945–1950* (London, 1995), 104–5.

empire need to be set against the contribution that the UK's colonies made to plugging the dollar gap in the short term. As Hyam writes:

> Although the colonies in no sense provided economic salvation, they certainly made a contribution to Britain's recovery. For the first half of 1948 the index of the volume of colonial exports was 148 compared with 100 in 1946 and 118 in 1936. The colonial contribution to the total value of UK imports went up from 5.4 per cent in 1938 to 10.2 per cent in the first half of 1948. . . [T]he colonial empire (which was in dollar deficit in 1945) was in July–Sept 1948 a net dollar earner at the rate of 200 million dollars per annum.[79]

Cheap dollar-saving food supplies from the colonial empire were especially important here. It is reckoned, for example, that the state monopoly purchase of West African cocoa subsidized British consumers to the tune of £12 million between 1940 and 1948 alone.[80]

By the early 1950s, French officials too became disillusioned with the prospects for colonial economic development, since the exchange controls and import restrictions of the Franc Zone and massive flows of public investment failed to turn overseas France into a net dollar earner—on the whole, overseas territories ran a large trade deficit with the dollar and other currencies (bar sterling).[81] Imperial protectionism introduced hopeless inefficiencies into French industry, while subsidized colonial production raised French costs vis-à-vis Western competitors, leading to a 'divorce' between French capital and overseas France by the later 1950s.[82] But there were short-term benefits to be had in putting French industry back on its feet. The survival of imperial preference allowed metropolitan goods to sell in the French Union at a price level on average around 20 per cent higher than world prices, while goods from the non-metropolitan French Union sold in France itself at a price level around 10 per cent above world prices. Thus, as Lynch writes, 'French industry benefitted to the extent that profits made on exporting to the French Union . . . could subsidize French exports to third markets'.[83] Moreover, as Fieldhouse notes, for the period of severe global commodity shortages in the

---

[79]  Hyam (ed.), 'Introduction', xlv.

[80]  Oberst, 'Transport Workers', 123–4 citing the work of the distinguished development economist, P. T. Bauer.

[81]  Lynch, *International Economy*, 195.

[82]  The central argument of Marseille, *Empire colonial*. For a summary in English see Jacques Marseille, 'The Phases of French Colonial Imperialism: Towards a New Periodization', *Journal of Imperial & Commonwealth History*, 13 (1985), 127–41.

[83]  Lynch, *International Economy*, 199.

late 1940s, France was indeed fortunate to be able to drawn upon its colonial empire.[84]

For The Netherlands, 170,000 soldiers deployed in Indonesia in the three years after the end of World War Two looks on the face of it like a complete waste of money, especially as Holland's dollar deficit continued and Sukarno's vision of a unified Republic rather than the Dutch-supervised federation came to prevail after 1950. But, as van der Eng argues, after the second Dutch 'police action' against the Republic in December 1948 and a further UN Security Council resolution, Dr. H. M. Hirschfeld, the Government Commissioner for the ERP, was able to convince the Hague cabinet that continued resistance to the Republic would endanger Marshall Aid to The Netherlands. Moreover, the retrieved Dutch economic stake in Indonesia could be preserved by meeting Republican constitutional de-mands. During the Round Table Conference of 1949, the Republic agreed that the new Indonesian state should inherit the colonial administration's debts, amounting to 4.9 billion guilders. Moreover, the transfer of profits *in foreign currency* back to Holland from Indonesia was guaranteed post-independence as were existing property rights for Dutch firms. In the ensuing Korean War boom, prices of Indonesian rubber, palm oil, tin, and fuel oil rocketed. With half of Indonesia's foreign investments still Dutch, the profits arriving in Amsterdam and Rotterdam, notwithstanding labour trou-bles, the doubling of wages, lack of security, squatting on plantations, and bureaucratic inconveniencies, were hardly inconsequential. In the East Sumatran plantation belt between 1949 and 1953 tobacco, rubber, and oil palm production increased by 50 per cent. In the second half of 1952—the peak of post-colonial income flow—495 million guilders-worth of foreign currency and gold reached The Netherlands from Indonesia. At the same time, The Hague was relieved of responsibility for Indonesia's reconstruction. Nationalization of Dutch enterprises, in the context of the West New Guinea dispute, did ensue in 1957–8. Even so, 'Dutch economic recovery in the 1950s was for a substantial part facilitated by the consent of [the] Dutch cabinet in 1949 to Indonesian independence'.[85]

What is clear from the Dutch case, however, is that the post-war develop-ment drive in the European empires created intense difficulties of local pol-itical management. The sterling-area system would have been more equitable had Britain been able to supply goods which net dollar earners, such as Malaya and the Gold Coast, wished to purchase outside the sterling area.

---

[84] Fieldhouse, *Black Africa*, 15.

[85] van der Eng, 'Marshall Aid', 347–52; C. L. M. Penders, *The West New Guinea Debacle: Dutch Decolonisation and Indonesia, 1945–52* (Adelaide, 2002), 265–71.

But UK manufacturing under-capacity, combined with the priority given to exporting to dollar markets and fears about running down sterling balances, ensured prolonged shortages of consumer goods, producing inflationary conditions in many colonies throughout the 1940s.[86] Waves of disturbances throughout post-war British Africa were directly related to this, most notably the Gold Coast riots of 1948, which had a major influence on the acceleration of decolonization in British West Africa. Strikes (of railway and dock workers in particular) consumed not just British but also French Africa in the period from 1945–48, reflecting a general shortage of goods and an increased cost of living across the continent.[87]

The Senegalese general strike of January 1946, and the epic five-month railway strike across the AOF from October 1947, are particularly instructive because they both reflected and frustrated the post-war French development drive.[88] A wage freeze in Dakar, and other West African towns, was part of a French policy to hold back astronomical inflation but also maintain the competitiveness of French colonial exports on world markets. Yet, this was blown apart in January 1946 as strikes extended from dock workers to civil servants to market sellers in Dakar and beyond, effectively closing French West Africa's leading port just at the point of the peanut harvest. By February ordinary labourers had achieved significant wage increases (more than doubling in many cases). After April 1947, the French Union's critical foreign exchange position led to another effort at controlling price and wage levels. Support from farmers, merchants and market sellers for the striking railway workers in West Africa demonstrated widespread disaffection with post-war economic policy. The railways strike undermined the dollar-saving and dollar-earning production push, while also exacerbating consumer goods shortages throughout AOF, threatening, in turn, to frustrate a further increase in cash crop output through providing a lack of incentive for peasant farmers to produce. The railway workers achieved a single scale of wages and benefits, the *cadre unique* (irrespective of race), the integration of the mass of auxiliaries into the cadre, and a 20 per cent wage hike. Significantly, the egalitarian rhetoric of the *Union Française* was utilized by African workers to claim not just wage increases but family allowances, housing improvements, and later pensions. As Cooper has argued, these escalating labour costs contributed towards French officials, politicians, and business leaders

---

[86] Fieldhouse, 'Labour Governments', 95–8.

[87] Oberst, 'Transport Workers'.

[88] This section relies upon Cooper, 'Senegalese General Strike' and Cooper, ' "Our Strike" ' as well as the relevant pages of Frederick Cooper, *Decolonization and African Society: The Labor Question in French and British Africa* (Cambridge, 1996).

increasingly questioning the benefits of colonial rule to the metropole by the 1950s. Moreover, emerging politicians like Léopold Senghor of Senegal, would exploit the networks created by trade unions and their strikes to build alliances and coalitions to accelerate decolonization.

In South East Asia, the ravages of war and Japanese Occupation resulted in galloping inflation rates, reaching 800 per cent in Malaya under the British Military Administration of 1945–46.[89] To try and keep a lid on price rises, however, the BMA in Malaya refused to raise wages, which fed into post-war unrest articulated by MCP-led trade unions representing rubber tappers, tin miners, and dockers. With the suppression of the trade unions, the MCP turned to insurrection after June 1948. Of course, the MCP was ultimately defeated, and the British transferred power to a remarkably Anglophile and foreign investor-friendly regime in 1957. But this process of decolonization came about far quicker than the British would have conceived back in 1942 when wartime planning for reoccupation and reconstruction commenced.[90] Dutch trade regulations from the beginning of 1947 in Indonesia were a de facto economic blockade of the Republic, aggravating an already perilous food situation and '[d]eteriorating living conditions fuelled anti-Dutch resentment, especially in urban areas, and increased the resolve of the pemudas [radical militias] to wage guerrilla attacks'.[91] By the 1950s, the French government recognised that a major source of disaffection throughout the French Union was the system of imperial preferences.[92]

Crashing into development projects also alienated peasant communities. In the British domains, draconian conservation measures designed to increase the efficiency of peasant agriculture in the late 1940s/early 1950s in Kenya (the compulsory construction of terraces), in Ghana (the compulsory cutting out of diseased cocoa trees), and in Tanganyika (de-stocking regulations) were deeply resented by African farmers. This allowed intelligentsia figures like Jomo Kenyatta, Kwame Nkrumah, and Julius Nyere to expand their constituencies beyond the towns.[93] In East and central Africa there

---

[89] F. S. V. Donnison, *British Military Administration in the Far East, 1943–46* (London, 1956), 312 cited in Oberst, 'Transport Workers', 124.

[90] Richard Stubbs, *Hearts and Minds in Guerrilla Warfare: the Malayan Emergency, 1948–1960* (Singapore, 1989); T. N. Harper, *The End of Empire and the Making of Malaya* (Cambridge, 1999).

[91] Frey, 'Indonesian Revolution', 92.

[92] Lynch, *International Economy*, 198–9.

[93] The best summaries of a huge literature here are David Throup, 'The Historiography of Decolonization', unpublished seminar paper, Institute of Commonwealth Studies, University of London, 31 January 1991; Hodge, *Triumph of the Expert*, 215–26.

was a wave of European immigration—with the number of white settlers in Southern Rhodesia, Northern Rhodesia and Nyasaland growing from about 76,000 in 1938 to 169,000 in 1950. This gave an added fillip to anti-colonial nationalism, and land improvement schemes for black Africans were regarded as subterfuges for further European encroachment.[94]

Scares over the alleged deleterious consequences of deforestation on climate and soils (desiccation) reached new heights in French Guinea in the late 1940s and early 1950s given a desire to secure high coffee yields. In a major wave of forest reservation, the expanded forestry service increasingly acted as a 'repressive police force', imposing prohibitions and fines—for example on the use of fire to clear forests—which 'rode roughshod over prior rights and livelihood concerns'. Not surprisingly, nationalist politicians found that they could easily rally rural support through slogans such as 'we promise to give you back your lands and forests'.[95]

Post-war Dutch development schemes in Indonesia had very little impact, given ongoing conflicts with the nationalist movement. Nevertheless, as Howard Dick demonstrates, the two military offensives to secure Indonesia's economic assets during 1947 and 1948 backfired:

> The flaw in the Dutch military strategy was the vulnerability of. . . plantations to guerrilla action. During the second offensive, Indonesian forces put much more effort into sabotage. Sugar mills and other plantations suffered more damage at this time than at the hands of the Japanese. Those recaptured intact soon had to be abandoned. Hill stations and road and rail traffic also became targets. Cooperating members of the 'native' civil service (*pamong praja*) were assassinated, paralysing the Dutch administration. The Dutch became bottled up in the towns, able to move only in daylight and even then not always in safety. This was very bad business.[96]

Meanwhile, the naval blockade encouraged massive Republican 'smuggling' of export crops to Singapore and Penang, the hard currency earnings from which financed the nationalist struggle (particularly the reverse illicit trade in weaponry).[97]

---

[94] J. D. Hargreaves, *Decolonization in Africa* (Harlow, 1988), 83; Hodge, *Triumph of the Expert*, 223–4.

[95] Fairhead and Leach, 'Desiccation and Domination', 43–51.

[96] Dick, 'Nation-State', 169.

[97] Twang Peck Yang, *The Chinese Business Elite in Indonesia and the Transition to Independence, 1940–1950* (Kuala Lumpur, 1998), ch. 6; Yong Mun Cheong, *The*

Political liberalization, designed to bolster colonial rule in a rejuvenated development partnership between Europeans and non-Europeans, also had unintended consequences. The British hoped to foster elected local councils and so divert nationalist attention away from the centre. But the African Local Self-Government Circular Despatch of 1947 had the opposite effect. As Gallagher wrote: 'territories which had been political deserts now seemed to pullulate with political parties that were the darlings of the masses, the tribunes of the people and the voice of the people'.[98] In French Africa's elections after 1945, the conservative assimilationist politicians were increasingly swept aside by a younger breed of more radical activists, leading to the formation of a cross-AOF and -AEF political party, the *Rassemblement Démocratique Africain* (RDA), which affiliated with the French Communist Party. It was the presence of African *députés* in the *Assemblée Nationale Constituante* which would lead to the abolition of forced labour in April 1946 three years ahead of the schedule laid down at Brazzaville.[99] With that emancipation and the end of the *indigénat* as well, French officials in the *Office du Niger* could no longer control the movement of their farmers, so much so that 15 per cent of settlers on the Sudanese irrigation scheme merely left between 1946 and 1949. Those remaining were buoyed up by new rights of association to collectively protest against Office policies—especially the growing of cotton instead of rice—and in the early 1950s went to the lengths of forming a union.[100]

Moreover, the reconstruction drive contributed to fundamental fissures within European imperial and colonial elites. As Hodge writes for the British experience, 'Debate and disagreement existed at every level of administration, from the lofty colonial secretary's room in Whitehall, with its impressive burr walnut map case, down to the most remote district boma at the farthest reaches of empire'.[101] Notwithstanding stresses and strains between generalists and experts in colonial administrations 'on the ground', the incoherence of central planning in London with a maze of policy-making committees, and the internecine turf wars between the Colonial Office, Treasury, Ministry of Supply, and Ministry of Food (the last having been put in charge of

---

*Indonesian Revolution and the Singapore Connection, 1945–1949* (Singapore, 2003); Teuku Mohamad Daud, 'Recollections of My Career' in Thee Kian Wee (ed.), *Recollections: The Indonesian Economy, 1950s-1990s* (Singapore, 2003), 254–6.

[98] J. Gallagher, *The Decline, Revival and Fall of the British Empire* (Cambridge, 1992), 148.

[99] Cooper, *African Society*, 186–9, 193.

[100] van Beusekom, 'Disjunctures', 84, 85.

[101] Hodge, *Triumph of the Expert*, 226.

Groundnuts due to perceived CO intransigence) have been identified as major limiting factors in the post-war British development project.[102]

The lack of integration of economic policy-making at colonial and imperial levels in the French Union was of an even higher order.[103] By 1951, this incoherence had come to alienate a leading figure in the French imperial business world, Paul Bernard, managing director of SFFC and a key adviser to both Vichy and the Fourth Republic in their plans for the industrialization of Indochina, which he had necessarily hoped would reap great rewards for his conglomerate. For Bernard the ineffectualness of the French Union was epitomized by the failure to secure sufficient guarantees for French capital in the establishment of the semi-independent associated states of Indochina after 1949, and concomitantly the non-materialization of his treasured secondary industries.[104] In the UK and the Netherlands too, leading imperial business figures, who their governments had hoped would play a central role in the post-war 'new imperialism', had become disillusioned with attempts to rejuvenate empire. During the struggle for independence, Paul Rijkens, chairman of Unilever NV, the Dutch half of the Anglo-Dutch soap and food manufacturing giant, had been very critical of the The Netherlands for not fully respecting the legitimacy of the Republic as outlined in the Linggajati agreement of November 1946, which, in turn, had 'given the Indonesians an excuse to deviate from what has been agreed'.[105] Although the decolonization settlement with Republican Indonesia had been in large part concerned with securing the future of Dutch capital, from 1950, Unilever executives—notably Rijkens—regarded Holland's stubborn refusal to surrender West New Guinea/Irian Jaya as liable to harm Dutch economic relations with the rump Indonesia. The best solution was Dutch acceptance of West New Guinea's transfer to the Indonesian Republic.[106] Frank Samuel, managing director of the United Africa Company, the trading arm of Unilever, had made the initial proposal for the Groundnuts Scheme to the Minister of Food, Sir Ben Smith, in 1946. By 1951, however, Samuel had concluded that 'there has been a great

---

[102] Billy Frank, 'The Formation of British Colonial Development Policy in the Trans-World War Two Period, 1942–53: With Special Reference to Central and Southern Africa', PhD thesis, University of Lancaster, 2003, ch. 3–4.

[103] Thomas, 'Roots', 146; Hardy, 'Paul Bernard', 833–4.

[104] Ibid., 830–5.

[105] Merseyside Maritime Museum, Ocean Archives, 2537/2, letter to Sir John Hobhouse, 4 March 1947; see also D. K. Fieldhouse, *Unilever Overseas* (London, 1978), 284 for the favourable attitude of Unilever executives towards Indonesian independence.

[106] Unilever Archives, Port Sunlight, Acc 1997/127, Box 41, Special Committee Minutes, 8 May 1950; Penders, *West New Guinea*, 218, 347.

deal of wishful thinking . . . since the war . . . that Tropical Africa is an El Dorado of wealth sorely neglected in the past and capable of being developed rapidly on a grand scale. I take a far more sober view of the position.' Rather than Europeans taking the lead in colonial development, the initiative in future would have to come from an African intelligentsia.[107]

On top of growing problems of colonial control, such attitudes amongst key business leaders in the metropoles contributed towards disengagement between Western Europe and the colonial world during the 1950s and 1960s. As such it was not the Second World War per se, but the intrusive and often haphazard imperialism of the era of reconstruction that followed it, which represented the fundamental watershed in the decolonization of Europe's three most significant maritime empires.

[107] Hodge, *Triumph of the Expert*, 251.

# Reconstructing the 'Plural Society': Asian Migration Between Empire and Nation, 1940–1948[1]

## Sunil Amrith

'Why should we expect that we're going to spend the rest of our lives here? There are people who have the luck to end their lives where they began them. But this is not something that is owed to us. On the contrary, we have to expect that a time will come when we'll have to move on again. Rather than be swept along by events, we should make plans and take control of our own fate.'[2]

The Second World War left few parts of Asia untouched. The suddenness of the Japanese conquest of the whole arc of territories from Burma to Indonesia following efforts at a full-scale invasion of China, and the dramatic collapse of European imperialism in the region, transformed its political and social history. Christopher Bayly and Tim Harper have called it, aptly, the Great Asian War: the most widespread and violent since the Mongol Invasions.[3]

Among the many social and political transformations it brought, the war shattered patterns of inter-Asian migration that had flourished for close to seven decades. From the mid-nineteenth century, the mass migration of young men from southern China and south India to the frontier lands of South East Asia—over 50 million in all—had been at the core of an inter-connected regional economy. The global depression of the 1930s dented this system severely, but it took the war to transform it. This chapter will examine the efforts to reconstruct and reorient patterns of migration across South and South East Asia during and after the war. The war posed with fresh urgency the question of how mobility would be governed in a post-imperial era, forcing a set of compromises between sovereignty and necessity, policy and

---

[1] The research for this article was made possible by a Large Research Grant from the British Academy.

[2] Amitav Ghosh, *The Glass Palace* (London, 2000), 310.

[3] Christopher Bayly and Tim Harper, *Forgotten Armies: The Fall of British Asia, 1941–45* (London, 2004); Christopher Bayly and Tim Harper, *Forgotten Wars: The End of Britain's Asian Empire* (London, 2007).

---

　　　　　　　　© The Past and Present Society

pragmatism, which would shape the history of Asian migration in the decade after 1945.

Historians of the war and of post-war reconstruction in Asia have long been preoccupied by the problem of nationalism. The war provoked new expressions of nationalism, and paved the way for ambitious post-war experiments in nation building. This chapter adopts a different lens on the period, by examining the impact of the war and post-war reconstruction on one of Asia's largest and most dispersed diasporas: the Indian diaspora in South East Asia. Focusing on the experiences of Indian communities in Burma and Malaya (both British territories, conquered by the Japanese in 1942) this chapter examines the ways in which circuits of migration—based on transnational family connections, and older networks of labour recruitment—broke apart during the war, and attempted to rebuild themselves after 1945. Migrant groups posed significant problems of government for the planners of post-war reconstruction. Faced with the human displacement of the war, the control of population movements was a central aim in plans for post-war reconstruction; differentiating between 'displaced people', 'refugees' and 'migrants', and identifying where they each belonged, became a pressing concern of state. Those whose locations had been fluid and shifting before the war—migrant labourers, and diasporas—complicated these calculations. Mobile people constituted an anomaly, to be reconciled in plans for new kinds of citizenship. Yet in trying to reconstitute themselves after the war, networks of migration between South and South East Asia also served as agents of economic and social reconstruction in their own right.

The war and the process of post-war reconstruction constituted a critical moment in the redefinition, across Asia, of the relationship between territory, mobility, and citizenship, in a world that was increasingly torn between embattled European empires and assertive nations-in-the-making. In examining the effects of this process on patterns of Asian migration, this chapter suggests that among the most lasting legacies of wartime planning and post-war reconstruction were the hardening of borders, and the advent of new, more exclusive notions of citizenship and belonging.

## Indian migrations to South East Asia

The movement of labourers, traders, merchants, and administrators from the eastern coast of India to the frontier lands of South East Asia—Burma, Malaya, and to destinations in the Netherlands East Indies, Indochina, and the Pacific—was one of the great circuits of migration that transformed Asia after 1870. The other, simultaneous, movement took young men from coastal southern China to the 'south seas': to Malaya, Indonesia, Thailand, the Philippines, and further afield. The movement from India totalled perhaps

29 million people altogether, over the century between 1840 and 1940: approximately 4 million to Malaya and 8 million to Ceylon (primarily from the Tamil region of the far south), and around 15 million to Burma (mainly from the Telugu districts north of Madras).[4] These migrants worked on rubber plantations and tin mines, on expanding frontiers of rice production, and in every corner of the urban economy of expanding port cities—on the docks and in the canteens, as sweepers and porters and rickshaw pullers. Asia's Indian and Chinese migrants, together with many other people on the move, were essential to the capitalist transformation of Asia under imperial rule. A characteristic feature of this migration was its circular nature. People rarely moved with the intention of settlement; rather, they moved back and forth between India and South East Asia, alternating between periods of labour overseas, and time spent in their home villages. For many, the Bay of Bengal was an easily passable space that made South East Asia a natural extension of the Indian world.[5]

The unravelling of this world of migration is one of the least understood aspects of Asia's destructive age of economic crisis and war that spanned the middle decades of the twentieth century. In 1931, there were over 620,000 Indians resident in Malaya and the Straits Settlements of Singapore, Penang, and Malacca, and more than a million in Burma. By this time, however, it was already a world under the pressure of a global economic crisis.[6] War came to Asia on the heels of an economic depression that had begun to untangle the bonds of commerce, trade, and migration that knit South, South East, and East Asia together into an interconnected regional economy in the half-century after 1870. For the first time since the 1870s, the number of Indians leaving South East Asia after 1930 exceeded the number of new arrivals. Nearly 200,000 Tamil plantation workers were repatriated from Malaya during the Depression, as, for the first time, the colony introduced immigration restrictions. Chinese labourers—coming from outside the British Empire—bore the brunt of these restrictions, but the state placed significant new controls on the movement of South Asians too.

Planning for post-war reconstruction, by British colonial administrators and Asian nationalists alike, had to take into account not only the effects of war, but also the longer-term impact of the 1930s on the region. The legacies

[4] Adam McKeown, 'Global Migration, 1846–1940', *Journal of World History*, 15:2 (2004), 155–89.

[5] Sunil S. Amrith, 'Tamil Diasporas across the Bay of Bengal', *American Historical Review*, 114:3 (2009), 547–72.

[6] Christopher Baker, 'Economic Reorganization and the Slump in South and South East Asia', *Comparative Studies in Society and History*, 23:3 (1981), 325–49.

of the 1930s—economic, social, and political—shaped, to a significant degree, the imagination of a post-war future.

## Indians and Burma, 1940–1945

On the eve of the war, the future of relations between Burma and India exercised many legal and administrative minds. In 1937, Burma ceased to be ruled as a province of British India, gaining constitutional autonomy and a limited franchise. Relations between migrant Indian communities and the indigenous Burmese majority had been fraught throughout the 1930s. During the millenarian Saya San rebellion, which swept rural Burma in 1931, anti-Indian violence erupted; in 1930 and in 1938, Rangoon too was beset by inter-ethnic violence. South Indian moneylenders of the Chettiar community, who had played a central role in advancing capital to Burmese cultivators and expanding Burma's rice frontier, took control of nearly a quarter of Burma's agricultural land during the depression, as struggling rice farmers were unable to pay their debts.[7] Many Burmese nationalists looked forward to a future free from Indian domination. In early 1941, a leading Burmese newspaper invoked Hitler approvingly in discussing the 'Indian problem'. The newspaper 'now remembers a speech delivered by Hitler before he came into power. Hitler said, "I have studied the histories of all countries; and I find that the retardation of a country's progress is not due to its economic affairs, but due to the influx of foreigners."' The article concluded that in Hitler's words lay a lesson for Burma.[8]

Throughout 1941, protracted negotiations between the colonial governments of India and Burma aimed to draft an 'immigration agreement' between India and Burma, which would recognize that borders that had, until 1937, been internal administrative borders within British India, were now international ones. The government of India 'depredated the proposal to have passports as a condition of entry to Burma', yet their pressure on the Burmese authorities proved ineffective.[9] At the heart of the controversy over the future position of Indians in Burma was the definition of 'domicile', a concept that would continue to shape debates about migration after 1945, not least the migrations during and after the Partition of India. 'The determination of intention'—to settle, or to return—was 'the principal content' of any

---

[7] Michael Adas, *The Burma Delta: Economic Development and Social Change on an Asian Rice Frontier, 1852–1941* (Madison, 1974).

[8] National Archives of India [hereafter NAI], New Delhi, Indians Overseas Department (Overseas Branch), File No. 144–1/38—L&O: translated extract from *Saithan*, 1 Jan 1941.

[9] NAI, Indians Overseas Department (Overseas Branch), File No. 144–1/38—L&O: Minutes of the Meeting of the Standing Emigration Committee, 15 May 1941.

definition of 'domicile': yet 'intention' was exceedingly difficult to prove, in a context where the vast bulk of migration between India and Burma had been circulatory. The lawyers sought, in vain, to recognize a distinction between Indians who were 'settled immigrants' in Burma, and those who were 'useful temporary residents of varying degrees of permanence', who would enjoy 'civil and political rights as British subjects', but not as Burmese citizens.[10] Already on the eve of the war, then, different kinds of citizenship— imperial, colonial, and national—came into contention, and came to redefine millions of people's entitlements, to residence, employment, and security.

The abstract debates over 'domicile' and 'intention' soon became very much more complicated, as Japanese forces swept through South East Asia in the first months of 1942. In the atmosphere of fear and panic that set in as Japanese aerial bombings intensified over Burma in early 1942, a great movement of Burma's Indian residents began in search of safety.[11] European residents, too, fled, and kept for themselves most of the places on the ships out of Burma: the racial discrimination at the heart of colonial rule was laid bare. The mass exodus of Indians from Burma took place mostly on foot, through Arakan and over the mountain passes to Assam. Historian Hugh Tinker has called the exodus a 'forgotten long march' of the Second World War.[12]

The Indian refugees who set out on the journey north numbered more than 140,000. Trekking through treacherous conditions, beset by malaria, and subject to attacks by groups of Burmese armed by the advancing Japanese forces, perhaps 40,000 of the refugees never completed the journey out of Burma, dying along the way.[13] Exhaustion alone killed scores of refugees, like K. N. C. Ayyar, a man of 58, who died of 'starvation, exposure, and exhaustion' four miles west of Tamu. Another refugee, named Abdolla, died in July 1942 of 'heart failure, exhaustion, and an amputated leg'.[14] These are but two names that came to the attention of the relief and rehabilitation authorities in Assam; thousands of victims remained nameless. When the rains came, malaria spread rapidly, condemning many of the refugees to death.

---

[10] NAI, Indians Overseas Department (Overseas Branch), File No. 144–1/38—L&O: File note [anon., no date (*c.*1941)].

[11] The following section draws on the account in Sunil S. Amrith, *Migration and Diaspora in Modern Asia* (Cambridge, 2011), chapter 3.

[12] Hugh Tinker, 'A Forgotten Long March: The Indian Exodus from Burma, 1942', *Journal of South East Asian Studies*, 6 (1975), 1–15.

[13] A vivid Tamil memoir by a survivor of the trek is V. S. Sarma, *Enatu Barma Vazhi Nadai Payanam* (Madras, 1979).

[14] NAI, *Burma Evacuee Register*, Part 2, No. 403 (B).

The 'evacuees' that succeeded in reaching India were housed in makeshift refugee camps in Assam, aided by the Tea Planters' Association, which was a dominant presence in that region of India. Conditions in the camps were dire. There were shortages of rice and water. One camp official reported that 'sanitation was at a standstill at the outset, but a force of sanitary sweepers was obtained from the refugees', many of whom had worked as sweepers and nightsoil removers in Burma before the war. Countless refugees died each day, 'people who died of exposure, undernourishment, and sheer exhaustion'.[15] The registers of 'evacuees' that survive in the National Archives of India give a poignant sense of how diverse the body of refugees—and, therefore, Burma's Indian population—really was. The 'occupations' listed included fishermen and cloth merchants, sweepers and milkmen, 'coolies' and cultivators, boatmen and machinists; a 'spare motor driver', a *paan* (betel leaf) seller, and a postman. Their destinations in India included, overwhelmingly, towns in the Telugu-speaking districts of Madras, and the Bengali-speaking regions bordering on Burma, particularly Chittagong, but also included destinations throughout the Tamil south, and as far afield as Lahore and Amritsar.[16] In extremis, the extent of the networks linking Burma with the four corners of the Indian subcontinent emerged in sharp relief.

The legal distinctions between Indian 'settlers' and 'immigrants' in Burma—already in place on the eve of the war—became more complex with the creation of a new class of 'evacuees'. Planning for the post-war reoccupation of Burma, British officials recognized the enormity of the problem. 'Indians owned large moveable and immoveable properties in Burma', one official wrote, but he pointed out that 'the destruction of property was accompanied by the destruction of title deeds also'. More seriously, however, he predicted that 'all those Indians who have been displaced from their homes in Burma . . . will find very great difficulty in establishing their claims'. The breakdown of the 'plural society' and its fragile bonds was complete. Many reports circulated about 'Burmese hostility towards Indians . . . exhibited in a most ruthless form immediately after the Japanese invasion of Burma'. British Indian officials feared that the Japanese retreat would 'leave behind a vast, armed Burmese population' and that 'there is thus a great danger to the life and property of the Indian community now in Burma'.[17]

---

[15] NAI, Commonwealth Relations Department: Overseas Section, File Number F. 45–21/44-OS: Lieutenant G. C. G. Brown, Burma to Commanding Officer, Burma, 11 September 1942: Report on Kyaukpyu Evacuation, dated 14 April 1942.

[16] NAI, *Burma Evacuee Register*, Part 2, No. 403 (B).

[17] NAI, Commonwealth Relations Department: Overseas Section, File No. 45–21/44-OS: 'Confidential: A Brief on Burma' [anon., no date, *c.* early 1945].

For many thousands of Indians with an intimate connection to Burma over years or generations, a temporary journey in search of refuge—the long march of 1942—resulted in a permanent and unexpected alienation from Burma. Many refugees who survived the trek would never return to Burma. The 'loss' of Burma to India and Indians would provoke influential cultural representations in the post-war years, not least one of the most famous Tamil films ever made: *Parasakti* (1951). Others would return in 1945 and 1946, in a desperate attempt to rebuild their old lives, in new and unpropitious circumstances.

## Migration and planning for Malayan reconstruction

The relationship between migration and planning for post-war reconstruction was different in the case of Malaya. Significantly, most of Malaya's pre-war Indian population remained in Malaya through the Japanese occupation. Unlike Burma, Malaya lacked a land border with India, so when shipping across the Bay of Bengal was abruptly curtailed during the war, there were few routes of escape. At most, a few thousand 'got away from Malaya' in the early stages of the Japanese occupation; 'most of these belong[ed] to the middle or upper class'.[18]

What emerged, instead, was a political problem: a significant number of Indians in Malaya had joined the Indian Independence League, or even the Indian National Army, both of which collaborated with the Japanese in their quest for Indian independence from British rule. When Subhas Chandra Bose declared the establishment of a Provisional Government of Free India—an Indian nation in exile—in 1943, many Indians in Malaya felt incorporated into a kind of citizenship for the first time.[19] Many more Indian labourers— mostly Tamil labourers from the rubber plantations of the Malay Peninsula— were used as forced labour by the Japanese in the construction of the notorious Thailand-Burma railway.[20] The 'problem' of Indians' role in Malaya's post-war future revolved around two distinct, but related, questions. The first surrounded the political status of long-settled Indians within polity that

---

[18] NAI, Commonwealth Relations Department: Overseas Section II, File No. 43/44—OS: file note by V. Viswanathan, 2 March 1945.

[19] Sugata Bose, *A Hundred Horizons: The Indian Ocean in an Age of Global Empire* (Cambridge, Mass., 2006).

[20] Nakahara Michiko, 'Malayan Labour on the Thailand-Burma Railway', in Paul H. Kratoska (ed.), *Asian Labor in the Wartime Japanese Empire: Unknown Histories* (Armonk NY, 2005); for detailed documentation, see Paul H. Kratoska (ed.), *The Thailand-Burma Railway, 1942–1946: Documents and Selected Writings*, 6 volumes (London and New York, 2006).

would emerge after the war; the second concerned the future supply of Indian labour migrants to Malaya, that is to say, the future of fresh migration between India and Malaya.

The position of Indians in post-war Malaya was tied up with British plans for sweeping reforms in citizenship upon their reoccupation of Malaya; plans to create a unified political community under Crown rule—a Malayan Union—were central to the whole enterprise, although they proved short-lived.[21] The question of Indians' political status had connections, in the official mind, with the parallel question of the future position of Malaya's Chinese. The new generation of colonial officials charged with planning for Malaya's post-war future—sitting in Wimbledon, or in Simla—sought to build a new kind of Malayan citizenship, within which the large Indian and Chinese populations would feel included. But this came up against serious obstacles early on. In discussion with Indian government officials over the future place of Indians in Malaya, one Malayan official 'touched on the difficulty of giving equal rights to all inhabitants in Malaya', fearing that this would bring into the political community 'large numbers of Chinese, whose status in Malaya was at best indeterminate and required a cautious approach'.[22]

The resumption of Indian migration to Malaya after the war—which, at its peak in the 1920s, had involved over 100,000 arrivals in Malaya from south India each year—proved a more contested issue. In 1938, relations between the colonial governments of India and Malaya had virtually broken down over the question of migration. Frustrated by their inability to secure an acceptable minimum wage for Indian migrant workers in Malaya, Indian government negotiators decided in 1938 to put an end to all government-assisted migration to Malaya. This ban covered, in effect, the majority of labour migration, since most working-class migrants had their passages paid for ('assisted') by the state.[23] Furthermore, the Indian government threatened to prohibit Indian emigration to Malaya altogether if their demands were not met. The Malayan government countered that 'the time is past when Indian immigration is essential to Malayan agricultural enterprise', stating explicitly that the 'racial constitution of estate labour forces' would

---

[21] T. N. Harper, *The End of Empire and the Making of Malaya* (Cambridge, 1999).

[22] NAI, Commonwealth Relations Department, Overseas Section II, File No. 43/44—OS: file memo by A. V. Pai, 30 June 1944.

[23] NAI, Department of Education, Health and Lands: Overseas Branch, File No. 44/38—L.&O.: Minutes of the Standing Emigration Committee, 13 February 1939. For further discussion of this ban on emigration, see Sunil S. Amrith, 'Indians Overseas? Governing Tamil Migration to Malaya, 1870–1941', *Past and Present*, No. 208 (2010), 231–61.

change: Chinese and Javanese workers would replace Indian migrants on the estates, with effects 'fatal to the well-being of the non-estate Indian population'.[24] A bemused civil servant in London wrote that 'the Government of India seems to be going very far in seeking to prevent the free movement of its people', in a way that was 'more suggestive of a totalitarian state than a part of the British Empire'.[25] The Japanese invasion of South East Asia cut off shipping across the Bay of Bengal, making negotiations over migration largely abstract during the war. Nevertheless, the rancour between the Malayan and Indian administrations continued, and the question of the future of migration between India and Malaya remained unresolved amid the plans for post-war reconstruction.

What was clear to all was that 'for years after the reoccupation of Malaya . . . the demand for rubber, both natural and synthetic, will be very large indeed'.[26] The corresponding demand for labour meant that the question of future migration from India to Malaya was crucial to plans for economic reconstruction. Indian officials, however, sought to 'keep on unaltered the ban on assisted emigration', and to reconsider the ban only when a comprehensive agreement on wages and conditions had been reached. 'If labour is to be assisted or indentured for migration', wrote the labour specialist B. P. Adarkar, 'it must receive the assurance of a minimum security of employment [and] income'.[27] The rather striking reference to the possibility of 'indenture'—even though indentured labour had been phased out in Malaya, and elsewhere in the British Empire, between 1910 and 1917—gives a sense of the uncertainty surrounding the nature and the terms under which labour would move in the post-war world. There was a clear sense of the urgent and unprecedented demands that post-war reconstruction would exert, and an equally strong awareness of the constraints facing policy-makers as they tried to think up new ways of mobilizing labour across long distances, and across the boundaries of empires and nations.

In 1945 it was unclear which circuits of migration, and what kinds of regional economic connections, would re-emerge after the end of the war. Malayan authorities insisted that they did not 'want Malaya to become a

[24] The National Archives of the UK [hereafter TNA], Colonial Office [CO] file 273/640/7: Chief Secretary, Straits Settlements to Secretary to the Government of India, 12 September 1938.

[25] TNA, CO 273/661/6: G. Orde-Brown, file note, 18 November 1940.

[26] NAI, Commonwealth Relations Department: Overseas Section II, File No. 43–44—OS: file note by 'rubber adviser' [no date].

[27] NAI, Commonwealth Relations Department: Overseas Section II, File No. 43–44—OS: note by V. Viswanathan, 2 March 1945; Note by B. P. Adarkar [no date].

province of either China or India', and instead favoured 'the importation of Javanese labourers who are Mohammedans like the Malays, speak the same language, and are easily absorbed by the Malay population'.[28] One of the most perceptive Western commentators on Asia—and on the question of Asian migration in particular—was Bruno Lasker, a German-born American who worked for the Institute of Pacific Relations. Lasker wrote, just before the end of the war, that 'a demand for labour in British Malaya and an oversupply of labour in Java admirably supplement each other', predicting that 'even an informal economic and administrative collaboration between the two dependencies would suffice to lay the basis for a comprehensive Javanese settlement in Malaya.'[29] The future composition of Malaya's population, the balance between old and new migration, between migration and settlement, remained open.[30] The Allied reoccupation of Indonesia just months later, followed by the outbreak of the Indonesian revolution and the ensuing Dutch blockade of the Indonesian Republic, meant that things turned out quite differently.

The war had unsettled the ways in which sovereignty mapped onto territory, and citizenship onto residence. In contention within these competing plans for post-war labour migration were very different perceptions of the region. On the one hand lay a 'greater Malaya', in which Javanese migrants were 'easily absorbed' into the economic reconstruction of the Malay Peninsula; on the other hand was a vision of a reconstructed of 'greater India', with India at the heart of British imperial networks that radiated across the Indian Ocean.[31] The place of China, and Chinese diasporic networks, within either of these visions was uncertain, and fraught with anxiety. All of these ideas of a reconstructed Asian region had soon to take account of the realities of colonial reoccupation, and postcolonial revolution.

### Reconstructing migration after 1945

The human detritus of war in Asia was on a scale almost unimaginable, and certainly comparable to that of Europe. Tens of millions of people found themselves 'out of place' in 1945—in one estimate, in China alone around

---

[28] NAI, Commonwealth Relations Department: Overseas Section II, File No. 43–44—OS: file note [anon., no date, c.1945]

[29] Bruno Lasker, *Asia on the Move: Population Pressure, Migration, and Resettlement in East Asia under the Influence of Want and War* (New York, 1945), 84–5.

[30] Joel S. Kahn, *Other Malays: Nationalism and Cosmopolitanism in the Modern Malay World* (Singapore, 2006).

[31] Cf. Thomas Metcalf, *Imperial Connections: India in the Indian Ocean Arena, 1860–1920* (Berkeley, 2007).

95 million people had been displaced by over a decade of fighting:[32] they had fled from armies or aerial bombing, they had been coerced into joining labour gangs on mines, building roads, railways, and airfields. There was no Asian equivalent to the massive European effort to rehabilitate and resettle refugees and displaced persons. Yet in Asia, too, these categories assumed importance. There was a clear distinction between—as Tony Judt has put it—'displaced persons (assumed to have, somewhere, a home to go to) and refugees (who were classed as homeless).'[33] There were also 'evacuees', and those that had been 'resettled'; and millions with no clearly defined status at all. Amid this uncertainty, the large number of Asians who had lived mobile lives before the war—as labour migrants and merchant diasporas—struggled to establish their claims, and to re-establish their connections. The debates on 'domicile' that had taken place behind closed doors during the war suddenly had a direct effect on millions of people, while the war had made the question of proving one's 'domicile' more complicated than the planners had ever imagined.

The return of Indians to Burma after the end of the war highlights the ways in which 'resettlement' and 'return' melded uneasily into one another in the conditions prevailing at the end of the war, under the new constraints provided by the rise of militant Burmese nationalism. Writing towards the end of 1945, B. N. Nanda, an Indian government official, determined that the 'return of evacuees' from India to Burma 'is likely to start by March-April 1946'; he predicted that 'a large number of Indian labourers will be in Burma very soon, and the labour problem will be very acute during the next year'.[34] The return began even sooner than he anticipated. Indian officials observed that, already by the end of 1945, Indian labour in Burma 'is employed in a large number of occupations, e.g. at docks, on rice fields, in saw mills, in oil refineries, in the Public Works Department, in Railways [and] as rickshaw coolies'.[35] Indian labour was essential to the piecemeal revival of economic life in Burma that was proceeding quite apart from grand plans for post-war reconstruction. In the chaos of the immediate post-war period, policies bore little relation to practice. Desperate to reopen the factories, the rice and saw mills, the Burmese government brought with them, on the reoccupation of Burma,

---

[32] Stephen MacKinnon, 'Refugee Flight from the Outset of the Anti-Japanese War', in Diana Lary and Stephen MacKinnon (eds), *Scars of War: The Impact of Warfare on Modern China* (Vancouver, 2001), 118–35.

[33] Tony Judt, *Post war* (London, 2005), 28–9.

[34] NAI, Ministry of External Affairs and Commonwealth Relations (CR Wing): 'Burma: Indian Embassy', File No. 4/2/46—OS IV: file note by B. N. Nanda, 29 December 1945.

[35] NAI, Ministry of External Affairs and Commonwealth Relations (CR Wing): 'Burma: Indian Embassy', File No. 4/2/46—OS IV: file note [anon.], Dec 1945.

'many hundreds [of Indians] who were not evacuees, nor even skilled or semi-skilled': precisely the kinds of Indian 'immigrants' barred from Burma under the Immigration Agreement of 1941. Indian labour was thus 'imported' into Burma by the Burmese authorities 'against the express legal prohibition' that the Burmese authorities had passed in 1941.[36]

Indian and Burmese authorities struggled to differentiate between 'returning' residents and fresh migrants; or between 'evacuees' and newly recruited labour. The Indian envoy in Rangoon sought to detail the different categories of people that made up the surging Indian population of Burma, which included 'numbers recruited by the military after the war' for help with post-war reconstruction; 'evacuees recruited from India after the Japanese collapse', and 'others brought over here from India who are not evacuees'. There was, in addition, the problem of rehabilitation for those Indians who had remained in Burma during the war, but 'compelled to leave their places of residence and to migrate to various places chiefly on grounds of personal safety': the problem of 'internally displaced' people.[37]

The difficulty of 'placing' Burma's Indian population after the war reflected, in a much deeper sense, the nature of Indian migration to Burma over many decades. Migration between India and Burma was invariably circular, with a constant exchange of population. After the war, migration recommenced, and it followed its 'usual' channels, that had always operated independently of the colonial authorities: migrants were channelled along family networks, or under the auspices of indigenous labour recruiters. Groups of kin and fellow villagers travelled to and from Burma, replacing each other in the factories and on the fields. This suggests, first, how resilient the migrant networks were, reconstituting themselves more or less spontaneously at the end of the war. It also shows how easily the 'old' diaspora could meld into a fresh wave of migration: 'evacuees', 'returnees', 'displaced persons' and new recruits may belong to the same families and at times these terms could even apply to the same individuals.

Faced with a population in flux, and with the unsettled conditions of the post-war world, migration proved difficult to regulate, and to care for. Jamnadas Mehta, the Indian envoy in Rangoon estimated that by April 1946 there were 600,000 to 700,000 Indians in Burma, 'scattered all over the country'. For most of them, 'housing conditions' were 'atrocious', and 'medical relief hardly exists'. Mehta lamented that 'in a country with an area

---

[36] NAI, Ministry of External Affairs and Commonwealth Relations (CR Wing): 'Burma: Indian Embassy'. File No. 4/2/46—OS IV: Janadas Mehta (Indian Representative in Rangoon) to R. N. Banerjee (Indian Civil Service), 8 April 1946.

[37] Ibid.

of 260,000 square miles, these thousands of unfortunate workers are scattered here and there absolutely at the mercy of their employers'.[38] As high political negotiations over Burma's future continued in London and in Rangoon, a militant Burmese nationalism, under Aung San's leadership, dominated the public sphere.[39] Old fears over Indian immigration emerged once again. Many Indians who had held property in Burma before the war, particularly Chettiar moneylenders, struggled to establish their claims; the Burmese government passed legislation that effectively dispossessed many Chettiar families.[40] As the immigration laws passed on the eve of the Japanese invasion began to be implemented, many Indians faced the challenge of documenting their pre-war residence in Burma. This proved impossible for many, whose papers along with their possessions had been destroyed as they fled the fighting in 1942.

Restrictions on entry and exit, and on the import and outflow of goods and currency, only seemed to stimulate border crossings of all kinds. Just one example of many can be found in the oral history narratives collected by the Burmese writer, journalist, and folklorist Ludu U Hla in the late 1940s. One of his interviewees was a Tamil youth called Kanniya, who gave an elaborate account of how Indian merchants and labourers maintained their links of commerce and travel with south India after 1945:

> The Indian merchants who did business on Moghul Street usually sent diamonds and jewellery to India on ocean-going steamers plying between Rangoon and Indian ports. The ships' officers acted as couriers, the gems being packed in boxes of Cuticura face powder. I remember seeing on one occasion the European captain of a ship being handed such a box. Other favourite places of concealment were false compartments in suitcases, hollow heels of European style shoes and handles of umbrellas and bicycles.

> The quickest way to send money to Madras was to buy postal order permits from Indian labourers who had been granted permission to remit money to their families in India. Another method was to send an Indian labourer on an expense paid trip home. The steamer fare costs sixty kyats, and meals and other incidentals perhaps forty kyats more. Each passenger was permitted to take a bank draft for three hundred kyats and Burmese currency worth one hundred

---

[38] Ibid.

[39] Bayly and Harper, *Forgotten Wars*.

[40] NAI, Ministry of External Affairs, Burma I Branch, 1950, File No. 48–65/50—B.I.

kyats. In addition a female passenger could take gold rings, gold bangles, earrings, necklaces and other items of jewellery with her. The Indian merchants in Rangoon would load down each labourer with the maximum permissible amount of jewellery and currency and send her to India, where she would be relieved of these by the merchant's agents and given a commission for her services.

Kanniya himself went back and forth between his father's family in Madras and his mother and stepfather in Burma in 1947, continuing a long tradition of circular migration, and the maintenance of transnational families, even under new constraints. At a time of acute food shortage and rationing in India, Kanniya sought, in 1948, to return to Burma; restrictions on entry and residence posed little obstacle to those, like himself, who knew how to circumvent them.[41]

In retrospect, the years immediately after the war appear as a small window, within which regional networks of migration and circulation could reconstitute themselves. The independence of Burma in 1948 brought sweeping new restrictions, and the eruption of a myriad of armed civil conflicts—pitting the Burmese state against Karen separatists, and competing 'Red Flag' and 'White Flag' Communist rebellions. This led a significant portion of the Indian population of Burma to return to India, this time permanently. Writing from a small intelligence post near the Burma-India border, an Indian Army officer reported, in early 1949, that 'many Indians are reported to be making ready to come back to India', fearing—yet again—that 'apart from creating serious security problems, these refugees will also create problems of relief and rehabilitation'.[42]

### Return to Malaya

In post-war Malaya, too, there was a permeable boundary between return migration, and new migration occasioned by the demands of post-war reconstruction. Compared with Burma, far fewer Indians had left Malaya during war, yet the problems of 'return' and rehabilitation were not insignificant. Of the 72,000 or more labourers coerced to work on the Thailand-Burma railway during the war, a significant proportion was made up of Tamil estate labourers. Perhaps 40 per cent of them never returned. Official allied figures recorded 29,634 deaths, but after detailed investigation,

---

[41] Ludu U Hla, *The Caged Ones* [1958], (Bangkok, 1986), trans. Sein Tu, 116–21.

[42] NAI, Ministry of External Affairs, B.I. Branch, File No. 3–8/49—BCI (B) [Secret]: From Army Headquarters Liaison Officer, Shillong, to Military Intelligence Director, New Delhi, 26 March 1949.

Michiko Nakahara concludes that this is probably an underestimate; she estimates, too, that over and above the number of dead, almost an equal number 'deserted' on the way to the railway's construction sites; many were lost in the jungle, and their whereabouts never determined.[43] The Indian Agent in Malaya, S. K. Chettur, toured the plantations to find social and family life devastated by the loss, during the war, of large numbers of able-bodied men. Particularly distressing for many estate families was not knowing what had become of their husbands, fathers, or sons who had been carted away by Japanese forces. The rubber estates of Malaya were filled with widows, and orphans.[44] In other cases, families had been separated during the war, and took the first opportunity after 1945 to reunite. The family of Palanisamy, a foreman on a rubber estate and a labour recruiter in his own right, found themselves on a visit to India when the war broke out, and were only able to return to their home and rebuild their livelihoods in Malaya in 1946.[45]

Malaya was utterly central to the post-war reconstruction of the British Empire. Malaya produced half the world's timber, a significant proportion of its rubber, and its dollar-earning capacities were essential to Britain's own economic reconstruction;[46] this created significant opportunities for a resumption of Indian labour migration. Yet the old problems that, as we have seen, bedevilled negotiations between the Malayan and Indian authorities over the question of migration, had not disappeared. The Indian government, on the verge of independence, decided to uphold and extend the ban on unskilled emigration from India: every Indian passport issued after 1946 differentiated between skilled and unskilled Indians seeking to depart from India's shores: only skilled workers received a stamp declaring that 'emigration clearance' was not needed. The Malayan government for its part, maintained a studied ambivalence: aware of the attractions of a steady supply of Indian migrant labour for post-war reconstruction, and yet reluctant to countenance fresh migration that might upset the conservative Malay nationalists that had emerged as the most important potential allies—and the most dangerous potential critics—of British authority in Malaya.[47]

Nevertheless, the process of post-war reconstruction, and particularly the reconstruction of the port cities, created opportunities for Tamil migrant

---

[43] Nakahara, 'Malayan Labour on the Thailand-Burma Railway'.

[44] S. K. Chettur, *Malayan Adventure* (Mangalore, 1948).

[45] Muthammal Palanisamy, *Nadu Vittu Nadu* ['From Shore to Shore'] (Chennai, 2007).

[46] Harper, *End of Empire and the Making of Malaya*; Nicholas J. White, *Business, Government, and the End of Empire: Malaya, 1945–1957* (Oxford, 1996).

[47] TNA, PRO, CO 717/181/2: Conditions of Indian Labourers in Malaya.

labourers to travel to Singapore and Malaya to work as cable layers, road builders, food vendors, petty traders, and as essential labour at the British military establishments. The resurgence of migration between South India and Singapore began in the interregnum after the end of the Second World War, working through the interstices of authority. The era of nation-states in Asia was on the verge of realization, but in 1946 and 1947, they were nations that had yet to come into being. Abdul Aziz, a Tamil Muslim who made his life in Singapore as a provision-shop keeper, remembers how easy the journey was, still, in 1946. 'India was still in the British Raj, and Indians were still British subjects—we could go elsewhere within the British Empire' without hindrance. Even as British rule in India teetered on the brink of collapse, Indians made full use of the imperial connections that remained open to them. Passports, Abdul Aziz recalled, were issued from Delhi, and checks on identity were rudimentary. 'You could fool them', he recalled, 'and come as Ramasamy, or Kuppusamy, or whoever [you liked]'. Often employers would arrange for the forty Rupee fee for the passport; sometimes this would add to the debt that the migrant began with on arrival in Singapore.[48]

Tamil newspapers in the late 1940s were full of advertisements for jobs in Singapore. Regular notices were posted in Tamil magazines, newspapers, and periodicals announcing the departure of the steamer services, which were deregulated in 1947, as the post-war shortage of shipping began to ease. A migrant from Kerala, M. K. Bhasi, who travelled to Singapore in 1946, had a similar memory of relative freedom of mobility: 'At that time there was no restriction, no immigration controls; you could just buy a ticket and come [to Singapore]'.[49] Fewer than 10 per cent of Indians resident in Singapore in 1946–7 had first arrived after the war. Of the remainder, those who had not stayed in Singapore through the war years might well have been second, third, or even fourth-time migrants to Singapore, reviving in new circumstances the patterns of circulation that they had followed in the 1930s.[50]

Indian authorities recognized the porous nature of the system of border and identity checks, even into the 1950s. The distinction between 'old residents' of Malaya and new migrants was complex. The certainty that the new tools of documentation—passports, in particular—sought to supply belied

[48] National Archives of Singapore [hereafter NAS], Oral History Department [OHD], Abdul Aziz, interviewed by Rajendran Supramaniam, 6 September 1990.

[49] NAS, OHD, M. K. Bhasi, interviewed by Ng Chang Wang, August 1985.

[50] M. V. del Tufo, *A Report on the 1947 Census of Population*, M. V. del Tufo, (Kuala Lumpur, 1947).

the contingency of separation and return: officials struggled to determine whether 'new' migration was not, in fact, family reunification. The Indian Passport Office conceded that passports had been issued 'liberally for Indian nationals bound for Malaya', and they were issued 'solely on the basis of the Statutory Declaration' of identity, and a 'certificate of *bona fides*' issued by the passport applicant's village *munsiff* (headman). K. S. Seshan, who acted as the 'controller of emigration' in Madras stated, bluntly, that 'my experience has shown that 9 out of every 10 Statutory Declarations are either faked or otherwise ungenuine [sic]'. He concluded that 'as an international document', the passport, 'certainly deserves much more respect than what it now receives'.[51] Seshan pointed to the durability of the old migrant recruiting networks, that operated outside the purview of the authorities; the cast of characters was a familiar one: 'the omnipresent tribe of landsharks known by a variety of denominations, such as passage brokers, travel agents, guides, etc.' indulging in 'recruitment on the sly'. He concluded that 'there will be a certain amount of legalised leakage of manpower from India into Malaya which is going to be very difficult to prevent'.[52]

By this time, however, the tide had turned, and migration between Malaya and India had come under increasing control. The shift from post-war reconstruction to counter-insurgency in Malaya, with the declaration of the Emergency in 1948, provided new security concerns to reinforce migration control: 'political and economic conditions had made it necessary', the Immigration Department decided, 'for Malaya to guard against any large influx of aliens'. In this context, 'strict control was particularly important in relation to adjacent countries'—among which the author included India—'from which there was continual pressure by large numbers of potential immigrants'.[53] As S. Arasaratnam concluded, in his classic study of Malaya's Indian communities: 'In the period after 1947, the Indian population settled down to a natural and internally-ordained growth, unaffected by the vagaries of inflow and outflow that had caused constant changes in the years before the war'.[54]

---

[51] NAI, Ministry of External Affairs (Emigration Branch), File No. F 11–5/53—Emi: K. S. Seshan (Controller of Emigration) to S. V. Sampath (Under Secretary, Ministry of External Affairs), 2 March 1953.

[52] NAI, Ministry of External Affairs (Emigration Branch), File No. F 11–5/53—Emi: K. S. Seshan, to T. V. Ramakrishna Rao (Acting Agent of Government of India in Malaya), 21 August 1953.

[53] Singapore, *Annual Report of the Immigration Department* (1953).

[54] Sinnappah Arasaratnam, *Indians in Malaysia and Singapore* (Kuala Lumpur, 1970), 41.

Through the rupture of the war and the vicissitudes of post-war reconstruction, migrants and diasporic communities sought a kind of reconstruction of their own: the reconstruction of family networks of migration and circulation. They worked with, and where necessary around, the new structures and the new constraints. The connections between South and South East Asia, shattered by the war, re-emerged at least in part through the agency of diasporas trying to reconstitute themselves. Yet by 1950, mobility across South, South East, and East Asia was much more restricted than ever before, and the constraints faced by diasporic communities escalated.

### Diasporas, states, and statelessness

'Reconstruction' produced new notions of citizenship, new bureaucratic markers of identity, and—most importantly—fundamental transformations in sovereignty. Within four years of the end of the war, India, Pakistan, Burma, Ceylon, Indonesia, and the Philippines had emerged as independent states; the Communist victory in China inaugurated the People's Republic, and brought an end to decades of civil strife. The imperial borders that mobile peoples had crossed with relative ease, now became international borders, policed by passports and new visa regulations. Yet imperial administrators in some ways anticipated this transformation on the eve of the war, bringing in new restrictions—as we have seen—governing movement within the British Empire in Asia. This new geographical imaginary of Asia as a succession of frontiers underpinned the process of planning for post-war reconstruction.

In the aftermath of war, large parts of the Asian continent witnessed an often bloody contest over sovereignty, between European imperial powers and Asian nationalist movements. Yet there was also a convergence on all sides around the norms of the international system of nation-states. Colonial administrators, too, began to see their task in terms of nation building, even as they retained a commitment to maintaining imperial control.[55] Many of the architects of the post-war order came around to the view that ethical citizenship was difficult to foster in a 'plural society'. Reflecting not only on the war, but also on the experience of social breakdown and communal tension in the 1930s, J. S. Furnivall—a veteran colonial administrator, scholar of Burma, and committed Fabian socialist—diagnosed the ills of the 'plural society', that is to say, the multi-ethnic societies that had emerged from colonial Asia's age of migration. In Asia's port cities and frontier zones, he argued, the 'various races . . . mix but do not combine'; 'as individuals they meet, but only in the

---

[55] Harper, *End of Empire and the Making of Malaya*; Frederick Cooper, *Colonialism in Question: Theory, Knowledge, History* (Berkeley, 2006).

marketplace, in buying and selling'. In contrast to a 'homogenous' society, the plural societies of colonial Asia were 'broken up into groups of isolated individuals, and the disintegration of social will is reflected in a corresponding disorganization of social demand'. 'Civilization', Furnivall declared, 'is the process of learning to live a common social life', and in a plural society, he stated baldly, 'men are decivilized'.[56] Within this post-war imagination of social citizenship, diasporas and migrant groups were agents of 'decivilization', rather than guarantors of cosmopolitanism and openness. Reconstruction, then, sought not merely a recovery from the devastation of war but also an entirely new relationship between—as Vazira Zamindar has put it—'birth, residence, migration, and citizenship'.[57]

A central tenet of the new order of things lay in dismantling the world of circulating labour and interlocking diasporas that shaped Asia's modern history from the last quarter of the nineteenth century; historians are only just beginning to recognize this. The Second World War was a crucial period in Asia's 'unmixing of peoples', to borrow a phrase from European history, but this was a process that began in the 1930s, and which continued well after 1945. The war closed borders that were already in the process of becoming more restrictive. By putting a stop to movement between India and China and the lands of South East Asia, the war brought about, suddenly and without warning, the kind of change in population that the Depression years had foreshadowed.

Borders opened again, for a brief period, after 1945, but by 1949, with the Communist victory in China, all further migration from China overseas virtually ceased, for several decades. Overseas migration from India, too, lessened in scale, though it did not cease, and began to seek new destinations, in the West and, later, the Persian Gulf. Thus, as a result of the war, the two great movements of people that had shaped modern Asia—from India and China to the frontiers of South East Asia—came to an end. The rich and vital connections that the Indian and Chinese diasporas maintained with their lands of origin also came under greater restriction, surveillance, and constraint. Remittances, for instance, became difficult if not impossible to send, in an age of closed national economies. Politically, too, the war and the process of post-war reconstruction marked a rupture in the connections between South and South East Asia. Speaking in India's Constituent Assembly in March

---

[56] J. S. Furnivall, *Colonial Policy and Practice: A Comparative Study of Burma and Netherlands India* (Cambridge, 1948), 302–12.

[57] Vazira Fazila-Yacoobali Zamindar, *The Long Partition and the Making of Modern South Asia: Refugees, Boundaries, Histories* (New York, 2007), 106.

1948, Jawaharlal Nehru indicated the attitude that his government would take towards the question of Indians overseas:

> But the real difficulty is the question of citizenship. How, these Indians abroad—what are they? Are they Indian citizens? Are they going to be citizens of India or not? If they are not, then our interest in them becomes cultural and humanitarian, not political . . . This House wants to treat them as Indians and, in the same breath, wants complete franchise for them in the countries where they are living. Of course, the two things do not go together.[58]

Nehru's essential question—'what are they?'—was faced by a great many of Asia's diasporas in the years after 1945; diasporas that had long lived across the boundaries of colonial territories, and often crossed the boundaries between different empires. The Jews of South East Asia, the Armenians, and many creole ('Eurasian') communities found themselves, literally, homeless; they became the 'orphans of empire', and the new age of nation-states.[59] Writing of the Hadrami Arab diaspora that lived across the British and Dutch empires of the Indian Ocean, Engseng Ho has shown that as 'diasporic persons became minorities within new nations, some were then expelled to homelands they had never known; others became permanently stateless'.[60]

Finally, tragically, this process of sealing borders and drawing new ones provoked a further, massive displacement of people across new frontiers. The making of new Asian states in the aftermath of war displaced people on a similar scale to the war itself. Close to 20 million people moved across the Partition boundaries between India and Pakistan, and several million more died.[61] Hundreds of thousands of Tamil labourers in Ceylon became stateless in 1948, when neither the state of Ceylon, nor India, would accept them as citizens. Tens of thousands more were 'repatriated' to an Indian 'homeland' they had never known.[62] Migrants and diasporas were immobilized;

---

[58] Jawaharlal Nehru, speech in the Indian Constituent Assembly (Legislative), 8 March 1948, in Jawaharlal Nehru, *India's Foreign Policy: Selected Speeches, September 1946—April 1961* (New Delhi, 1962), 128–9.

[59] Robert Cribb and Lea Narangoa, 'Orphans of Empire: Divided People, Dilemmas of Identity, and Old Imperial Borders in East and South East Asia', *Comparative Studies in Society and History*, 46:1 (2004), 164–87.

[60] Engseng Ho, *The Graves of Tarim: Genealogy and Mobility Across the Indian Ocean* (Berkeley, 2006), 307.

[61] See, *inter alia*, Zamindar, *The Long Partition*; and Yasmin Khan, *The Great Partition: The Making of India and Pakistan* (New Haven, 2007).

[62] Patrick Peebles, *The Plantation Tamils of Ceylon* (London, 2001).

long-term settlers were forced to become migrants. The Rakhain, Arakanese-speaking Buddhists, began an exodus across the borders of East Pakistan into Burma; conversely, the Bengali-speaking Muslims of the Rohingya community found themselves driven out of Burma, often by military force, to seek refuge in East Pakistan.[63] The life chances of vast numbers would be shaped, to a significant extent, by precisely the bureaucratic categories—'refugees', 'migrants', 'displaced people'—that had emerged during and after the war, in the effort to disentangle different kinds of migration, and to differentiate between migrants and refugees.

On many views, the aftermath of the Second World War marked the 'beginning of the end' for European empires in Asia. It also marked—with a final, bloody exodus—the end of Asia's great century of overseas migration, which would not resume, on the scale of the 1920s, until the final decade of the twentieth century.

[63] Willem Van Schendel, 'Guns and Gas in South East Asia: Transnational Flows in the Burma-Bangladesh Borderland', *Kyoto Review of South East Asia* (August 2006).

# Internationalism in Relief: The Birth (and Death) of UNRRA[1]

**Jessica Reinisch**

Susan Pettiss, an American relief worker, remembered that UNRRA—the United Nations Relief and Rehabilitation Administration—'caused quite a stir when it was established'. Its creation was 'a magnificent unprecedented feat', she thought: 'There was no background, tradition, system, common language or currency for UNRRA'; yet it brought together 'men and women of different nationalities, backgrounds and skills', all united in the ambition to build 'a true world community with new social systems and international relations'.[2] Other relief workers thought much the same. Francesca Wilson, a British relief worker with decades of experience, described how en route to begin her duties in continental Europe it suddenly dawned on her 'what a great experiment UNRRA was—the first international body to do something concrete and constructive, an attempt at an international civil service'.[3]

Nor was this sense of UNRRA's unprecedented internationalist tasks and character confined to the organization's foot soldiers. An editorial in *The Observer* enthused that the UNRRA agreement, 'one of the most important and pregnant events of the war', provided a forum for 'world-management', 'as bold, big and exciting a venture as any in the history of social organiza-tion'.[4] Jan Masaryk, Foreign Minister of the Czechoslovak government-in-exile, argued in March 1944 that the successes of UNRRA as 'the first great agency of the United Nations' would have 'great repercussions on the new forms of international organisation' at the end of the war.[5] In more measured tones, Philip C. Jessup, an American lawyer and diplomat who

---

[1] The research for this chapter was made possible by a Leverhulme Early Career Fellowship.

[2] Susan T. Pettiss and Lynne Taylor, *After the Shooting Stopped: The Story of an UNRRA Welfare Worker in Germany, 1945–1947* (Trafford, 2004), 5–7.

[3] Francesca Wilson, *Aftermath: France, Germany, Austria, Yugoslavia 1945 and 1946* (Middlesex, 1947), 19.

[4] *The Observer*, editorial, 13 June 1943, quoted in National Planning Association, 'UNRRA: Gateway to Recovery', *Planning Pamphlets*, 30–31 (1944), 15.

[5] NA, FO 371/38956, Jan Masaryk, 'Czechoslovakia looks East and West", 13 March 1944.

*Past and Present (2011)*, Supplement 6     © The Past and Present Society

served in the State Department's foreign relief office, agreed that UNRRA was 'an international organisation of a unique character', none like it having existed before on a comparable scale.[6] Others welcomed UNRRA as a great 'cooperative enterprise' of entirely new dimensions.[7] Even UNRRA's critics tended to agree about its uniquely internationalist ambitions (usually before going on to demonstrate how they had fallen far short from the ideal). One outspoken critic, the American Marvin Klemme, declared that UNRRA was populated with 'fanatical internationalists [who] felt sure that UNRRA was the vanguard of some sort of world order'. The body had been conceived by American 'super-idealists' and 'super-internationalists' who aimed 'for nothing less than complete world government', he proclaimed, but their idealism was then quickly exploited by 'a great many Europeans and Asiatics who thought that they saw the opportunity of getting a whole lot of something for very little or nothing'.[8] UNRRA's international fantasies were bankrolled by the American taxpayer, who got little benefit in return.

Supporters and critics alike concurred that UNRRA was a novel experiment in international collaboration—successful or not. This theme has also dominated more recent historiographical assessments. Many accounts of the nexus of activities accompanying the Allied war effort and post-war planning for a 'new world order' firmly anchor UNRRA's creation within a by now standard narrative: the rise of internationalism in the aftermath of the First World War, followed by its spectacular failure in the 1930s climate of fierce nationalism and protectionism, followed by its eventual triumph in the early 1940s and the second post-war era. In other words, a false inauguration of a new international order in 1919 was rectified by the successful second attempt in 1945.[9] UNRRA could be seen as its first manifestation, soon succeeded by a

---

[6] League of Nations Archives, Geneva (LON), R5809/50/42186/42186, 'Address by Mr. Philip C. Jessup . . . before the Summer Institute in International Relief Administration', 18 June 1943. In 1943/44 Jessup served as Assistant Secretary-General of UNRRA. He was also a delegate at the Bretton Woods conference, the UN General Assembly in 1948, and the UN Security Council which debated the Berlin blockade. He served on the UN General Assembly from 1951 to 1953, before resuming his teaching duties at Columbia University. Later he became a judge at the International Court of Justice at The Hague.

[7] James T. Shotwell, *The Great Decision*, 2nd edn (New York, 1945), 45, 171.

[8] Marvin Klemme, *The Inside Story of UNRRA: An Experience in Internationalism—a first hand report on the displaced people of Europe* (New York, 1949), 12, 1/2.

[9] E.g., Amos Yoder, *The Evolution of the United Nations System*, 2nd edn (Taylor & Francis, 1993). For more sophisticated versions of this narrative, see e.g. Akira Ariye, *Cultural Internationalism and World Order* (Baltimore, 1997); Zara Steiner, *The Lights that Failed: European International History, 1919–1933* (Oxford, 2005). Although Steiner insists that the 1920s should be seen as a 'post-war' rather than a 'pre-war' decade (i.e. within the

wide net of other international and transnational efforts. The causes of this apparent ascendancy of internationalism are often traced back to a 'seismic shift' in American foreign policy which precisely matched the path of internationalism's rise, decline and rise: American involvement in world affairs during the First World War came abruptly to an end as 'Wilsonian internationalism' failed to find support at home, and the following two decades were marked by the country's disentanglement from the world and its aloofness from foreign affairs, until it was once again thrust into renewed international involvement and leadership.[10]

However, historians have on the whole been so focused on the problem of American isolation and the apparent shift to internationalism and an international foreign policy that they have often failed to examine this internationalism itself, or considered what the different visions of the new international order actually amounted to.[11] This paper seeks to re-assess the international dimension and dynamics of relief work in the immediate aftermath of the war in this light. Relief in war-torn areas was one of the first subjects during the war to prompt consideration of future international co-operation and mechanisms. When UNRRA was formally established in November 1943 by 44 participating countries to oversee and direct relief programmes across the world, it continued and replaced the work of a joint Anglo-American committee for post-war relief, and it drew upon a curious amalgam of interwar lessons, war-time experiences and conflicting priorities for post-war reconstruction. This paper will contrast some of the different motives for and perspectives on internationalism which shaped

---

context of the aftermath of World War I, not as a prologue to the 1930s), her portrayal of the 1920s enthusiasm for international institutions and 1930s destruction of the international fabric does not contradict the standard narrative.

[10] See e.g. David C. Henrickson, 'The Renovation of American Foreign Policy', *Foreign Affairs*, 71:2 (Spring 1992), 48–63, at 52. Andrew J. Williams, '"Reconstruction" before the Marshall Plan', *Review of International Studies*, 31 (2005), 541–58. Andrew Williams, *Failed Imagination? The Anglo-American New World Order from Wilson to Bush*, 2nd edn (Manchester, 2007). Also see Ian Tyrrell, *Transnational Nation: United States History in Global Perspective since 1789* (Palgrave, 2007). Jerry Z. Muller, 'Us and Them: the enduring power of ethnic nationalism', *Foreign Affairs*, 87:2 (March/April 2008), 19. For a parody of this narrative, see William Appleman Williams, 'The Legend of Isolationism in the 1920s', *Science and Society*, 18 (Winter 1954), 1–20, reprinted in Henry W. Berger (ed.), *A William Appleman Williams Reader: Selections from his Major Historical Writings* (Chicago, 1974).

[11] Donald White, 'History and American Internationalism: The Formulation from the Past after WWII', *Pacific Historical Review*, 58:2 (May 1989), 169.

UNRRA and accompanied its activities throughout its short five-year existence.

## Planning for relief: premises and consensus

By the time UNRRA's international remits became a matter of debate, central premises on relief work were already in place. From 1941 onwards, 'post-conflict planning' in Washington and London proceeded from the assumption that the mistakes of the First World War and the interwar years were not to be repeated.[12] Allied planners now tended to agree that after World War I there had been a costly delay in getting relief into the devastated areas, and that when it finally arrived, it had been insufficient to cope with needs. American refusal to commit American aid to an inter-allied scheme for the allocation of supplies meant that there was no competent organization able to take charge in 1918, as a result of which '[m]uch time and valuable capital of experience and confidence had been wasted'.[13] Resources had also been squandered, analysts concluded, because the efforts of the many voluntary organizations had not been coordinated. One of the biggest problems had been the absence of a plan. Sir Frederick Leith-Ross, Chief Economic Adviser to the British government, reiterated in 1943 that thousands of people could have been saved after 1918, if only the Entente powers had planned relief ahead of time.[14]

Apart from these organizational problems, the situation had then been exacerbated, many planners agreed, by much wider political and economic 'failures of analysis' after World War I.[15] The failure to appreciate the close relationship between international reconstruction, stability and security weighed heavily. Nehemia Robinson, a Lithuanian-born Jewish economist, observed in 1945 in his gloomy forecast of European reconstruction problems that in 1918 insufficient emphasis had been placed on 'solv[ing] the problems of the economic consequences of the war on an international scale' and

---

[12] See Jessica Reinisch, 'Introduction: Relief in the Aftermath of War', *Journal of Contemporary History* special issue on 'Relief in the Aftermath of War', 43:3 (July 2008), 371–404.

[13] Arthur Salter, *Allied Shipping Control*, (Oxford 1921), 221, quoted in *Relief and Reconstruction in Europe—The First Steps: An Interim Report by a Chatham House Study Group*, (Royal Institute of International Affairs, July 1942), 20.

[14] Frederick Leith-Ross, 'Opening Lecture', in War Organisation of the British Red Cross Society and Order of St. John of Jerusalem (ed.), *Training Course of Pre-Armistice Civilian Relief Overseas, Report of Lectures, January 1943*, (London, 1943).

[15] Phrase from a prospectus for a course on 'Democratic Reconstruction' at Antioch College, Yellow Springs, Ohio, held in January-February 1943. New York Public Library, Central and Eastern European Planning Board (NYPL-CEEPB), 'The Institute of Democratic Reconstruction', Preliminary Prospectus [January 1943].

through international collaboration. Now, after the Second World War, he concluded, UNRRA, as 'the only working international organization', was in no state to help singlehandedly; the 'need for more far-reaching international cooperation' had already become apparent.[16]

In these analyses, failures in the organization of relief after 1918 appeared as part of a much bigger cluster of failures concerning inadequate reconstruction programmes, insufficient international agreement and an unstable international architecture, all of which had disastrous consequences. The insistence that key responsibility lay with the United States' absence in the new international structures was shared by many American and European thinkers alike. As Frank P. Walters, former Deputy Secretary-General of the League of Nations, later wrote, the League's 'immediate loss of power and influence . . . due to the absence of the United States was great; it was destined to show itself in a hundred ways as the years went by. The indirect effects were no less calamitous.'[17]

Some time before UNRRA took shape, relief planners had thus concluded that in order to avoid a repeat of earlier mistakes relief operations had to be carefully planned; they had to be coordinated as a joint problem and one to which the United States pledged its support; and they had to lead up to and prepare the ground for sound schemes of longer-term economic reconstruction. One institutional product of this new desire for planned coordination, the 'Inter-Allied Committee on Post-War Requirements', was established by Churchill under the chairmanship of Leith-Ross. At its founding meeting in London in September 1941 eight European allies, the Free French, British Dominions and the UK agreed to collaborate in the work of compiling estimates on likely requirements for relief materials in the occupied countries after their liberation.[18] Shortly afterwards the committee began to plan for the accumulation and use of supplies after the end of hostilities.

Other authorities soon followed. From the summer of 1942 voluntary relief organizations in Britain were coordinated under the umbrella of the 'Council of British Societies for Relief Abroad' (COBSRA), as the body through which the constituent societies would make suggestions to and receive instructions

---

[16] Nehemia Robinson, 'Problems of European Reconstruction', *The Quarterly Journal of Economics*, 60:1, (November 1945), 1–55, at 53. On Robinson's work, see e.g. Angelika Timm, *Jewish Claims against East Germany: Moral Obligations and Pragmatic Policy* (Budapest, 1997), 74.

[17] F. P. Walters, *A History of the League of Nations* (Oxford, 1952), 72–8.

[18] National Archives Washington, (NARA), 840.50 UNRRA/139, 'Report to Allied Governments by the Inter-Allied Committee on Post-War Requirements', June 1943, 3. Grace Fox, 'The origins of UNRRA', *Political Science Quarterly*, (December 1950).

from governments. In Washington, the 'Office of Foreign Relief and Rehabilitation Operations' (OFRRO) was established in November 1942 to organize relief abroad. President Roosevelt appointed Herbert Lehman, former Governor of New York, as its director. OFRRO's tasks were 'to undertake the work of organizing American participation in the activities of the United Nations in furnishing relief and other assistance to victims of war in areas re-occupied by the forces of the United Nations'.[19] OFRRO policies and activities were supervized by the State Department and its expenditures largely supplied by the Lend-Lease administration under Edward Stettinus.

Together, the Leith-Ross Committee, COBSRA and OFRRO treated relief primarily as a matter of procurement, as a logistical problem of matching estimated relief needs with available supplies and transporting essential items into affected areas. They urged allied governments not to earmark consignments for their own countries or to build up reserve stocks for their own use, since surpluses were to be pooled and diverted to where they were needed most. 'Coordination' was the magic process which could reduce waste and delay and prevent the duplication of relief efforts, both nationally (among the different government departments and voluntary bodies) and internationally (among the different allied governments). In this light, relief quickly appeared as more than simply a logistical matter of coordinating needs and supplies; it was a problem of collective, international action and agreement. As Roosevelt told Congress in December 1942, relief and rehabilitation in the liberated areas would have to be 'a common responsibility of all the United Nations'; it had to be 'a combined operation in the same sense as the military operations themselves'.[20] There was widespread agreement in Europe that since war, disease, hunger, and population upheavals were international in character, relief work, too, had to be international and collective.

Not only was relief a fundamentally global problem, the process of solving it internationally could also set in motion support for wider international cooperation. By the time UNRRA was established, discussions on how the international community could be rebuilt and how countries could govern together and secure peace had thus turned relief work into the testing ground for international cooperation after the demise of the League. After all, if the 'nations of the world should fail to work in mutual cooperation' in 'preventing and halting death by starvation, exposure, disease and neglect', declared

[19] George Woodbridge, *UNRRA: The History of the United Nations Relief and Rehabilitation Administration*, vol. 1 (New York, 1950), 21–2.

[20] F. D. Roosevelt, '7th Lend-Lease Report to Congress', 11 December 1942, in NARA, 840.50 UNRRA/131, 'Inter-Allied Committee on Post-War Requirements, Report to Allied Governments', 30 June 1943.

Lehman, 'what hope could we hold for political cooperation to banish war?'[21] Cooperation in relief was the first test. But on both sides of the Atlantic hopes were high that collaboration on a 'functional problem' such as relief could form the seed of greater and more far-reaching internationalism in other fields, and thereby allow a new international organization to develop almost 'as a kind of natural consequence'.[22] Even those who understood relief as a political, more than a technical, issue hoped that an agency such as UNRRA would help to define and strengthen channels of international communication, and that 'the habit of co-operation . . . would spill over into other, more complex areas of international relations'.[23]

In June 1943 the Department of State published a first draft of an agreement to establish UNRRA, with the concurrence of the governments of the United States, Britain, the Soviet Union, and China. Following discussions within the Senate's Foreign Relations Committee and the Foreign Affairs Committee of the House and comments from some of the Allied nations, a second draft was issued in September—eventually signed as the UNRRA Agreement in November 1943 by 44 participating nations.[24] OFRRO's small staff of 150 became subsumed into the brand-new, enormous UNRRA apparatus, as it assumed responsibility for the provision of relief to liberated populations and the return of refugees, and Lehman became UNRRA's first Director-General.

### Internationalism, but on whose terms?

By the time UNRRA was founded, relief thus appeared as an international problem, the solution of which lay to a significant degree in international collaboration. But within this broad consensus, a range of very different interests in and interpretations of internationalism co-existed and competed,

[21] LON, R5809/50/ 42186/ 42186, 'Address by the Honorable Herbert H. Lehman, Director of Foreign Relief and Rehabilitation Operations, before the Dinner of the Foreign Policy Association, Hotel Waldorf-Astoria, New York City, 17 June 1943'.

[22] Churchill College Archives, Noel-Baker papers (NBKR), 4/500, Noel-Baker to Harold [Butler], 24 August 1942. Also see Frank Walters to Noel-Baker, 2 April 1942. For one of the originators of this functional approach to international government, see Dorothy Anderson, 'David Mitrany (1888–1975): an appreciation of his life and work', *Review of International Studies*, 24 (1998), 577–92. Also see one of his most influential publications, David Mitrany, *A Working Peace System: An Argument for the Functional Development of International Organisation* (London, 1943, and later reprints).

[23] John Hutchinson, 'Disasters and the International Order: Earthquakes, Humanitarians and the Ciraolo Project', *International History Review*, 22 (2000), 1–36 at 35.

[24] National Planning Association, 'UNRRA: Gateway to Recovery', *Planning Pamphlets*, 30–31 (1944), 62.

**Fig. 1.** 'No Foreign Entanglements.' A 1935 Herblock Cartoon.
©The Herb Block Foundation.

even in the seemingly technical sphere of relief. Differences between perspectives centred particularly on the role of the United States and other allied powers within the international order, and on the relative rights and responsibilities of large and small nations in an international forum.

*American foreign policy, 'missionary internationalism' and the Four Policemen*
Both European and American analysts diagnosed the United States' refusal to participate in inter-Allied relief schemes and, more fundamentally, the country's lack of involvement in European and world affairs after World War I, as root causes of some of the subsequent decades' crises and upheavals. Of course, the extent to which the shifts in twentieth-century American diplomacy actually conformed to the narrative of international involvement, disentanglement, and renewed engagement has been fiercely fought over. The debate has tended to move between the two poles of 'isolation' on one hand and 'internationalism' on the other (and often still does). In the early 1950s a number of revisionist historians of the Left challenged the reality of such a path and juxtaposition of opposites. William Appleman Williams, for example, argued that the United States did not withdraw from world affairs, even after the defeat of Wilson's programme, but that it continuously pursued an active diplomatic, cultural, and above all expansionist economic policy abroad, particularly through developing markets and investments, and military interventions in Russia and Central America.[25] More recently, some diplomatic historians have argued that after Wilson's activities on the world stage America did not retreat to 'political isolationism' so much as to an 'independent internationalism';[26] that is, a focused pursuit of national interests, by multilateral means if desirable, but unilaterally if necessary.[27]

However, regardless of the reality of American isolation, in the aftermath of the attack on Pearl Harbor, throughout the war years and well into the

---

[25] Appleman Williams, 'The Legend of Isolationism in the 1920s'; William Appleman Williams, *The Tragedy of American Diplomacy* (New York, new edn 1972, 1st edn 1959). Also see Benjamin D. Rhodes, *United States Foreign Policy in the Interwar Period, 1918–1941*, (Westport CT, 2001), 4. Michael Cox and Caroline Kennedy-Pipe, 'The Tragedy of American Diplomacy? Rethinking the Marshall Plan', *Journal of Cold War Studies*, 7:1 (Winter 2005), 97–134.

[26] Michael Hogan (ed.), *The Ambiguous Legacy: US Foreign Relations in the 'American Century'* (Cambridge, 1999), 6. Joan Hoff-Wilson, *American Business and Foreign Policy, 1920–1933* (Kentucky, 1971). Ian Tyrrell, *Transnational Nation: United States History in Global Perspective since 1789* (Palgrave, 2007).

[27] Hoff Wilson, *American Business and Foreign Policy*, e.g. xvi, contrasted with 'Wilsonian Internationalism', 47.

post-war era, the notion of the United States' 'harmful' and 'selfish isolation' became a means to shake political opponents and a complacent or sceptical American public into action. Both a group of Roosevelt's New Dealers (within and outside the State Department) and an influential wing of the Republican Party used the spectre of isolation in their attempts to mobilize forces and to urge that the United States should now assume a leading role in international affairs, so as to make up for its earlier failures and broken promises. In Vice-President Henry Wallace's words: 'We of the United States can no more evade shouldering our responsibilities in this modern world than a boy of eighteen can avoid becoming a man by wearing short pants.' The United States now had 'a second chance' to heal the world and make it 'safe for democracy'.[28] This became the battle cry for planners and relief workers on both sides of the Atlantic.

The rhetoric of a second chance became a central rallying-point particularly in the early discussions on foreign relief and America's participation in UNRRA. Many echoed the call for the United States to set an international example at this crucial juncture, particularly in matters of European relief. As Lehman declared, it was 'given to us, twice within the span of a life-time, to attempt to devise a peace in which all men can live in freedom from fear and want. We failed last time. We dare not fail again.'[29] Relief supplies for war-torn areas, he added, could be provided easily from goods in abundance at home. Or as Wendell L. Willkie, defeated Republican Party nominee for the 1940 presidential election and thereafter an ally of Roosevelt, argued: if American isolation after the previous war had indeed been a contributing factor to the present calamities—'and it seems plain that it was'—then 'a withdrawal from the problems and responsibilities of the World after this war would be sheer disaster'. He urged the US to 'use the full force of our influence and enlightenment as a nation, to plan and establish continuing agencies under which a new world may develop—a world worth the fight and sacrifice we have made for it'.[30]

This portrayal of a second chance was often accompanied by an insistence that isolation was not only undesirable and selfish, but also plainly impossible to maintain. It had become a recurring theme in internationalist visions that scientific progress and technological innovations in transport and communication had made the world a smaller place. Already in the 1920s Arthur

---

[28] Henry Wallace, *The Century of the Common Man* (1944), 6.

[29] LON, R5809/ 50/42186/ 42186, Address by Herbert H. Lehman op. cit. 17 June 1943.

[30] Wendell L. Willkie, 'America's Real Task', in *The Peoples' Peace, by Representatives of the United Nations* (New York, 1943), 260–1.

Salter, long-time British Director of the Economic and Finance Section of the League and later Assistant Director of UNRRA, had been struck by the extraordinary pace of inventions. Rapid and easy communication in the form of 'transport and telegrams' had 'transform[ed] the world', and continued to open up new possibilities for international governance, but they also presented entirely new kinds of dangers.[31] These dangers became even more apparent after the world spiralled into war again. Self-proclaimed internationalists now went to great lengths to spell out the implications for both America's geographical place on the world map and its future security. James T. Shotwell, a historian and well-known American internationalist and former foreign policy advisor to Woodrow Wilson, argued that since war had become 'total war', no nation could 'adequately protect itself against a force which is bound more and more to conquer nature and thus change the basis of national security. To live well and prosperously in a world under the constant threat of war waged under these conditions is simply impossible.' The lesson was that isolation could no longer provide the kind of safety it had done in the past: 'There are no mountains or deserts on the airways of the stratosphere', and American defence and foreign policy had to take account of this fact.[32]

Some of these advocates identified the opposite pole of America's 'internationalism' not just as one of 'isolation' but also of 'imperialism'. Willkie thought that the United States had to choose 'one of three courses' after the war: 'narrow isolationism which inevitably means the loss of our own liberty; international imperialism which means the sacrifice of some other nation's liberty; or the creation of a world in which there shall be an equality of opportunity for every race and every nation'.[33] Surely the American people could see that there was really no alternative to the third path, he insisted. 'Internationalism', in relief as in other fields, thereby became a short-hand term for America's equitable and just world leadership. Fiorello H. La Guardia, Republican mayor of New York and Lehman's successor as UNRRA's Director-General, put it similarly a few years later in one of his radio broadcasts: 'We must not be soft. We must not get tough. We have no selfish interests. We want no land in Europe or elsewhere . . . Hence our duty is plain—to provide the kind of leadership to which European politics is

---

[31] Arthur Salter, 'World Government', in Mary Adams (ed.), *The Modern State* (London, 1933).

[32] James T. Shotwell, *The Great Decision*, 2nd edn (New York, 1945), xix, 89.

[33] Willkie, 'America's Real Task', 262.

unaccustomed; to stand by the right; to support such policies as are founded on justice, peace and understanding.'[34]

Although in these discussions the responsibility of leadership fell primarily to the United States, similar language was also used in Britain. Anthony Eden, for example, thought that because 'the world was shrinking before our eyes', there was no longer any 'room for isolation' or for 'selfish politics, or un-neighbourly policies. There will be but one village street from Edinburgh to Chungking.' Although Britain could not neglect British interests, Eden insisted, it could also not 'afford to disinterest ourselves [sic] from the interests of other nations. There can be no isolation for the British Empire, ever again. We must assume the burden of leadership. It is a burden which others will share with us. But a great part of the burden is for us.'[35] This was the language of America's and Britain's 'internationalism'.

This perspective—I am tempted to call it 'missionary internationalism'—drew strength from an analysis of the anticipated distribution of power at the end of war. James Shotwell's 'Commission to Study the Organization of Peace' (an influential study group making plans and recommendations on post-war policy in the US) was by spring 1942 under no illusion that the burden of global relief and reconstruction would rest mostly on the two or three nations, the United States definitely among them, which would emerge as the victors of the war.[36] 'Aside from the meritorious claims of each nation, and aside from the justice of the situation', a Commission report stated, 'the inescapable fact is that power will be exercised by those who remain strong

---

[34] La Guardia and Wagner Archives (LGWA), 26B7, Transcript of broadcast, 21 August 1946 and 18 September 1946.

[35] Anthony Eden, 'Sacrifices for Peace: Extract from Speech at Usher Hall, Edinburgh, 8 May 1942', in: *The Peoples' Peace, by Representatives of the United Nations* (New York, 1943), 70.

[36] The Commission to Study the Organization of Peace was set by the League of Nations Association in 1939, modelled on Wilson's 1917 'Enquiry' to make recommendations on the future peace settlements. It was directed by Clark Eichelberger and James Shotwell. Members came from a wide spectrum of opinion on international affairs, and included people such as Charles Taft, John F. Dulles, John W. Davis, Sumner Welles, Philip Jessup, Quincy Wright and Max Lerner. See Clark Eichelberger, *Organising for Peace: A Personal History of the Ffounding of the United Nations* (New York, 1977). Glenn Tatsuya Mitoma, 'Civil Society and International Human Rights: The Commission to Study the Organisation of Peace and the Origins of the UN Human Rights Regime', *Human Rights Quarterly*, 30 (2008), 607–30. Robert P. Hillmann, 'Quincy Wright and the Commission to Study the Organisation of Peace', *Global Governance*, 4 (1998), 485–99.

enough to exercise it'.[37] Shotwell himself argued that both 'logic and political necessity' demanded 'recognition on the part of the United Nations of a definite leadership by the Great Powers', as a result of which dominant executive authority in the future international organization had to lie in the hands of the Great Powers.[38] The US, together with Britain, he maintained, had to use its 'military and economic power to restore and maintain order in the world', while making clear that it sought for itself no special material or political advantages. It was about fair leadership in place of isolationism or imperialism. In an influential essay of 1942 he argued that whereas in 1918 the US had lacked a 'clear sense of [its] responsibilities as a member of a world community of nations', by now Americans had fortunately recognized their inescapable duties concerning post-war problems in the rest of the world. This new 'strategy of peace', he wrote, had to begin with the fight against disease and famine, the provision of relief goods, and the re-establishment of standards of dignity, equality, and tolerance across the world.[39]

These declarations on the Great Powers' (and particularly America's) past failures and present responsibilities accompanied OFRRO's first months of activities as it embarked on relief work with the Allied troops in North Africa. They were further strengthened by a rhetoric of economic and political self-interest: advocates were at pains to point out that whereas before American economic and military self-sufficiency had enabled a sense of detachment from European affairs, now it was undeniably in America's national interest to seek active international involvement.

From the start, arguments on economic self-interest played a significant role in plans for international relief. In American and British economic circles, thinking about relief and UNRRA began as a way of solving the problem of world surpluses. In the US, as Patricia Clavin and others have shown, there was a new, powerful constellation of interest groups whose well-being depended on the continued export of American goods.[40] Post-war relief became a means of disposing of surplus commodities accumulating in the Western hemisphere and British Empire as a result of the war's disruption of trade. As early as 1941, Dean Acheson, Assistant Secretary of State for Economic Affairs, also thought that relief could be used to make liberated countries

---

[37] Commission to Study the Organisation of Peace, 'Second Report—The Transitional Period', *International Conciliation*, 379 (April 1942), 162.

[38] Shotwell, *The Great Decision*, 49.

[39] James T. Shotwell, 'After the War', *International Conciliation* (December 1942), 32.

[40] Patricia Clavin, *The Great Depression in Europe* (London, 2000), 201.

pledge to avoid economic nationalism and to cooperate in the economic sphere.[41]

Here, too, Americans wanted to learn from previous mistakes. Lehman pointed out that relief should not be given as a 'selfless gift' but with the understanding that it would be repaid. And sometimes even giving gifts would be in the US' best interests. American relief operations in Europe after 1918 had highlighted the dangers of setting up loans which could not be repaid, he argued: American insistence that the aid be paid for had severely hampered receiving countries' possibilities for recovery, and ultimately ushered in a 'tragic cycle' of debt and repayment, leading 'first to a gigantic depression, then to the rise of Hitler, Mussolini and the Japanese depression, and finally to global conflagration'. The lesson was, he insisted, that in some cases it would be 'the course of prudence and wisdom' to provide goods for relief and rehabilitation as gifts and thereby put a faster end to the need for relief. After all, restoring peace and a stable world economy was 'what we want. . .', he insisted. It was 'merely enlightened self-interest'. Americans should not forget, Lehman went on, that after this war the US would once again 'be the greatest producers in the world' and would urgently require world markets for American grain, cotton, tobacco, steel, automobiles and 'the thousands of products of our mills and factories'. The self-interest argument was thus abundantly clear, Lehman concluded: providing relief to war-stricken Europe was the necessary first step towards creating a stable world economy and finding outlets for American surplus goods, providing jobs for America's returning soldiers and converting American industries back to peacetime production.[42]

This rhetoric became particularly useful when in January 1943, Lehman and a group of advisors, Herbert Hoover among them, began to draft plans for an entirely new, international relief body—UNRRA—, which could carry out relief work on a much larger scale than any of the existing bodies such as OFRRO. Their resulting blueprint for American participation in international relief, Arthur Krock wrote optimistically in the *New York Times*, should 'impress Congress and the public with its practical good sense and reassure those who may fear that the OFRRO will attempt to play the part of a world

---

[41] UN Archives, S-1021–0017–08, Grace Fox, 'Early Consideration of Post War Relief: The Problems of Surplus Commodities', 1 June 1944. On Acheson, see Robert A. Divine, 'Acheson, Dean Gooderham', *American National Biography Online*, February 2000, http://www/anb.org/articles/07/07/00002.html.

[42] LON, R5809/50/42186/42186, Address by Herbert H. Lehman, op. cit. 17 June 1943. Similar conclusions also in National Planning Association, *Relief for Europe* (Washington DC, 1942), 37–44.

Santa Claus or the forcible dispenser of "blessings" to those who do not view them as such'. The point of the proposals was to supply aid to enable the restoration of war-ravaged countries, so that eventually they themselves could pay for the material aid they required. Lehman did not propose, Krock wrote, 'to build utopia at the expense of the United States, but to invoke businesslike practices that will at the same time be humanitarian and effective in providing insulation against future war'.[43]

All in all, 'self-interest alone' was thus 'sufficient to make the United States deeply concerned with the contentment and well-being of the other peoples of the world'.[44] But as the declarations on moral responsibilities and just leadership suggested, these considerations transcended *Realpolitik* and simple self-interest. American advocates of leadership in international relief regularly used Christian imagery of charity and philanthropy, providence, morality, and the protection of individual dignity. Lehman thought that apart from the evident motives of economic and political self-interest impelling Americans to international relief, 'the deep moral motives' alone were justification enough.[45] 'Bread cast upon the waters does return', insisted Wallace: relief cast upon the waters of war-wrecked Europe would demonstrate the power of American charity and enable the US to take its rightful place of leadership in world affairs.[46] Together this was a powerful combination which proved to be of lasting significance for American, and to a lesser degree also British, perspectives on internationalism.

Even before UNRRA appeared on the scene, the arguments on the impossibility of isolation and the economic benefits of American leadership were first rehearsed by humanitarian groups' in their efforts to extend relief through the British blockade of German-occupied Europe. By the time UNRRA was founded, internationally-minded Democrats could thus agree with their outward-looking Republican colleagues on a number of crucial foreign policy issues and in matters of international engagement. To both groups, developments in the US seemed to form the pinnacle of history and progress. The application of American institutions and practices to world problems, which American guidance of relief would stimulate, would help to solve problems of war, poverty, famine, and tyranny. Some suggested that the American Constitution and Bill of Rights should become the basis of an International Bill of Rights to safeguard personal liberty, freedom of thought,

---

[43] Arthur Krock, 'In the Nation: The Lehman OFRRO Blue-Prints Its Task', *New York Times* (7 January 1943).

[44] Wallace, *The Century of the Common Man*, 57.

[45] LON, R5809/50/42186/42186, Address by Herbert H. Lehman, op. cit. 17 June 1943.

[46] Wallace, *The Century of the Common Man*, 68.

religion and expression, and perhaps even a model for a new 'Constitution of the United Nations'.[47] Many agreed that it was a major purpose of America's management of the relief project to internationalize New Deal achievements and teach the world how to enjoy higher standards of living. Through relief work, countries could be taught how to use their soils and resources more effectively, and shown how to raise their standards of production and consumption.[48] Some writers also compared the process of making devastated Europe habitable again with the hardships of the nineteenth-century pioneers who had forced their way through frontier wilderness.[49]

Of course, people like Shotwell were critical of simplistic identifications of 'progress' and 'freedom' as purely American inventions. This was, Shotwell argued, clearly a 'falsification of history', since the founders of the American Republic were influenced by Continental and British intellectual currents, and the antecedents of the American experiment went back 'across the whole history of the Western world'.[50] But he, too, insisted that American history offered a genuinely useful guide on how to solve problems inherent in international collaboration. The Constitution's principle of the division of powers, for example, was of immediate relevance and current application: 'It is not just the balancing of legislative, executive and judicial powers, important as that device has proved', Shotwell wrote, 'It includes as well the other devices by which communities preserve their liberties against the central power in a democratic federal system', and its notion of graded responsibility, he thought, should become a guiding principle for the United Nations.[51] Overall, American history provided the example to be followed by the rest of the world. 'Internationalization' was the process by which it could happen.

Even if such metaphors on the internationalization of American history did not always correspond with British ideas, two- or four-power thinking of the kind enshrined in the UNRRA agreement was also welcomed among British circles, not least since British planners were anxious to tie the United States into the rehabilitation of Europe. For example, Melville

[47] E.g. James T. Shotwell, 'After the War', *International Conciliation* (December 1942), 34. Ruth Bryan Owen, *Look Forward, Warrior* (New York, 1942).

[48] Wallace, *The Century of the Common Man*, 58.

[49] UN Archives, S-1021–0143–1/13, *In the Wake of the Armies: Raw-materials for Writers, Directors, Producers, Story Editors*, 8 November 1945.

[50] James T. Shotwell, 'The Constitution and the Guarantee of Freedom', in James T. Shotwell, *The Faith of an Historian and Other Essays: An Anthology* (New York, 1964), 259–260.

[51] Shotwell, *The Great Decision*, 96–97.

Mackenzie from the Ministry of Health, who also served on an UNRRA Expert Committee on Quarantine, welcomed the fact that UNRRA committed both the American and Soviet governments to collaboration and shared leadership in health and relief. A new international body such as UNRRA, he argued, had to devise mechanisms by which each member country exercised a vote proportionate to the importance of its resources. The failure to recognize this before had led to the absence of some of the most advanced nations in earlier international health projects. One could simply not expect the Great Powers to be overruled by a vote of less developed nations.[52] Or as Arthur Salter declared in the House of Commons in 1948, America, like Britain, followed a dual political and humanitarian purpose, namely to 'preserve her own and other peoples' freedom'. As the country's humanitarian record demonstrated, he argued, America had commendably 'developed a responsibility proportionate to her power'.[53]

In short, among American and British relief planners there was a consensus on the desirability and unavoidability of an Anglo-American leadership of the relief project, and a crucial role of the Great Powers in any future international organization. Shotwell, although much more sympathetic to the legacy of the League than some of his American colleagues, insisted that the distribution of power made a leadership by the Four Policemen (in UNRRA as in the future United Nations) simply unavoidable. In fact, in a number of essays Shotwell also suggested that if the seeds of the new international system lay in the relationship between the Great Powers, the kernel of that seed was the bond of 'understanding' between the United States and Britain, based largely on similar outlooks and ideals.[54]

*The view from Central Europe: the 'cooperative internationalism' of small states and federations*
Representatives of those countries seeking to qualify for aid proposed rather different priorities and interpretations of 'internationalism' and the international relief project. They were surrounded by the devastation caused by years

---

[52] Melville Mackenzie, *Medical Relief in Europe: Questions for Immediate Study* (Royal Institute of International Affairs, (4th impression February 1944, 1st published July 1942). Also see NA, CO 859/66/14, M. Mackenzie, 'Critical Review of the Work of the Office, and the Health Organisation of the League of Nations', Confidential Note, 21 September 1943, quoted in Sunil Amrith, *Decolonizing International Health: India and Southeast Asia, 1930–1965* (Basingstoke, 2006). Melville Mackenzie, 'International Collaboration in Health', *International Affairs*, 26:4 (October 1950), 515–21.

[53] Quoted in: Lord Salter, *Memoirs of a Public Servant* (London, 1961), 311–12.

[54] Shotwell, *The Great Decision*, 30.

of foreign occupation, war, racial conflict, and 'scorched earth'—or, in the case of the exile leaders, by passionate letters and appeals from their colleagues and compatriots. To them, international relief programmes were not an abstract exercise.[55] They were in no doubt about the enormity and urgency of the relief problem: the food shortage on the continent, they insisted, could result in a famine worse still than those seen in the Volga region two decades before. The potential for an epidemic crisis was at least as severe as it had been when the influenza pandemic hit the world in 1918, and when typhus and cholera ran wild in large areas of East-Central Europe. They also knew that the refugee problem was far greater in magnitude than before, as millions of people had already fled or were being expelled from their homes.[56] All in all, although there were many obvious similarities between the conditions after the previous world war and those likely to be faced now, there were also some crucial differences: in size, intensity and 'thoroughness' of genocidal policies this latest war far outstripped any previous conflicts.[57] An obvious corollary was that problems of relief and rehabilitation would also be greatly increased.

In these conditions, at the start thinking about relief involved above all thinking about medical relief, and the earlier precedent of the League of Nations' medical missions after World War I proved highly significant. Then as now, relief workers and politicians argued, only international action could help. As one Romanian doctor wrote to his former League colleagues in Geneva, the epidemic situation in Eastern Europe, particularly concerning typhus fever, was 'every bit as bad as it was in 1919': 'In the light of the statistics for 1944–1945 I foresee a catastrophic spread of the disease, and I can see no safety except by international collaboration like that accomplished by the International Epidemics Commission of the

---

[55] Relief was a central area of concern of many émigré groups, e.g. it was one of the fields of activity of the Central and Eastern European Planning Board in New York. NYPL-CEEBP, minutes, 26 October 1942.

[56] See e.g. National Archives, Kew (NA), FD, 1/6819, The Royal Institute of International Affairs, 'Immediate post-war measures of relief and reconstruction in Europe', 9 February 1942. Also see *Relief and Reconstruction in Europe—The First Steps: an interim report by a Chatham House Study Group*, (Royal Institute of International Affairs, July 1942); Mackenzie, *Medical Relief in Europe* ; Julian Huxley et al., *When Hostilities Cease: Papers on Relief and Reconstruction prepared for the Fabian Society* (London, 1943); Save the Children Fund, *Children in Bondage: A Survey of Child Life in the Occupied Countries of Europe and in Finland* (London, 1942); G. H. Bourne, *Starvation in Europe* (London, 1943).

[57] National Planning Association, 'UNRRA: Gateway to Recovery', *Planning Pamphlets*, 30–31 (1944), 3.

League of Nations in the years 1919–1922.' The work of the Commission had proved, he wrote, 'that the only way to protect the whole of Europe against epidemics moving Westwards was a common front of all European countries so that disease could be attacked at its source. This is the only method by which once again the spread of epidemics may be avoided . . . ' Nothing had fundamentally changed this time around: 'I can state positively', he concluded, 'that no government of any Eastern European country is in a position to cope, during the coming winter, by its own efforts with the threatened epidemics'; as before, relief supplies and expenditures would have to be provided by international and voluntary contributions.[58]

Apart from this sense of precedent, appeals for international aid also contained a clear notion of entitlement. Petitions frequently insisted that since the native forces were already doing everything possible to prevent an escalation of crises, in the interest of world health they surely deserved to be supported. As a Polish report observed, if the widely feared epidemic threat was still kept in check then it was thanks only to the 'tireless work' of the 'Extraordinary Commissariat for the Fight Against Epidemics', which the Polish National Liberation Committee had set up in September 1944. In the seven months of its existence it had divided the country into a thousand 'epidemic districts', each of which had to be policed individually, and it had trained over two thousand disinfectors and many more doctors in epidemic work. But so far it had received vaccines only from Russia.[59] Another Polish memorandum stated that the current health emergency had its direct origins in the German occupation and the Nazis' genocidal policy. The young Polish government and sanitary service were now rallying all forces to eradicate and overcome this legacy. But, it noted, the only effective means for combating epidemics would be international relief. After the First World War, when Poland had been in a similar situation, the League of Nations had sent an international sanitary commission to Poland's rescue. But until now only the Soviet government had provided any help, both through the work of Red Army sanitary organs and through the donation of drugs, sera, and vaccines. The Swedish Red Cross had also sent gifts. But none of this was enough, and much greater international support was needed.[60]

[58] LON, R6151/42789/41674, extract from letter by Dr. M. Ciuca (Cantacuzene Serum and Vaccine Institute, Bucharest, Romania) to Dr. Frank G. Boudreau, 15 September 1945, and forwarded to Dr. Yves Biraud, Section d'Hygiène, League of Nations.

[59] LON, R6151/8A/42758/41674, Dr. Blum, Polska Agencja Prasowa 'Polpress', Berne, to Dr. Biraud (head of Hygiene-Section of League of Nations), Geneva, 15 August 1945.

[60] LON, R6151/8A/42758/41674, Schweizerisch-Polnisches Koordinations- u. Hilfskommittee für das befreite Polen, 'Die Seuchenlage in Polen', 31 August 1945.

UNRRA's aid was indeed slow to arrive in Poland. UNRRA's negotiations with the London-based Polish government-in-exile began in summer 1944, but the creation of the Soviet-sponsored Polish Committee of National Liberation (known as the Lublin committee, but after January 1945 based in Warsaw) complicated matters. In September 1944, each of these two competing Polish authorities submitted their own formal request to UNRRA for aid and supplies. UNRRA's diplomats attempted to steer a neutral course between them, but with only limited success. While the London-based Poles heralded UNRRA aid as a welcome expression of American commitment to Poland's future,[61] the communist authorities were suspicious about precisely the nature of this commitment. UNRRA only established a Polish mission after Lehman had appointed the Soviet ambassador and member of the UNRRA Council, Mikhail Menshikov, to negotiate a formal agreement with the Lublin government. And even then the necessary entry visas for members of a first temporary UNRRA delegation were delayed until July 1945, the day after the United States and the United Kingdom formally recognized the newly reconstituted Polish Provisional Government.[62]

Appeals and petitions for relief supplies at times implied that if Britain and the United States had come to the rescue earlier, the world would not now have to revisit the scenes of suffering and devastation seen two decades before. Even where this accusation remained unspoken, the many long lists of estimated relief needs sent by the occupied countries to the Leith-Ross Committee in London, and then to UNRRA, in fact contained a particular view of international responsibilities. In Polish eyes, international relief programmes involved coming to the aid of one of the acknowledged greatest victims of Nazi aggression, which also had been a site of grave crises just decades before. In a speech to the citizens of Warsaw (as reported by a Swiss-Polish relief committee), Deputy Prime Minister Stanisław Mikołajczyk even referred explicitly to international 'rights' and 'obligations': not only did every Pole abroad have the 'right' (and duty) to return to Poland to take part in the country's reconstruction, but Poland, he declared, 'as the first country which took up arms, had a right to demand [international] help'.[63] Although both Anglo-American diplomats and representatives

[61] E.g. see Stanislaw Mikolajczyk, *The Rape of Poland: Pattern of Soviet Aggression* (New York, 1948).

[62] Woodbridge, *UNRRA*, vol.II, 204.

[63] LON, R6151/8A/42758/41674, Schweizerisch-Polnisches Koordinations- u. Hilfskomittee fuer das befreite Polen, 'Informationsbericht', 3 August 1945, my translation: 'Auf der anderen Seite hat aber Polen, das als erstes Land zu den Waffen griff, ein Recht zu verlangen, dass ihm geholfen werde.'

from the occupied countries thus spoke of international *obligations* and *duties* to provide relief, they did not share this language of countries' or populations' rights and *entitlement* to relief.

Some socialist and communist preparations for relief and reconstruction contained even more explicit accusations about the Great Powers' responsibilities. For example, Sava N. Kosanovich, a former Serbian minister and now member of the 'Central and Eastern European Planning Board' (a group of Czechoslovak, Greek, Polish, and Yugoslavian exile politicians) in New York insisted that after 1918 'the world' had been 'extremely charitable toward the Germans and preferred to find an excuse for all their sins'. The countries of Central and Eastern Europe had to face the consequences, left 'to the mercy of Germany to do with them what she liked'. No-one came to their rescue, and no-one stopped Germany—in fact, German actions in the area 'had, as a rule, the support of the other Great Powers'. [64] The provision of relief and means for rehabilitation could thus be seen as a form of compensation for past failures, but it would only be the first step. Relief programmes had to initiate lasting reconstruction which could eradicate economic injustices and transform the region's living standards forever. There could be no lasting peace, Kosanovich insisted, if 'the citizens of the small and devastated countries' were 'left at their present level of destitution from which they have not been permitted to rise in spite of all their efforts and the rich natural resources of the territories which they inhabit'. Countries of Eastern Europe and the Balkans could no longer be 'regarded as "inferior" to the rest of Europe'. The 'Jugoslavs, Czechoslovaks, Poles and Greeks' had suffered enough and had made enough sacrifices for 'the ideals of humanity' for them to 'deserve' a fair peace. The United Nations had to eliminate all forms of exploitation, including the inequalities between 'the high industrialized countries' and those undeveloped nations. As a result, 'this part of Europe' would 'become largely free from need'.[65] As a stepping-stone to far-reaching and radical transformations, international relief had here altogether different functions from those identified by diplomats in Washington and London.

Apart from a clear sense of precedent and a particular understanding of entitlement to international aid, how was internationalism in relief understood differently here? Opponents of the four-power model included former officials of the League of Nations, who tended to focus on the interdependence of nations and on the universality of rights and obligations within

---

[64] Savo N. Kosanovich, 'Eastern Europe Awaits a Common Man's Peace', in *The Peoples' Peace*, by *Representatives of the United Nations*, (New York, 1943), 134.

[65] Ibid., 133, 135.

international organizations. This line of argument had a number of important British and American supporters, but it was of particular significance to socialist and liberal advocates in Central and Eastern Europe, who highlighted a dual function of internationalism: to safeguard the rights of small nations, and to contain not just Germany but also the Soviet Union and tie it into a broad international system. International relief in this perspective would thus not only enable countries to rebuild themselves, to throw off the shackles of foreign occupation and to restore their sovereignty, it would also help to create international mechanisms to guarantee their future safety and global collective security. To economists and political scientists in Poland, for example, Polish relief and reconstruction appeared to be both central to future European stability and only possible within a broad international settlement. The Krakow-based academic Roman Dyboski insisted as early as 1937 that a Polish recovery had 'wide international bearings': a state of thirty-four million people in the centre of Europe could not 'be left economically in a blind alley without grave danger to the balance and the stability' of the continent and the world.[66]

The connection between UNRRA and past as well as future programmes of global health and stability was also made by Ludwik Rajchman, a Polish Jew and former director of the League's Health Organization. During the war he was based in Washington; he later returned to Poland and became a Polish representative on UNRRA. In 1942 and 1943 he drafted plans for UNRRA's medical programme and a future international health organization. UNRRA, he thought, should continue the spirit and tradition of international cooperation pioneered by the League's Health Organization, and provide a stepping stone towards a new permanent and much improved international health service. Not only were countries to be represented equally, but even within countries representation should be much improved. Whereas in the League health matters had been controlled by diplomats, in the new body the 'consumers of health' should be represented by their municipal authorities and social security agencies, in addition to representatives from the central governments. Whereas Melvin Mackenzie, as we have seen above, thought that an international health body was inherently and unavoidably unrepresentative, Rajchman argued against four-power thinking in international health and relief. After all, he wrote, '[t]he USA or Great Britain need international biological standards as much as does Greece. China is as interested in tests of mental fitness as Switzerland or Holland. Gt. Britain, France and USA would

---

[66] Roman Dyboski, 'Economic and Social Problems in Poland', *International Affairs*, 16:4 (July 1937), 592.

all derive advantages from international success in control of yellow fever or malaria'.[67]

Proponents of this perspective—let us call it a 'cooperative international-ism'—recognized the need for the Great Powers' participation in a global organization. But while Rajchman and his League colleagues agreed that American participation in international relief was vital for success, they insisted that American finances and supplies were to be pooled and jointly controlled. At the same time they also rejected many of the American claims. Max Czech, a member of the circle around the Polish refugee sociologist Feliks Gross in New York, thought the idea that post-war problems could be cured by universalizing the American outlook and by drawing up an American constitution for the world was altogether 'too pat and homely, too idealistic and oversimple'.[68] In fact, rather than applying American yardsticks and re-enacting American history, real 'internationalism', in Czech's and Gross' eyes, would be a means to preserve and protect the peculiar social, cultural, political, and economic needs and landscape of the European countries. As we have seen, Lehman reassured his American compatriots that knowledge of impending US aid would transform the 'down-trodden people of Europe' into a usefully 'cohesive group, ready and willing to co-operate in the battle of liberation'.[69] But these Europeans, by contrast, were dismayed by the American and British discussions' frequent lack of awareness of their peculiar settings and needs. Feliks Gross was under no illusion that 'the small nations' of Central and Eastern Europe seemed very 'remote to the American in Kansas', and '[e]ven most American tourists who have visited Western Europe never travelled in Eastern Europe'.[70] Such lack of familiarity bred enormous differences in perspective, concerning relief needs and requirements as much as future international collaboration more generally.

Ultimately, this became not so much a confrontation between Americans and Europeans so much as between UNRRA's diplomats in Washington and London on one hand, and its relief workers and relief recipients on the ground on the other. Relief workers of all nationalities frequently called for greater appreciation of and sensitivity to European cultural peculiarities on the part

---

[67] National Archives Kew (NA), FO 370/804, Rajchman, 3. Many thanks to Sunil Amrith for drawing my attention to this document.

[68] Max Czech review of Ruth Bryan Owen, *Look Forward, Warrior*, (1942), *New Europe* (1942), 33.

[69] LON, R5809/ 50/42186/ 42186, address by Herbert H. Lehman before dinner of Foreign Policy Association, 17 June 1943.

[70] Feliks Gross, *Crossroads of Two Continents: A Democratic Federation of East-Central Europe* (New York, 1945), 5.

of the Anglo-Saxon policy-makers. The Canadian Mary McGeachy, UNRRA's Director of Welfare, her biographer noted, had 'reservations about Americans riding roughshod over local sensitivities in war-torn Europe'—a 'pro-European stance' which was interpreted by some of her critics as 'anti-American'.[71] UNRRA's intention should be, McGeachy argued, to increase local participation and responsibility, and she disagreed with her American colleagues who were, as she put it, 'anxious that UNRRA shall convey American experience and standards abroad'.[72] Many other memoirs, letters, and accounts by UNRRA's relief workers document the geographical and psychological gap that separated their analyses from those of the planners in Washington and London.

Socialist and communist leaders tended to articulate this distinction as one between politicians and diplomats on one hand and 'the common people' on the other. Like Rajchman and Kosanovich, Feliks Gross, too, argued that in previous peace conferences diplomats had decided the fate of peoples and nations, but this time the people themselves had to control their own fate.[73] To them, the solution to creating such a peace and to satisfying the region's needs lay partly in the creation of regional federations as components of a larger international organization. This idea was supported within émigré circles and for a time had a number of important advocates among the re-sistance movements in Poland, Czechoslovakia, and Yugoslavia.[74] A feder-ation of Central and Eastern European nations, Gross and others argued, would not only 'preserve national and cultural characteristics', but would also be 'the only road to economic reconstruction of these devastated areas and the only method whereby the standards of living of the most underdevel-oped area in Europe can be raised'.[75] Moreover, such a federation would form a useful bridge between the Soviet Union and the Western democracies, or a 'crossroads' between East and West, and thereby become a vital component of any future global framework. Here, too, Gross rejected the American role model offered to the European federalists. Although Europeans could per-haps learn from the 'Jeffersonian optimism' of success against the odds, he

---

[71] Mary Kinnear, *Woman of the World: Mary McGeachy and International Cooperation* (Toronto, 2004), 160.

[72] Mary McGeachy to Derek Hoyer-Miller, 30 May 1944, quoted in Mary Kinnear, *Woman of the World: Mary McGeachy and International Cooperation* (Toronto, 2004), 160.

[73] Gross, *Crossroads of Two Continents*, 85.

[74] E.g. see NYPL-CEEPB, Feliks Gross to Malcolm Davis, Carnegie Endowment for Inter-national Peace, 16 June 1943, referring to article in *Robotnik*, London, 1 June 1943. The Central and Eastern European Planning Board, 14 January 1942.

[75] Gross, *Crossroads of Two Continents*, viii.

wrote, federalism in Europe could not 'imitate directly the American system, because conditions are altogether different. Although a melting pot, the United States is populated by a more or less homogenous people, who speak the same language. Our section of Europe is composed of many nations, who speak different languages and have various traditions, customs and cultures'.[76] Ultimately, the irony was not lost on Gross that these plans for regional federations were being developed just as relations between the different countries (and the different factions among their representatives) were becoming ever more fraught, and that it could not happen if the Soviet Union continued to reject any kind of federation in Europe.

These kinds of analyses all fed into debates about UNRRA's structure. Here, even the Americans and the British did not always see eye to eye. While the agreement was being drafted, confrontations about the degree to which power should be centralized in UNRRA's headquarters seem to have come out at least partially in favour of the Europeans: the Americans had demanded a strong executive at the headquarters in Washington, subject only to a committee advising on policy matters (since the bulk of supplies would be found and transported in and through the United States), whereas the British argued in favour of operating regional committees and regional Deputy Directors General, not least because the occupied countries demanded an active role in the relief programmes. Soviet officials also demanded a Soviet Deputy Director General and an extended scope of regional committees. The compromise solution was to establish a European Regional Office with its headquarters in London, which administered and supervised offices, missions, and displaced persons operations in Europe and the Middle East.

But as Grace Fox, one of UNRRA's archivists and official historians, noted, '[p]olitical philosophies and political interests . . . are seldom killed by compromise'.[77] Disagreements concerning the relative power of larger and smaller participating nations within UNRRA's policy-making bodies proved much more difficult to resolve. From the start, a number of European countries protested about the four-power composition of UNRRA's Central Committee. The Dutch Foreign Minister, van Kleffens, told Dean Acheson that UNRRA would set a precedent for future international collaboration which the Netherlands 'would find . . . extremely difficult to accept'. The problem was that in the occupied territories the composition of the Central Committee 'would be regarded as somewhat akin to the pattern of the three dominant states with the satellite states'. Membership should be enlarged by at least 2 or 3 countries, he insisted, including at least one occupied country

---

[76] Gross, *Crossroads of Two Continents.*

[77] UN Archives, S-1021–0017–23, Grace Fox to Larry Leonhard, 6 December 1944.

and one South American state.[78] The Polish Ambassador in Washington, Jan Ciechanowski, similarly protested about the absence of a representative from the receiving countries of Europe aside from the Soviet Union. Countries like Poland, he insisted, would eventually be in a position to become supplying powers themselves, if their rehabilitation proceeded smoothly.[79] To him, UNRRA 'consolidated the "dictatorial" policy of the major powers'. As he explained later, he 'understood that the final plan for UNRRA's organization, on which my government and . . . others would be asked to give advice, had already been definitely decided upon by the Big Four. There was nothing left for us to do but sign.'[80] He urged that membership of the Central Committee be broadened.

Even Lord Halifax had misgivings about the lack of European and Canadian representation within UNRRA. While ultimate control of military and political arrangements inevitably had to lie with the four powers, he thought that other allies should be allowed to participate in organizations such as UNRRA, since they would only be successful if they secured 'willing and full cooperation' of all interested parties. After all, individually the European allies might not be 'on a level with the great powers', but their aggregate population amounted to over 133,000,000 people and their aggregate trade before the war had been greater than that of either Britain or the US. Now, their governments could 'hardly be expected to agree that decisions, vitally affecting the economies of their countries, should be settled by a committee on which they have no representation'. Even if most of them would initially be recipients rather than suppliers of relief, they should not be disqualified from membership of the policy committee. This was all the more important since a number of them would in fact make important contributions to relief provision; Norway and Holland would assist with shipping, Holland and France with supplies, and so on.[81]

[78] Lehman Suite, Hugh R. Jackson papers, Folder 49–2, 'Meeting Mr. Van Kleffens and Mr. Acheson', 11 June 1943.

[79] Lehman suite, Hugh R. Jackson papers, Folder 49–2, 'Draft Agreement for a United Nations relief and rehabilitation administration—meeting with Mr.Ciechanowski (Polish Ambassador), Mr.Domaniewski (Commercial Counsellor of the Polish Embassy), Mr.Lychowski (Chief of Economic Section of the Polish Ministry and of Commerce, Industry and Shipping in London) with Mr.Acheson and Mr.Veatch)', 23 and 26 June 1943.

[80] Jan Ciechanowski, quoted in Marta Balinska, *For the Good of Humanity: Ludwik Rajchman, Medical Statesman* (Central European University Press, 1995, 1st English edn 1998), 1919. Jan Ciechanowski, *La rancon de la victoire* (Paris, 1971).

[81] Lehman Suite, Hugh R. Jackson papers, Folder 49–2, Halifax to Acheson, 24 January 1943.

These clashes also concerned the issue of control of other parts of UNRRA's machinery, particularly that of supply and shipping. Some early critics of UNRRA pointed out that although the 'United Nations' had signed up to it, the body was in fact 'wholly dependent for supplies and shipping space on four "Combined Boards" which are entirely an Anglo-American affair (with the exception of one, on which Canada is represented)'. Supplies were controlled not by an international body, but by the United States and Britain, 'with a small voice—a ninth part of a larynx, as it were—permitted to Canada'.[82] By contrast, a truly international relief agency had to bring together producers and consumers, suppliers and recipients, 'have and have-not nations'. In this sense, Spencer Coxe from the US National Planning Association argued that relief programmes had to be determined by a body in which every affected nation—'either as a recipient or a giver, whether large or small, victor or vanquished'—had an equal voice. Only in this way could relief be given impartially and efficiently. He thought it was quite wrong to assume that the United States would be able to feed Europe single-handedly. It might well be the largest single source of relief supplies, he wrote, but it would 'by no means furnish an overwhelming proportion, and there [was] no reason why we should have complete control over the administration'.[83]

In practice, these disagreements soon led to a split between Western European member countries of UNRRA and those from Central and Eastern Europe. Although all of them questioned, as one report put it, 'the pattern of Anglo-American control into which they were supposed to fit' to some degree, the representatives of Belgium, the Netherlands, France, Luxembourg, Denmark, and Norway were in comparatively better positions. Although their first priority was to sort out their own relief needs, they also possessed some foreign exchange to pay for goods; and they saw themselves as potential suppliers of resources, goods, or shipping in the near future. Once they had received assurances of aid from other Anglo-American sources, their perspective on UNRRA changed: they were determined to pursue their individual negotiations for relief supplies outside of UNRRA, under as little control as possible. They saw themselves as potential supplying countries and were above all concerned with representation on UNRRA's policy-making committees. By contrast, the Czechoslovak, Polish, Yugoslavian, and Greek

---

[82] Potiphar, *They Must Not Starve*, (London, 1945), 20–22.

[83] Spencer Coxe, 'Relief and Reconstruction in Western Europe', *New Europe* (March 1943), 6.

members did not only lack the means to pay for goods but also to oppose the Anglo-American domination in the allocation of relief needs.[84]

The political compromise upon which UNRRA's structure rested proved no longer viable once the competing interests between supplying and receiving countries were drawn into the Cold War split between East and West.[85] The rifts between the different internationalisms embedded within UNRRA ultimately tore it apart. Amid growing controversy over UNRRA's role in Poland, Byelorussia and the Ukraine, the United States announced its intention to withdraw from UNRRA. In response, the formal decision to terminate UNRRA was taken at the fifth Council meeting in Geneva in August 1946, amid the realization that the financial contributions for the 1947 budget were not forthcoming.[86] UNRRA's relief operations wound down at the end of 1946. The DP Operation was initially to be dissolved in 1946, but its mandate was extended until 30 June 1947. The last staff appointment terminated in March 1949. UNRRA's remaining assets and personnel were distributed among the Food and Agriculture Organization, the International Refugee Organization, the World Health Organization and the United Nations Children's Emergency Fund.

## Mobilizing history

Internationalism in relief could mean a number of very different things. To some, it simply represented the antithesis of American isolationism and the re-establishment of the US' relations with the world in a narrowly defined field; to others it referred more specifically to America's assumption of its long-overdue role of leadership and duty to supervise the post-war reshaping of the world. Alternatively, it could also stand for a radical transformation of the world (or at least parts of it), or the construction of a new international framework which contained the Great Powers and firmly tied them into specific obligations. Still others hoped international relief would inaugurate an international system which enshrined principles of universality, the equality of nations and national sovereignty and a new and improved League of Nations. UNRRA united a range of these different models of and rationales for international collaboration, each of which traced different antecedents and saw the future of international relief in different terms. While these

---

[84] UN Archives, S-1021–0017–012, Dorothy Clark, 'The Scope of UNRRA', 13 September 1946.

[85] Robert H. Johnson, 'International Politics and the Structure of International Organization: The Case of UNRRA', *World Politics*, 3:4, (July 1951), 520–38.

[86] 'UNRRA (Winding-Up)', *Hansard*, 29 November 1946, Vol.430, cc.1979–2018.

approaches undoubtedly shared important common ground, they have to be disaggregated in order to illumine both the fragile consensus on internationalism after the war and its eventual disintegration. Questions of 'internationalism on whose terms, and to what end?' have too often not been fully addressed. Ultimately, it seems, there was no *single* 'internationalism' able to bridge the different arguments about power and representation or the chasm between the suppliers and recipients of relief, particularly once these divisions began to pair up with the developing Cold War between East and West.

UNRRA and the relief project could be located within two very different genealogies. On the one hand, UNRRA appeared as the culmination of American humanitarian initiative and assumption of international responsibilities. Advocates of this position pointed to an apparently clear continuum, since in the American Relief Administration (ARA), as in OFFRA and then UNRRA, American money, experts and initiative helped to feed, clothe, and repatriate millions of people in Central Europe, a tradition then continued by Marshall aid. These continuities struck many commentators. Herbert Lehman, for example, thought in 1947 that this latest instalment of US humanitarian leadership was inspired by two honourable motives: 'One, the traditional policy of this country to relieve suffering and need; and two, a realization that we cannot isolate ourselves from the rest of the world behind the walls of our own plenty.'[87] Similarly, in a speech before the House of Commons in 1948 Arthur Salter recounted the American humanitarian record—from 'the time of Lend-Lease, and a pooling of resources which was without precedent in the history of war, to her UNRRA contributions, the American loans, and now Marshall Aid'—as a neat progression.[88] When Dr. Grace Fox recommended in 1944 that the organization would do well to adopt 'the philosophy of history embodied in the Hoover program [of the ARA]', she referred to the preservation of data and organization of records, but could in fact have been speaking about the mobilization of historical narratives.[89] Charles Maier has shown that American concepts of international economic stability and European reconstruction built upon domestic

---

[87] Lehman Suite, Lehman papers, Folder C54–13, Lehman, '2nd Draft Chicago Address (not used)', 1 October 1947.

[88] Quoted in Lord Salter, *Memoirs of a Public Servant* (London, 1961), 311–12.

[89] UN Archives, S-1021–0017–06, Grace Fox, 'A.R.A. Precedents for a Division of History and Records', 12 September 1944, 4. On Fox, see Allan Joseph Nevins, *Herbert Lehman and his Era* (1963), 416. See also Grace Fox, 'The origins of UNRRA', *Political Science Quarterly*, 65:4 (December 1950), 561–84.

solutions to social and political problems, which emphasized productivity and economic growth.[90] In a similar manner, internal debates about isolation and America's place in the world shaped the State Department's blueprint for internationalization and internationalism, in relief as in other areas. Their prime concerns were how the US could provide material and political solutions to the world while serving American interests, and details of international or supra-national collaboration appeared to be less relevant.

On the other hand, many European planners and relief workers of all nationalities saw UNRRA as a continuation of the League's achievements and lessons. For Rajchman and others there was one clear precedent to UNRRA's work: the League's Health Organization. Even though the League had failed in many of its tasks, to these internationalists it was an irrevocable precedent. Many of them had taken part in the creation of the new international bodies after 1919 and had served with the League or its associated offices. Similarly, many relief workers had participated in relief programmes in the 1920s and now returned to familiar areas and jobs. As a result, they insisted that there were some very practical reasons why international cooperation in relief on the League model now seemed more feasible than ever before: 'After all', thought the Labour MP Philip Noel-Baker in 1942, 'we are not where we were in 1919 with regard to the I.L.O., a Permanent Court of International Justice and International Council, the International Assembly, a Minority Protection Scheme, a Mandate System, etc. We have had tremendous experience; we have got the framework of institutions; we know the weaknesses'.[91] By contrast, OFRRO staff by their own account lacked this experience when they joined UNRRA.[92] As Philip Jessup warned in June 1943, to Americans relief work 'in a world at war with hundreds of millions of people affected' would be unfamiliar and challenging, and 'not the same kind of job' they had done in the United States, 'when a great natural disaster like fire, earthquake, or flood has brought suffering to several hundreds of several thousands of people'.[93]

---

[90] Charles Maier, 'The Politics of Productivity: Foundations of American International Economic Policy after World War II', *International Organization*, Autumn 1977, 31:4, 607–33. Also reprinted in Charles Maier, *In Search of Stability: Explorations in Historical Political Economy* (Cambridge, 1987), 121–54.

[91] NBKR 4/500, Philip Noel-Baker to Harold Butler, 24 August 1942.

[92] UN Archives, S-1021–0017–9, Grace E. Fox, 'The Development of the Administrative Structure', 19 October 1945, e.g. 24.

[93] LON, R5809/50/42186/42186, 'Address by Mr. Philip C. Jessup', 18 June 1943.

These two trajectories drew upon different points of reference and mobilized altogether different precedents, and they represented fundamentally different interpretations of internationalism. At one level these differences involved a juxtaposition of the Great Powers and the small nations, of the donating countries and those receiving aid, of an 'Anglo-Saxon' and a Eurocentric or 'Central-European' perspective. But they also reflected much more subtle disparities. In 1928 a syllabus for a course on international relations distinguished between two mindsets, that of the 'international mind' as contrasted with that of a ' "Foreign Policy" mind'.[94] Similarly, UNRRA's relief workers saw the reality and practice of international relief often in very different terms to policy-makers and diplomats in Washington and London. Together, these different approaches to internationalism in relief bring to light the rather delicate nature of the apparent consensus on internationalism in the immediate aftermath of the war.

Whether or not this collaboration in the field of relief formed a real moment of 'internationalism' is thus still up for debate. In his recent history of the United Nations, Paul Kennedy has posed a 'conundrum': on one hand the creation of a United Nations system formed a new world order by radically changing the political landscape and the structure of international politics from what it had been after 1648, 1815, and even 1919, not least because it brought all Great Powers 'into the tent'. But on the other hand, at the same time this multi-polar, largely Eurocentric order of states gave way to a bipolar world. The puzzle, Kennedy maintains, is how these different new orders could, if at all, relate to each other, since 'large nations are rarely good members of an international club designed to restrain the exercise of national power'.[95] It is precisely this conundrum which UNRRA embodied. Within UNRRA, the balance sheet indicates an undeniably Anglo-Saxon and American orientation of international relief. By 1947, Rajchman's and Gross' proposals on internationalism and federalist organizations proved unpopular and impractical in a world of spheres of influence. Moreover, the official American attitude itself changed in course of the post-war period: although the United States was initially committed to participating in an international forum, by the late 1940s it had retreated from full engagement in a universal United Nations, and instead created its own global alliance system.[96] The four-power notion of internationalism proved

---

[94] C. Delisle Burns, *Syllabus of a course of twelve lectures on the History of International Relations and the League of Nations* (London, 2nd edn 1928), 28.

[95] Paul Kennedy, *The Parliament of Man: The Past, Present and Future of the United Nations* (Random House, 2006), 45–6.

[96] White, 'History and American Internationalism', 169.

ultimately incompatible with proposals for a new international structure in which the Great Powers were securely tied in. Understanding the various internationalisms embedded in UNRRA thus becomes part of a much bigger challenge of assessing the United Nations and judging the feasibility of internationalist projects.

# The Multiple Contexts of Bretton Woods

**Harold James**

This paper examines why so much debate about the structure of the international economy revolves around a conference held at Bretton Woods in July 1944 which was not immediately conspicuously successful. There was a unique confluence of contemporary contexts—in terms of trade policy, stabilization policy, and policies with regard to capital movements—that meant that prevailing ideas (especially the ideas of John Maynard Keynes) and the interests of the United States coincided. It was fundamentally a victory of the United States, but dressed up as benign multilateralism. The myth of Bretton Woods was also created by a powerful retrospective interpretation or retrospective context that lent a golden halo to the whole exercise. In that sense our interpretation of a very specific historical event is inseparably intertwined with views of what happened *after* as well as *before* that event.

Bretton Woods has become a powerful myth. It is the only instantly recognizable location of the series of conferences of the wartime coalition (the United Nations) held shortly before and after the end of the Second World War. Hot Springs (the conference in May and June 1943 that discussed food and agriculture), Dumbarton Oaks (the meetings that sketched out a future international organization from August to October 1944) are easily forgotten; even the San Francisco conference (April–June 1945) that established the post-war United Nations system is scarcely identifiable to any but the expert in United Nations history. By contrast, the United Nations Monetary and Financial Conference, held in July 1944 at Bretton Woods, New Hampshire, is still instantly recognizable as a view of the world.

This paper suggests that this view stems from a unique confluence of contemporary contexts—in terms of trade policy, stabilization policy, and policies with regard to capital movements—but also from a powerful retrospective interpretation or retrospective context that lent a golden halo to the whole exercise. In that sense our interpretation of a very specific historical event is inseparably intertwined with views of what happened *after* as well as *before* that event. In retrospect, the Bretton Woods order looks like a solution, not just to the question of post-war reconstruction, but to the problem of recasting capitalism in such a way that it would not permanently destabilize both itself and the international political and legal order. As Robert Skidelsky has recently reminded us, in consequence it has a continuing actuality.[1]

Any contemplation of the Bretton Woods—especially one that is presented in Gordon Square in Bloomsbury—has to begin with the godlike (the phrase is Lionel Robbins's, not mine) figure who presided over it.[2] Bretton Woods was about reconstruction, but not simply about reconstruction after a war or about trying to return to the pre-war order. The conference continued a debate about the appropriate form of an international economic order that had already started in the war, as a competition of contrasting systems. When in 1940 the German Minister of Economics, Walther Funk, presented a plan after the fall of France and at the height of German euphoria about a Nazi 'New Order', the British government asked John Maynard Keynes to prepare a counterscheme. Funk had presented his plan as an alternative to the out-dated and discredited gold standard; Keynes insisted that any response could not offer reconstruction as it had been done after the First World War.[3] He did not want the solution that the United States preferred, extensive trade liberalization, as that would simply open up other, less competitive, economies to a renewed onslaught of the forces of depression. Bretton Woods was about reconstructing a system that had not been adequately reconstructed in 1919. But how could a world order, that had evolved rather than being created spontaneously, be negotiated by different powers that wanted to protect their national interest?

Keynes had a powerful reputation as a critic of counterproductive or de-structive attempts at international cooperation: of the Paris Peace Conference of 1919, but also of the attempts to deal with depression in the early 1930s. In 1933, Keynes had commented on the abortive London World Economic Conference that a pow-wow of sixty-six nations could never be expected to agree. A workable plan could only be realized at the insistence of

---

[1] Robert Skidelsky, *Keynes: The Return of the Master* (New York, 2009).

[2] This paper was originally presented in June 2008 at a conference in Birkbeck College London. For Lionel Robbins' description of the 'godlike' Keynes, Roy F. Harrod, *The Life of John Maynard Keynes* (Harmondsworth, 1972), 740; also Donald Moggridge, *Maynard Keynes: An Economist's Biography* (London, 1992).

[3] Walther Funk, *The Economic Future of Europe* (Berlin, 1940); Armand van Dormael, *Bretton Woods: Birth of a Monetary System* (New York, 1978), 6–7; Joseph Gold, *Legal and Institutional Aspects of the International Monetary System: Selected Essays*, volume 2, (Washington, 1984), 19; Donald Moggridge, *Maynard Keynes: an Economist's Biography* (London, 1992), 654.

'a single power or like-minded group of powers'.[4] In 1919, in *The Economic Consequences of the Peace*, John Maynard Keynes wrote plaintively: 'But if America recalls for a moment what Europe has meant to her, what Europe, the mother of art and knowledge, in spite of everything, still is and still will be, will she not reject these counsels of indifference and isolation, and interest herself in what may be decisive issues for the progress and civilization of all mankind?'[5] Was the turn in 1944 to a different post-war policy to that of 1919 a consequence of new power politics, or a new intellectual direction that overcome American isolationism? Was the key to success American power, or was it Keynes's powerful intellect that brilliantly confined and circumscribed the possibilities of applying American power?

Bretton Woods was obviously a unique occasion, whose magic was produced in part by the felicitous timing: just after the Normandy landings, when the prospect of a very speedy end to the European conflict appeared much greater than in reality it proved to be. Treasury Secretary Henry Morgenthau told a strategy meeting preparing for Bretton Woods quite candidly that: 'we felt that it was good for the world, good for the nation, and good for the Democratic Party, for us to move'.[6] Why was what was good for the Democratic Party really what was good for America or the world?

Was this naked power masked as idealism? At the inaugural session of the conference, Morgenthau had propounded a vision:

> I hope that this Conference will focus its attention upon two elementary economic axioms. The first of these is this: that prosperity has no fixed limits. It is not a finite substance to be diminished by division. On the contrary, the more of it that other nations enjoy, the more each nation will have for itself...

> The second axiom is a corollary of the first. Prosperity, like peace, is indivisible. We cannot afford to have it scattered here or there among the fortunate or to enjoy it at the expense of others. Poverty, wherever it exists, is menacing to us all and undermines the well-being of each of us. It can no more be localized than war, but spreads and saps the economic strength of all the more-favored areas of the earth...

---

[4] Cited in Robert Skidelsky, *John Maynard Keynes: The Economist as Saviour* (London, 1992), 482.

[5] John Maynard Keynes, *The Economic Consequences of the Peace* (London, 1919), 268.

[6] John Morton Blum, *From the Morgenthau Diaries, vol. 3, Years of War 1941–1945* (Boston, 1967), 248.

Along with the idealism, there were three specific lessons, in all of which idealism was tempered by a precise calculation of the balance of national interest: in trade relations, in internationalizing the New Deal, and in addressing the question of capital mobility. The American negotiators themselves were quite aware of their negotiating advantage, and knew that they should use it. As Morgenthau told Assistant Secretary Harry Dexter White, the principal negotiator of the Bretton Woods settlement, 'Now the advantage is ours here, and I personally think we should take it.' White replied: 'If the advantage were theirs, they would take it.'[7]

These lessons were substantively lost in a retrospective context.

### The trade lesson

The Bretton Woods Conference represented both an attempt to learn the lessons of the Great Depression (in the mind of the Democratic Party, the lessons of the New Deal), and a part of the preparation for peace and the post-war order. The conference was preceded by negotiations involving initially the United States and the United Kingdom, and then the other members of the United Nations (the wartime coalition against the Axis powers). The fundamental insight that made it possible to agree on an outcome was that destructive disputes over trade could be overcome by an agreement on monetary matters.

In this it broke through the paralysis that had afflicted interwar attempts at international cooperation. The World Monetary and Economic Conference held in London 1933 was generally seen as the last, and lost, opportunity to arrive at a settlement.[8] It had treated the trade and monetary issues separately. Even at the preparatory stage, work on the agenda of the London conference had been divided between two sub-committees. The Monetary Sub-Committee dealt with financial issues and with currency stabilization, and the Economic Sub-Committee with trade. The result of this division of labour was predictable, and would have been comic if the results had not been so tragic. The monetary discussion arrived at the conclusion that a prerequisite for stabilization was the dismantling of barriers to trade. 'Freer trade was a prerequisite of a return to normal economic conditions and a return to the gold standard.' On the other hand the trade debates produced agreement that nothing could be done without an overhaul of the international financial system since 'for ten years the world has been attempting to adjust the balance of payments by lending and borrowing instead of buying

---

[7] Armand van Dormael, *Bretton Woods: Birth of a Monetary System* (New York, 1978), 211.

[8] See Patricia Clavin, 'The World Economic Conference 1933: The Failure of British Internationalism', *Journal of European Economic History*, 20 (1991), 489–527.

and selling'.[9] This was patently a perfect recipe for a deadlock, in which trade and currency experts thought that the other side should be the one to take the first move.

The fundamental cause of the intellectual shift between 1932 and 1933 on the one hand and the wartime discussions on the other lay in the unflinching commitment of the world's most powerful state and economy to the principle of multilateral negotiations to reduce tariff levels and eliminate as far as possible trade quotas. This was a specifically Democratic (especially southern Democratic) vision: its major champion was Secretary of State Cordell Hull. Hull had been a Congressman and then Senator for Tennessee, and was deeply influenced by the traditional interpretation of southern interests, which saw free trade as beneficial to southern cotton exporters and other farmers, and protection as the imposition of the interests of the manufacturing states of the north-east and the mid-west. In the 1930s, as Secretary of State, he had used bilateral negotiations as a way of creating reciprocal commitments to trade liberalization. His wartime diplomacy simply followed this pattern.

The principle of the obligation to introduce currency convertibility, limits on discriminatory trading practices, and increased access to each other's markets had been inserted into Anglo-American relations as Article VII of the Lend-Lease agreement, which was generally known as 'the Consideration' and was regarded by Keynes with considerable bitterness. The original draft of the State Department specified that the two countries would commit themselves to 'promote mutually advantageous economic relations between them and the betterment of world-wide economic relations; they shall provide against discrimination in either the United states of America or the United Kingdom against the importation of any product originating in the other country'. The measure appeared in Washington as a sledgehammer to break the carapace of British Imperial Preference. The same language was used in Clause Four of the Atlantic Charter, drawn up in shipboard meetings on the ocean at the first visit of Winston Churchill to Roosevelt. The governments committed themselves 'to further the enjoyment by all States, great or small, victor or vanquished, of access, on equal terms, to the trade and to the raw materials of the world'.

Hull's strategy for limiting protectionist impulses rested on two pillars. First, following what had become a standard political science interpretation of the origins of the Smoot-Hawley tariff and the disasters of Depression-era trade policy, there was a need to limit congressional or parliamentary politics.

---

[9] League of Nations archive, Geneva (United Nations), R2672, 1 xi 1932 Second Meeting of Monetary Sub–Committee; R2671, 7 xi 1932 Third Meeting of Preparatory Committee.

Elmer Schattschneider had shown how the tariff had changed its nature in the course of congressional debate, as individual parliamentarians added on measures to protect particular interests associated with their locality. The logic of this argument is analogous to the collective action mechanism suggested by Mancur Olson: an accumulation of small interests will lead to a sub-optimal outcome, as each small interest will see major gains in a protectionist measure, and the collectivity is happy to accept this, as the overall cost of each measure is relatively trivial. Olson's suggestion is that only an over-arching articulation of a general interest can solve the collective action problem: in terms of concrete politics, this meant the strengthening of the executive and the presidency at the expense of the legislature. This was exactly the course adopted by Hull with legislation (the Reciprocal Trade Agreements Act of 1934) that allowed the president to conclude bilateral trade treaties.[10]

The second logic behind Hull's strategy lay in the perception that it is safer to anchor liberal arrangements in a legal or constitutional form, and in this way also remove them from party and parliamentary politics. Anchoring the open economy in international treaties would be a way of tying political hands, or—in today's political science terminology—embedding the liberal international order.[11] In this way, an international order might create permanent constitutional guarantees for preferences of the United States as a collectivity (but not necessarily of individual Americans or individual parliamentarians).

The uncompromising attitude of the United States brought the inescapable conclusion even to opponents and sceptics (such as Keynes) that trade liberalization could not be the subject of discussion or bargaining. How fortunate for the world that there were no trade negotiations! When after the conclusion of the war, countries started haggling about the exemptions they desired from a proposed International Trade Organization, the United States Congress revolted, and the proposed institution collapsed. Bretton Woods in this sense had already succeeded before the delegates even met because of the already established wartime consensus that trade should not

---

[10] E. E. Schattschneider, *Politics, Pressures and the Tariff; A study of free private enterprise in pressure politics, as shown in the 1929–1930 revision of the tariff* (New York, 1935); Mancur Olson, *The Logic of Collective Action : Public Goods and the Theory of Groups* (Cambridge, Mass., 1971).

[11] John Gerard Ruggie, *Winning the Peace : America and World Order in the New Era* (New York, 1996); G. John Ikenberry, *After Victory : Institutions, Strategic Restraint, and the Rebuilding of Order after Major Wars* (Princeton, 2001).

be debated, and thus that an initial conference should deal with currency stabilization. The order was already embedded in pre-existing diplomacy.

## The New Deal context

The second component was born out of the character of the conflict. Keynes was asked by the British government to prepare a counter-scheme to the German Economics Minister Walther Funk's remarkable (but insincere) plan for European prosperity of 1940. He rejected very decisively the idea that a return to 1920s internationalism might be attractive as a pattern for post-war relations. It would not be enough, he said, to offer 'good old 1920–1921 [the post-war slump] or 1930–1933 [the Great Depression], i.e., gold standard or international exchange laissez-faire aggravated by heavy tariffs, unemployment, etc., etc.'. In his proposals, Keynes spoke of 'the craving for social and personal security' after the war.[12] But there were as yet few details on how an international economy might be managed to promote such security.

Very different types of economy needed to be integrated in the common vision: ones that relied (as would the UK and the US) on Keynesian macro-economic demand management; as well as economies with central planning, including of external trade, on the Soviet model. The Soviet delegation was a part of Bretton Woods, and some of the more obscure wording of the agreement is the result of the need to take into account Soviet peculiarities.

How could domestic priorities be reconciled with peace and broad international objectives? There were three alternative possibilities:

1. States might come to see their self-interest as lying in international harmony. The experience of the 1930s however did not seem encouraging.
2. An international juridical framework might be established for economic issues, to arbitrate in cases where national and international objectives clashed.
3. An entirely automatic mechanism might point states in the direction of peace and prosperity without a complex and lengthy bureaucratic or juridical process.

Discussions of the post-war order swung between acceptance of the second and third of these choices, and ended by taking elements of both. Automatism

---

[12] Armand Van Dormael, *Bretton Woods: Birth of a Monetary System* (New York, 1978), 6–7. Joseph Gold, *Legal and Institutional Aspects of the International Monetary System: Selected Essays II* (Washington DC, 1984), 19. Donald Moggridge, *Maynard Keynes: An Economist's Biography* (London, 1992), 654.

was attractive because it was apolitical; but it might not always fit in with widely perceived needs. An element of discretion was needed, which might best be provided through the creation of an institution with legal powers established by treaty. The resulting compromise is the foundation of the Bretton Woods achievement.

Keynes's scheme proposed an international bank, which he called the Clearing Union, with a new unit of account that would be the basis for the issue of a new international currency. The proposed currency's name, *bancor*, indicates the way in which the new money was conceived as an artificially created replacement for gold, which should gradually be expelled from the civilized conduct of international economics. Gold might be sold by central banks to the new international bank for bancor, but would not be bought.

The object of the Union's activities would be to avoid balance of payments imbalances through the creation of a body of rules and practices relating to the overdrafts on the bank accumulated by debtors and the positive balances acquired by creditors. The quotas for each country in the Union were to be fixed as half of the average of imports and exports over the past five years. These quotas determined the limits up to which debtors could borrow (at interest rates that rose with the quantity of their debts). Creditors had to transfer to the Union surpluses above their quota, and pay charges to the Union if their balances rose above a quarter of their quota. The Keynes scheme created a nearly perfect symmetry: it was to be as unpleasant and as costly to hold credit balances as to be a debtor. The result would be the impossibility of policies such as those followed by the United States and France in the later 1920s: the rules of the Clearing Union would drive such creditor states to expand.

In subsequent drafts of his proposal, Keynes wrestled with 'the most difficult question', 'to determine . . . how much to decide by rule and how much to leave to discretion'.[13] An abstract and impersonal operation would give the most scope for the operation of markets, and also for the preservation of national sovereignty. The most extreme version of a rule-bound system, however, the gold standard, had led to deflation and depression. Successive British drafts, tossed forwards and backwards between Keynes and the British Treasury and the Bank of England, gradually increased the discretionary element in what had originally been a neat and simple automatic principle of operation. Monetary authorities preferred (often they still do) 'to operate by vague requests backed by vague sanctions, rather than by publishing

---

[13] J. Keith Horsefield, *The International Monetary Fund 1945–1965: Twenty Years of International Monetary Cooperation, vol. III* (Washington DC, 1969), 6.

definite rules'.[14] By the fourth draft, the balance had shifted towards discretion. The Governing Board of the International Bank might set conditions under which countries would be allowed to increase their debit balances, including the surrender of their gold reserve, the control of capital transactions, and a devaluation of the currency. But even with the introduction of consultations about policy in the place of rules of conduct, there still existed a symmetry between the constraints on debtors and creditors. If a credit balance exceeded half the quota, the country would be required to 'discuss with the Governing Board (but still retain the ultimate decision in its own hands)' an expansion of domestic credit and demand, an exchange rate revaluation, an increase in wages, tariff reductions, or international loans for the development of backward countries. The US gradually intervened in the negotiations to avoid being forced into expansionary policies simply by virtue of its debtor position. This was possible, because international capital movements would largely be controlled.

## The intellectual context

Keynes did not believe in what might be called the 'globalization paradigm': the theory, elaborated already by Montesquieu and celebrated by Richard Cobden and John Bright as well as by Norman Angell that commerce and commercial inter-connectedness would by themselves bring international peace and order. In the *Economic Consequences of the Peace* he had written:

> Bankers are used to this system, and believe it to be a necessary part of the permanent order of society. They are disposed to believe, therefore, by analogy with it, that a comparable system between Governments, on a far vaster and definitely oppressive scale, represented by no real assets, and less closely associated with the property system, is natural and reasonable and in conformity with human nature. I doubt this view of the world. Even capitalism at home, which engages many local sympathies, which plays a real part in the daily process of production, and upon the security of which the present organisation of society largely depends, is not very safe.[15]

The Bretton Woods scheme depended on a worldwide agreement on the control of capital movements, which was presented as a 'permanent feature' of the post-war system.[16] The Union would work closely not only with an

---

[14] Samuel Brittan, *A Restatement of Economic Liberalism* (London, 1988), 87.

[15] Keynes, *Economic Consequences*, 263–4.

[16] Horsefield, *International Monetary Fund, III*, 13.

agency dedicated to stabilizing prices (in order 'to control the Trade Cycle'), but also with a super-national peace-keeping agency ('charged with the duty of preserving the peace and maintaining international order'). The British draft concluded that the proposal was 'capable of arousing enthusiasm because it makes a beginning at the future economic ordering of the world between nations and the "winning of the peace", and might help to create the conditions and the atmosphere in which much else would be made easier'.

A new consensus on the causes of the Great Depression had shifted the emphasis away from the favourite villains of the 1930s literature—the uneven distribution of gold and the sterilizing policies of the Banque de France and the Federal Reserve System, or the allegedly excessive monetary inflation of the 1920s, or structural weaknesses in major industrial centres. Rather the new view looked at the transmission process of depression, and came to the conclusion that the large short-term capital flows of the 1920s and 1930s had led to disaster. These movements had made it impossible for states to pursue stable monetary policies, they threatened exchange rate stability, and they made fiscal stabilization highly hazardous.

This approach to the interwar economy, oriented towards the diagnosis of capital movements as the fundamental ill, had been developed by League of Nations economists in the 1930s. The most influential academic statement was Ragnar Nurkse's *International Currency Experience* (1944). 'In the absence of international reserves large enough to meet such speculative and often self-perpetuating capital movements, many countries had to resort to exchange control and to other less insidious means of correcting the balance of payments.' From this historical experience, Nurkse drew the conclusion that greater international cooperation was needed: 'But if, owing to anticipated exchange adjustments, political unrest or similar causes, closer control of hot money movements is inevitable, then some of its difficulties and dangers might be overcome by international understanding.' As a consequence, when he wrote about plans for an international bank or monetary fund, Nurkse added: 'If, in addition to trade and other normal transactions, such a fund had to cover all kinds of capital flight, it might have to be endowed with enormous resources. In fact, no fund of any practicable size might be sufficient to offset mass movements of nervous flight capital.'[17]

The restoration of a multilateral financial system thus depended in the view of almost every analyst on control of capital movements for an unlimited time. This approach appealed to Keynes, who had repeatedly asserted his scepticism about the benefits of both capital exports and capital imports.

---

[17] Ragnar Nurkse, *International Currency Experience: Lessons from the Inter-War Period* (Geneva, 1944), 220, 222, 188.

Keynes fully shared the belief that capital flight had been the major international inter-war problem: 'There is no country which can, in future, safely allow the flight of funds for political reasons or to evade domestic taxation or in anticipation of the owner turning refugee. Equally, there is no country that can safely receive fugitive funds, which constitute an unwanted import of capital, yet cannot safely be used for fixed investment.'[18] It is true that Keynes added that the new controls, which might become a 'permanent feature of the post-war system', should not bring an end to the 'era of international investment': but it would need states and international agreements to define (in accordance with national priorities) what was desirable investment and what was unwanted capital movement. The British economist Sir Hubert Henderson noted: 'It has been generally agreed in the United Kingdom that we must retain the right to regulate capital movements, effectively and indefinitely'.[19] Many Americans also shared this view.

In the United States, the feeling that the capital exports of the 1920s had been misused was a commonplace for the New Deal. Harry Dexter White, Assistant to the US Treasury Secretary, and the other major architect of what would be the Bretton Woods Agreements, fully concurred with Keynes that: 'The theoretical bases for the belief still so widely held, that interference with trade and with capital and gold movements etc., are harmful, are hangovers from a Nineteenth Century economic creed, which held that international economic adjustments, if left alone, would work themselves out toward an 'equilibrium' with a minimum of harm to world trade and prosperity . . . The task before us is not to prohibit instruments of control but to develop those measures of control, those policies of administering such control, as will be the most effective in obtaining the objectives of world-wide sustained prosperity'.[20] White's immediate superior, Treasury Secretary Henry Morgenthau, made the target of these controls much more explicit. The new institutions of the international order would be 'instrumentalities of sovereign governments and not of private financial interests'. The task that the statesmen should set themselves was to 'drive the usurious moneylenders from the temple of international finance'.[21] But this was primarily a political task.

---

[18] Horsefield, *International Monetary Fund, III*, 31; see also Moggridge, *Maynard Keynes*, 673.

[19] Bank of England archive OV38/49, Sir Hubert Henderson note of 1 August 1944.

[20] Horsefield, *International Monetary Fund, III*, 64.

[21] Richard N. Gardner, *Sterling-Dollar Diplomacy: The Origins and the Prospects of Our International Economic Order* (New York, 1969), 76.

Producing an agreement was possible because of the wide extent of agreement in the initial bargaining positions. [22] Keynes wrote of his proposals that they 'lay no claim to originality. They are an attempt to reduce to practical shape certain general ideas belonging to the contemporary climate of economic opinion, which have been given publicity in recent months by writers of several different nationalities. It is difficult to see how any plan can be successful which does not use these general ideas, which are born of the spirit of the age.'[23]

### The retrospective context

It took a long time for anything like the Bretton Woods system to come into operation. The right in the United States was hostile, and American bankers lobbied against the Bretton Woods agreements, which they saw as costly concessions to foreigners and to socialist and redistributive principles. For them, there was too much of the New Deal in the scheme. In the United Kingdom, the agreements were attacked by economic nationalists both on the left of the Labour party, and on the right of the Conservative party. For these politicians, the scheme was simply too American. The attempt to impose convertibility on Britain rapidly proved to be a fiasco in July 1947. The US administration took a different path to European reconstruction with the European recovery program (or Marshall Plan), whose administration was deliberately not entrusted to the IMF, but rather to the Basel-based Bank of International Settlements (BIS), a relic of the interwar years of bankers' diplomacy which the New Dealers hated, and whose termination had been provided for in the Bretton Woods Agreements. The European Payments Union, administered through the BIS, was a clearing mechanism restricted to Europe, and institutionalizing discrimination against the dollar.

The major European economies only restored current account convertibility, in line with the requirements of Article VIII of the International Monetary Fund's articles of agreement after 1958, and Japan in 1964. By 1968 the par value system was in obvious crisis, and between 1971 and 1973 it broke down. Despite the fact that it only 'worked' for a few years, it is held to constitute a success. Something like a modified capitalist order was indeed reestablished.

[22] A modern commentator speaks of the existence of a 'primitive epistemic community' of expert economic opinion-makers: G. John Ikenberry, 'A World Economy Restored: Expert Consensus and the Anglo-American Post-war Settlement', *International Organization*, 46 (1992), 293.

[23] Horsefield, *International Monetary Fund, III*, 21.

Interests and ideas had overlapped in creating the post-war monetary order. It is striking that in retrospect Bretton Woods appears as the only really successful example of a multilateral redesign of the world's international monetary order: Napoleon III had tried to establish a world money at the World Monetary Conference of 1867; the Genoa conference in 1922 was ineffective in proposing a blueprint for monetary stability after the First World War; in 1971 Richard Nixon termed the Smithsonian meeting the most important monetary conference since the birth of Jesus Christ, but the new exchange rates held for less than two years; and ever since the disintegration of the Bretton Woods regime in the early 1970s economists and policy-makers have been calling in vain for a new Bretton Woods. Such reforms never materialized because of monetary multilateralism: there is no single power or like-minded group of powers that can impose their plan on a complicated and perhaps uncontrollable market of ideas and interests.

Bilateral talks subsequently remained the key to every major success of large-scale financial diplomacy. In the early 1970s, when the fixed exchange-rate regime came to an end, the IMF seemed to have outlived its function. Its Articles of Agreement were renegotiated by the US, which was looking for more flexibility, and France, which wanted something of the solidity and predictability of the old gold standard.

Later in the 1970s, European monetary relations were hopeless when France, Germany, and Britain tried to talk about them, but were straightened out when only France and Germany took part. In the mid-1980s, when wild exchange-rate swings produced calls for new trade protection measures, the US and Japan found a solution that involved exchange-rate stabilization. Today the major focus of international economic diplomacy is again bilateral, between the US and China.

In recent years, a debate has developed about whether the world of the 2000s constructed a 'Bretton Woods II', in which rapidly growing export-led economies peg to the dollar (more or less) in order to obtain faster growth, and consequently accumulate reserves at spectacular rates. The issues raised in a series of articles by Dooley, Folkerts-Landau, and Garber concern the sustainability of the current monetary system (or non-system) and of the 'global imbalances'.[24] But they also raise the questions about how sustainable

---

[24] Michael P. Dooley, David Folkerts-Landau and Peter Garber, 'An Essay on the Revived Bretton Woods System' (NBER WP 9971, September 2003); 'The Revived Bretton Woods System: The Effects of Periphery Intervention and Reserve Management on Interest Rates & Exchange Rates in Center Countries' (NBER WP 10332 March 2004); 'Direct Investment, Rising Real Wages and the Absorption of Excess Labor in the Periphery' (NBER WP 10626 July 2004); 'The US Current Account Deficit and

the original Bretton Woods order really was; and obviously also about how appropriate the analogy of the 1960s and the 2000s can be, and what it was about this analogy that originated in a wartime conference.

The prevailing view is that the 1960s collapse of Bretton Woods was inevitable, and was only staved off by quite able and sophisticated management of the system through the 1960s, in particular through the action of the BIS and the creation of the swap system, and through the GAB (General Arrangements to Borrow). Two views are usually presented to explain the ineluctability of breakdown: the first, following the analysis given by Robert Triffin, in which the growth of other countries' dollar reserves (or claims on the US) would lead to an increasing probability of crises of confidence, as reserve holders might realize that their assets were not liquid in the sense that they might not be convertible into gold. Alternatively, if reserve accumulation did not occur, the world would face liquidity shortages.[25] For part of the 1960s, more attention focused on the latter part of the dilemma, and the construction of the SDR (Special Drawing Right) was intended to relieve liquidity constraints. It was thus ironical by the time that the SDR came to be issued, the world was perhaps suffering more from the first arm of the dilemma, namely that of excessive reserve creation leading to crises of confidence. The dollar appeared to be like the infamous Ford Edsel, which the burgeoning consumer movement in the US had condemned as being 'unsafe at any speed': threatening world deflation if too slow, or inflation and crises of confidence if too fast.

The second interpretation sees the problem in terms of the inconsistent trinity, that became well known from debates about whether a new version of Bretton Woods could be applied in the regional setting of the European Monetary System after 1979.[26] Fixed exchange rates, capital mobility, and independent monetary policies are inconsistent with each other. The presence of capital mobility in a fixed rate regime makes it impossible for countries to set their own monetary policies or determine their own monetary preferences. As applied to Bretton Woods, this interpretation emphasizes the frustration of some of the growing export economies about rising levels of inflation that were interpreted as being imported from the United States.

---

Economic Development: Collateral for a Total Return Swap' (NBER WP 10727 September 2004).

[25] Robert Triffin, *Gold and the Dollar Crisis* (New Haven, 1960).

[26] Tommaso Padoa-Schioppa, 'The European Monetary System: A Long-Term View', in Francesco Giavazzi, Stefano Micossi, and Marcus Miller (eds), *The European Monetary System*, (Cambridge, 1988).

Neither of these widely shared interpretations is completely watertight, either factually or logically. The problems of the 1960s look much more easily soluble in retrospect, when compared with the challenges posed by global imbalances in the new millennium.

In particular, if the world (that is the world outside the US) needed reserves, why should it worry that they might not be completely converted into gold at an instant's notice? The build-up of reserves looks more analogous to the accumulation of assets in a bank, where individual countries (depositors) might suddenly need to call on their assets, and could have a legitimate expectation of being able to do this). But there is also a recognition that all countries (depositors) cannot convert their assets at the same time, without bringing down the bank. This analogy, made by Kindleberger, Despres, and Salant,[27] at the time, was a minority view, but it is quite a convincing point (unless one assumes a widespread fixation with gold in an age in which actual metallic money, circulating through individuals' pockets, was a more and more dated historical memory).

The world had moved to current account convertibility in the late 1950s and early 1960s, but there was no generalized liberalization of capital accounts. The inconsistent trinity is properly applied as a problem of the European Monetary System's exchange rate mechanism in the 1980s and early 1990s, and the strains that resulted did produce the major crises of 1992 and 1993. But it is not a good description of the issues of the 1960s, in which the behaviour of the large and dynamic export economies, especially Japan and West Germany, bear a closer analogy to Chinese management of its currency up to 2005. The US tried to restrict movements with its increased taxation of foreign earnings of US corporations and with the 1963 Interest Equalization Tax, although it became clear that such measures were ineffective and also in part counterproductive as they reduced the return flow of income from American investments.[28] But the other industrial countries, with the exception of Switzerland, had much more restrictive regimes and controls on the movement of capital. Nevertheless, some capital movements occurred, because trade invoicing can be used to move capital, particularly if there is an expectation of exchange rate changes. There was also a substantial

---

[27] Emile Despres, Charles Kindleberger, and Walter Salant, 'The Dollar and World Liquidity: A Minority View', in *The Economist*, 5 May 1966, 526–9.

[28] See Allan H. Meltzer, 'US Policy in the Bretton Woods Era', *Federal Reserve Bank of St. Louis Review*, 73 (May-June 1991), 54–83; also Michael Bordo, 'The Bretton Woods International Monetary System: A Historical Overview', in Michael D. Bordo and Barry Eichengreen (eds), *A Retrospective on the Bretton Woods System: Lessons for International Monetary Reform* (Chicago, 1993).

pool of offshore dollars, unconstrained by US capital controls, as the Euro-markets developed. Capital inflows to Germany from January 1970 to May 1971 (when one of the two principal export surplus countries floated, without destroying the system) amounted to DM 35.3 billion ($9.6 billion). These were flows in expectation of a renewed German revaluation. In 1971, Japan, the other big surplus country, had an inflow of $4.91 billion. While these were seen as very substantial flows by the standards of the time, they are modest by comparison with the extent of capital movements in settings in which there are no capital controls (i.e. the world of the 1990s and beyond). The inflow to Germany amounted to 6.6 per cent of GDP, and to Japan 2.2 per cent. If we look at increases in total reserves (foreign exchange, IMF position, and gold), the increases for Germany amounted to 3.6 per cent of GDP in 1970 and 2.2 per cent in 1971; for Japan 0.4 per cent in 1969, 0.6 per cent in 1970, and 4.1 per cent in 1971.

The Bretton Woods order of the 1960s thus looks eminently sustainable in theory and more sustainable than it was in practice: especially when the movements of the 1960s are compared with the extent of modern behaviour of foreign exchange markets in a world with much higher capital mobility. Daily world foreign exchange transactions in 2007 amounted to $3,210 billion (BIS). Chinese reserves in the 2000s have increased at an annualized rate of $250 billion (with signs of the rate increasing), in other words at an annual amount equivalent to 10 per cent of GDP.

There is also no doubt that by most criteria the Bretton Woods order was stable and beneficent. As Michael Bordo put it in his comprehensive survey, 'The Bretton Woods regime exhibited the best overall macro performance of any regime. This is especially so for the convertible period 1959–70 . . . both nominal and real variable were the most stable in this period.'[29]

So what is the real story of the collapse of Bretton Woods? There is no doubt that exchange rates had become inflexible, because of the worry that the possibility of movements would set off speculative movements. The adjustable peg system created the potential for one way bets that could force countries into crisis measure adjustment. Unwillingness to adjust on the part of countries pegged to the dollar (the one country which could not change its exchange rate) increased the sense that the dollar's role was problematical.

The heart of the story lies in the political economy of the reaction in the United States to the surge of exports from the 'emergers' of the time, in particular from Japan. This was the theme that John Connolly took up again and again, notably in his May 1971 Munich speech at the International Banking Conference. It became a part of congressional politics with the

[29] Bordo, 'The Bretton Woods International Monetary System', 27.

6 August 1971 report of the Joint Economic Committee's Sub-Committee on International Exchange and Payments which presented the 'inescapable conclusion' that the 'dollar is overvalued'. Exchange rates were to be used as a weapon to secure market opening in Japan and Europe at a time when the question of Japanese textile exports to the US was producing major congressional pressure for immediate action, and was likely to be a central issue in the 1972 election. The dollar crisis, and the associated temporary import surcharge, was used by an administration that was not particularly engaged in multilateral international financial diplomacy, in order to deal with a pressing issue in domestic politics.

Exchange rate changes do not simply and directly affect trade performance and competitiveness in the way that simple textbook models or their political interpreters think. In particular, a literature has developed to show why exchange rate devaluations for big industrial countries do not immediately improve the trade balance (McKinnon).[30] And indeed the formal reduction of the dollar parity at the Smithsonian G-10 meeting in December 1971 did nothing to reduce the US merchandise deficit, which rose from $2.27 billion in 1971 to $6.42 billion in 1972. In terms of addressing the problem which it was supposed to resolve, the 'cure' was (like many medical cures in the pre-modern era) much worse than the malady against which it was directed.

The dollar remained the world's leading currency after 1971, contrary to almost all the doom-laden commentary after 15 August 1971 (but as Robert Mundell predicted in a short and quite remarkable essay of 1970, which also forecast European monetary integration and the collapse of communism).

Immediately after the 1971 crisis, Paul Volcker, the US Treasury official responsible for managing the crisis, set out in quite subtle terms what seemed a very ambiguous and half-hearted defence of continuing to negotiate internationally, even though it was not clear whether there would be an outcome in the conventional sense: 'This initial effort may well have a relatively high probability of failure—but, even if it fails in its immediate objectives, it could be important in keeping open the path to "benign regionalism" . . . To try and fail is not to lose. It will tend, in all probability, to maintain a more constructive attitude internationally than an appearance of turning our back.'[31] Monetary negotiations could in particular help to take off the political pressure from more sensitive and vulnerable elements of the world's economic framework. This justification was, as Volcker saw, an important motivation

---

[30] Ronald McKinnon, Brian Lee and Yi David Wang, 'The Global Credit Crisis and China's Exchange Rate', in *The Singapore Economic Review*, Vol. 55, No. 2 (2010) 253–72.

[31] Quoted in Harold James, *International Monetary Cooperation Since Bretton Woods* (New York, 1996), 235.

of the new European drive to have a miniature Bretton Woods, or what Volcker called 'benign regionalism'.

The principal achievement of 1971 is a negative one: by shifting political discontent directed at the trade regime (the undisputed source of the world's massive post-1945 wealth creation, and indeed the heart of Cordell Hull's vision) onto the prominent and emotional issues around the international role of the dollar, the world escaped (though only just) a big trade war, and a reversal to the interwar era and the story of the repercussions of the Smoot-Hawley tariff. The centrality of the American dollar was the real legacy of Bretton Woods.

In the earlier age of worries about globalization at the turn of the nineteenth century a backlash began, which in the end produced restrictions on migration and high levels of trade protection. When national protection became the major priority of most countries, in the 1920s and 1930s, the world became both poorer and less safe. There was a vicious cycle, in which external forces were blamed for loss and disaster, and high levels of trade protection destroyed national prosperity.

Most countries have avoided this sort of backlash in the second half of the twentieth century, although their citizens had the same angst. There are obvious parallels between British concerns about German competition with cheap labour and the power of the new German industries in the 1880s and 1890s and worries of Americans about the Japanese threat in the 1960s and that of China today. The changing of employment patterns is a constant accompaniment of growth. In the early 1970s and again in the 1980s US workers and producers were upset about the loss of jobs to Japan. Some of the most skilled jobs, in automobiles, were lost; household appliances like TVs were no longer made in the United States. On each occasion, the administration tried to respond to the job loss worries not by trade restrictions, but by exchange rate alterations that would make the US products more competitive: first the end of the gold convertibility of the dollar in 1971, and then in 1985 the Plaza agreement to depreciate the dollar. Monetary and exchange rate policy initiatives offered a way of absorbing adjustment pain. The focus of trade discontent was shifted to the monetary arena in a way that helped to undermine the legitimacy of institutional ways of regulating the international financial system.

The use of monetary policy and exchange rate adjustment to de-escalate trade conflict is harder today, since many of the countries whose products are entering the United States peg their own currencies in more or less formal ways to the dollar. Governments still feel that they need some response in an attempt to 'feel the pain', and to show that they are doing something. Like the Bush administration they adopt tariffs that may then be overruled by the

WTO. In this way they do nothing very harmful, but point out to the elect-orate that their hands are tied by international agreements and institutions. But this sort of action itself then produces a new kind of backlash, against the international institutions.

Trade problems are in fact routinely dealt with by shifting the emphasis to the monetary arena. The world has developed its institutional arrangements in the setting of globalization away from the Bretton Woods settlement by making them harder in the trade arena and softer in the monetary one.

In the future the offloading of adjustment problems to monetary policy (that was the most useful part of the 1971 exercise) will be more difficult because of widespread Asian exchange rate pegging and because of the new informal and largely privatized character of the international monetary system. Something of this reverse reaction is evident in the Schumer-Graham amendment passed by the US Senate in 2005, which provided for a 27.5 per cent tariff on all Chinese goods entering the United States unless China revalued its currency. Monetary issues now produce trade responses, and threaten the basic element of the Bretton Woods formula.

In the same way as the Versailles Treaty produced a negative mythology, in which all the bad and unstable elements of interwar politics were attributed to the peace treaty rather than to the destruction of the war, Bretton Woods took on a positive mythology. According to that version, an act of enlightened creative internationalism removed obstacles to aligning the interests of mul-tiple nation states and of economic agents, and providing a new synthesis of state and market. Bretton Woods was the intellectual sugar covering and masking the bitter taste of the pill of *Realpolitik* dollar hegemony. But it also provided a sugar coating for the unpleasant taste of internationalism in the domestic context of American politics.

In the post-1970s debate, which is still continuing today, two issues were conflated: the question of why there hasn't been another Bretton Woods; and the perception that the world economy is in a mess, and that an international market order (or capitalism) has not been properly restored. The conflation leads to the constant demand for another Bretton Woods, and indeed for another Keynes, or another US in its 1944 embodiment as a power standing for liberal international principles. In other words, it continually regenerates the myth of Bretton Woods, or of how benign multilateralism once rescued the world.

# 'A Blessing in Disguise': Reconstructing International Relations Through Atomic Energy, 1945–1948

Waqar Zaidi

## Introduction

Even as it was being waged, the Second World War was seen by many in Britain as a unique rupture in the global system of international relations. It provided, many believed, the opportunity for its reconstruction into a stable, peaceful, and lasting form. Histories of thinking on and planning for this reconstruction during and after World War Two have traditionally focused on the United Nations Organization and associated agencies.[1] This paper however adds to a growing interest in other powerfully imagined world orders, which although they did not materialize nevertheless left their mark on the post-war period.[2] I focus on proposals for the international control of

---

[1] Recently: Robert C. Hildebrand, *Dumbarton Oaks. The Origins of the United Nations and the Search for Postwar Security* (Chapel Hill, 1991); Stephen Schlesinger, *The Act of Creation: The Founding of the United Nations* (Cambridge, Mass., 2003); Paul Kennedy, *The Parliament of Man: The United Nations and the Quest for World Government* (London, 2006); Sean Greenwood, *Titan at the Foreign Office: Gladwyn Jebb and the Shaping of the Modern World* (Leiden, 2008), chapter 4. Henceforth the following abbreviations are used in this paper: AScW PAPERS (Records of the Association of Scientific Workers, Modern Records Centre, University of Warwick); CEIP PAPERS (Carnegie Endowment for International Peace Records, Rare Book and Manuscript Library, Columbia University); CHAT PAPERS (Records of the Royal Institute of International Affairs, Chatham House, London); DAVIES PAPERS (David Davies of Llandinam Papers, National Library of Wales); MO PAPERS (Mass Observation Archives, Special Collections, University of Sussex Library); PNB PAPERS (Noel Baker Papers, Churchill Archives Centre, Cambridge University); PRO (The National Archives, UK); UNA PAPERS (Papers of the United Nations Association of Great Britain and Northern Ireland, British Library of Political and Economic Science, London School of Economics).

[2] From the Centre/Centre-Left: Peter Wilson, 'The New Europe Debate in Wartime Britain', in Philomena Murray and Paul Rich (eds), *Visions of European Unity* (Boulder, 1996), 39–62; and R. M. Douglas, *The Labour Party, Nationalism and Internationalism, 1939–1951* (London, 2004). From the Right: Mark Mazower, *Hitler's Empire: Nazi Rule in Occupied Europe* (London, 2008).

*Past and Present (2011)*, Supplement 6

atomic energy, which I show to be a vital part of internationalist hopes for a new reconstructed world order.

Historians of proposals for the international control of atomic energy have not recognized such proposals as part of a wider ranging re-imagining of international relations. They have instead portrayed them as more narrowly focused attempts at disarmament—either pacifist endeavours motivated by fear or horror, or calculated attempts at diplomatic advantage by the American government and its supporters.[3] I show in this paper, on the contrary, that these proposals were not pacifist in nature, but incorporated a crucial militant element. Rather than simply limiting the use of the bomb, internationalists planned its use, alongside atomic energy more broadly, by supranational authority. International peace and security, and so the reconstruction of international relations itself, was to be achieved through an international force armed with the atomic bomb, and through the international cooperation of scientists and other technical experts.

Historians, following the American historiography, have placed scientists at the centre of Britain's initial internationalist response to the bomb.[4] I argue instead that the response came not only or primarily from scientists, but rather from a broad range of individuals, organizations, and press located at the centre of the political spectrum. Between late 1945 and 1948 liberal internationalists (many also vocal supporters of the UN) were the leading source of pronouncements on the effects of atomic energy on international relations. Although their rhetoric emphasized the uniqueness of the threats and opportunities latent in atomic energy, and argued that their own proposals for international relations were similarly new and novel, I show that actually these proposals re-expressed long-standing tropes, including that of an international police force and that of science's ability to transform international relations.

---

[3] See Greta Jones, 'The Mushroom-Shaped Cloud: British Scientists' Opposition to Nuclear Weapons Policy, 1945–57', *Annals of Science* 43 (1986), 1–26; Greta Jones, *Science, Politics, and the Cold War* (London, 1988), 38–45; Lawrence S. Wittner, *The Struggle Against the Bomb, Volume 1: One World or None: A History of the World Nuclear Disarmament Movement Through 1953* (Stanford, 1993), 80–98; Susanna Schrafstetter, ' "Loquacious. . .and pointless as ever?" Britain, the United States and the United Nations Negotiations on International Control of Nuclear Energy, 1945–48', *Contemporary British History* 16 (Winter 2002), 87–108; Douglas, *The Labour Party, Nationalism and Internationalism*, 147–153. The most influential work on the American case is Alice Kimball Smith, *A Peril and a Hope: The Scientists' Movement in America: 1945–47* (Chicago, 1965).

[4] Jones, 'The Mushroom-Shaped Cloud'.

**Fig. 1.** 'Tick-Tock, Tick-Tock.' A 1949 Herblock Cartoon. ©The Herb Block Foundation.

## A widespread response

Calls for the international control of atomic energy and for the formation of an international police force arose as soon as the bomb was dropped in August 1945, and reached their peak in mid 1946. One January 1946 poll gave a 74 per cent approval rating for 'control of atomic energy under the United Nations Security Council'.[5] Two Mass Observation surveys on 'World Organisation and the Future' found that 52 per cent of people polled favoured a UN international police force in February 1946, and 65 per cent in June 1946.[6] Mass Observation observed with some surprise, that, with regard to an international police force, 'Opinion breaks down along very definite political lines', with Labour supporters, compared to Conservatives, more likely to support an international police force.[7] This cleavage was also evident in press reaction to the atomic bombings. The Left-leaning press called for international control of atomic energy as soon as the atomic bomb was used. The Centre-right press, by contrast, did not. Indeed, an internationalist magazine, publishing in October 1945 a 'cross-section of opinion' on atomic energy, could only present editorials calling for international control from the *Manchester Guardian*, the *Observer*, and the *New Statesman and Nation*.[8]

The *Manchester Guardian*, a supporter (with some reservation) of the United Nations, called immediately for exclusive use of the bomb by a UN international police force as well as UN ownership of atomic raw material and plant. Its rationale largely focused on the argument that the destructiveness of the atomic bomb at last allowed the UN to grow the teeth it required for successful operation:

> If the United Nations Organisation has the atomic bomb at its disposal it will make it much easier to enforce its decisions on other nations. But if the United Nations Organisation has not got sole control of the bomb the position is reversed . . . When therefore the United Nations Organisation is set up (one hopes in the near future), its first task must be to see that the atomic bomb is placed under its control and, as a corollary, to see that no single nation is allowed to develop this fearful weapon.[9]

[5] 'The Quarter's Polls', *Public Opinion Quarterly* 10 (Spring 1946), 104.
[6] Mass Observation, 'World Organisation and the Future' (March 1946) and 'World Organisation and the Future—Changing Attitudes—February to June' (June 1946), Mass Observation File Reports 2370 and 2397, MO PAPERS.
[7] Mass Observation, 'World Organisation and the Future', 40.
[8] 'The Bomb', *The New Commonwealth* (October 1945), 324–7.
[9] 'The Charter', *Manchester Guardian* (23 August 1945).

However, UN ownership of just atomic bombs was not enough—after all, they could be produced by any nation with atomic research capabilities. Consequently atomic science itself had to be internationally controlled— 'For reasons of world security it would be ideal if the atomic plants and large-scale laboratories were centralized somewhere outside the borders of the larger nations.' This would require in addition a 'world-wide intelligence system to ensure that its monopoly was not infringed'.[10] The *Manchester Guardian* hoped that strengthening the UN in this way would allow it to evolve into a nascent 'world government'.[11] When the Baruch Plan was announced, the newspaper hailed it as advocating 'world government' in the 'atomic sphere'. The proposed controlling UN organization, an 'Atomic Development Authority', may even eventually become so powerful, the newspaper speculated, that it could 'supersede the Security Council and become the world government'.[12] The peaceful uses of atomic energy, mean- while, played a relatively minor role in newspapers' logic. Although the *Manchester Guardian* believed that atomic energy could provide 'power' which could 'change the whole character of human life labour', it also noted that this would come 'though only after long development' and that 'we cannot be certain that its general use might not be uneconomical beside the older sources of energy.'[13]

Other leading newspapers advocating international control included the *News Chronicle*, the *Observer* and the *Daily Herald*. Lord Astor's *The Observer* explained in some detail why atomic energy now made UN military forces practical. Here at last was the modern efficient 'weapon against which no criminal could stand':

> It is so powerful that it could be used effectively by quite a small, specially instructed Arm. It cuts out the need for elaborate inter- weaving of complex national and varied forces with all their separ- ate traditions, jealousies, and suspicions. Thus it enormously simplifies the recruitment and organisation of a World Police.[14]

[10] 'The Atomic Committee', *Manchester Guardian* (22 August 1945).

[11] 'The Challenge', *Manchester Guardian* (8 August 1945); 'The Atomic Committee', *Manchester Guardian* (22 August 1945); 'The Charter', *Manchester Guardian* (23 August 1945); 'Atomic Realism', *Manchester Guardian* (9 February 1946).

[12] 'The Control Plan', *Manchester Guardian* (17 June 1946). The Baruch Plan was the American proposal for international control put before the UN Atomic Energy Commission on 16 June 1946; see Larry G. Gerber, 'The Baruch Plan and the Origins of the Cold War', *Diplomatic History* 6 (Winter 1982), 69–96.

[13] 'The Challenge', *Manchester Guardian* (8 August 1945).

[14] 'The Bomb', *The Observer* (12 August 1945).

The *News Chronicle* and the *Daily Herald* used the most radical rhetoric by calling for world government. The *News Chronicle* reasoned that the UN was too weak to effectively control atomic energy, and called for it to be 'evolved' into a stronger 'world sovereignty': 'If this new invention, which opens up such appalling vistas, forces the nations to accept this basic truth, it will have proved a blessing in disguise.'[15] The *Daily Herald* reckoned that national sovereignty needed to be reduced much further than it was in the current UN, and called for it to be strengthened into a 'World Authority'.[16] These newspapers would, like the *Manchester Guardian,* later greet the Acheson-Lilienthal and Baruch plans with enthusiasm.[17]

This response to atomic energy built upon pre-existing stances on aviation and its relationship to international organization. The *Manchester Guardian* had long thought of aviation in liberal internationalist terms. In 1932 it had enthusiastically taken up (alongside many other British liberal internationalists) French proposals, made at the Geneva disarmament conference, for League of Nations control of military and civil aviation.[18] It continued to make these calls through to the end of World War Two.[19] The arguments were similar in striking ways to later arguments in relation to atomic energy. Aviation was too dangerous a weapon to be left in the hands of nations. Ceding control of aviation to international organization would allow for

---

[15] 'An End or a Beginning?', *News Chronicle* (8 August 1945).

[16] 'This New Power', *Daily Herald* (7 August 1945); 'Control it Or–' *Daily Herald* (9 August 1945).

[17] 'The American Plan', *Manchester Guardian* (9 April 1946); 'Atomic Proposals', *Manchester Guardian* (3 June 1946), 'The Control Plan', *Manchester Guardian* (17 June 1946); 'Atomic Progress Report', *The Economist* 150 (4 May 1946), 697–8; 'The Atomic Plan', *The Economist* 150 (22 June 1946), 995–6; 'Atom Plan', *News Chronicle* (15 June 1946). 'All-Nations Atom Power Corporation. US Plan for UNO', *Daily Herald* (29 March 1946). On the Acheson-Lilienthal plan, a State Department-sponsored proposal for international control made public in March 1946, see Barton J. Bernstein, 'The Quest for Security: American Foreign Policy and International Control of Atomic Energy, 1942–1946', *The Journal of American History* 60 (March 1974), 1003–44.

[18] 'A Plan for the Air', *Manchester Guardian* (21 May 1935); 'The French Plan', *Manchester Guardian* (14 October 1932). For more on this see Waqar Zaidi, 'Technology and the Reconstruction of International Relations: Liberal Internationalist Proposals for the Internationalisation of Aviation and the International Control of Atomic Energy in Britain, USA and France, 1920–1950', Ph.D. thesis, University of London (London, 2009).

[19] 'Air Transport', *Manchester Guardian* (13 March 1943); 'Australia and New Zealand', *Manchester Guardian* (24 January 1944); 'The New League', *Manchester Guardian* (10 October 1944); 'World Aviation', *Manchester Guardian* (18 October 1944).

the protection of civilization from the ravages of bombing, the development of aviation unfettered by interference from the nation-state, and the strengthening of the League of Nations. This focus on aviation in the service of international organization did not entirely disappear with the advent of the atomic bomb. The *Manchester Guardian*, noting that atomic bombs could best be delivered by bombers, announced that 'the argument for an International Air Force is now overwhelming.' To be able to effectively utilize this 'monopoly of the bomb', the UN, it argued, 'must have a separate territory for its manufacture and a separate Air Force for its delivery.'[20]

*The Times* and *The Economist*, by contrast, struck a much more ambivalent note. *The Economist* was initially sceptical about the possibility of international control, but expressed support for the Acheson-Lilienthal and Baruch plans once they were announced.[21] Although *The Times* did sometimes signal its support for international control, it more often than not either abstained from mentioning international control in its editorials on atomic energy, or rather weakly called for greater international cooperation, supervision or 'spirit of common understanding and action'. Its response to both the Baruch and Acheson-Lilienthal plans was guarded: it expressed support, but warned that the proposed Atomic Development Authority would be a step towards 'world government', with all its tyrannical possibilities.[22] In July 1946 it called for international co-operation through agencies such as the ILO, UNESCO, and FAO as it was 'easier to find common ground in the daily affairs of human beings than in strategic concepts, easier to agree about safety measures in the mines or standards of housing than about atomic bombs or the future of Italian colonies'.[23] The *Daily Mail*'s immediate reaction, meanwhile, was a call for Britain to develop an atomic arsenal, and for limited international cooperation consisting of 'all nations' getting together to 'establish their own controls of its use'.[24]

---

[20] 'The Charter', *Manchester Guardian* (23 August 1945).

[21] 'The Control of Destruction', *The Economist* 149 (18 August 1945), 225; 'Controlling the Atom', *The Economist* 149 (25 August 1945), 256–7; 'Atomic Progress Report', *The Economist* 150 (4 May 1946), 697–8; 'The Atomic Plan', *The Economist* 150 (22 June 1946), 995–6.

[22] 'Fulfilment', *The Times* (16 August 1945); 'Controlling the Atom', *The Times* (16 August 1945); 'Peace and the Atom', *The Times* (9 October 1945); 'The Explosive Atom', *The Times* (31 October 1945); 'Survival and the Price', *The Times* (28 November 1945); 'A Nuclear Plan', *The Times* (20 April 1946); 'Atomic Prospects', *The Times* (17 June 1946).

[23] Editorial, 'I.L.O. and U.N.', *The Times* (27 July 1946).

[24] 'Control or Perish', *Daily Mail* (8 August 1945); 'We Must Develop It', *Daily Mail* (9 August 1945); 'Future of the Atom', *Daily Mail* (22 August 1945).

## Internationalist organizations

Given the widespread nature of calls for the international control of atomic energy and the formation of an international atomic police between September 1945 and the end of 1946, it is of no surprise that internationalist organizations too put forward their own proposals. The two most influential organizations in this regard were the New Commonwealth Society and the United Nations Association.

The New Commonwealth, formed by David Davies in 1932 to agitate for the formation of an international air force and an international 'equity tribunal', had reached the apogee of its influence in the late 1930s, and declined into relative inactivity thereafter (Davies died in 1944).[25] The Society's Executive was quick however in using the bomb to resuscitate its activities whilst remaining true to its founder's vision of a modern technology-equipped international organization enforcing global order. For, in contrast to the then widespread claims for the uniqueness of the bomb's effects on international relations, many in the Executive viewed atomic destructiveness as an extension of aerial destructiveness: in the words of New Commonwealth-supporter Vivian Carter, the bomb 'only represents an extension of aerial warfare to the nth degree (total annihilation) . . . In short, it's the same old problem dressed up in a new and more devilish guise, not a new problem.'[26]

[25] Neil D. Bauernfeind, 'Lord Davies and the New Commonwealth Society 1932–1944', M.Phil. thesis, University of Wales at Aberystwyth (Aberystwyth, 1990).

[26] Letter, Vivian Carter to N. B. Foot (27 June 1946), B23/3—NC correspondence 1945—'C', DAVIES PAPERS. This juxtaposing of aviation and the atomic bomb was common amongst internationalists in 1945 and 1946. Philip Noel-Baker informed his audience at the inaugural meeting of the Preparatory Commission of the United Nations Organization that 'There is no doubt that the Governments of the world owe it to their people to do something about science pretty soon. For 40 years we have had aviation, and hitherto it has been nothing but an unmitigated curse to all mankind. Atomic energy may be controlled, or it will end us.' 'Organization to End War. Mr. Noel Baker on British Faith', *The Times* (26 November 1945). Aviation and the atomic bomb were at that time compared in other ways too; for a view from the Right see J. M. Spaight, *The Atomic Problem* (London, 1948); and from the Left: P. M. S. Blackett, *The Military and Political Consequences of Atomic Energy* (London, 1948). For more on this see Zaidi, 'Technology and the Reconstruction of International Relations', chapters 5 and 6; and Ralph John Desmarais, 'Science, Scientific Intellectuals and British Culture in the Early Atomic Age, 1945–1956: A Case Study of George Orwell, Jacob Bronowski, J. G. Crowther and P. M. S. Blackett', Ph.D. thesis, Imperial College London (London, 2009), chapter 6.

In December 1945 or early 1946 the Society's Executive passed a resolution adopting as policy the proposal that the atomic bomb be preserved for the exclusive use of an international air force.[27] The New Commonwealth was quick to organize meetings and lectures on atomic energy, and it sponsored the Mass Observation reports mentioned earlier. The Society proved remarkably successful in recruiting scientists for its cause, and in attracting energetic and newly elected MPs into its ranks.[28] The best known of these recruits was the newly elected Labour MP Raymond Blackburn (1915–1991)—an ardent anti-communist on the right of the party (he would leave it in 1950 to sit as an independent). Blackburn pushed for international control in Parliament, lobbied ministers directly, toured the United States as a representative of the New Commonwealth (meeting, amongst others, the Federation of Atomic Scientists), and participated in conferences and BBC discussions on international control.[29] By late 1945 Blackburn had carved out a reputation as the leading proponent of international control within Parliament. He was the principal mover behind the first tabled motion calling for international control, put to the House of Commons on 22 August 1945. Backed by nine other MPs, his amendment to a motion for approval of the UN Charter called for all research, development, and production of atomic energy to be placed exclusively in the hands of a UN 'international centre' manned by 'international scientists and experts'.[30] The New Commonwealth Society's muscular internationalism was reflected in Blackburn's reactions to the atomic bomb (though he himself did not explicitly call for the formation of an international atomic force). He greeted the Baruch Plan by emphasizing the need to back its proposed inspections by force, and to force hesitant nations to sign up to the Plan. No nation would then be able to 'contract out' of control measures.[31] He was also keen that the United Nations acquire

[27] Letter, N. B. Foot to George Cockerill (18 January 1946), B23/3—NC correspondence 1945—'C', DAVIES PAPERS.

[28] In October 1945 N. F. Mott, who would become in 1946 the first President of the Atomic Scientists' Association, published an article in the New Commonwealth's journal, and in November 1945 scientists M. L. Oliphant and William Chadwick explained the science behind atomic energy to the New Commonwealth Parliamentary Group. N. F. Mott, 'The Atomic Bomb and World Affairs', *London Quarterly of World Affairs* XI (October 1945), 187–90. *Minutes of the New Commonwealth Parliamentary Group*, in file titled 'NC Parliamentary Group Meeting', Box 101, DAVIES PAPERS.

[29] Raymond Blackburn, *I am an Alcoholic* (London, 1959), 86, 87.

[30] 'Use of Atomic Energy. Cabinet Acts. Advisory Panel of Experts', *Manchester Guardian* (22 August 1945).

[31] Raymond Blackburn, Letters to the Editor, 'Atomic Energy', *The Times* (20 June 1946).

as much as it could of the world's supply of uranium and thorium as soon as possible—a call he made in parliament in August 1946.[32]

The high point of the Society's advocacy occurred in March 1947 when it sent a statement, signed by a number of MPs and scientists, calling for international control to the Prime Minister and Foreign Secretary. Signatories included Raymond Blackburn, Lord Brabazon, Clement Davies, Michael Foot, Martin Lindsay, Harold Nicholson, A. M. F. Palmer and Arthur Salter, as well as the scientists H. S. W. Massey, M. L. Oliphant, and R. E. Peierls.[33] In response the Prime Minister (in a letter subsequently made public by the Society) suggested that 'the statement is somewhat optimistic' and that the Soviets were then unlikely to accept internationalization.[34] The Committee in reply suggested that Attlee bypass the United Nations altogether and approach Stalin and Truman directly.[35] This exchange received significant attention from the press—the *Manchester Guardian* in particular issued an editorial welcoming the 'note of urgency' in the approach to Attlee.[36] In May 1948, following the news that the UN Atomic Energy Commission was to suspend its discussions on international control, Blackburn reiterated in Parliament this call to bypass the UN.[37]

The United Nations Association (UNA, until late 1945 known as the League of Nations Association) was initially cautious in its response (calling for UN inspection rather than international ownership of atomic energy), though it was soon pushed in a more radical direction by the Chairman of its Executive Committee, the Earl of Lytton.[38] Lytton's proposal for international control, which included an international police armed with the atomic

---

[32] 'Parliament Atomic Energy Control, Merits of The Two Plans, House of Commons', *The Times* (3 August 1946).

[33] 'Banning Of Atomic Weapons Request for International Authority', *The Times* (8 March 1947).

[34] Letter, Clement Attlee to Raymond Blackburn (10 April 1947), File: 'NC Observer, World Army by Liddell Hart, NC Atomic Energy Committee 1947', Box 101, DAVIES PAPERS.

[35] 'Control of Atomic Energy Mr. Attlee's Reply to Committee', *The Times* (16 June 1947).

[36] 'A New Atomic Start', *Manchester Guardian* (16 June 1947). See also: 'Control of Atomic Energy Mr. Attlee's Reply to Committee', *The Times* (16 June 1947); and 'Atomic Energy Deadlock. New Commonwealth Committee Suggests Meeting', *Manchester Guardian* (16 June 1947). It even reached the *Bulletin of the Atomic Scientists*: 'Prominent Britons Urge Attlee to call Big Three Meeting', *Bulletin of the Atomic Scientists* 3 (August 1947), 218, 220.

[37] 'Parliament Atomic Energy Control, "Final" Approach Suggested, House of Commons', *The Times* (15 May 1948).

[38] *Resolutions Adopted by the General Council of the League of Nations Union at its Annual Meeting in London on September 6th and 7th, 1945* (14 September 1945), Folder

bomb, was circulated to UNA branches in November 1945, and accepted and adopted by the Executive in December.[39] The UNA's published proposal, based largely on Lytton's, called for an international 'Board' to 'own and to control the production of atomic energy, and to establish and maintain the central and most highly equipped research organization for the development of atomic energy.' Existing bombs were to be handed over to the Board, which would also produce new atomic weapons for a newly constituted Authority armed with international forces distributed around the world.[40] The report was propagated by leading UNA members such as Herbert Samuel (leader of the Liberal Party in the House of Lords), published in *United Nations News*, formed the basis of an Executive Committee-sponsored resolution at the June 1947 General Council meeting, and received some press coverage.[41] Following Lytton's resignation in late 1946, UNA interest in international control declined however, and the atomic sub-committee ceased to function by February 1947.[42]

Although both the UNA and the New Commonwealth proposed the formation of a powerful atomic-bomb-armed international police force, they were divided on how this force was to be used. The UNA position was that atomic bombs only be used against those countries that had violated

---

4X/124: 'UNA 1946 Onwards', PNB PAPERS. 'Controlling Use of Atomic Bomb L.N.U. Council's Hope of International Action', *The Times* (7 September 1945).

[39] League of Nations Union, *Annual Report for 1944* (London, 1945), 11; Earl of Lytton, *Can We Survive the Atomic Bomb?* (London, 1945); *Minutes of a Meeting of the Provisional Executive Committee. . . on Thursday, November 15th, 1945 at 2.15 PM*, 3/1/1, UNA PAPERS; *Minutes of a Meeting of the Provisional Executive Committee. . . on Thursday, December 6th, 1945 at 2.15 PM*, 3/1/1, UNA PAPERS; Memo, Earl of Lytton, *Appendix A: International Control of Atomic Energy. Stages by Which International Control of Atomic Energy can be Established* (undated, *c.*1 December 1945).

[40] *United Nations Association. Atomic Energy Sub-Committee Report to the Executive Committee* (5 December 1946), 3/1/1, UNA PAPERS.

[41] 'Appeal For Outlawing Of Atomic Bomb. Lord Samuel's Proposal', *The Times* (25 March 1947). United Nations Association, *Agenda of the Second Annual General Meeting* (London: June 1947), 2/1, UNA PAPERS. 'Atomic Energy Report on Control and Production, International Board Suggested', *The Times* (7 January 1947).

[42] *Minutes of a Meeting of the Executive Committee. . . on Thursday, 20th February, 1947 at 11 AM*, 3/1/2, UNA PAPERS. Earl of Lytton, *Memorandum by the Earl of Lytton* (undated, *c.* September 1947), 3/1/2, UNA PAPERS. Lytton was replaced by Air Vice-Marshall Donald C. T. Bennett, who incidentally was a proponent of an aerial international police force: D. C. T. Bennett, *International Security by Police Control* (6 June 1944), 8/1030, CHAT PAPERS; D. C. T. Bennett, *Freedom from War* (London, 1945); and D. C. T. Bennett, *Pathfinder: A War Autobiography* (London, 1958), 266.

international control of atomic energy.[43] The New Commonwealth's force on the other hand was to be used to implement global law and order on a comprehensive basis—particularly through the enforcement of the decisions of an international tribunal. General Secretary N. B. Foot explained what he understood to be the difference:

> It seems to me that in the joint conference with the other Societies the main conflict will arise between ourselves and the UNA. As you know, UNA have embraced an idea of Lytton's that an International Force should be formed simply and solely to serve as a sanction for the outlawry of the Atom bomb ... Our main thesis, as we say in the Resolution, is that the only satisfactory course is, in a sense, to make use of this 'Atomic Opportunity' to solve the problem once and for all and to bring into being a really satisfactory international machinery.[44]

Even within the UNA, though, there was a constituency which preferred a wider scope of activities for the international police force and its atomic bombs. A member of both the Commonwealth and the UNA wrote to the *United Nations News* in May 1946 protesting that under the UNA's plan 'a crisis might arise in which the International Force would stand by with folded arms during a major war purely because none of the contestants had used atomic weapons. Surely this is not our intention?' Instead, he proposed that the force be ready to use 'all necessary weapons' against any aggressor.[45] This constituency tried, in November 1945, to bring the two organizations to cooperate together on international control, and in February 1946 to get its proposals adopted as official UNA policy. It failed on both counts.[46] In fact, internationalist organization members expended almost as much effort urging unity amongst themselves as they did urging unity amongst nations. 'We must unite or perish' pleaded one letter to *Federal News*, referring not to antagonistic nations but to the UNA and Federal Union.[47]

---

[43] 'General Council Decisions', *International Outlook* 1 (March 1946), 11–12.

[44] Letter, Foot to George Cockerill (18 January 1946), B23/3—NC correspondence 1945— 'C', DAVIES PAPERS.

[45] R. E. G. Fulljames, Letter to the Editor, 'International Force', *United Nations News* 1 (May 1946), 26.

[46] 'UNA's First General Council', *International Outlook* 1 (March 1946), 7–12; *Minutes of a Meeting of the Provisional Executive Committee ... on Thursday, November 29th, 1945 at 2.15 PM*, 3/1/1, UNA PAPERS.

[47] Ronald E. Gundry, 'Letters: Two Roads—No Goal', *Federal News* 129 (December 1945), 12.

Other non-scientist internationalist organizations were much less interested in international control. The Federal Union, the National Peace Council
and the Crusade for World Government took little initiative with regard to
international control.[48] Of the three, Labour MP Henry Usborne's newly
formed Crusade for World Government was the only one to call for international control of the atomic bomb, alongside an atomic international force, in
its publications. It did little other advocacy on atomic energy.[49] Like Federal
Union, the prime aim of the Crusade was international federal union, though
with an emphasis on European federation first. Unlike the Union, Usborne
wanted an international atomic-bomb-armed force formed immediately
under the UN, rather than waiting for a world federation. The UN also
required, he reasoned, the ability to further develop atomic weapons, and
the right to control through inspection nationally owned atomic plants. His
logic, as explained in a National Peace Council pamphlet in 1946, was that a
European federal union would antagonize the Soviet Union because a
pan-European army would then face off against the USSR. To circumvent
this, the union would need to be disarmed at the time of its creation; and for
the European nations to agree to this the UN would first need to be bolstered
through control of atomic energy.[50]

The widespread support for the international control of atomic energy
described above cannot be solely or even largely attributed to the activities
and pronouncements of British internationalist scientists. They only organized themselves in late 1945; individual scientists speaking on atomic control in 1945 tended to speak on internationalist platforms alongside
non-scientists.[51] Although some scientists may have advised government

---

[48] These organizations however feature prominently in the secondary literature, see: Jones,
'The Mushroom-Shaped Cloud'; Wittner, *The Struggle Against the Bomb Volume 1*,
84–92. For a sense of the Federal Union and the National Peace Council's thinking on
atomic energy see: F. L. Josephy, 'Federate or Perish', *Federal News* 126 (September 1945),
3; F. L. Josephy, 'The Federal Implications of the Atom', *Federal News* 126 (September
1945), 1–2, 11; Mosa Anderson, 'The Approach to World Government', *One World* 1
(June 1946), 3–6.

[49] It is noteworthy that Usborne defected to the Liberals in 1962.

[50] Henry C. Usborne, *Towards World Government—The Role of Britain* (London, 1946);
Henry Usborne, 'What Holds us Back', *Federal News* 135 (June 1946), 2, 5. Like other
internationalist organizations, the Crusade invited scientists to talk on atomic energy; e.g.
Harold Urey: 'Atomic Warfare; No Defence Against the Bomb', *Manchester Guardian* (6
November 1947).

[51] For example, the November 1945 World Unity Movement symposium attended by
Leonard Hill, Kathleen Lonsdale, Ritchie Calder, and Lionel Penrose: Leonard Hill
et al., *Atomic Energy: Science v. Sovereignty* (London, 1946).

on the need for international control, support for such control was already widespread amongst senior ministers.[52] The secondary literature has focused on the Association of Scientific Workers (AScW) and the British Atomic Scientists' Association as the most significant scientists' organizations with regard to international control. Yet in actual fact the Atomic Scientists' Committee of the AScW, which had been meeting since late 1945, garnered little publicity that year. The most public interventions were a letter to *The Times* and a press release.[53] The Atomic Scientists' Association was not launched until the spring of 1946, and the major scientists' conferences on the implications of atomic energy took place in July 1946.[54] The liberal newspapers at the forefront of calls for international control in late 1945 barely referred to scientists at all in this regard. Instead, newspapers chose to print statements by politicians or leading liberal intellectuals such as Walter Layton on the international relations-transforming properties of atomic energy, or turn to H. G. Wells for an understanding and solution to this technological predicament.[55]

## Liberal intellectuals

That ideas for international control of atomic energy had predecessors in interwar internationalist thought is evident in the (somewhat contrasting) thinking of two prominent liberal intellectuals: Bertrand Russell and Arthur Salter. Russell's reaction to the bomb was immediate. In an article published on 18 August 1945 he turned to internationalization as a solution to the 'new and appalling problems with which the human race is confronted by its conquest of scientific power'. He called for humanity to 'bring to bear upon social, and especially international, organization, intelligence of the same high order that has enabled us to discover the structure of the atom'. Uranium ore, atomic plants, and atomic bombs were to be placed under the direct control of an 'irresistible' atomic-bomb-armed "international authority" which would then be able to bring to an end all wars. If the Soviet Union

---

[52] Margaret Gowing, *Independence and Deterrence: Britain and Atomic Energy, 1945–1952, Volume 1 Policy Making* (London, 1974), 70–2.

[53] J. D. Bernal, Letter to the Editor, *The Times* (5 September 1945); AScW, Press Statement, *Scientists and the Atomic Bomb* (1 November 1945), MSS.79/ASW/3/3/1, AScW PAPERS.

[54] The AScW Conference in London 20–21 July; the International Physical Conference at Cambridge 22–27 July; and the International Conference of the Atomic Scientists Associations 29–31 July.

[55] 'Atom: Boon or Doom? H. G. Wells Prophesised it in 1894', *Daily Herald* (9 August 1945); Editorial, 'The Lesson of Hiroshima', *Daily Herald* (5 September 1945); Walter Layton, 'Hiroshima', *News Chronicle* (9 August 1945).

did not agree to the provisions of international control, he suggested that it be forcibly disarmed through a pre-emptive war.[56] He stuck remarkably close to this early reaction over the following four years, and talked in the House of Lords of the need for the use of atomic bombs, and on behalf of the New Commonwealth Society during a lecture tour to Holland and Belgium in late 1947.[57]

Russell termed his reaction to the bomb 'new political thinking'.[58] Yet it was anything but. Russell himself had already called for the formation of a world government and an international air police in the late 1930s and during the war. In *Which Way to Peace?* (published 1936) he had joined liberal internationalist opinion in asserting that aviation had transformed war, giving attackers an insurmountable advantage. Aviation, along with gas and bacteriological weapons, would need to be handed over to an international force for its exclusive use. 'Permanent peace' required 'the existence of a single supreme world government, possessed of irresistible force, and able to impose its will upon any national State or combination of States.'[59] In January 1941 he wrote to Gilbert Murray: 'There can be no permanent peace unless there is only one Air Force in the world with the degree of international government that that implies. Disarmament alone, though good, will not

---

[56] Bertrand Russell, 'The Bomb and Civilization', *Glasgow Forward* 39 (18 August 1945), 1, 3.

[57] His later calls for international control include: Bertrand Russell, 'The Atomic Bomb and the Prevention of War', *Bulletin of the Atomic Scientists* 2 (1 October 1946), 19–21; and Bertrand Russell, 'Values in the Atomic Age', in M. L. Oliphant et al., *The Atomic Age* (London, 1949), 81–104. In the House of Lords his view was most vocally supported by A. D. Lindsay (who was linked to the New Commonwealth—he was President of the *London Quarterly of World Affairs*, previously the *New Commonwealth Quarterly*) and Viscount Samuel. HL DEB, 7 March 1946, volume 139, columns 1259–1260; and HL DEB, 30 April 1947, volume 147, columns 244–289. The New Commonwealth made full use of Russell's celebrity: his lecture was published in both their magazine and as a pamphlet: Bertrand Russell, 'International Government', in Bertrand Russell, *Towards World Government* (London, 1948), 3–12; Bertrand Russell, 'International Government', *The New Commonwealth* (9 January 1948), 77–80. Although historians have focused on his call for preventive war against the Soviet Union they have not noted that this was part of a wider militant liberal internationalism. See for example Ray Perkins, 'Bertrand Russell and Preventative War: A Reply to David Blitz', *Russell: the Journal of Bertrand Russell Studies* 22 (Winter 2002–03), 161–72; and Ray Monk, *Bertrand Russell 1921–70. The Ghost of Madness* (London, 2000), 298–305.

[58] Russell, 'The Bomb and Civilization'.

[59] Bertrand Russell, *Which Way to Peace?* (London, 1936).

make peace secure.'[60] His *Scientific Outlook* (1933), citing David Davies's *Problem of the Twentieth Century*, argued that the 'scientific outlook', the key to mankind's success, required a world state armed with 'a single highly efficient fighting machine, employing mainly aeroplanes and chemical methods of warfare, which will be quite obviously irresistible, and will therefore not be resisted'.[61] The notion that modern science and science-based industry made possible new articulations of power was a reoccurring theme in Russell's writings from the twenties to the early fifties.[62]

Arthur Salter's internationalist credentials (he had worked on Anglo-American transport planning in both the World Wars, for much of the twenties was head of the economic and financial section of the League's secretariat, and was known in 1945/1946 for his concern about world food shortages) ensured that his pronouncements on atomic energy received significant publicity. During the prominent August 1945 Commons debate on the UN Charter he claimed that the 'public shock' created by the bomb may help statesmen to strengthen the UN, and that international control could help restore the European economy. A speech to a joint Federal Union and UNA meeting in October 1945 was widely reported and printed in the United States.[63] In the latter he explained how the current 'international anarchy between sovereign States', required 'supranational authority' and the dilution of national sovereignty. The atomic bomb, he announced, provided a 'new lever of power to compel action'. It could transform world order, 'its power to achieve a constructive purpose will thus be as great as its destructive potency'.[64] He echoed these sentiments in BBC radio Brains Trust discussions, informing listeners in November 1945 (the other discussants were educator

---

[60] Letter, Bertrand Russell to Gilbert Murray (18 January 1941), reprinted in Bertrand Russell, *Autobiography* (London, 2010), 471.

[61] Bertrand Russell, *The Scientific Outlook* (London, 1954, first published in 1933), 219. Davies was a leading British proponent of an international police force and the international control of aviation in the 'thirties. His major written work on international relations was David Davies, *The Problem of the Twentieth Century: A Study of International Relationships* (London, 1930).

[62] On this see Peter Denton, *Bertrand Russell on Science, Religion, and the Next War, 1919–1938* (New York, 2001).

[63] 'Charter of Nations Cooperation for Peace, Commons Debate', *The Times* (23 August 1945); 'House of Commons', *The Times* (23 August 1945); 'Safeguard against Atomic Bomb Sir Arthur Salter's Proposal', *The Times* (9 October 1945); 'Sir Arthur Salter's Proposal', *Manchester Guardian* (9 October 1945); Arthur Salter, 'The United Nations and the Atom', *International Conciliation* 417 (January 1946), 40–8.

[64] Salter, 'The United Nations and the Atom'.

William Hamilton Fyfe, scientist Julian Huxley, Bertrand Russell, and Herbert Samuel) that 'atomic energy is after all a very powerful forcing hot-house to the development of political institutions'. Brains Trust discussions on atomic energy were characterized by almost complete agreement on its effects on international relations. Participants disagreed over the powers of future supranational authority which was to control atomic energy. This was the case during the November 1945 discussion, when Salter envisaged a powerful international supranational organization controlling 'armaments' and 'foreign policy', whereas Russell argued against such a 'thorough-going international authority' though for one with a powerful international force armed with 'all the really important weapons of war'.[65]

Salter too had a long history of pronouncements on science, technology and international relations. In lectures such as *Modern Mechanization and its Effects on the Structure of Society* (1933) he had emphasized mechanization and its creation of 'technological displacement' and a lag of social institutions behind the effects of mechanization.[66] His talks at the BBC, also in 1933, had linked 'scientific inventions' to the need for a limited form of 'world government'. One important task of world government would be to 'see that this Frankenstein remains our servant and does not become our master'. He imagined a techno-internationalist future in which delegates to the League of Nations in 1957 would travel by aeroplane and remain in instantaneous contact through wireless receiving sets in their waistcoat pockets.[67] In 1943 and 1944 he, like many others, saw in international Allied organizations the seeds of a post-war 'world government'.[68] Salter continued to hold many of these views into the late 1940s and expressed them again in his short biography of H. G. Wells, published in 1947.[69]

---

[65] 'Extract from "The Brains Trust"', *Federal News* 130 (January 1946), 4–5. On the significance of the BBC Brains Trust discussions for liberal intellectuals see Desmarais, 'Science, Scientific Intellectuals and British Culture in the Early Atomic Age, 1945–1956', chapter 4.

[66] Arthur Salter, *Modern Mechanization and its Effects on the Structure of Society* (London, 1933).

[67] Arthur Salter, 'World Government', in Mary Adams (ed.), *The Modern State* (London, 1933), 253–316.

[68] Arthur Salter, 'From Combined War Agencies to International Administration', *Public Administration Review* 4 (Winter 1944), 1–6; Arthur Salter, 'Pressing the Fight for Freedom', *Proceedings of the Academy of Political Science* 20 (May 1943), 74–84.

[69] 'H. G. Wells: Apostle of a World Society', in Arthur Salter, *Personality in Politics: Studies in Contemporary Statesmen* (London, 1947), 120–37.

## Chatham House and the decline of international control

Developments on the diplomatic front gradually dashed internationalist hopes for atomic energy from mid-1946 onwards. The Soviet Union reacted negatively to the American Baruch Plan, presented to the United Nations Atomic Energy Commission in June 1946, and by the end of the year it was clear that no agreement on international control would occur in the near future. Negotiations dragged on through to 1947 against a backdrop of worsening relations between the Soviet Union and the United States.[70] This decline is evident in the work of the international relations think tank Chatham House, whose Atomic Energy Study Group held its first meeting in September 1946, and continued to meet roughly every two months through to mid-1948. The Group was chaired by the scientist Henry Dale and composed of a mix of scientists, civil servants, academics and military men. Regular attendants included Oliver Franks, Air Marshal Roderic Hill, H. S. W. Massey, Arthur Salter, and Charles Webster. Others attending included Lord Hankey, James Chadwick, Marcus Oliphant, R. E. Peierls, Cecil Edgar Tilley and J. D. Cockcroft. Some, such as Arthur Salter, had been involved in earlier discussions on atomic energy at the New Commonwealth Society, but were attracted to the more agenda-free environment on offer at Chatham House.[71]

The two most vocal supporters of international control in the Group were Arthur Salter and Charles Webster. Salter's views, which he propounded during the Group's discussions, have already been explored above. Webster (1886–1961) had been in the interwar years an ardent supporter of the League, and worked during the war with the Foreign Research and Press Service and eventually with the Foreign Office on UN planning. His last post prior to his retirement from the Foreign Office in April 1946 was as Special Advisor to Philip Noel-Baker, the Minister of State responsible for United Nations Affairs. Webster became a strong supporter of the newly formed UN in 1945, and of international control through to 1947. Like other internationalists he would announce to his public audiences that international control afforded the 'opportunity' to 'see the United Nations transformed by action, into something much more powerful than it is today'.[72] He was also in keeping with a swathe of internationalist opinion in his belief that international control was not simply about preventing war, but also sowing the seeds of world government. He pushed this view within the Chatham

---

[70] Gerber, 'The Baruch Plan and the Origins of the Cold War'.

[71] *Dinner and Discussion on Atomic Energy* (6 May 1946), Folder 9/42b: Atomic Energy Subcommittee. Minutes Correspondence, CHAT PAPERS.

[72] Charles Webster, 'The Making of the Charter of the United Nations', in Charles Webster, *The Art and Practice of Diplomacy* (London, 1961), 70–91.

House Group, and, mindful of Chatham House's connections to political scientist David Mitrany (then already well known for this 'functional' approach to international relations), described this evolution from international control to 'World State' as an example of 'functional development'.[73] Webster emphasized that an international controlling authority's power would derive not only from its ability to control the manufacture of atomic bombs, but also from its ability to control the distribution of power generated by atomic energy—power which held 'great potentialities for the welfare of the world.'[74]

The Group published its report on atomic energy and international relations in January 1948.[75] The differing views of the Group's members led to a publication consisting of individually authored papers and lacking a single coherent viewpoint. Chapters dealt with a variety of topics, including scientific theory, the bomb's use in warfare, and the mining of raw materials. Only one, by Arthur Salter, Charles Webster, and Oliver Franks, propounded a plan for international control. They maintained that international control of atomic energy was of significance not only because it controlled the atomic bomb and atomic energy and allowed for the production of abundant electricity, but also because it would lead to co-operation in other areas. It would be the harbinger of a new international 'efficient system of direction and control' and would make possible the 'creation of a world community with practical institutions strong enough to control national States'.[76] The fact that someone like Oliver Franks would add his name to this proposal for internationalization alongside Salter's and Webster's is of some significance. Franks, a career diplomat, was at that time chairing the European organization formulating requirements for the Marshall Plan, and serving on the government's Advisory Committee on Atomic Energy. He would later serve as ambassador in Washington, DC. Out of the three he is the one who would have been the least obviously identifiable as a supporter of international control. His involvement signifies a certain attraction within

---

[73] Charles Webster, *The International Aspect of Atomic Energy Control* (25 November 1946), Folder 9/42e, CHAT PAPERS.

[74] Ibid.

[75] Royal Institute of International Affairs, *Atomic Energy. Its International Implications. A Discussion by a Chatham House Study Group* (London: RIIA, 1948). The significantly worsened atmosphere for international control ensured that it had little impact, though its publication was noted in Parliamentary debates and in international relations and internationalist publications.

[76] Charles Webster, Arthur Salter, and Oliver Franks, 'The Control of Nuclear Energy and the Development of International Institutions', in RIIA, *Atomic Energy*, 91–101.

mainstream British liberalism—that is outside the world of overt or activist liberal internationalism—to American-led proposals for international control.

The only other internationalist chapter in the Chatham House volume was produced by the interwar director of scientific research at the Air Ministry; Harry Wimperis, who served as rapporteur for the Group. He had already published in 1946, under the auspices of Chatham House, his own detailed plan for comprehensive UN-based international control. He had advocated UN control of all atomic bombs and their use for peace-keeping, as well as UN scientific development of the peaceful uses of atomic energy. He had acknowledged the need for a thorough overhaul of 'the relationship of States to each other', but recognized that for the moment the bomb could be used to strengthen the fledgling UN:

> Obviously an immense impulse is given towards the creation of a World State; but that must take time. Fortunately we have in the throes of creation a new almost world-wide United Nations Organization with a Security Council acting under it having the duty of preserving world peace. It is now possible, should it be so desired, to arm that Council with the most potent weapon ever discovered by man.[77]

By late 1947, when Wimperis penned his chapter for the Study Group report, the Soviets were well into their stride in rejecting American proposals for international control. He, much more so than Salter, Franks, and Webster, reflected this awkward reality in his chapter. Although based on similar assumptions about the internationalizing and integrative nature of science and technical work, he started with the assumption that international control would not be agreed. He instead took up a suggestion made by Air Chief Marshal Roderic Hill during Group discussions that the UN form its own atomic research and development laboratory. Nation-states would be allowed to retain their own atomic research programmes, but in this thinking such programmes would be overshadowed by the UN effort, and so wither away over time. Hill had argued that a new United Nations Atomic Research Institute would:

> tend to gain an ascendancy because national bodies would become so dependent on it that in practice they could not get on satisfactorily without it. Thus perhaps, might arise a form of 'control'

[77] H. E. Wimperis, *World Power and Atomic Energy: The Impact on International Relations* (London: RIIA, 1946), 1.

which while operating actively and efficiently, would avoid awkward questions of national sovereignty.[78]

Hill had claimed, echoing arguments made in the Acheson-Lilienthal Report (and indeed prevalent in much of the rhetoric on scientists and politics of the time) that the working methods of scientists could be relied upon to gradually arrive at international peace and security—that international cooperation amongst scientists would eventually spread to administrators and politicians.[79] Wimperis argued in his chapter that scientists' co-operation on atomic matters could become a template for international technical cooperation in other areas.[80]

For all the Study Group discussion on internationalizing atomic energy, the final chapter of the Group's report was written by the most vocal opponent of international control within the Group, Lord Hankey. Hankey had been dead-set against international control since discussions began, informing the Group in November 1946 that it was too intrusive to be acceptable, and even if successful would anyhow not prevent all warfare. For it to work, international control would have to be extended to 'other scientific developments', which he took to be 'biological warfare, rockets and other V weapons—radar and the rest'. That would require 'a vast increase in the scientific and technical personnel engaged in control and inspection' and would ultimately be 'too great a burden to place on the infant UNO.' He had pointed out that current fears about the atomic bomb were simply a replication of interwar fears of aerial bombardment. Civilization would survive the coming of the atomic bomb just as it had survived the dangers of air bombing.[81] His final chapter for the published report declared that Britain and the United States should continue to develop atomic weapons, though perhaps agreeing a treaty banning their use in war.[82]

Discussions within the Group continued for a few months after the publication of its volume, though by March 1948 all the Group's members

---

[78] Roderic Hill, *Memorandum* (15 January 1947), Folder 9/42e, CHAT PAPERS.

[79] *Verbatim Report of the Second Meeting of the Atomic Energy Group* (10 December 1946), Folder 9/42e, CHAT PAPERS.

[80] H. E. Wimperis, 'International Co-operation in the Development of Atomic Energy', in RIIA, *Atomic Energy*, 102–11.

[81] Lord Hankey, *Control of Atomic Warfare: Political Aspects* (25 November 1946), Folder 9/42e, CHAT PAPERS.

[82] Lord Hankey, 'The Human Element', in RIIA, *Atomic Energy*, 112–24. Hankey noted, during an extended denouncement of proposals for international control at the House of Lords, that he had written his chapter in May 1947. HL DEB, 18 February 1948, volume 153, columns 1190–1198.

accepted that international control was no longer a realistic option. They turned instead to the threat of communism. For Salter the 'immediate and urgent danger' became 'not the bomb but the overthrow of freedom by the methods adopted in Czechoslovakia'.[83] Wimperis in a Chatham House lecture suggested that a regional scheme, with 'United States as its chief organizer' was still possible, though 'the great menace now overshadowing the world' was not the atomic bomb but 'the steady attack by a fanatical ideology'.[84] Hope for the atomic reconstruction of international relations had died.

## Conclusion

The advent of atomic energy provided internationalists with a powerful arena over and through which they fought for their differing visions for a reconstructed international relations. Some wanted to create a United Nations-centred world order, whilst others wanted newer and more radical forms of international organization or international government. Powerful technologically superior military forces played an important role in many of these visions, as did the purported peace-spreading and integrative effects of international scientific and technical co-operation. British atomic culture held it to be self-evident that the atomic bomb heralded a new era of international political relations and warfare. Older weapons were assumed to be, if not quite obsolete, then much diminished in their usefulness for war. The underlying dynamics of international relations, if not the system itself, was assumed to have been transformed. Larger states now had the ability to further bully or even conquer smaller ones, leading to more conflict and deadlier warfare. The atomic bomb required, consequently, drastic transformations in societies, militaries, and international relations. Supranational organizations such as the UN assumed an even greater importance in the eyes of intellectuals and the public—as did the idea of supranational organization itself. The bomb was assumed to be a product of science, so scientists acquired a peculiarly high status as experts not only on scientific, technological, and industrial matters related to the bomb, but also on its effects on society and government policy.

This British response was similar in many ways to the American internationalist response, though there were two crucial differences. First, the concept of an international police force was much more commonly heard in Britain. Although some in the US called for it in late 1945, by mid 1946

---

[83] Arthur Salter, *The Atomic Problem* (March 1948), Folder 9/42g, CHAT PAPERS.

[84] H. E. Wimperis, 'Atomic Energy Control: The Present Position', *International Affairs* 24 (October 1948), 515–23. Similarly see Roderic Hill, *The Atomic Problem*, revised draft (17 April 1948), Folder 9/42g, CHAT PAPERS.

such calls died out. Prominent American proposals such as the Acheson-Lilienthal and Baruch plans did not envisage the formation of such a force. Secondly, scientists in America were much more at the forefront of internationalist rhetoric: they were more organized, cohesive in their action and statements, and prominent in shaping public understanding of the effects of atomic energy. In Britain, by contrast, scientists were relatively unorganized, politically and ideologically fractured in their understanding of international relations, and less effective in shaping public discourse and government thinking.[85]

Recognizing these approaches to international relations and atomic energy allows us to reconstruct important elements of post-war British culture now lost or forgotten. Historians are apt to associate the interwar, but not the post-war, with British liberal internationalism and its thinking on international relations and the control of weapons and warfare. Similarly it is generally assumed that the atomic bomb generated new or radically different thinking on international relations. This paper demonstrates that actually liberal internationalism remained of continuing importance in early post-war Britain, and in fact underlay an important British response to the atomic bomb. Recognizing this response's militant nature, its appeal to science, and its lack of opposition to a British bomb may help to explain why Britain did eventually acquire the bomb.

---

[85] Notwithstanding the more prominent role of scientists in the US, their significance has been exaggerated in the secondary literature. For a fuller comparison see Zaidi, 'Technology and the Reconstruction of International Relations', chapters 5 and 6.

# 'A Human Treasure': Europe's Displaced Children Between Nationalism and Internationalism

## Tara Zahra

In 1948 the United Nations Convention on the Prevention and Punishment of Genocide labelled 'forcibly transferring children of one group to another group' enacted 'with intent to destroy, in whole or in part, a national, ethnical, racial or religious group, as such', a form of genocide. A year later, Vinita A. Lewis, a social worker with the International Refugee Organization (IRO) in Germany, insisted, 'The lost identity of individual children is *the* Social Problem of the day on the continent of Europe . . . Even if his future destiny lies in a country other than that of his origin, he [the displaced child] is entitled to the basic Human Right of full knowledge of his background and origin.' Children, it seems, enjoyed a 'human right' to a nationality after World War II. Where did this strikingly nationalist understanding of human rights come from? And what does post-war activism around displaced children reveal about the broader relationships between nationalism and internationalism in the process of post-war reconstruction?

Children were at the symbolic heart of efforts to reconstruct Europe in the aftermath of the Second World War. International humanitarian organizations, government officials, and child welfare experts were particularly concerned about the fate of Europe's so-called 'lost children'—hundreds of thousands of children who were separated from their families or uprooted by bombings, military conscription, occupation, forced labour, deportation, and the death of their parents. Policy-makers considered the rehabilitation of these children to be essential to the biological, moral, and economic reconstruction of the nation. At the same time, however, refugee children were contested between states. And they stood at the centre of a host of new international humanitarian relief efforts that were animated by explicitly internationalist ideals.

The history of Europe's refugee children after World War II sheds light on how Europeans navigated the tensions between nationalism and internationalism that shaped the reconstruction of Europe. On the one hand, the end of the Second World War was accompanied by a wave of idealistic internationalism that gained new moral force after the Second World War.[1] The practical outgrowth of this 'new internationalism' was an explosion of intergovernmental and non-governmental international organizations. A United Nations survey conducted in January 1951 counted 188 officially recognized international organizations, one-third of which were founded after 1945.[2] In the realm of child welfare, the United Nations Relief and Rehabilitation Administration (UNRRA, 1943–47) and the International Refugee Organization (IRO, 1947–51) were at the forefront of efforts to re-habilitate and repatriate displaced children after the war.

None of the new post-war international institutions and conventions were premised on the death of the nation-state. But they did promise to usher in a new era of international cooperation and to uphold universal values that transcended state borders. The foot-soldiers of post-war relief efforts in Europe were themselves animated by this internationalist spirit. Susan Pettiss, an UNRRA social worker, recalled joining the organization with the hopeful conviction that 'the chaos immediately following the end of World War I with clogged roads, epidemics, widespread hunger could not be repeated. We would, this time, achieve a permanent peace and help establish a unified world.'[3]

The experiences of military conscription and occupation, population dis-placement, and deportation meanwhile created tens of thousands of trans-national families, transforming matters such as marriage, divorce, child custody, adoption, and child welfare into central concerns of diplomats, military officials, and humanitarian workers. The family was internationa-lized to an unprecedented extent in Europe during the Second World War. But internationalism as an ideology stood on shakier ground.[4] For beneath the surface of the lofty rhetoric adopted by United Nations' workers and

---

[1] On the rhetoric of individualism and human rights in post-war Europe, see Samuel Moyn, *The Last Utopia: A Recent History of Human Rights*, chapter 1 (Cambridge Mass., 2010); Tony Judt, *Post war: A History of Europe Since 1945* (New York, 2005), 564–5; Paul Lauren, *The Evolution of International Human Rights* (Philadelphia, 1996); Mark Mazower, 'The Strange Triumph of Human Rights, 1933–1950,' *The Historical Journal* 47:2 (2004), 386–8; A. W. Brian Simpson, *Human Rights and the End of Empire: Britain and the Genesis of the European Convention* (Oxford, 2001), 157–220; Akira Iriye, *Global Community: The Role of International Organizations in the Making of the Contemporary World* (Berkeley, 2002), 41–52.

[2] Iriye, *Global Community*, 40–52.

[3] Susan T. Pettiss with Lynne Taylor, *After the Shooting Stopped: The Story of an UNRRA Welfare Worker in Germany, 1945–47* (Victoria, BC, 2004), 5–6.

[4] On the relationship between internationalism and internationalization, see Martin Geyer and Johannes Paulmann, 'Introduction: The Mechanics of Internationalism', in *The*

officials, the liberation of Europe was an explosively nationalist moment. Reconstruction was understood as an explicitly nationalizing project, an effort to recover the national sovereignty and rehabilitate the national honour compromised by the Nazi occupation.

This project was brutally gendered. The sovereignty of the nation was symbolically located in women's bodies and in the bodies of children. Reconstructing national 'honour' meant purging and punishing collaborators of all kinds, but especially women who had (allegedly) enabled the national enemy to penetrate their bodies. In France, but also in Germany, Czechoslovakia, and elsewhere in Europe, women suspected of consorting with occupying soldiers were publicly humiliated. French partisans and villagers shaved women's heads in spectacles of violent retribution, while in Czechoslovakia, local 'people's courts' charged so-called 'horizontal collaborators' with the newly invented crime of 'offending national honour'. Many Czech women were fined, interned, or even stripped of their citizenship and expelled for the offence of having relations with Bohemian German-speakers who had been their neighbours, business partners, classmates, and friends for decades before the Second World War.[5]

The project of reclaiming national sovereignty in liberated Europe was also linked directly to sovereignty over children. Like women, children were seen as a form of national 'property' that required protection from foreign invasion and appropriation. Repatriating and renationalizing 'stolen' children in Germany and Austria was linked to post-war justice and denazification, the defence of 'human rights' and the family, and the acquisition of the productive and reproductive labour necessary for reconstruction. But officials in both Eastern and Western Europe did not only demand the return of 'lost children' in the name of national sovereignty. They also invoked the more universalist values of European security and children's individual 'best interests'.

This article focuses on the place of 'lost children' (both displaced children and children of occupation) in the reconstruction of France and Czechoslovakia. The imagined link between reconstruction and sovereignty over children transcended boundaries between East and West, but East European

---

Mechanics of Internationalism: Culture, Society, and Politics from the 1840s to the First World War (Oxford, 2001), 1–25.

[5] Fabrice Virgili, *Shorn Women: Gender and Punishment in Liberation France* (New York, 2002); Perry Biddiscombe, 'The Anti-Fraternization Movement in the U.S. Occupation Zones of Germany and Austria, 1945–48,' *Journal of Social History* 34 (Spring 2001), 611–47; Benjamin Frommer, *National Cleansing: Retribution against Nazi Collaborators in Postwar Czechoslovakia* (New York, 2004); Heide Fehrenbach, *Race After Hitler: Black Occupation Children in Postwar Germany* (Princeton, 2007).

policy-makers were far more dependent than French authorities on the good-will of the Allies and of international organizations such as the UNRRA and the IRO. But even United Nations workers who explicitly espoused interna-tionalist ideals ultimately came to favour the renationalization and repatri-ation of displaced children from Eastern Europe. Like French and Czechoslovak policy-makers, they linked the repatriation of children uprooted by war to overarching values of justice, democratization, and human rights. In the campaign to reconstruct Europe's children after World War II, international organizations reinforced nationalist ideals and policies, and collectivist understandings of child welfare and pedagogy were translated into the individualist and universalist language of children's 'best interests'.

### Displacement and demography

One of the most potent manifestations of post-war nationalism in Europe was the wave of populationism that swept the continent. Replacing the dead had particular meaning and urgency for European Jews after the Holocaust, but every European government sought to replenish its dead soldiers and civil-ians, recover its 'lost children', and secure the labour power needed for post-war reconstruction. These concerns encouraged pro-natalist social pol-icies and an expansion of European welfare states, and ultimately generated spirited competition among European governments to claim refugee chil-dren and orphans as immigrants. In 1946, Pierre Pfimlin, representing the French Ministry of Public Health and Population, described displaced chil-dren as a valuable 'blood transfusion' who could replace dead soldiers and thereby counter a 'menace of extinction' that threatened the French nation:

> During the war years Germany was an immense prison, where humans belonging to all of the nations of Europe rubbed shoulders . . . This mixing of humans without historical precedent has left human traces—children were born. A lot of children. A good number of them have French blood in their veins . . . From a demographic point of view the child is the ideal immigrant be-cause he constitutes a human asset whose value is all the more cer-tain since his assimilation is guaranteed. It is impossible to say the same of any adult immigrant.[6]

Pfimlin's view of displaced children as a potential demographic windfall reflected more than just perennial French anxieties about its low birth rate. In contrast to earlier pro-natalist movements in France, French authorities

---

[6] Conférence de presse de M. Pierre Pfimlin, 5 April 1946, 80/AJ/75, AN.

also claimed displaced children in the name of restitution for the Nazi demographic war on occupied Europe. Just as post-war governments and individuals demanded the restitution of apartments, furniture, bank accounts, artwork, and factories that had been plundered by the Nazi regime, they also demanded the return of lost human capital. Post-war European governments and social welfare activists saw displaced children, in particular, as a precious form of national patrimony that had been 'stolen' by the Nazi regime and/or biologically weakened by hunger, bombings, deportations, and forced labour. In a report recommending the transfer of refugee children in Germany to France for adoption, one military official explained, 'By initiating massive deportations and inflicting a long captivity on adults, one of the goals pursued by the Nazis was to reduce natality in the states that they planned to destroy . . . The Direction of Displaced Persons is now working to repair in part the damage inflicted on the Allies in this domain by Germany, by depriving Germany of the benefit of births that were due to the presence of millions of deportees on its territory.'[7]

The French government's decision to transform displaced children into French citizens was also shaped by the conviction that German overpopulation represented an inherent threat to French sovereignty and to European security. Demographers incessantly compared relative population losses in Europe after World War II, noting with dismay that the Nazis seemed to have triumphed in their demographic assault on Europe. Even worse, Germany's own population had actually grown by 7.5 per cent since 1939, with menacing implications, according to a 1946 report by the *Comité International pour l'Étude des Questions Européen*: 'The danger resulting from this state of affairs is extremely grave. It is all the greater since while the German population has grown from 67 to 72 million, German territory has been reduced by about one-fourth since 1945, due to the loss of Eastern Prussia and Silesia.'[8] General Pierre Koenig, the military governor of the French occupied zone of Germany warned in March 1946, 'All of this part of Europe will find itself in an unstable situation, and a tendency toward expansion will naturally arise in Germany. Given that such an expansion is inevitable, it is necessary, beginning now, to plan it and direct it.' Koenig hoped to forestall another German campaign for

---

[7] Entrée en france des enfants nés en Allemagne, undated, PDR 5/274, Archives des Affaires étrangères, Bureau des Archives de l'Occupation française en Allemagne et en Autriche (MAE-Colmar).

[8] Comité International pour l'Étude des Questions Européen, 'Les Resultats de la Guerre de 1939 à 1945 en ce qui concerne la population de l'Allemagne et celles des pays alliés en Europe,' 13 April 1946, volume 105, Allemagne, Z-Europe, Archives des affaires étrangères, Paris (MAE).

Lebensraum by encouraging the selective emigration of Germans to France. Not surprisingly, he identified children as the most assimilable (and therefore the most desirable) immigrants of all. 'On this subject it is worth noting that the ideal solution would not be to introduce young people in France who are already formed—or rather deformed—but children, even babies, who are easily assimilable. For example, in Germany there are thousands of children of French origins, born during the years of war. This emigration should be organized in the very near future, while Germany is still under the effect of a moral crisis in consequence of the defeat.'[9]

The decision to make French citizens out of children of Germans seems counterintuitive, to say the least. But the imperative to reconstruct French national sovereignty after World War II did not only entail protecting borders from military invasion. It also meant control over the nation's population. In a memo to the Commissaire du Plan, which was responsible for economic planning in post-war France, Raymond Bousquet suggested that France required 1,400,000 to 1,500,000 immigrants in order to meet its future labour needs. The problem, as he saw it, was that introducing such a large number of foreigners into the French population threatened to leave it 'invaded, peacefully or not, by a growing number of foreigners. All national character will disappear'. Bousquet therefore insisted on the need to carefully to select immigrants who would easily assimilate. Germans, he believed, ranked among the most desirable candidates: 'Aside from our interest in compensating for the Latin contribution to our population . . . with a Nordic contribution, this immigration will have the advantage of absorbing, at least to a certain degree, the overpopulation of Germany which represents a perpetual menace to France.' Like Koenig, he suggested that the French government should target displaced children in particular. 'The immigration of young German orphans, currently refugees in Denmark, would be particularly precious from a demographic perspective.'[10]

The fraternization of French prisoners-of-war and occupation soldiers with German women in the French occupation zone of Germany created a particularly seductive opportunity to augment the French population at German expense. In May of 1946, one French newspaper wildly estimated that 300,000 occupation children had already been born to French men and

---

[9] Problème démographique allemand, 10 March 1946, volume 105, Allemagne, Z-Europe, MAE.

[10] Raymond Bousquet à Monsieur le commissaire du plan, 80/AJ/75, AN. On demography in post-war France, see Paul-André Rosenthal, *L'Intelligence démographique: Sciences et politique de populations en France (1930–1960)* (Paris, 2003).

German women. While dismissing such projections as 'pure fantasy', Henri Fesquet, writing in *Le Monde* in August 1946, agreed that occupation children were promising candidates for French citizenship. But French officials would have to act fast to claim these children, before the Germans beat them to it. 'In spite of their racist theories, they [the Germans] don't ignore that the cross-breeding of French and Germans sometimes produces excellent results', Fousquet warned. 'It is advisable to remove these half-French children who we would like to form in our image from German influence as soon as possible.'[11]

French occupation authorities soon devised and implemented a plan to 'repatriate' all children born to French-German couples in wartime and occupied Germany. In a confidential memo in 1946, French Ambassador to Baden Jacques Tarbé de Saint-Hardouin outlined the plan to Georges Bidault, the Minister of Foreign Affairs. Leaving the children in Germany, he reasoned 'would allow Germany to benefit from a demographic growth that it doesn't deserve and would go against our principle . . . of reducing the German population. These children of unknown parents represent a human treasure that a country with low population density cannot ignore.'[12] By August 1946, French occupation authorities had established infant's homes in the French Zone of Occupation in Tübingen, Bad Durkheim, and Unterhausen.[13] After several months of physical and moral 'rehabilitation', the babies were transferred to France and handed over to the to the Assistance Publique. They were issued new French 'certificates of origins' to replace their German birth certificates. These certificates erased all record of the children's origins and birthplace. The infants were then given new French names and then placed in French adoptive families.[14] Quick adoption, Pierre Pfimlin hoped, would guarantee the assimilation of the occupation children, and meet the growing demand for children in France. 'The large majority of little immigrants will have a family without delay, a French family that will make them into true French citizens . . . That is doubtlessly the best way to resolve the problem of assimilation', he maintained.[15]

[11] Henri Fesquet, 'Les enfants nés en Allemagne pendant la guerre,' *Le Monde*, August 8, 1946, PDR 5/238, MAE-Colmar.

[12] Recherche en Allemagne des enfants resortissants des nations unies, 16 February 1946, PDR 5/284, MAE-Colmar.

[13] Rapport du Service Sociale du 28 avril au 26 mai 1945, Stuttgart, 26 May 1945, PDR 5/284, MAE-Colmar.

[14] Note relative au rapatriement des enfants française né en Allemagne, 5 August 1946, PDR 5/238, MAE-Colmar.

[15] Conférence de presse de M. Pierre Pfimlin, 5 April 1946, 80/AJ/75, AN.

French policy-makers and social workers justified the adoption scheme by depicting German mothers as immoral or negligent. They contrasted the sad future faced by occupation children in post-war Germany to the happier prospects they would enjoy as French citizens. German mothers, argued French social workers, typically 'abandon the child out of a lack of maternal sentiment or out of loyalty to their true family that would be compromised by the presence of a bastard child'.[16] A 1946 French military report noted that the number of occupation children was increasing, due to 'the promiscuity of German women'. These women abandoned their children out of 'disappoint-ment in the refusal of the presumed father to marry her, desire to make a new life with a German man who is not inclined to welcome the child of a stran-ger', or 'fear of the possible return of a German husband'. French authorities rarely mentioned the severe economic distress of many single mothers as a factor that contributed to abandonment. They instead depicted the adoption programme as a humanitarian gesture to rescue unwanted children from neglectful mothers.[17]

But in spite of high hopes, the adoption scheme produced meagre rewards for France. It turned out that most German women were reluctant to aban-don their babies to the French state. French authorities, meanwhile, rejected almost one-half of the abandoned babies for eugenic reasons, generating accusations of French racism among local Germans. Children of French co-lonial soldiers were explicitly excluded from adoption in France unless they had white skin.[18] By 1949 the French military's Child Search division had identified 14,357 illegitimate children with French or allied fathers. Of this number, however, only 484 had actually been repatriated to France for adoption.[19]

Even as the adoption scheme failed to augment the French population, it reflected the perceived centrality of children to post-war reconstruction of France. It also reflected the interlocking nationalist and universalist logics of reconstruction. French officials rhetorically justified their claims on occupa-tion children in humanitarian terms, and in the name of maintaining European peace and security. But they clearly pursued children from

---

[16] Rapport du Service Sociale du 28 avril au 26 mai 1945, 26 May 1945, PDR 5/284, MAE-Colmar.

[17] Activités, prévisions et besoins de la Section 'Enfance' de la Division PDR, 30 December 1946, PDR 5/242, MAE-Colmar.

[18] Recherche et rapatriement d'enfants nés en Allemagne de père français, 6 June 1946, Folder 5/370, MAE-Colmar.

[19] Compte rendu d'activité du service recherches enfants depuis sa creation 1949, PDR 5/285, MAE-Colmar.

Germany for more self-interested reasons, namely, to enhance the French nation's biological and economic power. The adoption scheme also reflects the extent to which the re-establishment of national sovereignty was linked to national homogeneity in post-war Europe, as assumption that would profoundly shape the politics of migration in the post-war era. Within this framework, refugee children came to be seen as 'most valuable immigrants' by virtue of their perceived ability to assimilate.

### The children of Lidice

The campaign to claim displaced children as lost 'national property' was even more politically and emotionally charged in liberated Eastern Europe. When the Nazis overran Eastern Europe during the Second World War, they deliberately attempted to enrich their demographic power through the forcible Germanization of Slavic children deemed to possess valuable German 'blood'. The Nazi regime's use of the term 're-Germanization' to describe these policies was no empty euphemism. It was a product of the long-standing battle for the souls of nationally ambiguous children in bilingual regions of Eastern Europe. During and after the Second World War, Nazi officials had justified Germanization policies as a form of restitution for alleged losses to the German population through interwar Czechification, Polonization, and Slovenization.[20]

Actual efforts to forcibly Germanize children in Eastern Europe met with determined resistance and only spotty success. After the war, however, East Europeans remembered the forcible Germanization of children as one of the Nazi regime's greatest crimes. Stories of children from Eastern Europe who had been 'stolen' or 'kidnapped' for Germanization circulated widely among relief workers and Western journalists, as well as within Eastern Europe. In 1951 the American journalist Dorothy Macardle reported that during the Nazi occupation, 'Children were taken from orphanages, from streets and parks, and even from their homes. It was the sturdy, fair-haired boys and girls who were lost, as a rule . . . The German motives were obscure, and appalling rumors and conjectures added to the torment of parents whose children had disappeared.'[21]

Meanwhile, the number of children reportedly kidnapped for Germanization by the Nazis was wildly exaggerated by Polish, Yugoslav, and

---

[20] On the history of nationalist claims on children in Eastern Europe before 1945, Tara Zahra, *Kidnapped Souls: National Indifference and the Battle for Children in the Bohemian Lands, 1900–48* (Ithaca, 2008).

[21] Dorothy Macardle, *Children of Europe* (Boston, 1951), 54–6.

Czechoslovak officials.[22] The Polish government and Red Cross declared that at least 200,000 Polish children had fallen victim to Nazi Germanization during the Second World War. Historian Isabel Heinemann has more credibly estimated that around 20,000 children were kidnapped from Poland, and up to 50,000 from all of Europe. [23] But precise numbers are difficult to come by, as they depend both on the definition of 'kidnapping' and the definition of 'Germanization' in a context in which national loyalties were ambiguous and bilingualism was commonplace. Many East Europeans voluntarily applied for German citizenship, and others abandoned their children to German families and institutions while working as forced or voluntary labourers in Germany or living in displaced persons' camps after the war. In any event, East European officials in the 1940s would have made no distinction between the forced removal of a child from his or her parents, and an orphaned or abandoned Slavic child placed with a German family for adoption. According to the nationalist logic of the time, children could be 'kidnapped' not only from their parents, but from the national collective.

The orphaned children of Lidice were Europe's most famous and celebrated lost children immediately after World War II. Their recovery from occupied Germany, like the repatriation and adoption of French-German children, came to represent a broader project of reconstruction and restitution after World War II. And while the French government relied primarily on its own military authorities to repatriate occupation children to France, Czech officials depended on international organizations such as UNRRA and the IRO to recover their lost human patrimony.

On the morning of 21 May 1942 Reichsprotektor Reinhard Heydrich had been attacked in Prague by Czech partisans, and died a few days later. In retaliation, on 10 June 1942, German soldiers rounded up all of the men in the small village of Lidice and shot them into a mass grave. The village was burnt and razed to the ground. Meanwhile, the town's women and children were shaken out of bed at 3 a.m. and dragged to a high school in Kladno. Nine children were selected for Germanization, and the rest of the women and children sent on to concentration camps. Nazi officials brought these children to an SS Lebensborn home in Puschkau, near Poznan, for Germanization and adoption. Hana Spotová, two years old at the time, was one of the children selected for Germanization. She received a new identity as Hanna Spott. After a brief stay in Puschkau, Hana was adopted by a German woman named Klara Warner. Warner later testified that Lebensborn officials told her that Hanna

---

[22] Memo from M. Thudicum to Sir Arthur Rucker, 31 January 1949, 43/AJ/600, AN.

[23] Isabel Heinemann, *'Rasse, Siedlung, deutsches Blut': Die Rasse und Siedlungshauptamt der SS und die rassenpolitische Neuordnung Europas* (Göttingen, 2003), 508–9.

was a German orphan whose parents had been killed in an aerial bombardment. But she soon heard disturbing rumours about the child's origins:

> When I picked up the child, a kindergarten teacher said, 'What a
> pity that the child is leaving, she was the prettiest here and learned to
> speak such nice German.' I was naturally surprised and asked, what
> do you mean, where is the child from? 'Don't you know? These are
> Czech children whose parents were killed', answered the kindergar-
> ten teacher. At the urging of my husband I later wrote to the regional
> home for Posen and asked for information about the origins of the
> child. But the only response I received is that the child is racially
> flawless . . . I had Hanna Spott in my care until March 1944. One day
> an NSV sister came and took her away without any explanation.[24]

Spotová was among the lucky few, as she lived to return to Czechoslovakia.
Only 17 out of 105 children from Lidice ultimately survived the ordeal—82
were gassed in Chelmno shortly after the 1942 massacre.[25] But immediately
after the war, the fate of Lidice's 105 missing children remained a mystery.
Czech government officials, the Red Cross, UNRRA, the press, and a broader
international public still hoped that the children remained hidden and that
they would be recovered for the Czech nation.

The hunt for the Lost Children of Lidice became a public spectacle that
dramatized the post-war campaign for justice and restitution. A radio address
on 8 January 1946 rallied all Czech citizens for the search, asking that they
immediately report any clues or sightings of the 105 missing children to their
local national council.[26] In liberated Berlin, meanwhile, German anti-fascists
circulated flyers and posters with the names and pictures of the missing Lidice
children. The posters appealed, 'There can be no town hall in Germany, no
police officer, no office, no church, no newspaper, no radio station, no political party, no union, no rally, no home, no family, which does not cry out,
"What happened to the children from Lidice?" '[27] The Czechoslovak Ministry
of Interior, meanwhile, published a booklet entitled *Kidnapped Czech
Children* that same year, listing 890 missing Czech children altogether,
including 93 children of Lidice.[28] By the time that the Ministry of Social

---

[24] Protokoll der Frau Klara Werner, Ministerstvo ochranu práce a sociální péče-repatriace
(MPSP-R), Carton 849, Národní archiv, Prague (NA).

[25] Jolana Macková and Ivan Ulrych, *Osudy lidických dětí* (Lidice, 2003).

[26] Ohledně pátrání po lidických dětech, Carton 849, MPSP-R, NA.

[27] An alle Frauen, an alle Familien in Deutschland, Wo Sind die Kinder von Lidice?, Carton
849, MPSP-R, NA.

[28] *Pohřešované československé děti* (Prague, 1946), Carton 846, MPSP-R, NA.

Welfare ended its search for deported children, in January of 1949, only 740 children had been located and 629 repatriated.[29]

Across Europe, the search for a relatively small number of children assumed extraordinary symbolic significance. The Czechoslovak press continuously denounced and publicized the villainy of German civilians and allied authorities, who allegedly deliberately hindered the return of Czechoslovak children to their homeland. 'Kidnapped children are enslaved by Germans', reported *Svobodné noviny* in March 1947. Two years after the defeat of Nazi Germany, the newspaper claimed, many deported Czech youth continued to labour for German employers, unaware of the possibility of returning home. According to *Svobodné noviny*, these forced labourers 'receive only small amounts of food and have no possibility of contact with the outside world. The majority were deported to Germany in their tender youth.'[30]

As the Communist party gained in power and influence in post-war Czechoslovakia, Czechoslovak newspapers and officials joined Polish and Yugoslav authorities in denouncing American military authorities and the IRO, accusing them of conspiring against the return of the nation's 'stolen' children. *Národní osvobození* reported in October 1947 that 13-year-old Hana Š. from Lidice was living with German foster parents who refused to relinquish her. When the conflict continued with no forseeable resolution, Czech repatriation officials decided they had no choice but to take matters into their own hands. 'Our people decided to abduct the girl. And so Hanička finally returned to the Czech land of her birth. This solution was dramatic, but what a tragedy! In 1947 Czechs must kidnap Czech children from German families, who were stolen in 1942 from Lidice! This abduction was made necessary by the American authorities, who guard the children kidnapped during the war by the Nazis,' accused the paper.[31]

Real-life family reunions were major media events. When seven-year-old Hana Spotová finally returned to Czechoslovakia on 2 April 1947, her train was greeted at the Wilson Train Station in Prague by 'an unusually excited and tense crowd of simple men and women, among whom mingled the khaki uniforms of the employees and representatives of UNRRA and our soldiers', reported the newspaper *Obrana lidu*. This festive crowd joined film-makers, photo-journalists, and newspaper reporters, who 'feverishly prepared to

[29] 'Po stopách zavlečených dětí,' *Lidové noviny,* 13 January 1949. Carton 409, Ministerstvo zahraničních věci-výstřižkový archiv (MZV-VA), NA.

[30] 'Zavlečené děti musí otročit Němcům,' *Svobodné noviny*, 16 March 1947, Carton 409, MZV-VA, NA.

[31] 'Neuvěřitelná případ,' *Národní osvobození*, 12 October 1947, Carton 409, MZV-VA, NA.

capture the extraordinary moment of reunion of parents with their children who had been robbed from them for years by the barbarous German regime, and who were cold-heartedly and consciously detained by German civilians even after the war'.[32]

Tales of Germanized children even inspired a popular children's story by the Czech writer Zdeňka Bezděková. *They Called Me Leni* (*Řikali mi Leni*) was first published in 1948 and later translated into English, German, Dutch, Slovene, Swedish, Japanese, Ukrainian, Slovak, and Sorbian. It was eventually reprinted eight times in Czech (most recently in 2001), and followed by a sequel. In the preface Bezděková wrote that she had been inspired by newspaper reports about real-life stolen children: 'In 1947 I read a newspaper report about a little Czech girl who returned to her home country after having lived for many years with a German family . . . I pondered over her sad fate and the fate of all these stolen children, and I decided to write this story.'[33]

Leni Freiwald, the heroine, was born Alena Sýkorová. In 1946, Alena was living in Herrnstadt, Germany with a Nazi family, completely unaware of her origins. But she had a vague sense that she didn't belong. Bit by bit, clues about her past life return to Leni in her dreams. She overhears her adoptive mother and grandmother fighting behind closed doors. A vindictive German classmate calls her a 'foreign Czech bastard'. Eventually she discovers a suitcase from home, locked in the attic, in which she finds clues about her past—a peasant doll, a white hat, a pair of stockings with the initials AS embroidered into them. Finally recalling her true origins, Leni runs away to a local UNRRA office, where she declares 'I have a mother in Czechoslovakia!' With the help of a friendly teacher and an UNRRA social worker, Leni's mother is located, and she returns to her native family, language, and nation. But the story ends on a sad note, as Leni acknowledges what has been lost in exile: 'For the first time, I felt love. But I couldn't say anything. I didn't know how to say Mummy in Czech.'[34]

### 'Every child needs a strong sense of national identity'

Leni's story highlights both the symbolic place of lost children in the process of post-war reconstruction, and the important role of international organizations such as UNRRA in the hunt for Lost Children from Eastern Europe. For post-war UNRRA and IRO social workers, tracing children uprooted by

---

[32] 'Návrat uloupených dětí do vlast,' *Obrana lidu,* 3 April 1947, Carton 409, MZV-VA, NA.

[33] Zdeňka Bezděková, *They Called me Leni,* trans. Stuart R. Amor (New York, 1973), 6. Most recent Czech edition: *Řikali mi Leni* (Prague, 2001).

[34] Bezděková, *They Called me Leni,* 82.

the Nazi war machine became central to their own goals of promoting democratization and human rights in post-war Europe. United Nations' social
workers claimed, at least officially, to stand above nationalist concerns. In an
expression of their individualist ethic, they pledged to uphold the 'best interests of the child' as the guiding principle of child welfare. The 'best interests'
principle was itself intended to mark the repudiation of Nazi racial hierarchies. Focusing on the best interests of individual children implied a rejection of
other possible criteria for making social welfare decisions, such as the goal of
creating a master race. But the meaning of these 'best interests' was far from
transparent. Based on the belief that children's psychological rehabilitation
depended on the cultivation of a firm national identity, UNRRA and IRO
social workers, as well as European governments, ultimately came to define
the individual 'best interests' of displaced children and adults in distinctly
nationalist terms. In the words of UNRRA child welfare worker Susan Pettiss,

> At first I couldn't understand why the Army and UNRRA almost
> immediately set up different camps for Poles, Ukrainians, Jews,
> Western Europeans, etc. Imbued with the idealistic sense of 'one
> world' I felt disillusioned when that unity didn't materialize right
> away. I soon realized, however, that for both psychological and
> practical reasons, national grouping was best during the insecure
> and traumatic times in the lives of the displaced.[35]

A central mission of UNRRA's 'Child Search Teams' was to comb the German
countryside in search of children like Leni. Simply identifying these children
required tremendous detective work. The nationalities of many East
European children were ambiguous, since displaced children often came
from bilingual regions, where blurry lines between so-called *Volksdeutsche*
(ethnic Germans) and Poles, Czechs, and Yugoslavs had become blurrier
during the Second World War.[36] To complicate matters, Nazi officials systematically changed the names and destroyed the records of children designated for Germanization. Many young children had no memory at all of their
native languages or families of origin. In 1947, Jean Henshaw described Polish
and Yugoslav children in the Children's Centre in Prien who had 'renounced
their country, language, and culture and vehemently claimed they were
Germans'.[37]

---

[35] Pettiss, *After the Shooting Stopped*, 62.
[36] See for example File 10, Report, S-0437-0013, United Nations Archive (UN); W. C.
Huyssoon, 'Who is this Child', S-0437-0013, UN.
[37] Report on International Children's Centre, Prien, 28 April 1947, S-0437–0012, UN.

Once identified, UN Child Search Officers typically sought to remove allied children from German families as quickly as possible. But even when the children were orphans, UNRRA workers typically sought to repatriate them to their national homeland. The children sometimes had to be removed from their foster-parents by force. In one such case, Child Care Consultant Eileen Davidson noted in her daily log for 19 October 1946: 'Conference with Polish Repatriation Officer re two adolescent Polish children who have been for two years with a superior German family and are asking permission to remain. They are orphans and have no family to return to. Permission refused. Children to be repatriated. Picked up both children at Ansbach much against their will.'[38]

Custody battles over displaced children generated sharp tensions between UNRRA, British and American military authorities, East European governments, family members, displaced persons themselves, and local German foster-parents. In the name of the 'best interests of the children', British and American military authorities often preferred to leave the children in German homes, insisting that the children would be emotionally scarred by removal from their German foster-parents.[39] It is likely that Allied military authorities also objected to the repatriation of East European children for more pragmatic reasons—in order to smooth relations between military authorities and local Germans, and ultimately out of anti-communist sympathies. UNNRA and IRO child welfare officers, however, consistently favoured removing displaced children from German homes and repatriating them to Eastern Europe.

In 1948, Eileen Davidson, then Deputy Chief of the IRO's Child Search Section, wrote a memo arguing that this policy represented the 'best interests of the child' from a psychological, moral, and political perspective. Her argument rested largely on the conviction that German society had not yet been purged of Nazi racism; the possibility of true integration for East European children in post-war Germany was therefore slim, in her view. She cited the case of 'two Polish children whose father had been in the SS and who were known as Volksdeutsche. The older girl worked long hours in the kitchen . . . She said that she always was told that she was a "dumb Pole".'[40]

---

[38] Daily Log of October 19th, 21st, from District Child Search Officer Eileen Davidson, S- 0437-0014, UN.

[39] On British and American military policies toward repatriation, see Provisional order no. 75 and the British Zone Policy, 9 November 1948, 43/AJ/599, AN; Removal of Children from German Care, 30 June 1947, S-0437–0017, UN.

[40] Eileen Davidson, Removal from German families of Allied Children, 21 February 1948, 7, 43/AJ/599, AN.

East European children left in German foster-families, she concluded, would surely suffer permanent psychological damage, even if they were loved and well cared for. 'Far from securing the best interests of the child [she wrote], one has run the danger with the passage of years of contributing to the development of a warped and twisted personality, a misfit with roots neither here nor in his home country.'[41]

Davidson's position was typical of UN social workers, and reflects the extent to which nationalist ideals were appropriated by new international institutions after World War II. Her insistence that national ambiguity would lead to the development of 'warped and twisted personalities' strongly echoed the concerns of earlier nationalists and educational reformers in Habsburg Central Europe, who had also insisted that bilingual education threatened to deform children's intellectual and moral character.[42] Davidson's memo also reflects how humanitarian workers defined ideals such as democratization, justice, and the individual psychological 'best interests of the child' so as to privilege the 'renationalization' of displaced children. Children, in this view, required a stable national identity in order to thrive as healthy individuals.

In policy terms, this meant that UNRRA and the IRO generally respected the demands made by East European governments for the repatriation of children. Officially, only representatives of an orphan's country of origins were legally entitled to approve decisions about the child's adoption, resettlement, or repatriation.[43] In addition, unaccompanied East European children could not legally be adopted by foster-parents of a different nationality, in accordance with domestic laws in Poland, Yugoslavia, and Czechoslovakia. The UN did not simply respect these national 'rights' to children out of deference to Eastern European nationalists. In a 1948 memo one IRO official elaborated, 'Every child's future is too important to be decided by a representative of a foreign nation . . . There can be no doubt that in order for things to run smoothly, the guardian must be of the same nationality as the child. If such a line is followed, nobody will be able to reproach the IRO for its desire to assimilate, denationalize children or to develop cosmopolitans.'[44] Jean Henshaw boasted of the UNRRA Children's Centre in Prien, 'One of our major tasks has been a program for renationalizing children. Where we have

---

[41] Davidson, Removal from German Families, 14.

[42] Zahra, *Kidnapped Souls*, chapter 1.

[43] Intergovernmental Committee on Refugees, Displaced Orphan Children in Europe, 13 November 1946, 43/AJ/45, AN.

[44] Comments on the guardianship problem of unaccompanied children, 5 March 1948, 43/AJ/926, AN.

had adequate DP staff from the children's home country . . . we have had outstanding success in awaking the spirit of national pride and feeling.'[45]

These views also shaped the pedagogy of rehabilitation within UNRRA and IRO camps and children's homes. In many explicitly internationalist projects to rehabilitate displaced children, young refugees were organized in separate national houses in order to cultivate national pride. In the Pestalozzi Village in Trogen, Switzerland in 1950, 132 orphans were housed in eight distinctive national houses, each appropriately 'decorated and furnished in national style'.[46] Each house had its own school where children were given lessons in their mother tongue with textbooks from their native lands. A teacher in the children's village boasted, 'It is really amazing to observe with what toughness and vitality even the smallest group preserves its national character if soundly organized. In each of these small colonies the very best elements of national culture come to the fore, the colourful variety of literary and musical talent, folklore, jest, and humour.'[47] The cultivation of each child's national identity was essential to his or her individual psychological well-being, according to Thérèse Brosse, writing for UNESCO:

> In the course of our visits to the children's communities, we saw indeed how much the children need a country of their own if they are to be psychologically normal and to feel 'like other people' . . . Their youthful independence is not strong enough for them to become world citizens immediately without first being a citizen of a smaller community . . . The all-important requirement for children who have been moved from one country to another: to settle the child and provide him with a country of his own and a language and culture which that implies.[48]

The argument that children constituted a form of national, collective property had been born in Eastern Europe in the nineteenth century and strengthened by the experience of Nazi occupation and persecution. After the Second World War, international humanitarian organizations and post-war governments launched a campaign to renationalize and repatriate displaced children in order to right the wrongs of Nazi Germanization policies. In the name of a radical break with the fascist past, they insisted that the material and

---

[45] Report on International Children's Centre, Prien, 28 April 1947, S-0437–0012, UN.

[46] Thérèse Brosse, *Homeless Children: Report on the Proceedings of the Conference* (Paris, 1950), 24.

[47] W. R. Corti, 'A Few Thoughts on the Children's Village,' *News Bulletin of the Pestalozzi Children's Village*, May 1948, 9, 43/AJ/599, AN.

[48] Brosse, *War-Handicapped Children*, 21–2.

psychological 'best interests' of individual children should guide post-war social work. Simultaneously, however, they defined those 'best interests' in distinctly nationalist terms.

This focus on children as national patrimony was not limited to Eastern Europe after World War II, however. Contrary to histories of nationalism, of World War II, and of reconstruction that posit radical differences between Eastern and Western Europe, the history of Europe's lost children reveals a set of shared challenges and assumptions in post-war Europe. In both France and Czechoslovakia, the 'repatriation' of children was linked to the reconstruction of national sovereignty and of the nation's biological and economic strength. Both French and Czechoslovak authorities demanded the return of 'lost children' in the name of restitution for a Nazi demographic assault on Europe. They claimed displaced children as part of an ostensible effort to prevent future outbreaks of German imperialism, and to guarantee the peace and security of Europe. Finally, both linked the security of Europe to the creation of homogenous nation-states. While post-war policy-makers across Europe were intent on increasing their war-battered populations after the war, they did not wish to do so at the expense of national homogeneity. In Czechoslovakia, this meant focusing on the repatriation of Czech lost children while expelling three million Germans (including, initially many children of German-Czech marriages).[49] In France, this entailed transforming occupation and refugee children into French citizens because of their perceived capacity to assimilate.

There were also key differences between the French and East European cases, however. As an Allied power, the French government could freely determine policies toward both 'lost children' and occupation children in its own occupation zones. Czechoslovak, Polish, and Yugoslav officials were by contrast constrained by Allied military authorities, representatives of international organizations (namely UNRRA and the IRO), and local German welfare authorities. In addition, the onset of the Cold War dramatically transformed the political stakes of international custody disputes. The campaign to repatriate East European 'lost children', initially imagined as a conflict between Germans and East Europeans, was translated into a battle between East and West. Many displaced youth, like adults from Eastern Europe, themselves refused to return home, whether due to political or religious loyalties or a desire for better social and economic opportunities. While representatives

---

[49] See Frommer, 'Expulsion or Integration: Unmixing Interethnic Marriage in Post-war Czechoslovakia,' *East European Politics and Societies* 14:2 (March 2000), 381–410; Tara Zahra, *Lost Children: Displacement and the Family in Twentieth-Century Europe* (Cambridge, Mass., forthcoming), chapter 6.

of UNRRA and the IRO continued to insist that it was in children's best interests to return to Eastern Europe after the consolidation of communist power, American and British authorities increasingly blocked the repatriation of East European youth out of explicit anti-communist sentiments. Aleta Brownlee, the Chief of UNRRA and IRO's child welfare division in the American zone of Austria recalled that as Cold War divisions hardened, 'United Nations worked against each other, ex-enemies became friends, West was set upon East, the Catholic Church against communism'. The preponderance of displaced children in Austria were of Slavic nations, and at least one high-ranking representative of an occupying power stated the position that 'there are too many Slavs anyway'.[50]

In 1951, Hannah Arendt famously observed that the refugee camps of interwar France had exposed the limits of the universal ideal of 'human rights'. Ultimately, such rights were nothing but empty promises to displaced persons who lacked national citizenship. 'The conception of human rights, based upon the assumed existence of human beings as such, broke down at the very moment when those who professed to believe in it were for the first time confronted with people who had indeed lost all other qualities and specific relationships—except that they were still human', she maintained.[51] After World War II, humanitarian activists and international organizations responded to the perceived failures of the interwar system of minority protection and child protection. They proudly proclaimed a new era of democracy, human rights, and internationalism in Europe. Through their efforts to rehabilitate Europe's displaced children, however, UNRRA and IRO workers ultimately anchored long-standing nationalist ideals at the heart of new international regimes of refugee relief and rehabilitation. Post-war European policy-makers, meanwhile, attempted to manage post-war population displacement to their own advantage in the name of biological and economic reconstruction. Arendt's insight, it seems, applied to the post-war world of the displaced persons camp, the children's home, and the orphanage, as well as to the interwar refugee camp. Reconstructing Europe after Nazi occupation required affirming a form of national sovereignty that was located as much in the control of children's futures as in the control of state borders.

---

[50] Aleta Brownlee, UNRRA Mission to Austria. Child Welfare in the Displaced Persons Camps, 6, Programme, Box 5, Aleta Brownlee Papers, Hoover Archive (HA), Stanford University.

[51] Hannah Arendt, *The Origins of Totalitarianism* (New York, 1951), 299.

# List of Contributors

**Sunil Amrith** is Lecturer in History in the Department of History, Classics and Archaeology, Birkbeck College, University of London.

**Pamela Ballinger** is Associate Professor of Anthropology in the Department of Sociology and Anthropology, Adams Hall, Brunswick.

**Richard Bessel** is Professor of Twentieth Century History in the Department of History, University of York.

**Holly Case** is Associate Professor at the Department of History, Cornell University, Ithaca.

**Fred Cooper** is Professor of History in the Department of History, New York University.

**David Edgerton** is Hans Rausing Professor of the History of Science and Technology, at the Centre for the History of Science, Technology and Medicine, Imperial College.

**David Feldman** is Professor of History at Birkbeck, University of London.

**Mark Harrison** is Professor in the Department of Economics, University of Warwick.

**Harold James** is Professor of History and International Affairs at Princeton University.

**Pieter Lagrou** is Professor at the Université Libre de Bruxelles.

**Mark Mazower** is Ira D. Wallach Professor of History at Columbia University.

**Silvio Pons** is Professor of History of Eastern Europe in the Departemento de Historia, Universita di Tor Vergata, Rome.

**Jessica Reinisch** is Lecturer in Contemporary History in the Department of History, Classics and Archaeology, Birkbeck College, University of London.

**Adam Tooze** is Professor of History at the Department of History, Yale University.

**Nick White** is Reader in Imperial and Commonwealth History in the Faculty of Media Arts and Social Science, Liverpool John Moores University.

**Tara Zahra** is Assistant Professor of East European History in the Department of History at the University of Chicago.

**Waqar Zaidi** is a Doctoral (PhD) Student in the Centre for the History of Science, Technology and Medicine, Imperial College London.

# Post-war Reconstruction in Europe index

and international law 23
internment camps 153
as model for socialist state in
    Yugoslavia 165
new generation of leaders 110
post-war planning 25
rapid post-war recovery data 111–14
rejection of Marshall Plan 79, 133, 134
relief effort 276
repression in 114–20
trade figures 83
and UNRRA 264, 282
wartime destruction 104–6
wartime information on subjects'
behaviour 118–20
Spain 98
Spencer, Herbert 44
Spotová, Hana 341–2, 343–4
Stalin, Joseph 48, 51, 75, 79, 127–8, 165, 318
    agreement with Beneš 125
    agreement with Churchill 124
    and Athens uprising 126–7
    dissolution of the Comintern 123
        n.3, 131
    and European communist parties 122–3
    Great Breakthrough (1929) 104
    Great Terror (1937) 113, 115–16,
        117, 118
    and Italy 135
    'popular democracies' doctrine
        131–2, 137
    post-war reassertion of authority
        109–10
    post-war repression 115–20
    and spheres of influence 124, 129
    'the dictator's dilemma' 118
    and Tito 135–6, 137
    vengeance over reconciliation 107
Strauss, Franz Josef 50
strikes 193, 198, 204, 231
Sukarno, President of Indonesia 199,
    214, 230
Sumatra 214, 218–19, 230
summary executions 166, 167, 181–95
Sweden 80
Swedish Red Cross 276
Switzerland 279, 304, 348
Syria 197

Taft, William Howard 59
Tamils 239, 243, 249, 250, 251–2, 256
Tanganyika 221, 232
tank manufacture 35, 39
taxation 62–3, 67
Taylor, A. J. P. 38–9
tea production 219
technological innovations 268
textile industry 221
Thailand 238
Thorez, Maurice 124, 133, 134
thorium 318
Thuringia 143, 149
Tilley, Cecil Edgar 326
*Times, The* 315, 322
tin 214, 216, 230
Tinker, Hugh 241
Tito, Josip Broz 82, 126–7, 127, 131, 135–6,
    137, 158, 162, 163, 166
tobacco 219, 230
Togliatti, Palmiro 123, 124, 126, 135
Togo 218
Tomlinson, Jim 31, 32, 42 n.56
torture 183, 185, 202, 203
tractor production 35, 37
trade 300, 305–6
    Bretton Woods Conference and 293–6
    colonial 34, 40–1, 212–36
    competition 307–8
    integration 47
    liberalization of 45, 66–7, 291, 295
    protectionism 43, 259, 294, 302, 307
    with Soviet Union 83
    war's disruption of 270
trade unionism 42 n.57, 205, 227
travel documentation 240, 251, 252–3, 254
Trees, Wolfgang 188
Trieste, city of 166–7, 168, 171, 175
Triffin, Robert 303
Truman, President Harry 318
Truman administration 58
Truman Doctrine (1947) 17 n.1, 97, 220
typhus 145, 275

U Hla, Ludu 249
Ukraine 285
UN (United Nations) 21, 24, 26, 219, 270,
    288, 289, 318